ROUTLEDGE LIBRARY EDITIONS:
INDUSTRIAL RELATIONS

Volume 7

CHANGE IN INDUSTRIAL RELATIONS

CHANGE IN INDUSTRIAL RELATIONS

The Organization and Environment

P.B. BEAUMONT

Routledge
Taylor & Francis Group
LONDON AND NEW YORK

First published in 1990 by Routledge

This edition first published in 2025
by Routledge
4 Park Square, Milton Park, Abingdon, Oxon OX14 4RN

and by Routledge
605 Third Avenue, New York, NY 10158

Routledge is an imprint of the Taylor & Francis Group, an informa business

British Library Cataloguing in Publication Data
A catalogue record for this book is available from the British Library

ISBN: 978-1-032-81770-5 (Set)
ISBN: 978-1-032-84492-3 (Volume 7) (hbk)
ISBN: 978-1-032-84496-1 (Volume 7) (pbk)
ISBN: 978-1-003-51350-6 (Volume 7) (ebk)

DOI: 10.4324/9781003513506

Publisher's Note
The publisher has gone to great lengths to ensure the quality of this reprint but points out that some imperfections in the original copies may be apparent.

Disclaimer
The publisher has made every effort to trace copyright holders and would welcome correspondence from those they have been unable to trace.

Change in Industrial Relations

The Organization and Environment

P. B. Beaumont

ROUTLEDGE

London and New York

First published 1990
by Routledge
11 New Fetter Lane, London EC4P 4EE

Simultaneously published in the USA and Canada
by Routledge
a division of Routledge, Chapman and Hall, Inc.
29 West 35th Street, New York NY 10001

Reprinted 1991

Typeset by Pat and Anne Murphy, Highcliffe-on-Sea, Dorset
Printed in Great Britain by
Richard Clay Ltd, Bungay, Suffolk

British Library Cataloguing in Publication Data

Beaumont, P.B.
Change in Industrial Relations: The Organization and Environment.
1. Great Britain. Industrial relations
331'.0941

ISBN 0-415-04344-1
ISBN 0-415-04345-X (pb)

Library of Congress Cataloging in Publication Data

Beaumont, P.B. (Phil B.)
Change in Industrial Relations: The Organization and Environment / P.B. Beaumont.
p. cm.
Includes bibliographical references.
ISBN 0-415-04344-1. — ISBN 0-415-04345-X (pbk).
1. Collective bargaining — Great Britain. 2. Industrial relations — Great Britain. 3. Trade-unions — Great Britain.
I. Title.
HD6664.B353 1990
331'.0941—dc20 89-39096 CIP

To PAT and TOM who in their different, but complementary, ways made this book possible.

Contents

Contents

List of tables

Preface

The basic purpose of this book is to examine the actual practices of, and existing research on a collective-bargaining-based system of industrial relations in an advanced industrialized economy. In view of the author's position in a British university, it should occasion little surprise that the book is overwhelmingly concerned with the British system of industrial relations. However, reference is frequently made to both the experience of, and research findings in, other national systems of industrial relations, particularly in the United States. As the book is *not* explicitly based on a comparative or cross-country framework of analysis, this tendency to draw on material from other countries clearly requires some word of explanation, not to say justification. In defence of this practice I would make two basic points. First, the value of any set of research findings in any system of industrial relations is always enhanced by seeing whether such findings are essentially system-specific in nature, as opposed to transcending the particular institutional arrangements of the system concerned. In other words, the findings and experience of other systems of industrial relations, be they similar or dissimilar in nature, constitute a potentially valuable reference point for the work of researchers in any one system of industrial relations. Second, studies from other national systems may be particularly important to students and teachers of industrial relations in Britain (and elsewhere) because of the particular question they have examined and the approach or methodology they have employed in their research work. In general, I would rather refer a student to a 'good quality' US study (perhaps with some appropriate caution about the limited potential generality of the findings) than to simply say that there are no relevant British studies on a particularly important issue or question, or make reference to an 'inferior' piece of work whose only virtue was the fact that it was conducted in a British setting.

The contents of the book have resulted from some 10 years'

experience of teaching a variety of courses in industrial relations at the University of Glasgow. These courses have included specialist ones to students on a Master's-level degree in industrial relations as well as a number of service-based, shorter courses to students in economics, management, and accountancy. To attempt to produce a book whose entire contents were of equal interest and value to such a diverse set of students) as well as one's own professional colleagues) might be viewed as a difficult, not to say rather foolhardy, undertaking. However, I was determined *not* to write a textbook whose relatively uniform treatment of a variety of traditional subjects was designed to be read from cover to cover by students on a single (specialist or non-specialist) course. The aim has rather been to produce something in the way of a reference book whose varied contents can be 'selectively dipped into' by students from a variety of industrial-relations courses.

The production of industrial-relations textbooks is one of the few growth industries in Britain at the present time, so that a few comments seem appropriate concerning the way in which the contents of this book differ from some of those currently available; the necessity for such comments reflects the author's view that this book will almost inevitably come to be regarded as something of a textbook. One such difference has already been mentioned — namely, the amount of reference that will be made to research conducted in other national systems of industrial relations. A number of other differences include (i) a relatively critical perspective being taken on some existing research studies, with gaps and weaknesses in the extent of our research-based knowledge being frequently highlighted; (ii) there is considerable reference to the research findings of scholars in other fields of study (e.g. economists, organization theorists, and urban and regional researchers) that are rarely incorporated in traditional, textbook treatments of industrial relations; and (iii) rather more attention is given to the currently changing nature of the system of industrial relations as a whole (and where it might be going) than tends to be provided in books that essentially aim to synthesize the findings of books and journal articles already published (i.e. the latter approach is, by definition, very 'status quo' orientated which is clearly more acceptable in some periods of time than others). Furthermore, considerably more information is presented here in tabular form than is typically the case in British industrial-relations texts, and the manner in which arguments and material is presented deliberately seeks to avoid individual chapters with essentially self-contained discussions of individual topics and subjects — i.e. there is considerably more in the way of cross-referencing of subjects across individual chapters.

The book that has most influenced the approach adopted here is Kochan's *Collective Bargaining and Industrial Relations* (1980) which is one of the most important books recently published in industrial relations. The essence of the conceptual approach adopted by Kochan (in what is an exclusively US-material-based book) is that certain independent variables — notably the external environment, the bargaining characteristics of management, the organizational characteristics of unions, and bargaining structure (an intervening variable) — impact on certain dependent variables associated with collective bargaining, namely the negotiations process, bargaining outcomes, the administration of the agreement and the union–management change process which, in turn, feed through to shape the goal attainment of the parties concerned and the public at large. This basic approach is used here to order and structure much of my subsequent discussion and presentation, although only to the extent that similarities between the British and US systems of collective bargaining warrant, and the available research literature in Britain permits. The approach adopted here also differs from that of Kochan in tending to treat the industrial-relations domain as somewhat less of a discrete, self-contained entity, both in the individual-organization and larger-society settings. At various points in the subsequent treatment, for example, it will be emphasized that some of the most important impacts and effects on industrial-relations phenomena arise from decisions in an organizational or political context that were not solely taken by industrial-relations professionals, nor taken for exclusively industrial-relations reasons. In other words, it is suggested that some of the most important influences on industrial relations are to a considerable degree exogenous to the control of the leading actors in the industrial-relations sub-system, as conventionally defined – a fact that has important implications for the research, teaching, and practice of industrial relations.

The plan of the book is essentially as follows. In the first chapter I review the changing nature of industrial-relations research in Britain, contrasting it with that in the United States, examine various proposed theoretical treatments of the field of study, and consider some of the more recent calls for new approaches and emphases in industrial-relations research. Chapter 2 examines the larger external environment of collective bargaining. This discussion of a key independent variable looks at various possible effects flowing from changes in the labour market, product market, and political and social environment. In Chapter 3 my concern is with the organizational characteristics of unions, with the individual topics covered including a number of traditional ones – such as union structure and union democracy – as well as some of the more recent work of labour economists that has attempted to develop deductive models of union behaviour in wage bargaining. Chapter 4 then turns to the management side of the collective-bargaining process. Inevitably, a good deal of attention is given here to the extent of development of, and influences on, the personnel management function. However, in an attempt to place this specialist functional role in a more precise organizational context I also examine the larger issue of organizational structure and strategy, and consider some of the relevant insights that emerge – for example, from product-life cycle theory and the 'companies of excellence' literature.

In Chapter 5 I begin to examine the nature of the collective-bargaining process as the major mechanism of union–management interaction in Britain. The discusssion here considers issues such as the essence and value of collective bargaining, the concept of the social or public interest in collective bargaining, the extent of bargaining coverage, and some criticisms that have been frequently levelled against this institutional arrangement. This chapter also contains an extensive discussion of the subject of bargaining structure, which is viewed as an important intervening variable in the larger system of industrial relations. Chapter 6 continues the examination of collective bargaining by considering various theories of the process of bargaining – identifying various organizational-level influences (e.g. size of establishment) that have been held to strongly shape the nature of collective bargaining structures, processes, and outcomes in Britain – and then draws together some of this material through means of a discussion of the concept of union power. The contents of Chapter 7 cover various outcomes of the collective-bargaining process such as the union-relative-wage effect, the possible relationship with the extent of money and real-wage change, productivity, and the distribution of national income between wages and profits. The prior discussion of the concept of union power is particularly used to inform the nature of the review undertaken here, while the latter part of the chapter considers the question of what is a 'good' collective-bargaining relationship at the individual organizational level. The Government role in industrial relations is touched upon in a number of preceding chapters, but it is in Chapter 8 that we most fully and directly examine this subject – through a consideration of third-party-dispute resolution procedures, incomes policy, and the industrial relations of the public sector. Chapter 9 then looks at a number of different issues, arrangements, and practices which appear to constitute a challenge to the position (or place) of collective bargaining as the key or central institutional mechanism of the British system of industrial relations. Finally, Chapter 10 draws together some of the findings of previous chapters in order to pose a number of questions about the possible future shape of the industrial-relations system in Britain.

Acknowledgements

I am, as always, grateful to Andrew Thomson for initially encouraging me to think about producing a book along these lines. The presentation of some of the issues raised here benefited greatly from discussions with a number of colleagues at Glasgow University, particularly with individuals in psychology, history, and economics, while a particular word of thanks is owed to Richard Harris in the Department of Economics at Queen's University, Belfast; collaborative work with him in recent years has been quite simply a pleasure, which is not always the case when an industrial-relations researcher gets together with an economist. A number of individuals in organizations such as ACAS and Incomes Data Services were also extremely generous in providing information, while some of my own students have been a most useful source of feedback on some of the material presented here. Finally, I am grateful to my secretary, Eithne Johnstone, for her tolerance in coping with my numerous 'final' revisions.

Chapter one

Industrial relations as a field of study

Origins and tendencies in research

Industrial relations as a separate and specialist field of study, which through time has come to be centrally concerned with the institutional determination and regulation of the terms and conditions of employment, largely had its origins in the institutional-economics movement in both Britain and the United States. Although not the first individual in the field, the founding father of industrial relations in the US is typically held to be John R. Commons, whose work at the University of Wisconsin is still widely and approvingly cited.[1] In Britain it is rather more difficult to attach such a title to any single individual, although the work of the Webbs was clearly a strong, formative influence on the field.[2] The aspects of the Webbs' work which still continue to be most discussed by students of industrial relations in Britain concerns the essential nature of collective bargaining (see Chapter 5) and how this method relates to others used by trade unions (e.g. mutual insurance, legal enactment) to maintain or improve the conditions of their members' working lives. In fact, the Webbs' larger, more enduring contribution was arguably to highlight a number of the leading normative premises of the field of study which distinguish it from the value orientation of both economists and organization-behaviour theorists. The premises that are particularly important here include recognition of the fact that labour cannot be viewed or studied as simply another factor of production, an emphasis on the inherent conflict of interest (at least to some extent) between employees and employers, and the fact that there is such an inequality of bargaining power involved in the individual employee–employer relationship. It is such premises that led the Webbs, in keeping with the larger, institutional economics movement, to favour the use of inductive-historical analysis over the deductive methodology of the neo-classical price theorists.

In a recent paper, Clark Kerr has classified the individuals making a contribution to industrial relations prior to the Second World War into the following groups: (i) neo-classicists (e.g. Marshall or Hicks); (ii) marxists; (iii) the administrative and the structuralists (e.g. the Webbs or Sumner Slichter); (iv) the institutionalists (e.g. Commons); (v) the anti-monopolists (e.g. Hayek); and (vi) the human relations school of thought (e.g. Mayo).[3] According to Kerr, the leading figures in the development of industrial relations as a field of study in the US in the period 1945–60 were not so much followers of Commons's institutional tradition, but rather a group that he labelled the 'neorealists'. These particular individuals (e.g. Dunlop) differed from the institutionalists in the following ways:

(i) they were relatively more interested in the influence of market forces, albeit forces constrained by customs, rules and regulations, and the power of combinations;
(ii) they were relatively more interested in collective bargaining than unions *per se*, hence their study of the management function and activities; and
(iii) they were relatively interested in the development of inter-disciplinary, or at least multi-disciplinary, work which involved other researchers from political science, sociology, and psychology.[4]

A sizeable group of industrial-relations researchers with the above orientation was relatively absent in the formative years of the subject's development in university settings in Britain – with the result that the nature of research in the two systems has increasingly diverged through the course of time. The leading individual researchers (as opposed to the majority of researchers) in Britain, such as Clegg and Flanders, were mainly from sociology and history – rather than economics, as in the United States – and were more wedded to (in Kerr's terms) the structuralist and/or institutional approaches. One useful indication of the nature of the divergence that has occurred in British and US industrial relations research through time is provided by Cappelli's observation that:

> Most of the research presented in the *Industrial and Labor Relations Review* over the past three years has applied deductive hypotheses from the social sciences. In contrast, only about 2 per cent of the research appearing in the same period in the British journal, *Industrial Relations Journal*, made use of deductive approaches based on social science theories.[5]

Specialist industrial relations researchers in Britain, who exist in some departments of economics, sociology, law, and (increasingly) in management or business schools, still overwhelmingly favour the inductive/historical approach of the institutionalists, utilizing case studies as their basic analytical tool of investigation. There will always be questions raised about whether case studies can adequately meet the standards of *internal validity* (i.e. can causal inferences be drawn by accepting or rejecting all possible rival hypotheses or explanations?) and *external validity* (i.e. can the findings generalise to the larger population?).[6] Certainly, in the United States it is clear that case-study-based work has increasingly acquired an unfavourable reputation in industrial-relations research, and is now relatively rarely conducted. This is an unfortunate development, as a well-designed series of case studies can be particularly important in (i) generating (as opposed to testing) new hypotheses, particularly those involving behavioural dynamics; (ii) providing an essential time-perspective on the evolution of particular structural arrangements identified in cross-sectional surveys; (iii) investigating in some depth the reasons why unusual or atypical situations (that depart, for example, from the industry norm) appear to have emerged and been maintained; and (iv) being one important component or element of the 'triangulation', or multiple-methodology, approach that is so important when one is undertaking any investigation of a large, multi-faceted issue and question in industrial relations, or indeed in the social sciences more generally.[7]

Industrial-relations research in both Britain and the United States does, however, have at least one feature in common at the present time – namely, that both have passed their zenith. In other words, both streams of research have passed through their respective 'golden ages' in the sense of the total amount of funded research being undertaken on socially important and pressing problems. There has always been something of a tension in the industrial-relations-research community between (i) the desire to be a socially relevant field of study that responds smoothly and quickly to the problems of the day, with the outcome being a capacity to offer useful guidance and direction to practitioners and policy makers, and (ii) the desire to be taken seriously as a separate field of study (with a distinctive subject matter and analytical approach) by other academics from the mainstream disciplines. If, however, we look across countries, or at changes through the course of time in a single country, then we find that industrial relations research has always been most active in systems or periods of time when industrial-relations problems are widely held to be most socially acute. Furthermore, as Government funding for research rises and falls according to the perceived extent and nature of such problems, so the 'popular' subject matter of industrial-relations research in any system will exhibit a similar pattern of movement. In Britain it is relatively easy to chart the changing fads in industrial relations research: shop stewards in the 1960s, followed by industrial democracy, corporatism and, now, management style. The 'golden age', or high-water mark, of industrial-relations research in Britain was approximately the period of time between the Donovan Commission (1965–8) and the Bullock Committee of Inquiry (1977), when the nature of research took roughly the following form: unionized relationships = collective bargaining = trade unions (particularly stewards) = plant level. However, since the Bullock Committee of Inquiry, and particularly in the 1980s, the emphasis has changed quite substantially – with non-union relationships, management structure, strategy and behaviour, and company-level analysis coming much more to the forefront, at least in terms of funded research.

To some researchers such short-run changes in subject matter and emphasis are both inevitable and desirable, whereas to others such a pattern of movement is viewed as having hindered the longer-run theoretical development and maturity of the field of study, with a resulting loss of reputation among academics from the mainstream disciplines. Many specialist industrial-relations researchers may be prepared to accept the latter criticism and 'cost' in an attempt to produce findings and results that will be of interest and value to practitioners and policy makers. However, this is a far from easy task to accomplish. The point here is that the different value-systems of researchers and practitioners (policy makers) means that the criteria for judging the worth and quality of research are very different. The result is that industrial-relations researchers are often forced to face up to important choices and trade-offs in their research design, depending on whether they are essentially seeking to speak to their academic peer group as opposed to practitioners. Clearly, the more that attention is given to the latter the more likely the field of study as a whole and individual researchers in it are open to the charges of loss of objectivity and conducting poor-quality research (e.g. the line between consultancy and research becomes increasingly blurred). Accordingly, the real challenge for industrial-relations researchers (with at least two potential audiences) – as for so much of social-sciences research – is to find ways of minimizing the conflict between conducting good-quality research and adequately conveying or disseminating the results of such research in a manner or form that is accessible and acceptable to practitioners.[8]

One recent review of US industrial-relations research contained a number of passing references to research in Britain, one of which was the claim that there has been rather more interest in the development of theory in the latter system.[9] At first glance this observation might appear inconsistent with a number of the comments made above (e.g. Cappelli's observation), but in fact what was specifically being referred to was the continued interest in Britain in searching for and developing one grand, or single, theory of industrial relations. It is to this matter that we now turn.

The search for the single, grand theory of industrial relations

The starting point for discussion of this topic is almost inevitably the book by John Dunlop which, although published more than a quarter of a century ago, still continues to attract a good deal of criticism – suggested modifications/additions to its basic structure have been put forward and, rather less frequently, it is utilized as the conceptual framework for single-industry, empirical (largely qualitative) studies.[10] The basic point from which Dunlop proceeded was that:

> To the date the study of industrial relations has had little theoretical content. At its origins, and frequently at its best, it has been largely historical and descriptive. Although industrial relations aspires to be a discipline, it has lacked any central analytical content. It has been a cross-roads where a number of disciplines have met – history, economics, sociology, psychology and law.[11]

The approach adopted by Dunlop was to develop the concept of a system of industrial relations to try and counteract the problems of competition between the contributing disciplines. The industrial-relations system at the national level (the possibility of industrial and regional sub-systems was noted) – which was a sub-system of the social, political, economic and legal systems – comprised three basic groups of actors: workers and their organizations; employers and their organizations; and government agencies. These groups confronted an environmental context composed of three inter-related elements: (i) technology; (ii) product market (or budgetary) constraints; and (iii) the power relations (and status) of the respective actors. The system was essentially an equilibrating one, bound together by an ideology or shared understanding between the actors which, at the very least, was the interest in 'mutual survival' or the maintenance of institutional arrangements. The outcome of the actors' interaction in this environmental context was a web of rules to govern relationships in the workplace. These rules, which were both substantive and procedural in nature, could be embodied in collective agreements, statute law, arbitration awards, etc. And the central task of a theory of industrial relations was to explain why particular rules are established in particular systems and how and why these rules change in response to changes affecting the system.

The work of Dunlop can be viewed as helping (particularly with the addition of certain modifications/additions proposed by subsequent writers) to delineate the central subject matter of industrial relations, namely the web of rules governing job regulation that emerges from the interaction of workers, management, and government actors – influenced by market, technology, and power forces.[12] Dunlop's work could also be viewed as having made a useful contribution to broadening the subject matter of industrial relations beyond collective bargaining – because of his emphasis on the fact that the web of rules could emerge from other mechanisms such as stature law and arbitration awards. There are also a number of specific insights that can be, and indeed have been, drawn upon in subsequent empirical studies. Witness, for example, the importance of the secular fall in product demand in shaping industrial-relations structure, behaviour, and outcomes in the British coal-mining industry.[13]

The Dunlop approach has, however, been subject to a very considerable volume of critical comment, although the seriousness of the individual criticisms made does tend to vary quite substantially. Undoubtedly the most damaging criticism is the claim that Dunlop has really only produced a classificatory system or heuristic device, which is not a theory capable of being operationalized and hence subject to potential testing and verification; having said this, at least one quantitative, sectoral study based on Canadian data does claim (perhaps rather generously) to have produced such an examination of his framework of analysis.[14] A further line of criticism has been that it is very much a structural, deterministic model, with the all-important environmental forces producing a mechanical, uniform effect on the behaviour of all the actors in the system. In other words, there is no recognition in Dunlop's treatment of the possibility (some would say likelihood) that different actors may have differing perceptions of a common environmental change which will, in turn, lead to quite different responses and patterns of behaviour. Accordingly, there is no 'social action' frame of reference accorded any role or importance in the actors' definition of situations. Dunlop's work has also been subject to the criticism that it is inadequate for analysing change and conflict. This criticism has involved the implied values or normative premises of the model (i.e. it is essentially a consensual one), and also the fact that its essentially static structure is only appropriate for analysing marginal, incremental changes in an industrial-relations system. In a period of time characterized by non-marginal changes, driven by fundamental value-shifts among at least one group of actors, it is held to be an inadequate framework of analysis; witness, for example, the recent call for a 'strategic choice' framework of analysis to help understand the nature, and determinants, of the recent fundamental changes occurring in the US system of industrial relations.[15] Finally, other researchers have been critical of the model's essential focus on only structured, formal levels and methods of union–management interaction – with a consequent slighting of the less formal, unstructured aspects of such processes (e.g. the neglect of historically determined 'custom and practice' in individual workplaces).

The search for a single, grand theory of industrial relations certainly did not end with the appearance of Dunlop's work. In one sense, the approach of marxist scholars can be viewed as the ultimate in single, grand theories of industrial relations, although in another sense it can be viewed as quite the opposite – due to its insistence that there is no autonomous sphere of industrial relations that can be adequately analysed as a closed, self-contained system. The view that industrial relations is simply derivative of relationships in (and of) production – which are, in turn, the result of historically shaped patterns of economic ownership and political control – contains at least two important implications or suggestions for industrial relations researchers:

(i) the key forces that bring about changes in industrial-relations structure, behaviour, and performance may not solely (or even mainly) derive from (or have their origins in) the industrial-relations sphere of activity as conventionally defined; and
(ii) as a consequence of the above, attempts to reform aspects of industrial relations by utilizing only those levers of change that exist in the industrial-relations sphere may have limited success due to the countervailing power of larger economic and political forces.

There has been something of a tendency, particularly in US industrial-relations research, to discount the role and importance of marxist analysis – on the grounds that its predictions about the nature of social and economic developments have not been borne out by time, and that it is of such a general, abstract nature that it does not readily lend itself to empirical examination. In fact, as will be apparent at various points in subsequent chapters, it has been the work and insights (often centring around the two implications identified above) of individual radical or marxist scholars that have been most important in sparking off some of the major contemporary debates in industrial-relations research in Britain.

There still continue to appear periodically a number of proposals for single, if rather less grand (than that of Dunlop), theories of industrial relations. These have essentially argued the case for a particular influence, or variable, to constitute the central analytical core of industrial-relations research. In some cases, what has been proposed is a potential *dependent* variable (such as industrial conflict or industrial democracy); in other cases, the proposal has been for focusing on an all-important, *independent* variable (such as bargaining power).[16] In the latter category has been Clegg's comparison of a number of national industrial-relations systems in which he accords key importance to the level of bargaining, or bargaining structure, within such systems.[17] In Clegg's view, certain leading industrial-relations phenomena – such as the extent and nature of strike frequency, union demoncracy, and industrial democracy – are explicable in terms of the level at which collective bargaining is conducted in the system(s) concerned.

Individual, disciplinary orientations in research

The alternative to seeking a single, grand theory of industrial relations is, or at least has been in practice, to favour the deductive, middle-range-theory(ies) approach of US industrial-relations research. The essence of this approach is to reject any suggestion that industrial relations is or should be a discipline in its own right. Instead, so the argument goes, it is a field of study which is a meeting ground for a number of disciplines – with the methodology, analytical tools, hypotheses, and insights that one uses to be drawn selectively from the individual contributing disciplines, according to the particular issue or question being researched. For example, if one is interested in trying to explain an aggregate, time-series problem (such as the year-to-year variation in total union membership in Britain), then the hypotheses to be tested should be drawn from the disciplines of economics, political science, history, and law; whereas, if one is investigating a micro, cross-sectional issue (such as the differing behavioural patterns of two workgroups in a single plant), then one will need to look to psychology and sociology for the relevant hypotheses and insights. There are various potential criticisms that can be made of such an approach to industrial-relations research. The leading ones are, arguably, the following:

(i) the field of study will diversify and fragment to such an extent that knowledge does not accumulate in a systematic, coherent fashion;
(ii) individual researchers will have disciplinary blinkers and ignore much of each other's work, with the result that comparisons across studies are difficult to make and/or individual results and findings are frequently rediscovered; and
(iii) genuine inter-disciplinary, as opposed to multi-disciplinary, work can only be undertaken by a relatively small number of unusually trained individuals.

There are numerous articles from researchers from individual disciplines identifying what they see as the particular contribution they can, should, and have made to industrial-relations research.[18] It is certainly no secret that individuals from one discipline do not always have a high regard for the work and contribution of industrial-relations researchers from others. Economists are often inclined to be quite dismissive of the work of specialist industrial-relations researchers,[19] arguing that it is highly descriptive and prescriptive in nature, while, at the same time, industrial-relations researchers from a non-economics background are frequently highly critical of the work of economists in the industrial-relations area.[20] The criticisms typically made of the contribution of economists to industrial relations have been as follows:

(i) they have studied only a relatively narrow range of subjects (e.g. wages, strikes);
(ii) they have largely employed *ex post facto* research designs – i.e. relied overwhelmingly on existing, published-data sources to test their hypotheses, rather than generating their own primary data;
(iii) their analysis has been conducted at highly aggregative levels far above the 'ideal' level of analysis where collective bargaining, for example, actually takes place (and the explanatory power of their aggregative models often falls dramatically when any attempt is made to replicate their work at more disaggregated levels of analysis); and
(iv) their focus on, for example, *the* union effect, or impact,

> ignores the extremely heterogeneous nature of the union movement in matters of structure, administration, and behaviour.

Moreover, pursuing point (i) above a little further, it is undoubtedly true that the research questions which have particularly attracted the attention of economists in the industrial-relations field have been overwhelmingly those to do with, what Freeman and Medoff have labelled, the 'monopoly face' of unions.[21] In their view, economists have been overly preoccupied with studying the particular issues of:

(i) unions raising wages above competitive levels, with the result that too little labour is employed relative to capital in unionized firms (the result being allocative inefficiency);
(ii) union restrictive practices and strikes;
(iii) unions increasing income inequality by disproprotionately increasing the wages of skilled (manual) workers; and
(iv) unions creating horizontal inequities as a result of establishing wage differentials among comparable workers based on the seniority (as opposed to ability) criterion.

In the past, only relatively small numbers of economists have been involved in industrial-relations research in Britain, but as the availability of survey data has increased quite substantially in recent years (especially as a result of the 1980 and 1984 workplace surveys) then it is a reasonably safe prediction that their relative contribution will rise in the future, a fact that has important potential implications for the subject matter and methodology of the field of study.

Some new directions in industrial-relations research?

From what has been said to date it should be clear that the area or field of industrial relations research has always been characterized by a good deal of debate and controversy about its basic nature and desirable orientation. There is rarely a lack of arguments and recommendations for industrial-relations researchers to reassess their priorities, orientations, and approaches, and here we consider a number of the more recent ones along these lines. At present, the one consistent theme that tends to run through such varied calls is for industrial-relations researchers to *broaden* their subject matter and frameworks of analysis. Accordingly, what we consider in the remainder of this chapter are the recommendations in favour of (i) more comparative or cross-country research, (ii) a greater integration of industrial-relations and organization-behaviour research, and (iii) industrial-relations researchers paying more attention to non-union plants and firms.

A variety of questions have prompted or motivated cross-country research in industrial relations. The following have been among the most important in this regard.

1. Are various national systems of industrial relations exhibiting any sort of tendency to increasingly converge or diverge through time, and what are the factors involved in such processes?
2. Are there 'model' systems of industrial relations, some of whose features can or should be 'exported' to other systems?
3. If various national systems are experiencing essentially similar problems of performance, are there any useful 'best-practice' policy lessons or guidelines that can be drawn from the different attempts to cope with these difficulties?
4. Do certain individual research findings (e.g. the relationship between highly competitive product markets and multi-employer bargaining arrangements) transcend the particular institutional details of individual systems?
5. Do multinational corporations have essentially similar industrial-relations arrangements in the various countries in which they are located, and do these tend to produce much the same results and outcomes in these different settings?

Some of the earliest interest in 'the industrial relations of other countries' arose from the visits of individual researchers from, let us call them, country A to country B which produced highly favourable reports of arrangements in B, with the suggestion that practitioners and policy makers in country A could usefully model themselves on country B. In a useful review of this literature, Kassalow has suggested that the particular countries that were cast in this 'model role' were: Britain (in the closing decades of the nineteenth century); Germany (before the First World War); the United States (1945–60); Sweden (in the 1960s); Germany (in the 1970s); and Japan (in the 1980s).[22] This is a far from analytical body of literature, but, according to Windmuller,[23] the three pre-requisites for the industrial-relations arrangements of any one country to constitute a viable model for others to emulate are: first, a fundamental consensus among the three groups of actors in the system concerned; second, a demonstrated capacity for high achievement or success within its own society along one or more relevant lines; and, third, a will to demonstrate or export to others on the part of the model system.

However, it was in the context of the larger discussion and debate of the late 1950s and early 1960s – about the alleged convergence of market and non-market economic systems – that comparative industrial-relations research began to be undertaken on a substantial scale. The best known work from this era is that of Kerr, Dunlop, Harbison, and Myers – which argued that the common values and orientation of the elite decision-makers in various countries were particularly important in working to produce certain similarities in industrial relations systems. Furthermore, systems would, over time, follow an increasingly convergent path, due to facing the common problems of industrialization.[24] This prediction has not in fact been borne out by experience, as the members of the original research team have themselves conceded in a subsequent publication,[25] due to changed circumstances invalidating certain of their key assumptions. For example, Goldthorpe highlighted their belief that pragmatic, mature unions, which were concerned overwhelmingly with collective-bargaining activities, would constitute an increasingly well-integrated component of a pluralistic, industrialized society. However, as he went on to argue:

> In particular, liberal theorists of industrialism failed to appreciate the importance of two developments that became increasingly apparent, even if with some significant cross-national variation, within trade unionism over the post-war period: first, the emergence of a new 'maximising' militancy in collective bargaining, encouraged, one would suggest, by the weakening of traditional legitimations of class inequalities and traditional limitations on wants and life-styles, as well as by the rising confidence of trade-unionists in the bases of their organised power; and secondly, a growing concern shown by unions, especially through their central federations, with the direction of macro-economic policy, which they increasingly recognised as capable of exerting a crucial influence on the bargaining strength of labour as a whole.[26]

The impact of such trade-union activity on market forces was alleged to have produced inherently inflationary tendencies from the late 1960s,[27] an outcome which led to a further wave of comparative industrial-relations research which was basically 'problem-orientated'.[28] In other words, studies of the extent and nature of 'union militancy'[29] (particularly on the part of the union rank and file) were followed by studies of union decline from the late 1970s,[30] and then by examinations of the means by which various industrial-relations systems attempted to adjust to, and cope with, the varied 'economic shocks' of the 1970s and 1980s.[31] One of the more recent, broad-ranging contributions to the comparative industrial-relations literature emphasizes the continued diversity of national systems and offers a conceptual framework (involving environmental conditions, intervening conditions, proximal conditions, and the strategic choices of actors) to help try and understand the nature of the observed differences.[32] However, whether this framework will prove capable of being operationalized and tested in a systematic and analytical way remains somewhat questionable.

There is undoubtedly a great deal of interest in pursuing comparative industrial relations research at the present time. However, for such work to proceed usefully it will be essential to move away from the traditional, highly descriptive approach of previous studies and to develop more systematic and analytical research designs.[33]

In order to achieve more analytical studies, one methodological approach that industrial-relations researchers are increasingly likely to pursue in the future is that which has been 'pioneered' by industrial sociologists in Europe. This is the *paired comparison* method, which involves selecting and studying in depth certain organizations in different societies that are matched on key matters such as size, technology, and product.[34] Finally, it is worth noting that although comparative studies of policy initiatives continue to be undertaken, particularly of incomes policy,[35] most industrial-relations researchers are now relatively sceptical of the value of comparative work for the purposes of drawing 'best-practice' policy lessons;[36] the reason for this being the belief that a common policy introduced into two systems of industrial relations with quite different traditions, structures, and patterns of behaviour will produce quite divergent outcomes, due to the system differences overriding the common-policy provisions.

In practice (if not necessarily in principle) industrial-relations researchers have overwhelmingly concentrated on group or collective relationships, with the research that has emerged from Britain and the US being overwhelmingly centred around collective bargaining as the major mechanism for the joint determination and regulation of the terms and conditions of employment; as indicated earlier, the emphasis in such research has only tended to shift between unions and management according to who was perceived to be the 'pace-setter' in the relationship in a particular period of time. The result of this focus, or orientation, is that the aims, aspirations, and goal attainments of the *individual worker* have received remarkably little attention in the resulting stream of research; one of the earliest criticisms of the Dunlop 'systems' approach centred around this very omission.[37] The individual employee figures much more prominently in the work of the younger, more radical labour historians in both Britain and the United States,[38] but it has really been the behavioural scientists (psychologists and sociologists) who have dominated the study of the individual employment relationship. The nature of their research efforts has been strongly shaped by the fact that both the scientific-management and human-relations schools of thought are premised on the belief in a strong, positive, direct relationship between job satisfaction and productivity. In the former theory, high productivity (stemming from a high degree of task specialization) is held to lead (via the operations of payment-by-results schemes) to high job satisfaction, while in the latter theory the line of causation is held to go the other way – i.e. high job satisfaction (through employee-centred supervisory practices, good communications, and non-directive employee counselling) will lead to high productivity.[39] In fact, the resulting research efforts of behavioural scientists have shown that the relationship between job satisfaction and productivity is not a particularly strong, direct one.[40] These accumulated studies have therefore meant that it is the behavioural scientists, rather than industrial-relations researchers, who have contributed most to answering questions about, for example, the nature and determinants of individual employees' attitudes and orientations to work, job satisfaction, and work performance.[41]

The existence of these two parallel streams of research has had two results. First, organization-behaviour researchers have criticized traditional industrial-relations books centred around the institution of collective bargaining for the lack of attention given to individual topics such as job motivation, job design, leadership styles, etc.[42] Second (and more positively), there have been a number of calls during the 1970s and 1980s in both Britain and the United States for a closer integration of the respective research efforts.[43] The latter have been useful in identifying some of the major, historical reasons for the separation of the two streams of research (e.g. different normative premises regarding the nature and value of industrial conflict),[44] and for proposing certain concepts (e.g. the nature of the 'psychological contract')[45] that could potentially constitute the centrepiece of collaborative research efforts. The momentum behind calls for more integrated research along such lines would appear to have been particularly enhanced by Fox's contention that an industrial-relations system based on a pluralist ideology will inevitably experience a secular decline in performance due to the mutual low-trust/high-conflict relationships that exist between workers and employers.[46] In his view, employer and union demands, tactics, and behaviour centred around, for example, the collective-bargaining relationship, are increasingly incapable of solving organizational problems and responding effectively to the expectations of individual employees.

At the present time there appear to be few formal, large-scale collaborative projects involving industrial-relations and organization-behaviour researchers in either Britain or the United States. It is clear, however, in recent years that industrial-relations researchers, particularly in the United States, have come to devote increased attention to the topics of job-satisfaction and productivity – subjects that were traditionally the preserve of organization-behaviour researchers.[47] Moreover, some of the more recent individual employee-centred working arrangements (e.g. quality circles, autonomous work groups) that have been introduced in Britain and the United States, in the larger context of increased employer interest in obtaining flexible working practices, will undoubtedly have the effect of encouraging industrial-relations researchers to examine more closely the nature, determinants of, and relationships between (i) job satisfaction, (ii) aspects of industrial relations performance, (iii) productivity, and (iv) measures of larger organizational performance;[48] the result of this will clearly be to bring the interests of industrial-relations and organization-behaviour researchers closer together.

One particular manifestation of the relatively limited attention given to the individual employment relationship by industrial-relations researchers is the fact that they have virtually ignored the existence of non-union firms. It was again the behavioural scientists, particularly those coming out of the 'human relations' school of thought or tradition (which tends to view unions as unnecessary if 'good' management meets the on-the-job needs of their employees) who were most interested in such organizations – in terms of providing advice and consultancy, as well as in conducting research. Not surprisingly, the nature of their involvement with such firms has not endeared such individuals to the union movement.[49] As indicated earlier, industrial-relations researchers concentrated very much on the union pace-setter in the joint relationship during the years (up to the late 1970s) when unions were growing, which has meant that even the more up-to-date books in British industrial relations only tend to refer to non-union firms when discussing (i) organizations that are not affiliated to employers associations, and (ii) the *unitarist* frame of reference of management within organizations; the latter holds that firms are analogous to sports teams in having a single focus of authority and loyalty and, as such, denies the legitimacy and value of the union role and industrial conflict.[50] Admittedly Fox's proposed taxonomy of employee-relations patterns, with their differing management styles, classified non-union firms under the heading of the *traditional* pattern, but he provided only the most limited discussion of this sub-group;[51] the elaborations of this classification which have been subsequently put forward will be discussed in Chapter 4. Similarly in the United States, industrial-relations researchers have not traditionally devoted much attention to non-union firms, although a long-standing distinction is drawn in the literature there between firms following a union-substitution (better standards) as opposed to a union-suppression (low standards) approach.[52] However, as the level of overall union density has fallen substantially in the US in recent decades, some researchers have begun to examine more systematically the organizational arrangements and practices of non-union firms.[53] Interestingly, this re-orientation of interest has attracted some criticism from older students of the subject, as being inconsistent with, and hence potentially capable of undermining, the historical roots and traditions of the field of study.[54]

Industrial-relations researchers in Britain have always acknowledged that the sub-set of non-union firms in the system at any point in time is extremely heterogeneous in nature, exhibiting considerable differences in matters such as (i) the level of terms and conditions of employment, (ii) workforce composition, (iii) key organizational characteristics, and (iv) in the nature of their larger operating environment. The extent and nature of such differences can be appreciated by contrasting individual cases of relatively large-sized, US-owned manufacturing establishments (such as IBM, Hewlett-Packard, and Motorola) with small-sized, domestically-owned, service-sector establishments in Britain. However, it is only with the appearance of large and nationally representative survey-data sets from the late 1970s that industrial-relations researchers in Britain have been able to examine more fully and comprehensively the extent and nature of such firms in the system at large. One such set of information is shown in Table 1.1, which indicates that the proportion of manual employees in non-union establishments increased quite substantially in the years 1980–4 in most regions and certainly for the country as a whole, with above average levels of 'non-union employment' being particularly associated with the southern regions. Further analysis of these two data sets has revealed that the non-union status of establishments is significantly associated with variables such as small-establishment size and younger-aged establishments.[55] As will be discussed more fully in Chapter 3, the level of overall union density in Britain has fallen

Table 1.1 Proportion of manual workers in private-sector establishments where trade unions were recognized or not, by region, 1980 and 1984

Region	*Proportion of manual employees in private-sector establishments where trade unions were:*					
	(i) Recognized		*(ii) Not recognized*		*(iii) Not present*	
	1980	*1984*	*1980*	*1984*	*1980*	*1984*
Scotland	85.4	67.2	1.9	13.9	12.7	19.0
Wales	85.7	73.3	6.5	5.8	7.7	20.9
North	91.5	84.1	2.7	5.3	5.9	10.5
North-West	89.4	83.6	7.2	5.9	3.4	10.3
Yorks./Humberside	86.5	85.4	2.8	3.8	10.7	10.8
West Midlands	90.9	77.1	2.6	6.8	6.6	15.5
East Midlands	93.0	63.1	1.9	10.9	5.1	26.1
East Anglia	82.1	66.1	8.1	19.5	9.8	14.4
South West	79.2	61.2	9.5	10.8	11.4	28.0
South East	69.4	51.5	10.1	15.4	20.5	33.2
London	75.8	68.3	5.2	4.3	19.0	27.5
Great Britain	83.7	70.3	5.5	9.1	10.8	20.6

Source: Based on the 1980 and 1984 *Workplace Industrial Relations Surveys*, with figures provided by Richard Harris (Queen's University).

quite substantially in the years since 1979, a change which has raised the question of whether the relative size of the non-union sector will increase quite significantly in the system as a whole in the years to come. In such discussions it is frequently suggested that *newer*, more recently established organizations will contain a relatively high proportion of non-union establishments, particularly if the organization is (i) small sized, and (ii) in a high technology industry; it is important to note here that our most important sources of survey data on industrial relations (i.e. the 1980 and 1984 workplace surveys) exclude establishments with less than twenty-five employees and contain only a relatively small proportion of new establishments.[56] Accordingly, the remainder of this chapter considers these two potential contributors to the possible growth of the non-union sector in Britain, and highlights some of the particular issues that can be usefully addressed by industrial-relations researchers if, and when, they begin to look more seriously at such organizations.[57]

The rate of small-business formation in Britain has been alleged to have increased in recent years, as a result of both the environment of high and rising unemployment and the substantial change in the nature of Government policy towards the small-firm sector from the late 1970s.[58] On the latter point, encouragement of the small-firm sector is particularly favoured by the present Conservative Government in Britain for, among other things, industrial-relations reasons[59] (i.e. as leading to reduced overall levels of union density and strike activity in the system as a whole). There are numerous aggregate statistics which are currently cited concerning the relatively favourable employment-generation performance of small firms in Britain. For example, it has been reported that manufacturing enterprises with less than 20 employees (100 employees) increased their employment share from 7(17) per cent in 1976 to 10(21) per cent in 1982, while for the period 1971–81 small firms with under 20 employees were responsible for 36 per cent of all new jobs generated (with these being the only creator of *net* new jobs in these same years).[60] However, such aggregate statistics need to be put in the context of the following, more detailed research findings.[61]

1. At least 30 per cent of new manufacturing businesses fail to survive for four years.
2. The median level of employment of a wholly new business is ten employees.
3. The median new business shows no tendency to increase its employment after it has been established for 5 years.
4. The probability of a wholly new business reaching 100 employees in a decade is between 0.5 and 0.75 per cent.
5. There is no evidence of more rapid growth in the so-called 'high technology' sectors.
6. Of all new business starts, 4 per cent created 34 per cent of all employment in new firms.

There is some survey evidence concerning, for example, the new towns of Scotland, which indicates that a relatively high proportion of newly established firms are both small-sized and non-union ones,[62] while a recent analysis of recognition-claims involving conciliation by officers of the Advisory Conciliation and Arbitration Service (ACAS) in one region of the country revealed that unions were least likely to obtain recognition in the claims involving small, single, independent establishments.[63] However, a number of substantial research issues still remain to be systematically addressed by industrial-relations scholars in this particular subject area. For example, urban and regional researchers have suggested that the founders of new small businesses are disproportionately likely to have an immediate employment background in small-sized plants.[64] This finding suggests that regions or sub-regions of Britain with a relatively high proportion of overall employment in small-sized plants are likely to generate above-average levels of new, small-business formation. It will therefore be important for industrial relations researchers to see if inter-area variation in the extent of such formation rates complements and reinforces the existing, industrial-relations practices and traditions of such areas. Specifically, it will be useful to examine the extent and ways in which the particular employment background of small-business founders shapes the nature of the 'organization culture' (e.g. non-union status) that they may seek to create for their own organization.[65] Furthermore, it is widely held that, as small firms grow (in terms of size), significant changes need to be made in the nature of their management and organizational arrangements – in order to avoid dysfunctional consequences for employee behaviour and performance.[66] The necessity for such changes inevitably raises questions about the extent of institutionalization of the particular culture created by the founder. Whether the industrial-relations components of the original culture (particularly any desire for non-union status) can survive the test of time is clearly an important subject for examination. Finally, a number of individual unions in Britain have recently initiated special campaigns to try and obtain increased levels of recognition among small-sized firms.[67] The processes and outcomes of such campaigns could usefully be the subject of some detailed research, given the long-standing difficulties of unions in making substantial inroads into such organizations, at least via traditional recruitment methods.

Turning now to the subject area of high-technology industries, the first question to pose is whether there is any such thing as a high-technology industry; is it a valid and useful concept, or is the notion of high technology much more of an individual, organization-centred concept? There has, in fact, been considerable discussion and debate over this particular question, both in Britain and the United States.[68] The proposed criteria for identifying high-technology industries typically include the level of research-and-development activity and the proportion of scientists, professional engineers, and technicians in the workforce. The Department of Trade and Industry has recently produced a definition and classification of high-technology industries along these lines; in 1986 these high-technology industries accounted for approximately 6 per cent of total employment.[69] The existing discussions of high-technology industries by industrial-relations researchers have suggested that a disproportionate number of firms in such industries are non-union, operate with a particular style of management (i.e. 'sophisticated paternalism') in which human-resource-management practices figure prominently, and are increasingly constituting the 'role model' that influences the individual employment practices of other organizations.[70] There are a number of *a priori* reasons why non-union status and relatively well-developed human-resource-management policies might be expected to be strongly related to organizations in these particular industries; these reasons include the younger age of such organizations, their operation in tight labour-markets and developing product-markets, the fact that they employ relatively high proportions of professional and technical staff, can readily incorporate new technology into their operations, and are still frequently run by their original founders. A recent analysis of the 1984 survey data has, in fact, revealed that (i) non-union status is significantly associated with establishments in high technology industries, and (ii) establishments in these particular industries have undertaken a relatively large number of recent employee-involvement initiatives.[71] However, many questions still remain concerning the details of such initiatives, and their possible implications for non-union status. In short, a very full and important agenda still awaits the attention of industrial-relations researchers in this particular subject area.

Conclusions

In this chapter I have indicated some of the trends and issues in the subject matter and methodology of industrial-relations research, considered the question of the role and place of theory in such research, and highlighted some of the major challenges and questions facing the field of study at the present time. In covering such topics it will, hopefully, be apparent that industrial relations, although not attracting the research funding and student numbers of the 1970s, is anything but a field of study lacking a lively, important, and controversial research agenda. Inevitably I have touched here on certain concepts and arguments that remain to be more fully examined in subsequent chapters. This task is begun in the next chapter, which examines the nature of some of the larger environmental forces operating on the process of collective bargaining.

Chapter two

The larger environment of collective bargaining

In systems of industrial relations in which collective bargaining has been the leading mechanism of union–management interaction for determining and regulating the terms and conditions of employment there have been long-standing discussions and debates concerning the extent to which collective bargaining outcomes diverge from those that would have resulted from the operation of market forces. In Chapter 7 I review a good deal of the empirical literature concerning the impact of collective bargaining on the economic environment, whereas here I view the larger external environment as an independent variable that shapes the structures, processes, and outcomes of collective bargaining, and present various facts and figures pertaining to *selected* aspects of this environment – namely, the labour market, the product market, the legislative and legal environment, and the larger societal and political context. In essence, I present here a 'check-list' of certain key facts and figures that should help the reader appreciate the larger setting of collective bargaining, with many of the more analytical issues and questions raised by such facts and figures being the subject of discussion in later chapters.

There are at least two important, introductory points that need to be made about the particular aspects or dimensions of the external environment identified and discussed here. The first is that these individual aspects of the environment will inevitably overlap and interact together in terms of their effects on the structures, processes, and outcomes of collective bargaining, so that it becomes a difficult task to disentangle their individual impact, *ceteris paribus*. In other words, one might observe certain changes in particular measures of industrial-relations activity in a given period of time, but, if there has been a rise in unemployment, an increase in the extent of product-market competition, and the passing of certain legislation in these particular years, then it becomes difficult to identify which of these three factors has been primarily responsible for the change observed. The second point to make is that my discussion of the external environment is, perhaps invariably, to some extent a selective and partial one. That is, I discuss here only certain of the more *objective* features of the *contemporary* external environment that are typically held to be important in influencing some of the contemporary features of collective bargaining. There are, however, other, *less tangible* aspects of the external environment – in particular the influences of historically determined values and patterns of behaviour – whose contemporary relevance cannot be ignored. Indeed, Alan Fox's recent book places a great deal of emphasis on the role of 'a social context itself marked by continuities of individualism and of a state seen in terms of instrumental convenience rather than intrinsic or transcendental value' in producing certain significant, historical continuities in British industrial relations.[1] David Marquand's broad-ranging discussion of the adverse effects of highly developed and well entrenched individualistic values, and the absence of a strong state tradition, on economic readjustment in Britain also has many important industrial-relations consequences and implications.[2]

The labour-market environment

The first, selected dimension of the external environment examined here is the labour market, with our discussion beginning with the fact of a high and rising unemployment rate in Britain in recent years. Table 2.1 sets out the published unemployment rates for the United Kingdom for the years 1975–85.

The substantial rise in unemployment from the late 1970s has involved a total of around three million unemployed persons at any

Table 2.1 Unemployment rates for the United Kingdom, 1975–85 (in percentages)

1975	4.0
1976	5.5
1977	5.8
1978	5.7
1979	5.3
1980	6.8
1981	10.4
1982	12.1
1983	12.9
1984	13.1
1985	13.3

Source: Central Statistical Office (1987) *Annual Abstract of Statistics 1987*, no. 123, p. 114, London: HMSO.

one point in time in recent years, a figure that is forecast to change relatively little by the end of the decade.[3] There have been numerous discussions and debates about (i) the extent to which the officially recorded unemployment figures (the basis of which has been changed a number of times in recent years) reflect the full number of unemployed individuals, and (ii) the individual factors that have been primarily responsible for the observed rise in unemployment.[4] The OECD-adjusted unemployment figures, for example, certainly indicate that the recent UK figures are above the average for OECD countries,[5] and that, furthermore, such levels of unemployment are above that necessary to keep inflation constant.[6] The position of the present Conservative Government is that the current levels of unemployment are not the result of a shortage of demand, a lack of public-sector investment, or the pace of technological change, but rather are due to the existence of a labour market whose operation, at both the macro and micro levels, is beset with rigidities. Accordingly, their general approach, as enunciated in the 1985 White Paper, for example, has been to try and bring about a labour market characterized by reduced costs and increased incentives, flexibility, and freedom from regulation.[7] The result has been, for example, the repeal of specific measures which, in their view, cause the floor level of wages to be set too high (e.g. repeal of Schedule 11 of the Employment Protection Act 1975) and, more positively, the introduction of measures designed to increase the training and mobility of the workforce.[8] On the latter matter, there were some 801,000 individuals covered by seven special employment and training schemes in the financial year 1986–7, a figure that had increased from 306,000 persons covered by three schemes in 1979–80.

This is not the place to review the general nature and influence of rigidities in the operation of the labour market,[9] nor attempt any overall assessment of the record of the present Government's employment strategy.[10] It is more important for present purposes to consider the general direction and extent of change in certain measures of industrial-relations activity in recent years. The rise in unemployment from the late 1970s has certainty been associated with a fall in both the level of union membership and strike activity. However, there has not been the level of moderation in the rate of real wage change that the Government has been looking for, particularly compared to that achieved in other countries in more recent years.[12] The contents of Table 2.2 provide some indication of the position in this regard.

In Chapter 7 I will consider some of the empirical research that has been concerned with the determinants of real wage change in

Table 2.2 The rate of change in consumer prices and hourly earnings in manufacturing in the United Kingdom for selected periods

Period	*Consumer prices (average annual rate)*	*Hourly earnings in manufacturing (average annual rate)*
1964–73	5.9	9.1
1973–82	14.7	15.8
1983	4.6	9.0
1984	5.0	8.7
1985	6.1	9.1

Source: OECD Economic Outlook, no. 41, December 1986, pp. 39 and 43.

Britain, but for the present the basic point to note is that the rate of earnings increase in recent years still remains above that of inflation. There are a number of further observations that can briefly be made here about the nature of wage movements in Britain in recent years. First, individual instances of negotiations involving pay freezes or pay cuts have occurred, but they have been relatively few in number,[12] particularly in comparison with the United States where such concessions occurred in some 44 per cent of all major collective bargaining contracts negotiated in 1982 and 1983.[13] Second, there is some evidence to suggest that the size of the union-relative-wage effect (i.e. the average wage of unionized workers compared to that of their non-union counterparts, *ceteris paribus*) has increased as unemployment has risen in the 1980s.[14] Third, it is apparent that there has been a quite substantial fall in the relative wage position of unskilled workers in the years since 1979.[15] Fourth, an analysis of some information contained in the 1984 workplace industrial relations survey provides an indication of the major factors alleged by management to have influenced the level of pay in the most recent settlement. The results of this examination are set out below in Table 2.3.

The most frequently cited influences were profitability/productivity, increasing cost of living, going rate in industry, external pay structure and all the establishment could afford, which are (i) generally in line with the reponses contained in other data sources,[16] and (ii) have been viwed as supporting 'insider–outsider' theories of wage determination;[17] such theories stress the key roles of firms' internal activities and financial performance. In order to round off this discussion of the nature of wage movements in recent years it is important to relate such movements to those in productivity. Table 2.4 presents some relevant evidence on the latter measure.

The much improved productivity performance of the British manufacturing sector in the 1980s has been the subject of a good

Table 2.3 Factors influencing the level of pay in the most recent settlements (in percentages)

	Union sector (manuals)	*Non-union sector (non-manuals)*	*Union sector (non-manuals)*	*Non-union*
All establishment could afford	11	5	9	7
Increasing cost of living	34	29	37	32
Going rate in industry	15	23	13	19
Merit/individual performance	4	20	5	33
Published norms	3	2	3	4
Internal pay structure	2	3	6	15
External pay structure	15	15	9	11
Government regulation	6	3	10	2
Strikes	1	0	0	0
Profitability/ productivity	34	35	37	38
Economic climate	9	2	13	3
Other	13	7	15	6
Not answered	8	3	11	1

Source: D. G. Blanchflower and A. J. Oswald (1987), 'Internal and external influences upon pay settlements: new survey evidence', Centre for Labour Economics, LSE Discussion Paper no. 275, March, Table 2, p. 7.

Table 2.4 Average annual percentage change in output per head, manufacturing

Years	*UK*	*Average of seven major industrial countries*
1964–73	3.8	5.0
1973–79	0.7	3.2
1979–86	3.6	2.8

Source: D. Metcalf (1988), 'Water notes dry up', Centre for Labour Economics, LSE Discussion Paper no. 314, July, p. 4.

deal of discussion, with considerable controversy surrounding questions such as whether the rate of increase can be sustained in the future, and the particular contribution that various types of industrial-relations changes have made to the increases observed.[18] The latter issue will be discussed in more detail in Chapter 7.

The influence of the labour-market environment on the

contemporary structures, processes, and outcomes of collective bargaining is more than simply a function of relatively short-term movements in variables such as unemployment. One also needs to consider the effect of longer-term, *structural* changes in the labour market, such as, for example, (i) the relative growth of white collar, service-sector employment, (ii) the increased workforce participation rates of women, (iii) the relative growth of part-time, temporary work and self-employment, and (iv) the urban-to-rural shift in the location of manufacturing-sector employment.[19] A number of relevant, individual statistics in these regards are as follows.

1. The Institute of Employment Research at the University of Warwick has forecast that two-thirds of all net new jobs in Britain in 1985–90 will be in the private-services sector.[20]
2. Women constituted some 37.5 per cent of the workforce in 1971, a figure that is estimated to rise to some 42–44 per cent of the employed workforce by 1990–1.[21]
3. Full-time employment in the UK fell by some 1.2 per cent in 1979–85, whereas part-time employment grew by 5 per cent, with the result that the share of part-time employment in total employment in the UK was some 21.2 per cent in 1985 (compared to an average of 15.7 per cent for all countries examined by the OECD).[22] Self-employed (with or without employees) rose from 7.7 per cent of the total working population of the UK in 1975 to a figure of 9.5 per cent in 1985.[23]
4. Manufacturing employment in the years 1960–78 fell by 42.5 per cent in London and by 26.5 per cent in conurbations, whereas it increased by 15.7 per cent in small towns and by 38 per cent in rural areas.[24]

These sorts of structural changes, particularly in association with changes in the size and organizational arrangements of individual employment establishments and the pace of micro-electronics-based technological developments, have led some commentators to raise questions about the longer-term viability of the traditional (socially-constructed) work ethic, and its accompanying arrangements in terms of standard lengths of the working day, week, year, and lifetime.[25] In the industrial relations area, one of the most obvious questions raised by such changes in the composition and distribution of the workforce concerns the future level of overall union membership in Britain and elsewhere. In addition, such workforce compositional changes have potentially important implications for the character of the union movements concerned. The need to increasingly recruit white-collar and service-sector employees has been viewed as raising three basic possibilities for the union movements of Europe:[26]

(i) in those countries where unions fail to recruit an increasing proportion of the new workforce, they will be better able to retain their old sense of direction, but will represent a declining minority of the workforce;
(ii) where the new categories join unions, but in separate white-collar or professional confederations, as in Scandinavia, the old social democratic component of organized labour will gradually cede dominance to 'bourgeois', or non-partisan, unions; or
(iii) in those countries where manual and non-manual workers are successfully organized within the same confederation (i.e. Austria, and UK and, increasingly, West Germany), the main conferations themselves will be vulnerable to changes in character.

The sort of structural changes in the labour market referred to above have predictably raised questions about whether orientations to work and levels of job satisfaction have changed substantially in recent times. On the matter of work orientation, the European-values study of the early 1980s painted a picture of British workers as being strongly committed to work, readier than most to accept the existing patterns of authority and ownership in industry, as not being particularly hard driving, but who responded well to crisis situations, although they were particularly sensitive to perceptions of exploitation and being pushed around.[27] Furthermore, a review of the available survey evidence for manual workers and routine clerical workers reported that (i) pay and security have been increasingly emphasized as work priorities relative to the 1960s, and (ii) there were no clear-cut, observable trends through time in the levels of reported job satisfaction.[28] In the 1970s, figures contained in the General Household Survey revealed that, in any one year, between 82 per cent and 89 per cent of those interviewed reported themselves as being either very, or fairly, satisfied with their job in general terms. These levels of reported job satisfaction, with the essential absence of any notable changes (in either an upwards or downwards direction) through time, are very much in line with those typically obtained from similar surveys in other advanced industrialized economies (with the interesting exception of Japan).[29] However, it is only appropriate to acknowledge the fact that the value of such survey evidence has come in for a good deal of critical comment.[30] To some commentators, the whole approach of trying to investigate the complex, multi-faceted concept of job satisfaction by means of responses to a single question is a misplaced exercise, while others have pointed to the fact that the responses obtained are relatively sensitive to the precise wording of the question asked and that such responses are likely to embody substantial elements of both rationalization and defensiveness on the part of respondents. In short, the belief of many individuals is that findings for reported job satisfaction substantially overstate the levels of actual job satisfaction, and hence one must carefully distinguish between 'satisfaction with a job', as opposed to 'satisfaction in a job'.[31] The nature and implications of job satisfaction (or dissatisfaction) need to be much more thoroughly and systematically examined by industrial-relations researchers in Britain, particularly in view of some recent American research which indicates that (i) job dissatisfaction is an important source of demand for union representation, and (ii) there are significant differences in the reported job satisfaction of union and non-union employees, with unionized employees reporting relatively high satisfaction with some aspects of their job (e.g. pay and job security) and relatively low satisfaction with other items and issues (e.g. job content and relationships with supervisors).[32] More generally, a particularly important question for future study follows from the fact that the particular industries which are in relative decline (e.g. coal-mining, shipbuilding) are those that industrial sociologists have shown to be traditionally associated with a strong sense of employee identification. And this structural change has led to some speculation as to whether individual organizational identification can (and will) increasingly substitute for occupational/industrial based sources of work identification.[33]

The product-market environment

Industrial-relations researchers have had a long-standing, if somewhat limited, interest in the impact of the nature of the product-market environment on the structures, processes, and outcomes of collective bargaining. It has, for instance, been widely contended that a highly competitive product-market environment will tend to limit the extent of union organization due to the difficulties of effectively organizing a relatively large number of individually small-sized firms, particularly in the face of considerable employer opposition to unions and collective bargaining arrangements stemming from the limited ability to pass on negotiated wage increases in the form of higher product prices.[34] It is also clear that when unions do make organizational inroads into such industries, both unions and employers are particularly likely to favour the establishment, and maintenance, of multi-employer, industry-level collective bargaining arrangements in order to try and take wages out of competition – i.e. set a floor to the level of wage competition in the industry concerned.[35] Thirdly, the nature of the product market environment has been viewed as an important determinant of the wage outcomes of collective bargaining. There has, in fact, been a considerable volume of empirical studies in both Britain and the United States concerned to see whether both the level and rate-of-change of wages is higher and greater in environments characterized by the relative absence of product-market competition.[36]

However, in more recent years it has been increasingly argued that the inescapable fact of life for most business organizations is that of substantially increased product-market competition from both domestic and foreign sources. This fact is apparent from both the subjective responses of managers in various survey studies,[37] and objective information on matters such as import penetration ratios;[38] by the early 1980s Britain's trade in manufactures was in deficit for the first time since the industrial revolution. This increased product-market competition (especially from foreign sources) when taken in conjunction with a general shortening of product life-cycles, is seen to have resulted in a fundamental reassessment of corporate and business strategies in advanced industrialized economies. A broad distinction is often made between individual competitive strategies involving (i) low labour cost and high volume production, and (ii) high product quality and/or technological advantage orientated towards serving more specialized market niches.[39] The latter, which is designed to support a high-wage/high-productivity employment relationship, is generally held to be the more desirable and feasible strategy for firms in advanced industrialized economies, given the difficulties they face in competing with the low labour costs of the newly industrializing nations.[40] The needs of such a competitive strategy have resulted in the current upsurge of management interest in obtaining organizational structures and practices that emphasize above all else the need for flexibility of operation. One view of the key aspects of this new, flexible organizational form is set out in Table 2.5.

The extent, nature, and implications of tangible moves in the direction of such flexible organizational forms will be discussed at various points in subsequent chapters. The particular role of product market forces in stimulating flexible working arrangements should be viewed in the light of Kelly's argument that

Table 2.5 Features of traditional and new organizations

Traditional	*New*
The technological imperative	Joint optimization
Man as an extension of the machine	Man as complementary to the machine
An expendable spare part	A resource to be developed
Maximum task breakdown, single narrow skills	Optimum task grouping, multiple broad skills
External controls (supervisors, specialist staffs, procedures)	Internal controls (self regulating sub-systems)
Tall organizational chart, autocratic style	Flat organizational chart, participative style
Competition, gamesmanship	Collaboration, collegiality
Organization's purposes only	Members' and society's purposes also
Alienation	Commitment
Low risk-taking	Innovation

Source: Michael Cross (1985), 'Flexibility and integration at the workplace', *Employee Relations* 17(1), p. 4.

product- rather than labour-market influences have historically been important in the introduction of job re-design arrangements.[41]

The larger social and political environment

The central contention of a number of general discussions of the changing economic, political, and social features of contemporary Britain is that there has been a substantial reduction in the traditional homogeneity and cohesiveness of social classes.[42] This line of argument would appear to have a number of important implications for industrial relations, given that:

> The working class thrust itself into the centre of Britain's social and political life during an upsurge of militancy lasting from 1910 to the early 1920s . . . This massive growth in the industrial and political strength of workers established the twentieth-century pattern of British politics. Henceforth, support for the Labour Party, together with membership of the unions, would be seen as part of what it meant to be working class. More importantly, the representation of the class would come to depend upon the combined fate of the workers' industrial organisations, of their political party, and of the links that held together the unions, the party and the class.[43]

This observation provides the basis for structuring the material presented in this section which largely revolves around the issues of (i) the relationship between the working class and the Labour Party, (ii) the relationship between the unions and the Labour Party, and (iii) the attitudes of society in general towards trade unions.

From the 1950s and into the 1970s there has been a substantial body of research conducted by sociologists concerned with the extent and nature of the impact of a relatively full employment environment, together with rising living standards and the development of the Welfare State, on traditional working-class attitudes in the employment, social, and political spheres of life; much of this was concerned to examine the extent to which material affluence had resulted in a process of 'embourgeoisement'.[44] The election victories of the Conservative Party in 1979, 1983, and 1987, in a context of high and rising unemployment, have been major factors in producing a renewed research interest in this subject, albeit with a substantial change in the basic parameters of the discussion; if 'affluence', 'privatization', and 'instrumental collectivism' were the watchwords of this research theme during the 1960s and 1970s, then by the 1980s they were 'stagflation', 'fatalism' and 'authoritarian populism'.[45] The more recent discussions of the cultural, political, and ideological implications of changes in, for example, the occupation, gender and geographical composition and distribution of the workforce have raised major questions about, for example, the validity and value of the traditional definition of the working class in terms of a manual/non-manual employee distinction.[46] Furthermore, as one major recent review has suggested:

> Sociologists have exaggerated the extent to which the sphere of production generally, and work in particular, does now provide workers with a clear sense of collective social identity which could form the basis for class action. For many people, work is now part of the world which is not regarded as amenable to either personal or collective control, and is thus approached instrumentally and fatalistically. Such empirical findings as are available point to a combination of increasing sectionalism and increasing fatalism in the sphere of production . . . In the sphere of consumption similarly, post-war changes in patterns of working-class culture and community are tending towards a relative privatization of individual households or families, which is in turn reinforced by patterns of private consumption, particularly of housing. Both in the sphere of production and in the

sphere of consumption, groups of workers are coming to occupy increasingly diverse social positions (in terms of their potential interests) which traditional working-class organizations such as the Labour Party and the trade unions have failed to articulate or constitute in terms of collective class identities.[47]

A number of the elements in this argument still await detailed empirical examination, but there is little doubt about the extent of decline of the Labour-Party/working-class vote in recent elections. Table 2.6 provides one set of relevant figures on this particular phenomenon.[48]

Table 2.6 Decline of the working-class vote for the Labour Party (as percentage of popular vote)

Year	*Percentage of manual vote for the Labour Party*
1959	62
1964	64
1966	69
1970	58
1974 (February)	57
1974 (October)	57
1979	50
1983	38

Source: Extracted from Dennis Kavanagh (1986), *Thatcherism and British Politics: The End of Consensus?*, p. 168, Oxford: Oxford University Press.

The figures in Table 2.6 should be placed alongside those for the proportion of trade-union members who voted Labour; these were 73 per cent in 1964, 71 per cent in 1966, 66 per cent in 1970, 55 per cent in both the General Elections of 1974, 51 per cent in 1979, 39 per cent in 1983, and 42 per cent in 1987.[49] Political scientists in recent years have actively debated the question of whether 'class dealignment' is undermining the strength of the party identification model in explaining the voting patterns of the electorate.[50]

It has been argued that trade unions in advanced industrialized societies will almost inevitably be drawn into a concern with politics, although the unions' natural and legitimate interest with the course of macro-economic policy does not fully and adequately explain (i) any emergence of a more general political interest on their part, or (ii) why formal links have frequently been established with particular political parties.[51] As regards the latter point, there appear to be certain paradoxes and contradictions involved in the extent and nature of the union's position, in that:

> British trade unions, like those of nearly all other countries, are deeply involved in politics. In this country they founded the Labour Party and remain today its main paymasters and by far the bigest voting strength at the annual conference; whatever political party is in office, they have dealings with it and offer it advice on a range of policy issues; and on several occasions in the past three decades they have become involved in agreements with governments over wage restraint. On the other hand, opinion polls report widespread dissatisfaction among union members with unions playing any political role at all . . . More strangely, there is considerable evidence that unions themselves do not take their wider political role very seriously. A fact commonly noted is that, while the major union leaders ensure that they themselves sit on the General Council of the TUC, they send a lower level of official to represent their unions on the National Executive Committee of the Labour Party.[52]

The traditionally limited political objectives of unions in Britain (i.e. keep politics out of the industrial sphere of activity) began to change from the mid-1960s as the basic nature of Government macro-economic policy changed from simply monetary/fiscal policies to include policies of wage restraint, and restrictive industrial-relations legislation was proposed. The establishment and operation of formal policies of wage restraint was a major factor in white-collar unions increasingly affiliating to the TUC,[53] but, at the same time, was a major source of increased tension between the unions and the Labour Party in the 1960s and 1970s.[54] Indeed, it was incomes policy (1965–70) and the Labour Government's 1969 White Paper, *In Place of Strife*, that were of major importance in calling into question the continued viability of any working separation and distinction between the industrial and political spheres of activity, with adverse consequences for the relationship between the unions and the Labour Party.[55] The Labour Party/union difficulties of the years 1968–70 were, in Minkin's view, 'all the more dangerous for the relationship now that the unions' channel of influence direct to the government seemed secure whatever government was in office'.[56]

On the latter point it is important to note Middlemas's argument that the pressures on the Government during the First World War produced 'a corporate bias in the British state' (with trade unions and employers organizations becoming heavily involved in policy-making) that resulted in a low level of class conflict relative to that of other European countries in the years 1914–64.[57] The extent to which such relationships were maintained in the inter-war years has, however, been strongly challenged by a number of other historians.[58] Furthermore, the ability to develop this relatively informal corporate bias into relatively formal, stable, tripartite structures and arrangements appears to have been relatively limited in Britain. The subject of corporatism or neo-corporatist labour-market arrangements became of considerable interest to industrial-relations researchers in Europe as a number of countries sought to develop such political bargaining arrangements in the wake of the rank-and-file militancy and stagflation of the late 1960s and the world economic shocks (particularly the oil price increases) of the 1970s. To some commentators, the development of such arrangements was both inevitable and desirable[59] (particularly when viewed alongside possible alternative lines of development such as those of free collective bargaining or the approach of the present Conservative Government), whereas other individuals, from a variety of political persuasions, have spoken of the threat posed by such arrangements to the sovereignty of parliament,[60] and the inability of rank-and-file employees to derive gains under them.[61] In Britain, the ability to fully develop and operate successfully such arrangements was seen to be limited by factors such as the decentralized nature of the trade-union movement, the limited co-ordination powers of bodies such as the Confederation of British Industry, and the autonomous strength of the financial sector.[62] Admittedly, the Labour Party/union relationship of the years 1974–8 (the social contract years), whereby the TUC sought to deliver wage restraint in return for various legislative and economic gains, has been very much discussed in terms of corporatism,[63] although existing studies of corporatism and centralization in labour-market arrangements across countries invariably accord a relatively low position or rank to Britain. This is indicated by the contents of Table 2.7.

There are a number of comments to make about these cross-country rankings and the findings of some economists that corporatist labour-market arrangements are positively associated with relatively superior macro-economic performance, particularly in the face of exogenous, economic shocks to the system.[64] First, some of the individual elements or components of the ordinal indexes which underlie these rankings are far from clear-cut and unambiguous in nature.[65] Second, there is the issue of the relevant length of time over which such relationships are studied, as internal changes can undoubtedly operate to undermine the longer-term stability of such arrangements.[66] Third, some more recent work has suggested that *both* highly centralized and highly decentralized systems have relatively favourable levels of macro-economic

Table 2.7 Rank orderings of countries according to their degree of centralization

Calmfors–Driffill	*Schmitter*	*Cameron*	*Blyth*	*Bruno–Sachs*
1. Austria	1. Austria	1. Sweden	1. Austria	1. Austria
2. Norway	2. Norway	2. Norway	2. Norway	2. Germany
3. Sweden	3. Sweden	3. Austria	3. Sweden	3. Netherlands
4. Denmark	4. Denmark	4. Belgium	4. Denmark	4. Norway
5. Finland	5. Finland	5. Finland	5. Finland	5. Sweden
6. Germany	6. Netherlands	6. Denmark	6. New Zealand	6. Switzerland
7. Netherlands	7. Belgium	7. Netherlands	7. Australia	7. Denmark
8. Belgium	8. Germany	8. Germany	8. Germany	8. Finland
9. New Zealand	9. Switzerland	9. UK	9. Belgium	9. Belgium
10. Australia	10. US	10. Australia	10. Netherlands	10. Japan
11. France	11. Canada	11. Switzerland	11. Japan	11. New Zealand
12. UK	12. France	12. Italy	12. France	12. UK
13. Italy	13. UK	13. Canada	13. UK	13. France
14. Japan	14. Italy	14. US	14. Italy	14. Italy
15. Switzerland		15. France	15. US	15. Australia
16. US		16. Japan	16. Canada	16. Canada
17. Canada				17. US

Source: Calmfors, Lars and Driffill (1988), 'Bargaining structure, corporatism, and macroeconomic performance, *Economic Policy*, no. 6, April, p. 18.

performance, with the intermediate systems being the least successful performers.[67] Fourth, it would appear that employers and governments have become relatively dissatisfied with the neo-corporatism of the 1970s. This is because either union confederations could not deliver wage restraint from their affiliates (Denmark, Italy, the UK) or else they demanded *quid pro quos* that employers and governments felt were too high (Germany, Sweden).[68] For these and other reasons, governments in Europe have increasingly begun to favour, in Goldthorpe's terms, the dualism approach – whereby authority and control mechanisms are increasingly centred on the individual employment establishment through enlarging the areas of the economy (small firms, contracting, and sub-contracting arrangements) exposed to market forces.[69] In short, some corporatist arrangements remain well entrenched, others have declined or face increased internal pressures, but certainly the 1980s have seen the development of few new corporatist arrangements in Europe. Indeed, corporatist arrangements appear to be difficult to develop in the absence of certain prior conditions, such as relatively centralized bargaining structures and a long history of relatively well-accepted government intervention in the industrial-relations system; in this sense, findings about relationships with the level of macro-economic performance appear to have only limited, short-term policy relevance.

In terms of more recent relationships between the unions and the Labour Party in Britain, some reference needs to be made to the requirement of the Trade Union Act of 1984 that union ballots concerning the existence and use of political funds should be held at least every 10 years. The outcome of the ballots conducted in 1985–6 was that all unions concerned were in favour of maintaining such a fund, with the overall membership vote in favour being some 83 per cent.[70] Indeed, some fifteen unions in Britain in the 1980s have established political funds for the first time.

The question of why this 83 per cent 'yes' vote on a 51 per cent turnout rate only translated into a 42 per cent union membership vote for the Labour Party on a 75 per cent turnout rate in the General Election of 1987 has led to the suggestion that union members want their unions to have a voice and influence in politics, but that they do not want their unions to be a party-political organization;[71] such an interpretation is certainly consistent with the findings of some existing studies of political activity in individual unions.[72]

The sort of relationships discussed to date in this section need to be set in the larger context of social or public attitudes towards trade unions at large. In Britain, public opinion polls conducted in the years 1975–84 have consistently found that the majority of the public (typically 73 per cent) hold the view that unions are essential to protect workers' interests, but that majority opinion also believes that unions have too much power (68 to 75 per cent) and that most unions are controlled by a few extremists and militants (typically 66 per cent).[73] In short, there consistently appears to be considerable public support and approval for the institution of unionism, although considerably less for individual aspects of the administration and behaviour of unions. There is obviously variation in answers to such questions among different segments of the population, although over the period 1964–79 it is worth noting that the proportion of Labour Party supporters who held the view that trade unions have too much power rose from 41 to 64 per cent;[74] the high-point figure coincided with the so-called 'winter of discontent' of 1978–9.

The legal and legislative environment

When a longer-run, historical perspective is taken on the place of labour law in the British system of industrial relations, the following points are typically made: (i) the essential legal basis has been the common-law relationship between the employer and the individual employee; (ii) parliamentary or statute law has not provided, unlike the position in the US or other European countries (e.g. France and Italy), positive rights to organize or strike; (iii) collective agreements are not directly enforceable in law so that little distinction has been made, again unlike the position in other national systems, between 'conflicts of interest' (i.e creation of new standards) and 'conflicts of rights' (i.e. interpretation of existing standards); and (iv) the traditional history of parliamentary or statute law has been to provide immunities from common-law judgements concerning criminal conspiracy (the first part of the nineteenth century) and subsequently civil liabilities. These features of the system, which essentially came into place in the years 1870–1914, have been attributed to a conjunction of three basic factors – namely, a relatively strong, but essentially industrial-based labour movement, a gradual but incomplete extension of the male franchise, and, third, the relatively late emergence of the Labour Party – all of these being located in a larger setting of early industrialization and well-entrenched *laissez faire* values.[75] This system of labour law has been variously described as one of negative law, abstentionist law, or collective *laissez faire*, because:

> The Acts of 1871, 1875 and 1906 aimed to push back the boundaries of illegalities in the common law that would hamstring the unions. In trade disputes, 'the law' (the common law) which once intervened could not now do so in respect of these excluded liabilities. The critical exclusions were the removal of the doctrine of 'restraint of trade' that made unions unlawful associations (1871), the two doctrines of conspiracy to injure in 'trade disputes' (1875, criminal liability; 1906, civil liability), and the tort of inducing breach of an employment contract in 'trade disputes' (1906). Without these exclusions, unions and collective bargaining would encounter immediate illegality, then and now. These and parallel legal provisions came later to be known (perhaps unfortunately) as 'the immunities'.[76]

These immunities, particularly those of the Trade Disputes Act of 1906, have been the source of a great deal of recent discussion. There have, for example, been discussions of their historical origins,[77] critical contentions concerning their adverse implications for the macro performance of the British economy,[78] and arguments about whether trade unions should seek (via the legislation of a future Labour Government) to return to the 1906 immunities position or look to the establishment of a set of positive legal rights.[79] It was essentially these provisions of the 1906 Act that led to the British system of industrial relations being traditionally labelled a 'voluntarist' system, one characterized by the relative absence of statute law of either an auxiliary or restrictive nature.[80] However, as the volume of statute law began to build up from the mid-1960s (the Contracts of Employment Act 1963, the Industrial Training Act 1964, and the Redundancy Payment Acts 1965) into the 1970s and 1980s, industrial-relations researchers have increasingly questioned the accuracy and value of the label of voluntarism for the contemporary system of industrial relations in Britain. Although, in Kahn-Freund's terms, regulatory labour law is a relatively long-standing feature of the system (e.g. Factories Acts, wages-council legislation) it has been noted that there were only five general Acts of Parliament regulating employment passed in the years 1950–9, a figure that rose to sixteen in the years 1960–9, to thirty in 1970–9, with a further eight being passed in 1980–2.[81] This legislation of the 1970s and 1980s can be categorized and viewed as follows: (i) the Industrial Relations Act 1971 of the Heath Government which, initially viewed as an alternative to incomes policy, was influenced by the provisions of the Taft Hartley Act 1947 in the United States; (ii) the Labour Government legislation of 1974–8 which, influenced to some extent by Britain's membership of the EEC, sought to add to the floor of individual employee rights and extend the coverage and scope of collective bargaining; and (iii) the four major Acts of the Thatcher Government, namely the Employment Acts of 1980, 1982, and 1988, and the Trade Union Act 1984. The varied aims and provisions of this legislation over the last 15 years or so reflect a number of factors, notably changes in public opinion towards organized labour, attempts to alter the balance of power between unions and employers and between unions and individual union members, and different perceptions of the Government's role and responsibilities in the industrial-relations and economic systems.

There now exist a number of volumes which summarize the background, provisions, and impact of the individual pieces of legislation that are currently operative in Britain;[82] in addition to the four major Acts of the present Conservative Government mentioned above, the relevant legislation also includes the Equal Pay Act 1970 (as amended, with effect from January 1984), the Trade Union and Labour Relations Act 1974 (as amended in 1976), the Health and Safety at Work Act 1974, the Employment Protection Act 1975, the Sex Discrimination Act 1975, the Race Relations Act 1976, and the Employment Protection (Consolidation) Act 1978. Accordingly, the remainder of this chapter will be limited to a number of selective issues, namely (i) some general comments on the nature of the present Government's legislation, (ii) a few observations concerning some of the research undertaken on the impact of individual pieces of legislation, and (iii) a brief reference to some of the issues that have been raised about the future role of law in the industrial relations system. On the first matter, the Conservative legislation of 1980–8 has lowered the floor of employment protection rights (e.g. raised the length of the employment qualifying period for workers in small businesses to claim unfair dismissal), removed measures (e.g. Schedule 11 of the Employment Protection Act 1975) designed to extend the coverage of collectively bargained wages and limited the extent of the immunities which are involved in industrial action. In the latter area, both secondary picketing and secondary industrial action are no longer legally permissible, action to extend union recognition or the use of union labour only are outlawed, the definition of a trade dispute has been much more narrowly defined (i.e. it must now exist between workers and their *own* employer and must wholly or mainly relate to the list of employment matters affecting workers of that employer), the management ability to dismiss employees on strike (without risking an unfair dismissal claim) has been enhanced, and a union (and its officials) only have immunity in authorizing or endorsing strike action when a majority of members approve such action in a ballot. There is also much more legal regulation of closed shops and provisions for the election of the executive committee of unions.[83] The Conservative Government legislation of 1980 to 1988 is highly consistent with their overall view of, and strategy towards, the operation of the labour market and economy more generally. As such, it can be viewed not so much as an attempt to reform collective bargaining (by, for example, changing the power balance in favour of employers), but rather as an attempt to increase the relative importance of the individual (as opposed to collective) employment relationship which is based in common law;[84] it is significant to note here the role of common law liabilities in a number of disputes (particularly the miners' one) in recent years.[85]

In terms of research activity it has undoubtedly been the provisions concerning unfair dismissal (originally of the 1971 Act) that have attracted the most attention, as the number of unfair dismissal claims in individual years in the 1980s has frequently exceeded 30,000.

There has been a considerable variety of research concerning these particular provisions, which so many managers view as the centrepiece of labour law in Britain. For example, industrial-relations researchers have examined the characteristics of claimants (disproportionately employees from small, non-union establishments), and documented (i) the relatively low success rates of claimants, (ii) the limited amounts of monetary compensation obtained by them, (iii) the limited usage of the re-instatement and re-engagement remedies, and (iv) the increased incidence of legal representation before tribunals.[86] In 1984, for example, only 7,587 claims out of 28,052 complaints went to the industrial tribunals, just under 29 per cent of these were upheld and orders for re-employment were made in only 78 instances; in the 5 years 1980–4 the median awards to successful complainants at the tribunals were £598, £963, £1,201, £1,345, and £1,345, respectively (i.e. well below the available, maximum level).[87] A number of changes and reforms (e.g. the use of arbitration) have in fact been proposed to try and bring the workings of the tribunals more into line with the original aims of the legislation.[88] Economists have also examined the impact of the unfair dismissal provisions, and other employment protection legislation, on the level of labour demand and unemployment.[89] In general, such studies have not identified such provisions as having had a significant, adverse impact on the level of unemployment in Britain in recent times, a finding that is clearly in line with the results of a recent CBI enquiry which reported that only 10 per cent of employer respondents suggested that abolition or reduction of unfair dismissal rights would definitely or possibly lead them to increase their levels of employment.[90]

Economists have also conducted statistical studies which have sought to identify the wage impact of the Equal Pay Act 1970 and the Sex Discrimination Act 1975, with significant, positive effects tending to be reported;[91] the average level of women's wages tended to move from some 65 per cent of men's in the early 1970s to around 75 per cent by the latter years of that decade, since when there appears to have been relatively little change.[92] However, beyond the specific studies mentioned to date, the existing research on industrial-relations law has been overwhelmingly of two basic types, namely (i) surveys of management respondents seeking their subjective assessments of the impact of the existing legislation, and (ii) reviews of individual Acts and provisions via a 'content analysis' of key, reported cases and decisions.[93] There are two individual findings to emerge from this body of research which are worthy of particular attention here. First, some of the individual Acts and measures appear to have had offsetting or non-complementary effects. For example, Daniel has argued, in a recent discussion of the Redundancy Payments Act 1965, that its lump-sum-compensation approach has in practice limited the effectiveness of Part IV of the Employment Protection Act 1975, which provides for joint discussions and consultations over the procedures for handling redundancies.[94] Second, the 1980 and 1984 workplace industrial-relations surveys have revealed that considerably more use has been made of the provisions of the Employment Protection Act 1975, which provide for the disclosure of information for collective bargaining purposes, than has been suggested by analyses based on 'head-counts' of the number of complaints (under such provisions) that have come before the Central Arbitration Committee,[95] (i.e. the peak level of such complaints was 62 in 1978, a figure which has fallen to between 10 and 20 in the 1980s). This particular finding would appear to have some important methodological implications for the traditional labour-law research approach of assessing the impact of individual pieces of legislation by analysing the contents of key, reported decisions and cases.

Finally, it is relevant to note the recent appearance of a number of proposals from individuals sympathetic to the labour movement, to (i) extend the coverage of legislation to 'marginal' groups of workers (e.g. part-timers, temporaries, etc.), (ii) reduce the complexity and 'excessive legalism' of various procedural arrangements, and (iii) provide statutory supports for the right to organize and strike that are relatively immune to being undermined through the course of time by 'restrictive' legal interpretations and judgements.[96] Indeed, as was mentioned earlier in this section, there is now a considerable debate within the trade-union movement concerning the relative advantages of legal immunities and positive rights in law. With the present Conservative Government in its third, successive term of office, there is no immediate likelihood of such proposals coming into effect, although it is important to note that some questions have already been raised about the longer-term strength and staying power of the principles of such proposals; the major question raised has been whether statutory rights can safely and successfully be built on the traditional 'corner-stone' of the common law contract of service.[97] In the more immediate future, one of the most interesting and important questions for industrial-relations researchers and practitioners will be the way in which the nature of the industrial-relations legislative and legal environment in Britain continues to move under the present Conservative Government relative to that of other European countries. This question arises from the fact that the extent of important, EEC-wide initiatives in the employment-legislation area has declined in recent years, relative to the level that was apparent in 1975–80,[98] when there were, for example, major Directives on collective redundancies, employee rights in the transfer of undertakings and protection of employees in the event of employers' insolvency. Admittedly, the present Government did amend the Equal Pay Act 1970 to bring it into line with an EEC equal-pay directive which provided for equal pay for 'work of equal value'. This amendment came into effect from January 1984, with nearly 1,500 applications having come before industrial tribunals in 3 years; only around 60 employment organizations have, however, been involved in these particular cases. The case of *Pickstone* v. *Freemans plc* (1987), in which the Court of Appeal decided arguments about the relative supremacy of European and domestic employment law in favour of the former, is likely to be particularly important here as one moves towards the integrated European market developments of the 1990s and the British trade unions look increasingly to Brussels, as opposed to Whitehall, as the source of 'progressive' developments in labour legislation and regulations.

Conclusions

The basic purpose of this chapter has been to identify a number of the key dimensions of the contemporary environment which constitute important determining forces on the structures, processes, and outcomes of the collective bargaining process. A good deal of basic information has been presented here, particularly in tabular form, on the environment as an independent variable in the collective-bargaining-based system of industrial relations in Britain. A number of issues touched on here will be returned to in the more detailed discussion of later chapters, but already we have highlighted some of the key forces (e.g. intensified product market competition) that constitute potential sources of change in the system at large.

Chapter three

Trade unions as organizational entities and bargaining agents

An historical perspective

In considering the organizational characteristics of unions as a determining factor or independent variable in the system of collective bargaining, we can usefully begin with various theories of the labour movement that have been advanced by individuals such as Tannenbaum, the Webbs, Hoxie, Perlman, Commons, and marxist writers. These theories have offered a variety of answers to the following basic questions:[1]

(i) How is one to account for the origin or emergence of labour organizations?
(ii) What explains the pattern of growth and development of labour organizations?
(iii) What are the ultimate goals of the labour movement?
(iv) Why do individual workers join labour organizations?

All of these questions will be considered in this and other chapters, but for the moment we confine ourselves to question (i) above.

In seeking to account for the origins of trade unions, the existing theories of the labour movement have variously emphasized the key importance of technology (Tannenbaum), the crystallization of a group consciousness (Hoxie), the emergence of a scarcity mentality (Perlman), and the geographical widening of product markets. The latter influence was central to Commons's inductive theory of union development, being based on a detailed, historical-case study of the evolution of employee protective arrangements through time in the shoe manufacturing industry in the United States.[2] The essence of the Commons view was that developments (such as those of improved internal transportation) towards a more integrated economy, increased the extent of product market competition among employers (by breaking down spatial monopolies) which, in turn, resulted in attempts to keep down the level of wage costs.

These attempts, which involved the increased use of less skilled labour, changes in technology and in the size of individual employment establishments, posed an obvious threat to the living standards and job status of skilled workers, who reacted by demanding the protective services of unions. The major insights or implications of this study were (i) some minimal level of integration in an industrializing economy is a necessary prerequisite for the emergence of trade unions, (ii) unions will initially be concentrated among skilled manual workers, (iii) the basic orientation of such unions will be defensive or reactive in nature, and (iv) unions have evolved out of, or have historical linkages with earlier, less formal, and permanent employee-protective structures and arrangements.

The approach of Commons in the United States, and that of the Webbs in Britain, had the effect of making labour history very much (i) the history of the organized working class, and (ii) the study of trade unions – the latter being viewed particularly from the perspective of national officials directly involved in the establishment and maintenance of collective bargaining arrangements with employers.[3] This view that labour history was essentially the history of trade unions came under substantial attack in both Britain and the United States from the 1960s.[4] The essence of this criticism, which has been very much led by radical or marxist scholars, has been the belief that the central dynamic of labour history has been the struggle between workers and employers for control of the labour process (i.e. the frontier of control) which leads to labour institutions being viewed as expressions of a deeper class consciousness; the result has been the appearance of individual studies of the workplace (and the community) concerned with the larger, industrial working class and not simply the organized sub-set of it.[5] Moreover, 'from a view of institutions expressing the deeper interests of social groups, however problematically, to that of institutions as constraints on those interests, is a short step which an increasing number of labour historians were prepared to take in the late 1960s and 1970s.'[6] The essential elements of this latter view have been identified as follows:

> The exponents of what can be termed 'rank-and-filism' argue that collective bargaining with employers is vital to the institutional survival of trade unions, but has as its cost the acceptance of managerial prerogatives and the capitalist ownership of industry. The 'rank-and-filists' maintain that as a result trade union leaders had themselves been forced to moderate the demands of their members and deflect them from struggles for control at work on to an economistic terrain which can be made

> acceptable to employers; while the officials' responsibility for upholding collective agreements ultimately leads them to become a bulwark of managerial discipline in the factory.[7]

This sort of perspective will be returned to when we consider some of the criticisms of the institution of collective bargaining in Chapter 5.[8] There are numerous individual arguments and findings that have emerged from both the institutional and social historical approaches to British labour history, but all agree on the fact that the basic contours of trade union organization and collective bargaining arrangements in Britain are *relatively old and long established* compared to that of other national systems. For example, Zeitlin has commented that 'few nations have the unbroken record of trade union organization and collective bargaining which distinguishes the history of industrial relations in Britain',[9] while Hyman has observed that 'to a large extent, the current pattern of organization was established in Britain by 1920, when 45 per cent of the labour force was unionized.'[10] This 45 per cent unionization rate of the United Kingdom in 1920 was above that of Australia (42 per cent), Sweden (26 per cent), and the United States (17 per cent).[11] This relatively early basis of union organization is one of the factors highlighted in Phelps Brown's recent discussion of the origins of union power in Britain,[12] while, more generally, it is clear that so many key organizational characteristics of the contemporary union movement – such as the extent of multi-unionism, the basic orientation and authority of the TUC, and the emergence and development of shop-steward systems – derive from the fact that the basic contours of union organization and collective-bargaining arrangements in Britain are relatively old and long established. A number of these key organizational characteristics will be discussed in turn in the sections of this chapter.

Union structure and the TUC

Discussions of the subject of union structure in Britain invariably begin by listing the following sorts of factual points: (i) the total number of unions has fallen through the course of time (from, for example, 507 in 1974 to 371 in 1984); (ii) not all unions are affiliated to the TUC, but the ones with the largest membership are (in 1984, 91 out of the 371 unions in Britain were affiliated to the TUC, and the membership of the TUC affiliates was 9,855,204 out of a total membership of 11,086,000 in that year); and (iii) the majority of unions have small membership totals, but the majority of union members are in a relatively small number of individually large unions (in 1984, only 2.7 per cent of all unions had memberships greater than 250,000, but fully 60.9 per cent of all union members were in these particular unions); the tendency towards membership being increasingly concentrated in a small number of individually large unions is not unique to Britain, as Windmuller's comparative study of nine western countries over the 20-year period 1957–78 has demonstrated.[13] Finally, the financial assets and resources of unions in Britain are relatively limited (i.e. the entire funds and gross assets of all unions in 1983 were approximately £980 million, or some £90 per member), with the average membership subscription levels being low by international standards (i.e. approximately some 0.36 per cent of members' earnings, compared with figures of 0.6 to 1 per cent in Italy and France). Interestingly, the substantial membership losses of unions since 1979 do not appear to have seriously damaged the overall financial position of the majority of unions. A survey commissioned by the Department of Employment, for example, reported that most unions in 1985 were as well off financially as ten years previously, largely as a result of increasing their subscription incomes, raising the proportion of income deriving from investments, and by the selling off of assets.[14]

Over and above the presentation of such factual material, discussions of union structure have frequently pointed to the limitations of the traditional categorization of craft and industrial unions for understanding the essential nature of union structure in Britain, and have offered alternative categorizations of the recruitment and growth orientation of individual unions; the latter are frequently variants of the notion of 'open' and 'closed' unions.[15] It is, however, the particular issue of *multi-unionism* – i.e. the main occupational groups in an establishment are organized by different unions and/or more than one union competes for membership within a given group of workers – that has been so prominent in discussions of union structure in Britain. A number of commentators have pointed to the allegedly substantial costs of multi-unionism in Britain (e.g. strikes, restrictive practices and 'leap-frogging' in pay claims),[16] but such discussions are not based on the findings of systematic empirical research; rather, single statistics and examples tend to be cited for individual industries such as steel and shipbuilding. Secondly, it is not these essentially 'managerial costs' that have motivated the trade unions to attempt to reform their structures but rather concerns about duplication and waste of resources and the inability of smaller unions to deliver a comprehensive range of benefits and services to their members.

There is some evidence to suggest that unions have made

pragmatic adjustments to the fact of multi-unionism at the level of the individual workplace. For example, one study has reported that the nature of shop-steward arrangements (i.e. the presence of full-time stewards, executive committees, and the regularity of meetings) in the manufacturing sector is significantly and positively influenced by the existence of a multi-union structure.[17] It is, however, at the level of the system as a whole that reforms to union structure and multi-unionism have been most strenuously urged, and various union initiatives have occurred. For example, over the course of time, the TUC has discussed the alleged virtues of industrial unionism, sought to encourage more mergers and amalgamations, and attempted to limit the extent and nature of inter-union competition and rivalry, as possible contributions to easing such structural issues and problems. In the 1980s, however, it is employer initiatives involving a demand for single-union recognition arrangements in new plants that have, as we shall see, had important implications for the nature of union responses to the alleged problems of multi-unionism in Britain.

In the early years of this century, theoretical arguments in favour of industrial unionism tended to view it as one means of developing a broader, more politically orientated union movement, but any periodic TUC discussion and endorsement of the concept (as in 1924) has been based much more on notions of administrative efficiency; it is relevant to note here that an industrial union structure was one of the widely admired features of the West German model system of industrial relations in the 1970s. In Britain, any large-scale movement in this direction has always been considered impractical, although Bell has also questioned some of the 'principled advantages' of such arrangements.[18] Undoubtedly, the most well-known TUC measure in relation to union structures is that of the Bridlington principles (embodied in a resolution passed by Congress in 1939) which is 'a code of conduct which unions are advised to follow in order to avoid what experience has shown to be the more common causes of inter-union conflicts about membership'.[19] In the years 1979–84, for example, the annual number of inter-union disputes reported under the TUC disputes machinery ranged between 55 and 99 with conciliation being the increasingly used settlement technique and the number of disputes referred to committees for adjudication or arbitration being very much a minority (i.e. from 8 to 17 cases in these years). The general, longer-term effect of these principles has been viewed as limiting the emergence of new, small unions,[20] although in more recent years it has been the EETPU single-recognition agreements in new plants that have posed the most awkward questions for these principles and arrangements.[21] In 1985, the TUC General Council's amendment of its dispute principles and procedures sought to eliminate single-union recognition agreements that were at the expense of previously recognized unions, and in the case of greenfield sites sought to ensure that such agreements were consistent with existing industry arrangements and practices. In June 1988, the EETPU were suspended by the TUC for non-compliance with a TUC-disputes-committee decision which instructed the union to terminate its single-union agreements with Orion Electric and Christian Salvesen, and to exclude employees in these plants from membership of the union. Subsequently, the EETPU was expelled from the TUC at the annual meeting of Congress in September 1988. The same meeting considered the first report of the Special Review Body established by the General Council of the TUC, the report being concerned with an extended role for the TUC in regulating inter-union relations through a code of practice, the development of designated organizing areas, and a change to its current disputes principle no. 5 (which concerns union organizing in areas where other unions have an interest). This report was adopted at the 1988 annual meeting, with the new code of practice being particularly directed at the controversial issue of inter-union relations in seeking single-recognition arrangements at new employment sites; it covers the individual subjects of prior notification, no-strike clauses and arbitration, inward investment, and the general level of terms and conditions involved in such agreements. Interestingly, the first single-union agreement following the code of practice coming into force in October 1988, which involved the AEU, did not apparently comply with the pre-notification provision, while the issue of other unions 'poaching' members of the EETPU has been a major concern of the General Council of the TUC.

The process of union mergers and amalgamations over time has been facilitated by, among other things, significant legislative changes in 1917 and 1964. The 1964 Act distinguishes between two types of merger, namely a transfer of engagements (i.e. one union transfers members to another and loses its legal identity) and an amalgamation (i.e. two or more unions merge to produce a new organization that replaces the merging bodies); the former is the more common as it does not require a vote by members of the union to which the engagements are being transferred. The disproportionate concentration of union mergers and amalgamations in particular periods of time (e.g. 1911–22) has resulted in a number of studies of the features and associated characteristics of such merger waves[22] (e.g. periods of substantial company mergers).

Moreover, most of the leading, 'open' or 'growth orientated' individual unions in Britain have tended to growth in this manner (over 80 unions have merged with the TGWU, for example, since its foundation in 1922),[23] a process that is expected to continue in the future. Indeed, it has been claimed that any membership growth in individual unions in the future is likely to be inextricably linked to the occurrence of mergers,[24] and in a speech at the CBI conference in 1986 Gavin Laird, general secretary of the Amalgamated Engineering Union, suggested that the number of TUC affiliates could be as low as twenty by the year 2000;[25] the ten unions each with more than 50,000 members that recruit in both the public and private sectors (e.g. TGWU, ASTMS) have been identified as likely to take the lead in aggressive merger activity.[26] In 1986, the certification officer reported that thirty-two transfers of engagements had taken place (the highest number in any year since the office was established in 1976), while in 1987 the most significant union mergers were that between ASTMS and TASS to form Manufacturing, Science, Finance (MSF), which is currently the sixth largest TUC affiliate, and that between members of the Civil Service Union and the Society of Civil and Public Servants to form the National Union of Civil and Public Servants. Although further mergers seem to be the wave of the future, it is questionable whether the outcomes of such processes will always necessarily involve more rational structures and greater collective-bargaining effectiveness; increased problems of intra-union co-operation, coordination, and democracy may also result, particularly in very sizeable individual unions with an increasingly heterogeneous membership.

Some aspects of the role and authority of the TUC (established in 1868, but only a significant confederation after its re-organization in the early 1920s) have already been touched on above, so that here I will only attempt to provide some further perspective on this body by considering a number of individual research findings and issues of contemporary relevance. It has been increased government intervention in the industrial-relations sphere which has been the major determinant of the TUC's role as an intermediary between government and individual unions, and, since the Second World War, there has been increased TUC representation on advisory committees, Royal Commissions, departmental committees, and agencies. Allen, for example, reported that the General Council of the TUC was only represented on 1 Government committee in 1931–2, 6 in 1934–5, 12 in 1938–9, but 60 in 1948–9, 31 in 1953–4, and 65 in 1957–8.[27] However, Allen went on to allege that the impact of the individual unionists on such committees was rarely more than that of 'preventing decisions being taken which are inimical to the interests of trade unions more by being present than by argument'.[28] Some more recent assessments of the TUC influence within the decision-making process of, for example, the National Economic Development Council (the leading tripartite decision-making body in Britain) have tended to reach conclusions not too dissimilar from that of Allen.[29] However, it was the increased use of incomes policy by governments of both political persuasions in the 1960s and 1970s that has been such an important determinant of TUC–government relationships. Under such policies, governments have initially sought the co-operation of the TUC General Council in trying to ensure wage restraint, often in return for procedural and substantive concessions in other areas, but through the course of time have found that the basic nature of the TUC's authority structure has not been adequate to the task of ensuring the observance and maintenance of top level 'commitments' to wage restraint at the all-important decentralized levels of bargaining.[30] These same problems and difficulties were apparent as the basic nature of incomes policy became more one of 'bargained corporatism' in the years 1974–8.[31] The contents of Table 3.1 help place the nature of the TUC's role and authority in something of a comparative context.

Table 3.1 Estimate of authority of central union bodies in selected countries

	Percentage of total union revenues received by central bodies	*Intervention in internal union affairs*	*Involvement in collective bargaining*
Highly centralized			
Austria	80	High	High
Norway	18	Moderate	High
Sweden	18	Moderate	High
Moderately centralized			
Belgium	40	Moderate	Moderate
Denmark	9	Moderate	Moderate
France	21	Moderate	Moderate
Decentralized			
West Germany	12	High	Low
Great Britain	2	High	Moderate
USA	3	Moderate	Low

Source: John P. Windmuller (1975), 'The authority of national trade union confederations: a comparative analysis', in David B. Lipsky (ed.), *Union Power and Public Policy*, Ithaca: Cornell University Press, Tables 2 and 3.

Undoubtedly the most 'pessimistic' assessments of the limited authority and powers of the TUC have been based almost exclusively on the records of incomes policy,[32] a fact that Martin has critically commented on in his more broad-ranging examination of the TUC's political role in the light of the theory of pressure group politics.[33] Within the TUC itself there has been periodic controversy concerning the basis on which individuals were elected to the General Council of the organization, a criticism very much associated with the relative growth of white-collar union membership from the 1960s. This relative growth of white-collar and public-sector membership has to some extent been reflected in the changing composition of the General Council over time. Minkin, for example, reported that there were 10 white-collar union representatives out of a Council of 38 in 1972, which was twice as many as sat on the 35-man Council in 1960.[34] However, complaints from such unions of under-representation on the General Council persisted throughout the 1970s with, for instance, Clive Jenkins of ASTMS claiming (in the mid-1970s) that the way in which members were elected to represent the eighteen trade groups into which the TUC was then subdivided was 'a reflection of a ghostly membership of long-dead trade unionists'.[35] The 1982 annual meeting of Congress approved a report on the structure of the General Council which gave effect to a 1981 Congress resolution in favour of automatic representation for unions with more than 100,000 members. The result is that the General Council now consists of three sections – namely, members (N = 37) from unions with 100,000 or more membership, members (N = 11) of unions with less than 100,000 membership and women members (N = 6). The 1981 meeting of Congress also adopted the TUC Development Programme which followed a wide-ranging review of TUC organization, structure and services. One of the potentially most important, tangible developments under this heading has been the growth of industry committees (from 7 at the 1972 meeting of Congress to 9 at the 1982 meeting and 11 at the 1985 meeting), although it is only the steel committee (the first one established in 1967) that is both an active lobbying and collective-bargaining body.[36] Finally, it is important to note that the present Conservative Government has deliberately sought to minimize the extent and nature of TUC involvement in national-level, policy-making structures and processes. The decision in 1988 of the TUC to boycott the Government's Employment Training Scheme is likely to encourage and facilitate further Government moves in this direction.

The role orientation of shop stewards and the issue of incorporation

It has been suggested that the move from regional/district-level bargaining to the industry-level bargaining in Britain in the years 1890–1918 (approximately) had the effect of (i) limiting the scope of formal collective bargaining to wages/hours matters only, which, in turn (ii) made the rise of shop-steward bargaining over non-wages/hours matters almost *inevitable* at some point in time (predictably in circumstances of a relatively full-employment environment).[37] Hinton's examination of the skill-dilution issue in the munitions and engineering industries during the First World War views shop stewards as embodying the anti-bureaucratic character of the craft tradition, with their activities being the only major source of opposition to forces working towards incorporatist solutions and outcomes.[38] However, subsequent research on the war years has tended to be highly critical of many aspects of Hinton's work, raising questions about the extent and generality of both the dilution issue and the differences that existed between shop stewards and union district officials.[39]

Prior to the appearance of the Hinton book in 1973, research on shop stewards involved little more than the surveys undertaken for the Donovan Commission which in themselves did little more than refute certain 'characterizations' (i.e. almost strawmen hypotheses) concerning the attitudes and behaviour of stewards, although such work did confirm that shop stewards' bargaining activities very much concerned non-wage/hours matters and that such activities, it was suggested, had had major (adverse) implications for the extent and nature of joint consultative arrangements.[40] However, throughout the 1970s (and into the 1980s) a substantial body of research literature on shop stewards has appeared, with the two major themes being (i) the development of typologies of shop stewards based on their role orientation and (ii) the extent and nature of developments in shop-steward organization since the Report of the Donovan Commission, centring particularly around the question of their possible incorporation into 'the management way of doing things'.

There have been individual studies and discussions of the way in which shop stewards come to occupy their roles, the nature of the learning processes involved, and the pressures they face in performing their duties,[41] but the major concern and interest of the case-study-based, shop-steward literature of the 1970s has been with identifying differences in patterns of behaviour in role occupancy. The most widely discussed of these studies involves a dichotomy between (i) stewards who are 'leaders', being highly committed to union principles and performing a representative (initiator) role or function *vis-à-vis* their constituents; and (ii) stewards who are 'populists', having a relatively limited commitment to union principles and performing a delegate (responder) role or function on behalf of their workforce constituents.[42] Although widely quoted, this particular typology has been criticized for, among other things, (i) proposing that an individual steward will be a leader (or populist) on all issues and matters encountered, (ii) equating leaders with blue collar stewards and populists with white collar stewards, (iii) basing the categorization on rather vague and ambiguous constructs and measures (e.g. commitment to union principles), and (iv) failing to develop and elaborate on certain other categories and groupings which appeared to be present.[43] To these criticisms of the content and manner of construction of the typology can be added one concerning the relevant determinants of differing patterns of shop-steward behaviour. Specifically, this typology (and indeed others of steward behaviour) is not based on, or related to, variations in the attitudes and behaviour of the individual workgroups that the stewards represent. The classic study of workgroup behaviour still remains that conducted by Sayles in the United States in the late 1950s which, on the basis of the level and nature of grievance activity of some 300 workgroups in thirty plants, identified apathetic, erratic, strategic, and conservative groups:[44] the apathetic groups were quiet, lacked unity and leadership; the erratic exhibited highly variable grievance and output levels; the strategic were highly productive, united, and continually pressured management; while the conservative groups only periodically exerted pressure to achieve objectives of particular interest to them. Sayles's work has been subject to the following criticisms: that variation in inter-group grievance activity is overwhelmingly viewed as a function of technology; that all relevant influences on workgroup behaviour are treated as exclusively in-plant in nature; and that the typology is constructed on the basis of only a single aspect of behaviour.[45] Nevertheless, it is this study which needs to be replicated and extended in Britain, particularly with a view to examining whether observed variations in the attitudes and behaviour of shop stewards derive from, and indeed adjust to, variations in the attitudes and behaviour of the individual workgroups they represent. The possibility of such a contingency-based explanation of steward behaviour is in fact suggested by some findings of at least one study of the role orientation of safety representatives.[46] This particular study found that safety representatives who held that their priority task was to take up workers' health and safety complaints with management, viewed the employees they were responsible for as having an above average level of concern with workplace health and safety; in contrast, representatives who saw their key functions as inspections and accident investigations tended to feel that their workgroups were not sufficiently concerned about health and safety matters.

Earlier in this chapter we made reference to the work of some labour historians (those individuals that Zeitlin has labelled the 'rank-and-filists') which argued that shop stewards had historically held out against the forces of bureaucracy and incorporatism that had ensnared the national- and district-level officers of individual unions. This theme of incorporation has been taken up and developed in a number of industrial-relations researchers' assessments of the impact of the Donovan Commission's recommendation in favour of a move towards single-employer bargaining structures. The essence of the Donovan Commission's recommendation involved seeking a more stable and predictable set of bargaining outcomes through the medium of two primary sources of change – namely, first, an increase in the status and authority of the personnel-management function (see Chapter 4) and, second, through the increased recognition accorded to shop-steward arrangements. Some radical commentators have claimed that the Donovan strategy has been effective in the sense that (i) there have been significant changes in the nature of shop-steward organization throughout the 1970s (namely, more hierarchical and centralized arrangements, such as increased numbers of full-time, senior stewards and of shop-steward committees), (ii) the nature of these changes have derived, in the main, from management-initiated actions (e.g. the provision of facilities and involvement in formal, plant-level bargaining arrangements) which, in turn, has produced a set of 'institutional' interests for shop stewards that have more in common with those of management (i.e. stability and predictability through institutionalization) than with those of the rank-and-file employee, and (iii) such processes of incorporation have limited the ability of shop-steward systems to effectively oppose any substantial employment reductions and changes in collective-bargaining arrangements and practices sought by management in the high-unemployment environment of the 1980s.[47]

In order to test this hypothesis fully and adequately, one would first require data and evidence that meet the standards of both external and internal validity (see Chapter 1). This would require the existence of large and representative survey-data sets that can be compared for two points in time (e.g. 1968 and 1978) to see whether the alleged changes in the nature of shop-steward organization have occurred on a widespread basis. Second, one would require a detailed set of closely related and integrated case-studies in order to see whether these alleged changes in organizational arrangements have derived from the forces and influences that those advocating the incorporationist view have claimed to be the case. The fact of the matter is, however, that the nature of the available evidence for the 1970s is too partial and fragmentary to adequately and comprehensively test this thesis for the system as a whole, although both advocates and opponents of the contention can, and do, point to selective evidence in support of their respective lines of argument.[48]

The 1980s continue to witness the appearance of individual arguments and contentions about the nature of shop-steward arrangements and behaviour. It has, for example, been claimed that shop stewards' substantial dependence on the resources and facilities provided by management (as opposed to those provided by the external, union organization) has made them increasingly more inclined to identify with, and be concerned about, the economic fortunes and performance of their individual company, as is the case in Japan;[49] in fact, the nature of this resource-dependency effect may be producing more of an individual plant-orientation, rather than an individual company- or enterprise-orientation. This sort of argument (and indeed others) about the nature of shop-steward systems is potentially much more capable of detailed and systematic examination in the 1980s, as a result of the existence of the two workplace industrial-relations surveys. A comparison of the results of the 1980 and 1984 surveys has already revealed, for example, that: (i) the total number of shop stewards in the economy as a whole increased from some 317,000 to 335,000 in the years 1980–4 (although important differences occurred between manufacturing and other sectors); (ii) non-manual stewards were nearly as common as manual stewards in 1984; and (iii) the proportion of establishments with senior and full-time stewards changed little in these years.[50] These two surveys also provide useful information on a number of other individual matters – such as the average constituency-size of stewards, the extent of their training, and the extent of contact with union full-time officials – with the more general conclusion from the evidence of these years being that the stability and maintenance of shop-steward systems, at least in structural terms, has been considerably greater than might have been predicted on the basis of the movement in overall union membership in these same years.

The incorporationist thesis is closely bound up with a number of important differences between the attitudes and roles of shop stewards and those of full-time, national and district union officers.

In the workplace bargaining of the 1960s it was commonly reported that (i) shop stewards personified the trade union to individual members, (ii) management was relatively well disposed towards dealing with stewards because of their close knowledge of the situation and the speed with which joint decisions could be reached, and (iii) a trade-union movement with limited financial resources, and a formal structure that rarely went beyond the geographically-based branch and into the workplace, was heavily dependent on the functions and services performed by stewards, although such individuals were only rarely explicitly mentioned in the rule-books of individual unions at that time. Moreover, it was widely recognized that the particular constituency responsibilities of shop stewards (i.e. representatives of, and hence ultimately responsible to, the individual workgroups that had elected or appointed them), when combined with differential access to information, would produce differences in their attitudes and orientation from those of the full-time officers of the union; in general, stewards were more likely to be short-term, individual employee-gains orientated, whereas the full-time officers would have more of a longer-term concern with the union as an organizational entity. In individual disputes such differences in responsibilities and orientation could raise important questions about the right and ability of the official union hierarchy to control the actions of such stewards; such questions have had increasingly important legal implications for the unions as evidenced by the Heatons Transport Case of 1972 and the workers' occupation of the Caterpillar plant in Scotland in 1987. More generally, individual commentators have tended to disagree on the larger implications of such differences in the responsibilities and orientations of shop stewards and full-time officials, particularly as regards their implications for the internal democracy of unions. It is to the subject of union democracy that we now turn.

The issue of union democracy

In discussing the subject of union democracy, the major questions which need to be explicitly addressed are as follows. First, is the concept of democracy relevant to unions and can it be achieved at relatively little cost – to individual union members, to unions as organizational entities, and to society at large? Second, if the attainment of such a goal is deemed desirable (by unions, society, etc.), how does one measure the democracy of unions, what are the major determinants of its presence or absence, and, in particular, are such determinants of democracy amenable to control by the major industrial relations actors at any point in time? To individuals who view trade unions as essentially analogous to voluntary organizations,[51] democracy is likely to be seen as a desirable aim, whereas those who feel that firms or business organizations are the more appropriate analogy[52] are rather less likely to urge the value of union democracy as an end in itself and/or to recognize that the attainment of such democracy (however defined) may not be without its costs to individual members, unions as organizational entities, and, indeed, to society at large. The latter line of argument essentially views a union as a self-interested body operating in an uncertain, competitive environment (i.e. dealing with a self-interested management that makes few concessions to democracy in its own organizational arrangements) whose sole, or at least primary, responsibility is to be an effective bargaining agent which delivers a level of benefits and services that is acceptable to at least the majority of its current membership. And the essential administrative basis for such a level of delivery will be a bureaucratic, organizational structure characterized by formalization, standardization, centralization, and specialization, which may be less a function of the choices of individual union leaders and more a reflection of the inevitable forces of their historically determined operating environment.[53] As to the potential costs of democracy to individual members and union bodies, Undy *et al.* have criticized existing studies of union democracy in Britain for ignoring the implications of democratic arrangements for the quality and effectiveness of union-leadership decisions.[54] A detailed study of the 1980 national steel strike constantly points to the potential tensions and conflict between a commitment to union democracy and the effective conduct of the strike action,[55] while one study, based on Canadian data, reports some positive correlations between bargaining outcomes and aspects of bureaucracy in unions.[56]

It is not uncommon to hear arguments to the effect that (i) democratic trade unions are an important element of, and safeguard for, a system of parliamentary democracy, and (ii) democratic unions can contribute to an extension of democratic principles and practices in the industrial, as opposed to political, sphere of activity – as only they (as opposed to all unions) can legitimately put forward demands for 'industrial democracy'. These, and other arguments in favour of the larger virtues and implications of union democracy need to recognize, however, that moves in that direction may not be without their social costs. For example, Clegg's examination of the influence of bargaining structure across national systems (see Chapter 1) suggested that a relatively decentralized bargaining structure is associated with more democratic unions, but also with relatively high strike frequency. This suggestion of a substitute, as opposed to complementary, relationship between the extent of union democracy and the extent of strike frequency has been documented in at least one empirical study in the United States.[57] In short, Hemingway's[58] rather narrow notion of a 'democracy dilemma' for individual unions (i.e a trade-off between discipline and democracy) can arguably be broadened as a concept, and generalized to the level of society at large.

The relevant literature on the measures and determinants of union democracy consists, first, of papers that present overall, conceptual frameworks for the study of the notion and, second, empirical studies of an individual union or a relatively small number of unions.

The potential limitations of the former check-list type of approach[59] are that: first, we have no idea of the relative importance of the sorts of individual factors listed; second, the listed factors frequently appear to be a mixture of both measures and determinants of union democracy; and, third, some of the individual propositions involved come dangerously close to being little more than truisms (i.e. statements that are true by definition). The available empirical studies of union democracy also have their limitations – i.e. they have overwhelmingly focused on democracy at the national-union level and have largely utilized a single measure of democracy.[60] According to Strauss, the various single measures of union democracy which have been employed by researchers can be classified into the following schools of thought:[61] (i) scholars from the legal school who have utilized measures such as constitutional provisions, honest elections, regular meetings, freedom for opposition to develop; (ii) the behavioural school which has emphasized institutional opposition, close elections, high participation rates, and (iii) the responsiveness/control school which has been more concerned with factors such as the ability of officials to reflect members' interests, the responsiveness of officers to members' demands and the existence of a substantial element of control residing with the membership.

The use of these various, single measures of union democracy in the existing empirical literature raises the all-important question of whether a comprehensive, systematic study would find that they are significantly and positively inter-correlated. In other words, is it the case that the unions that score high on one measure of democracy also score high on all the other measures, and, conversely, are the unions that are relatively undemocratic on one measure similarly undemocratic according to the other measures? One of the few studies to examine this particular question was based on information concerning local government unions in Canada, with the basic finding being that the various measures of union democracy (i.e. the dependent variables) were far from strongly inter-related.[62] The same study also examined a wide range of potential determinants of union democracy, which were basically grouped under the headings of (i) environmental factors (e.g. perceived degree of union–management hostility), (ii) structural factors (e.g. complexity and control), and (iii) internal factors (e.g. electoral process and communication processes), with the results indicating that different determinants were significantly correlated with different measures of democracy. Moreover, not all of the relevant determinants of the different measures of union democracy were found to be under the control of individual unions at any point in time. This latter finding is consistent with those of a number of recent single-union-based studies of democracy in Britain. For example, a study of one branch of NALGO concluded that 'democracy cannot be sensibly judged solely within the confines of the organization . . . this study has demonstrated the importance of educational levels and background political socialization factors for the development of the individual's capacity to participate and to participate effectively. These are factors beyond the ambit of the unions' control or direct influence.'[63]

The present Conservative Government's belief that union democracy (or at least some measure of it) is amenable to short-run policy influence received tangible expression in Part I of the Trade Union Act 1984 which stipulates that the principal executive committee of each union must be elected at least once every 5 years by means of a direct postal ballot of all members. This 'universalist' requirement is at variance with the traditionally diverse practices and pattern of arrangements among unions in Britain. For example, Undy and Martin's 1980 survey of the rule-books of some 103 unions, found that 65 of them used a membership vote to elect their executive committees, with only 15 of these using a full or half postal ballot for these purposes;[64] this was, in fact, the largest number of unions using postal ballots in any of the elections that they considered. This study considered the role of union ballots in relation to the larger issue of union democracy and suggested that:

> Legislation which seeks to promote union democracy will depend for its effect on democracy on the interaction between the method promoted and the union's existing processes of decision making, both formal and informal. As there is no common pattern of formal, much less informal, procedures in British unions, the result for democracy of enforcing postal ballots is problematical . . . formal factors are less important than informal

> and structural factors in promoting union democracy . . . unions with many of the same formal provisions, such as similar division of powers, tenured general secretaries and branch ballots for electing conference delegates may be more or less democratic in practice. Significantly, the development of factions and parties is not dependent on specific types of ballots or even on the election of full-time officials.[65]

Finally, one needs to note the availability of public funds for union ballots from 1980. By mid-1985, 28 non-TUC affiliated unions had applied for such funds for 79 ballots (more than 50 of these relating to elections), but official TUC policy (as laid down at the Wembley Conference of 1982) was that affiliated unions should not apply for such grants. However, the engineering union (awarded £1.2 million for 154 ballots for election of its officials in 1985) and the EETPU, both of which have used postal ballots for many years, have done so with their actions in this regard being a major source of controversy and debate at the TUC meeting of 1985. In 1986, some 15 of the 40 unions which applied for refunds for ballots were TUC-affiliated ones, with 13 of the former being first-time applicants.

Variation and change in union membership

In this section we are primarily concerned with what the available literature has to say about the determinants of changes in total union membership through the course of time, and with the determinants of variation in union membership levels and status (at various levels of analysis) at a single point in time. However, before considering these matters, there are one or two introductory comments that need to be made about the accuracy, value, and meaning of the available statistics on trade-union membership in Britain. First, the desirability of being able to calculate the proportion of the reported membership of individual unions which comprises the 'active membership' in the sense of employed, full-dues-paying members has frequently been raised, but is not something which can currently be undertaken – given the nature of the internal information systems of many unions.[66] Second, in calculating levels of overall union density there have been disagreements about the inclusion of certain categories of the workforce in the denominator of the ratio, so that differences will exist between the figures reported in individual studies. For example, depending on whether the denominator included the unemployed and self-employed, and the numerator involved TUC-affiliated membership only or that of all unions, a range of union-density figures was obtained for 1979 of 47.4 per cent to 58.3 per cent and, for 1985, figures ranging from 35.8 per cent to 51.4 per cent.[67] Third, economists in particular (see Chapter 7) have utilized changes in union membership and density as one of the leading statistical proxies for the extent of union power, but the use of these figures as indicating union power or reflecting the development of a 'genuine trade union consciousness' has been much criticized.[68]

It has long been recognized that the overall levels of union membership and density in any national system of industrial relations will exhibit considerable variability through the course of time. In the UK, for example, the level of union density was nearly 11 per cent in 1892, 45 per cent in 1920, 23 per cent in 1933, 39 per cent in 1945, 43 per cent in 1960, 55 per cent in 1979, and 45 per cent in 1984 (these figures include the unemployed in the denominator).[69] In seeking to understand the nature of such changes over the course of time, the essentially qualitative literature prior to the 1970s made two basic points,[70] namely (i) union membership rose in the upswing and fell in the downswing of the business cycle, and (ii) growth in union membership was disproportionately associated with relatively short, atypical periods of time (i.e. war years and the upswing of the business cycle immediately following a deep depression). The later pattern or finding has led one US commentator to describe unions as having been the 'beneficiaries of social disasters'.[71]

The study by Ashenfelter and Pencavel in the United States stimulated a major upsurge of interest from the 1970s in attempts to formally model the relationship between movements in total union membership and in aggregate levels of economic activity.[72] One of the most well-known studies along these lines is that of Bain and Elsheikh which examined the change in total union membership in four countries (Australia, Britain, Sweden, and the US) over something like a 70-year period of time (i.e. approximately 1900–1970).[73] Their basic explanatory model contained individual variables for the rate of change in money wages, the rate of change in prices, the level and rate of change in unemployment and the level of overall union density. The level of overall explanatory power of the model was considerable, with particular support being found for the following relationships: (i) increases in total union membership were positively associated with years of rapidly rising prices, a result attributed to the threat that such price rises posed to the living standards of employees; and (ii) increases in total union membership were positively associated with years of rapidly rising money wages, a finding attributed to employees crediting union activities with having brought about such rises. However, this particular study, and other subsequent ones along similar lines, have been subject to a certain amount of statistical and conceptual criticism.[74] One major statistical criticism has centred around the question of the structural stability of the estimating equations. The concern here is, first, that a single-equation model may in fact be a statistical average of two (or more) quite separate and distinctive relationships, given the sharp discontinuities or breaks in union membership figures over time; statistical tests for stability have suggested the existence of quite distinctive sub-periods of time which need to be analysed separately, in quite different terms. Second, there have also been criticisms centred around the fact that such models do not incorporate, or control for, certain important, structural changes in the composition and distribution of the total workforce (e.g. industrial and occupational shifts) over the period of time in question. Third, when such models, which are predominantly economic ones, seek to capture the influence of important political and legislative changes, the resulting dummy variables are often statistically significant, although whether such variables are solely picking up the particular hypothesized influence is somewhat questionable. Finally, some individuals have been critical of the 'micro-foundations' of such models which are overwhelmingly demand-side-dominated ones, and which involve individual employees in making exclusively rational, economic cost/benefit-based judgements about the worth of union membership; hence they ignore supply-side influences, such as inter-union competition for recruitment and the level of individual-union organizing activity.

In Britain, the overall level of union density changed little during the course of the 1960s (i.e. 44 per cent in 1960 and 45 per cent in 1969), grew substantially in the 1970s, and has fallen quite substantially in the 1980s. Table 3.2 sets out some relevant figures for the years 1975–86.

The existing literature contains a good deal of information on the characteristics and features of the union growth of the 1970s. For example, we know that such growth was disproportionately associated with the already relatively well organized manufacturing and public sectors, and with the very large unions (i.e. the 22 unions in 1983 which had more than 100,000 members each and which accounted for some 80 per cent of total union membership). In contrast, the extent of our knowledge about the characteristics and causes of union decline in the 1980s is much more limited: in addition to Britain, union decline in the 1980s is most obviously apparent in the US and Japan, although some decline also appears

Table 3.2 Trade unions: numbers and membership, 1975–86

	Number of unions at year end	*Total membership at end of year (millions)*	*Percentage change in membership since previous year*	*Membership as a percentage of working population*
1975	470	12.0		47.2
1976	473	12.4	+3.0	48.5
1977	481	12.8	+3.7	50.1
1978	462	13.1	+2.1	50.7
1979	453	13.3	+1.3	51.1
1980	438	12.9	−2.6	49.5
1981	414	12.1	−6.5	46.6
1982	408	11.6	−4.2	44.8
1983	394	11.2	−3.1	41.6
1984	375	11.0	−2.2	39.9
1985	370	10.8	−1.6	38.9
1986	335	10.5	−2.6	37.6

Source: Industrial Relations Review and Report, no. 417, 1 June 1988, p. 10.

to have occurred in Italy and the Netherlands. The one time-series study which has included the 1980s is that by Carruth and Disney, which reported that unemployment, a Conservative government in office, and nominal and real wage growth were all significantly associated with changes in total union membership.[75] Interestingly, they found a negative relationship between nominal and real wage growth and the level of union membership, in contrast to the earlier cited work of Bain and Elsheikh, and also favoured a measure of union density which excluded the unemployed from the denominator (the latter is more akin to the approach of US, rather than previous British, studies). It is also worth noting here some calculations performed by Price and Bain which suggested that the relative increase in women workers, in white collar workers and changes in the industrial composition of the workforce would have caused overall union density to have fallen by 4 percentage points between 1979 and 1990, even if the unions had been able to maintain the levels of union density reached in all areas in 1979.[76] The work of Carruth and Disney, however, reported that the composition of changes in employment played little part in explaining the 1980s decline in union membership.

In recent years there have been a number of studies in Britain which have examined the determinants of differences in union-membership levels and status at a single point in time. These cross-sectional studies have sought to account for the extent of differences in union membership between industries, plants and, most recently of all, between the status of individual employees.

The major conclusion to emerge from this body of literature is that generally the characteristics of plants (e.g. large plant size) and industries (e.g. public-sector status) are rather more important determinants of the extent of union membership than are the personal and demographic characteristics of the workforce or individual employees. This being said, the latter are not without their influence, as evidenced by, for example, the study by Bain and Elias of individual employee membership status (based on the National Training Survey of 1975), which concluded as follows:

> An individual who is self-employed, who works part time, who is a member of a white collar occupation, or who possesses a degree or related professional qualification is generally less likely to be a union member, whereas a person who is male, who left school before the age of sixteen, who currently holds more than one job, who works in Wales or in the North of Britain, or who is employed in industries characterised by labour intensity or product market concentration is generally more likely to be a union member. The probability of being a union member also generally increases, but at a decreasing rate, with size of establishment, work experience and level of earnings.[77]

Some other cross-sectional work has also revealed that: (i) union recognition at the establishment level (a major determinant of union membership there) is significantly associated with the northern regions of Britain, even when inter-regional differences in the occupational/industrial structure of the workforce are controlled for;[78] (ii) the existence of a union, recognition of that union, and public sector employment are major determinants of the union-membership status of managers in Britain;[79] and (iii) the likelihood of an individual union obtaining recognition under statutory provisions (i.e. Sections 11–16 of the Employment Protection Act 1975) which operated in the years 1976–80 was significantly and positively related to small bargaining unit size, a relatively short length of time being involved in the hearing and deciding of the claim, and the absence of inter-union competition[80] (the relative absence of these factors particularly limited the success of white collar claims in the years 1976–80).

There are a number of final comments to make about the present state of the research literature on union membership in Britain. First, one needs to recognize that the statistical significance of certain individual variables in the cross-sectional studies does not always reflect the existence of a single, self-contained influence. For example, the positive relationship between union membership and large plant size may reflect a demand-side influence (i.e. an above average employee demand for union services due to the non-monetary job dissatisfaction often alleged to be associated with large-sized employment units and the limited feasibility of individual bargaining), or a supply-side influence (i.e. organizing economies of scale for unions in such circumstances), or a combination of both. Second, there has been a quite sizeable 'instrumentality versus general principled commitment' debate concerning white-collar employee attitudes towards unions, which essentially revolves around the question of whether such individuals are relatively indifferent (or not) as to which particular union represents them.[81] This debate could usefully be taken a stage further by examining the nature of the influences (e.g. larger value systems of employees or particular union recruitment traditions) that leads some employees to join one union in preference to others in employment settings where more than one union is recognized for collective bargaining purposes. Research along such lines would be particularly useful in certain white-collar employment areas (e.g. nursing and teaching) where the character of the unions or employee representative bodies appears to be very different in nature. Third, there is a need for systematic empirical research to examine the claim of Undy *et al.* that the overall level of union membership can be substantially affected by the organizing activities of individual, 'growth orientated' unions, as opposed to being largely shaped by environmental factors (e.g. inflation, unemployment) essentially exogenous to union control.[82] A further subject for more research in Britian, particularly in relation to white-collar employees, involves the question of dual loyalty or dual allegiance among employees – i.e. can an individual employee who is a union member be positively committed to both the organization and the union? There is some existing research on this subject in Britain,[83] but nothing like the volume that is currently being undertaken in the United States.[84] Finally, one needs to consider some of the potential limitations of the existing studies of union membership based on the individual employee. The particular data sources on which they have been based (e.g. the National Training Survey) permit the identification of the characteristics associated with union membership status, but do not allow us to formally test the nature of the underlying decision-making processes involved. Indeed, the fact that the majority of recognized bargaining units have had this status for many years raises important questions about the appropriateness of treating the union status of a sample of contemporary workers as involving an individual choice process by them.[85] This is particularly the case where closed shop arrangements exist, which is the subject of the next section.

The rationale for, and the incidence and effects of, closed shops

As the contours of collective-bargaining arrangements are relatively long-established in Britain (and recognition of an individual bargaining unit is for the jobs, as opposed to the particular workers, of the unit) the basic choices which confront *contemporary* workers are, first, whether to seek employment in a recognized or non-recognized bargaining unit situation and, second, if an individual opts for the former position, whether (or not) to be a member of the union(s) which is the recognized bargaining agent for the unit concerned. In seeking to understand the nature of the latter decision, Commons has argued that a *reasonable* individual is aware that individual freedom can only be achieved through a collective adherence to duties that define and protect individual rights for everyone[86] (so that they are likely to voluntarily opt for union membership), whereas Olson has argued that the influence of trust, friendship, social pressure, or altruistic concern for the welfare of the group as a whole will have relatively little influence on a *rational* individual being asked to contribute towards the provision of collective or public goods in large group settings.[87] To Olson, the closed shop is an essential and legitimate institutional demand and response to such individual employee attitudes and motives, with the relative absence of such institutional arrangements in any national system of industrial relations likely to produce, and raise, the following features and issues:

1. There will be a substantial difference between the overall extent of collective bargaining coverage (particularly for wage determination) and the level of union density at any point in time. In the 1970s this difference in Britain was of the order of 25 percentage points, where in the United States it was only some 6–7 percentage points.[88]
2. In such a system, closed shops are only likely to be established in individual circumstances of already high levels of union density, which raises the question of whether closed shops will have a significant, independent effect on industrial relations processes and outcomes, *ceteris paribus*?
3. In such a system, closed shops are likely to be disproportionately associated with older industries which are in relative decline in employment terms. The result is that such arrangements will act to maintain the level of union density in such firms and

industries, but will make relatively little contribution towards increasing total union membership in the system at large.

4. In such a system, the limited presence of closed shop arrangements in the newer, relatively growing industries will require the union movement increasingly to emphasize the provision of private (e.g. legal representation) or semi-public (e.g. grievance processing) goods and services to members in order to increase the overall level of union membership and prevent the occurrence of an increasingly sizeable gap between collective-bargaining coverage and the level of union density.

The relative growth of closed shop arrangements in Britain during the 1970s has been documented by a number of studies.[89] For example, the 1980 workplace industrial-relations survey suggested that some 27 per cent of employees were covered by such arrangements, compared to an estimated coverage of some 16 per cent in the early 1960s.[90] This growth during the 1970s largely involved the post-entry form of closed shop, with overall coverage being disprotionately associated with manual workers (i.e. 44 per cent coverage compared to a figure of 9 per cent for non-manual employees), nationalized industries, and relatively large-sized establishments and organizations. However, the natural limits to this growth appeared to have been reached by the end of that decade, and certainly the 1984 workplace industrial-relations survey reported that the membership of closed-shop arrangements (i.e. some 3.5–3.7 million in mid-1984) had fallen by some 1.2 million in the early 1980s.[91] This reduction was particularly associated with the manual, post-entry, closed-shop arrangements of relatively large-sized, manufacturing-sector establishments. The same survey also revealed certain changes in the characteristics of closed-shop agreements (e.g. more written agreements), noted that newly established arrangements were few in number, and emphasized that the nature of the relationship between closed-shop and check-off arrangements (i.e. some six million employees covered by such arrangements in mid-1984) was a relatively loose one.

Research concerning the closed shop is likely to focus increasingly on two major questions or themes. First, what has been the impact of the existence of closed-shop arrangements on certain industrial-relations outcomes? A number of surveys by industrial-relations researchers have obtained subjective information from management respondents concerning the perceived impact of such arrangements, with one such study concluding 'that the impact of the post-entry closed shop on industrial relations tends to be elusive. The majority of managers interviewed were either unable to identify the costs and benefits involved with any certainty or considered them peripheral.'[92] Moreover, formal examinations (involving the use of multivariate statistical analysis) of the impact of such arrangements, *ceteris paribus*, on the processes and outcomes of collective bargaining have traditionally been few in number.[93] In recent years, however, some studies by economists have revealed that:

> The closed shop has a worse effect on labour productivity than just recognition without a closed shop. Similarly, the amount of extra pay that union members get over comparable non-union members is twice as high for those covered by a closed shop (9–14 per cent) than it is for those where there is recognition only (4–7 per cent).[94]

The second focus of future research activity is likely to concern the impact of the relevant provisions of the Employment Acts of 1980, 1982, and 1988 on the extent and nature of closed-shop arrangements. These legislative provisions, together with the relevant code of practice which has been issued, are designed to limit the growth of new closed-shop arrangements and to increase the range of individual employee exemptions under existing arrangements. For example, exceptions to the right to insist on union membership in a closed shop have been broadened (beyond religious belief) to that of 'conscience or other deeply felt personal conviction', while dismissal for non-membership is only 'fair' if the closed shop has been approved in a ballot by 80 per cent of those entitled to vote or 85 per cent of those voting. However, despite the public sector being used to provide something of a 'role model' here, with British Rail, British Gas, British Telecom, the water authorities, and the Post Office all having withdrawn from agreements providing for such arrangements, the ACAS Annual Report for 1986 observed that in that year they were only aware of some 9 ballots concerning closed shop or union membership agreements; this brought the total of such ballots to 116 (since the introduction of the relevant provisions), with fully 91 of these being in favour of the maintenance of the existing agreement. However, future research efforts will clearly need to advance our knowledge considerably beyond that of the present stage, which largely involves the citing of such figures and detailed discussions of individual disputes and cases (e.g. the NGA dispute with the Messenger Newspapers Group in 1983–4) before one can adequately hope to assess the full consequences and impact of the present Government's legislation concerning closed-shop arrangements.

Modelling union behaviour in wage bargaining

The question of whether one can usefully and meaningfully analyse the nature of union demands in wage bargaining by constructing a simple model of a union as a maximizing agent has produced one of the classic debates in the industrial-relations literature. According to Dunlop, a union is essentially a supplier or seller of labour services and hence, as the supply-side counterpart to the firm, can be treated as an economic decision-making unit whose primary objective is the maximization of some wage/employment dimension of its current membership.[95] Dunlop, in fact, outlined several possible wage/employment objectives that a union might have in formulating its wage demands in collective bargaining, such as that of maximizing the individual member's wage rate or maximizing the total wage bill of its membership. The essential aspect of all the possible aims outlined (except that of maximizing the individual member's wage rate) was that the union would take explicit account of the level of employment (of its current membership) that was associated with various possible wage demands. In other words, the union would make some estimate of the elasticity of demand for the services of its members when framing its basic wage demands, and the more inelastic the demand for labour function (i.e. the less employment changes in response to a given change in its price) the more the union could make higher wage demands without risking a displacement of members from employment.

This concept of the elasticity of labour demand still remains central to many economists' discussions of the nature of 'union power' in wage bargaining, with more sizeable union relative wage effects held to be positively associated with, and derivative from, situations of relatively inelastic demand for labour functions.[96] And, according to the Marshallian derived demand conditions, a labour-demand schedule is relatively inelastic: (i) the more essential is (union) labour to the production of the final product; (ii) the more inelastic is the demand for the final product; (iii) the smaller is the ratio of (union) labour cost to total production cost; and (iv) the more inelastic is the supply of other factors of production. These individual determinants of the elasticity of the demand for labour function have been the basis of certain important hypothesized relationships, namely that the relative wage effects of craft unions will exceed those of industrial unions and that such effects for public-sector unions will exceed those of their private sector counterparts. The former hypothesis has been subject to considerable *a priori* criticism,[97] while the latter has enjoyed only relatively limited support in the relevant (largely US based) empirical literature.[98] More generally, Dunlop's basic view of the union as an economic decision-making, maximizing agent was strongly criticized by Arthur Ross on the grounds that (i) collective bargaining was a wage, and not a wage/employment bargain because of the inability of unions to make estimates of the wage elasticity of their membership, and (ii) a trade union was not a homogeneous body because important differences existed between the aims of the union leadership and the aims of the rank and file members.[99]

According to Ross, the primary aim of a union leadership (whose goals, rather than those of the union rank and file, shape the nature of wage demands) was to maintain the union as a viable institution (i.e. survival and growth), with their secondary aim being to ensure their own position of authority and power within the organization. In seeking to achieve these particular aims, the union leadership has to try and reconcile the potentially conflicting objectives of three particular interest groups – namely the union rank and file, the employer(s), and the Government – and, so the argument goes, this is most likely to be achieved by basing their wage demands on notions of equity and fairness. The major criteria of equity and fairness is the level of settlements negotiated elsewhere in the economy, particularly by other unions in the same industry or by other unions in closely related industries (i.e. these being Ross's 'orbits of coercive comparison'). The alleged value of the union leadership framing their wage demands along these lines was that it satisfied the rank-and-file demand for equity, did not seriously undermine the competitive position of the employer, and would not lead to them being singled out by the Government for 'irresponsible wage behaviour'. In short, it is these sorts of 'political' considerations and inter-relationships, rather than the forces of supply and demand, that are all important in Ross's explanation of the nature of union wage demands in collective bargaining.

There are individual aspects of Ross's argument that are open to some criticism. For example, his contention that wage demands based on the 'orbits of coercive comparison' will not seriously undermine the competitive position of an individual employer, assumes that all major sources of competition are domestic in nature. Second, his wage-follower emphasis does not really offer any insights into how the wage demands of the original wage leaders (who establish the going rate) come to be first formulated. Third, he tends rather to gloss over the issues involved in one union, basing its wage *demands* on the wage *outcomes* of (as opposed to the demands of) other unions. Nevertheless, it is the Ross, as opposed to the Dunlop, approach to the formulation of union wage demands that has arguably found more favour with industrial-relations researchers, although Mitchell has proposed a distinction between 'resistance' and 'economic' unions which, he argues, goes some way towards reconciling their different positions on the question of whether unions perceive, and act upon, the existence of a wage/employment tradeoff;[100] the former type of union never confronts a wage/employment trade-off due to facing strong management resistance, whereas, for the latter unions, such resistance is absent and it is the trade-off relationship that puts a brake on their wage demands.

The 1970s and 1980s have seen economists in both Britain and the United States returning to a number of the issues raised in the original Dunlop–Ross debate, although the approach of this recent work is a distinctively economics one.[101] This recent work initially involved 'implicit contract' theory which basically sought to provide an economic rationale for certain macro-phenomena (e.g. the general absence of money wage cuts) and micro-practices (e.g. internal labour-market arrangements, labour hoarding in economic downturns, and redundancies based on the seniority principle) which did not clearly accord with the predictions of neo-classical, labour-market theory. In conjunction with this theoretical work on the nature of the labour contract has been the increased attention given to the micro-economics of trade unions, which has been primarily concerned with the mix of wage and employment levels that unions seek to achieve. There has, for example, been discussions of (i) monopoly models (of the Dunlop type) in which the union sets wages and the employer sets the levels of employment (on the labour–demand curve), (ii) efficient bargaining models in which the union and employer seek to set both wage and employment levels (off the labour–demand curve), and (iii) the median model (sometimes labelled a seniority version of the efficient-bargaining model) in which the union as a bargaining agent reflects the preferences of its average (as opposed to marginal) member who is a relatively older individual with considerable accumulated seniority.

This body of literature is overwhelmingly theoretical in nature, with empirical tests of the models being relatively few in number.[102] One might have expected, or at least hoped, that such work would have stimulated increased research collaboration between economists and industrial-relations specialists but, in practice, this has not occurred. In fact, industrial-relations researchers have largely tended to ignore this particular stream of research, or else be highly critical of it. Marsden, for example, has criticized these trade-union models: first, for their artifical separation of joint-regulation and wage-determination activities and, second, for the fact that 'trade unions are not coalitions of individual members, or median members plus leaders, but . . . are coalitions of groups.'[103] Industrial-relations researchers have also been critical of the related, implicit-contract-theory literature, and even some economists have acknowledged that some of the predictions of this work are at variance with the facts of the real world.[104]

Conclusion

Ideally, one would like to be able to summarize the discussion of this chapter by precisely identifying the factors involved in measuring and determining the effectiveness of individual trade unions as bargaining agents. In practice, however, this would be, to say the least, an extremely difficult task: first, because of the considerable variation in the internal administrative arrangements and practices of individual unions; and, second, because of the potential conflicts and trade-offs between the various aims and objectives of unions. Further complications for such an exercise arise from the fact that effectiveness can be judged from a number of different perspectives within a single union. In the US, there is a considerable volume of empirical reseach concerning rank-and-file assessments of their union's bargaining performance,[105] and Table 3.3 sets out some basic information along these lines for Britain.

Table 3.3 Union members' views of union activities at their workplace, 1979

Statement/Answer	*Percentage of union members*
Union at own place of work does a good job for self and family	71
Your union adequately represents your interests to the employer	65
Your steward adequately represents your interests to employers	57
Sufficiently consulted by your union	56
If disagreed with branch policy, how easy to make your views felt?	
Easy	59
Difficult	25
Never tried	16
Union at your workplace is:	
Too ready to take industrial action	12
About right	53
Not ready enough	30

Source: Michael Fogarty with Douglas Brooks (1986), *Trade Unions and British Industrial Development*, p. 95, London: PSI.

This sort of basic data gathered by opinion surveys reveals considerable inter-member variation in responses, and if such data could be made available to outside researchers one could seek to identify any systematic sources or bases of such variation; this would greatly assist in the task of helping to develop a 'client based' view of union-bargaining effectiveness. Obviously, however, not all of the relevant determinants of union effectiveness as a bargaining agent in its dealings with management are under the control of individual unions, a perspective that is pursued in the next chapter's discussion of the management role and function in collective bargaining.

Chapter four

Management strategy, structures, and policies for industrial relations

In this chapter we review the nature of the management role in industrial relations by considering a number of conventional subjects such as employer associations and the personnel-management function. However, the relevant literature of more recent years contains two particular arguments or suggestions which are reflected in the contents of this chapter. The first contention is that the range of personnel or industrial-relations policies is broadening and becoming more individual-employee orientated, with the result that some managers prefer to describe their policies as 'employee relations' ones, as opposed to industrial relations policies (which have the connotation of being collective-bargaining centred), or personnel policies (which have the connotation of bearing little relationship to larger business strategy).[1] The second argument is that the structures, processes, and outcomes of collective bargaining, at the level of the individual workplace, are increasingly influenced by (i) larger environmental forces (e.g. product market factors) affecting the company or corporation as a whole (as opposed to the individual plant), and (ii) the resulting decisions made at these organizational levels, which are not exclusively, or even mainly, industrial-relations ones (in substantive content) taken by the specialist industrial-relations function of management.[2] There are a number of practical and research implications which follow from these tendencies, one of which is that industrial-relations researchers must increasingly utilize the insights and findings of industrial economists and organizational researchers. Material from such research is certainly drawn upon here, although we begin this chapter with an examination of the traditional subject of employers' associations.

Employers' associations and the CBI

A discussion of the management role in collective bargaining in the context of the traditional system of industrial relations in Britain (i.e. very approximately, 1920–50), with its multi-employer, industry-level, collective-bargaining arrangements, was in effect a discussion of employers' associations. A number of explanations have been offered for the emergence of employers' associations and their subsequent levels of activity in different industries and in different periods of time.[3] For example, it has been suggested that employers associations were essentially an institutional response to the growth of union organization – which was designed to restrict collective bargaining to wages/hours matters, limit the official union presence in the plant, and thus maintain a wide scope of unilateral management decision-making over non-wages and hours issues. Furthermore, these associations were particularly likely to emerge, and be maintained, in individual industries in which relatively high labour to total cost ratios provided employers (and unions) with a relatively strong incentive to try and set a floor to inter-firm wage competition. More generally, employers' associations have been relatively active bodies as employer spokesmen in certain periods of time (such as the war-time years) which were characterized by considerable government intervention in the labour-market and industrial-relations spheres of activity. Similar influences on the origins of employers' associations have been noted in other countries.[4]

In recent years, there have been a number of examinations and discussions of the differing implications and determinants of the historical and contemporary role of employers' associations in Britain in comparison with other countries. For example, Phelps Brown has argued that the macro-performance of the British economy would have been superior since the Second World War if there had been stronger employers' associations (as in Germany) to have 'held the line against wage claims'.[5] In addition, the relatively greater historical role of employers' associations in Britain (and Western Europe more generally) compared to the position in the United States, which was attributed to relatively greater government involvement in the labour market, has been viewed as having strongly shaped the general nature of management attitudes towards trade unions (i.e. making them relatively more favourably disposed).[6] There have also been a number of discussions of the major determinants of variation in the presence and influence of employers' associations in a number of national systems of industrial relations. One such study along these lines argued that high levels of industrial concentration, relatively simple technical and business structures, and high levels of product specialization in the small-scale Scandinavian countries were responsible for their more highly centralized employers' associations in comparison with

Britain.[7] This particular argument, however, has been subject to considerable criticism.[8]

If one moves away from a comparative context to concentrate solely on inter-temporal change in Britain, the first relevant point to note is that the number of employers' associations has declined. For example, the number of listed employers' associations (which meet the legal definition of the Trade Union and Labour Relations Act, 1974) has fallen from 212 in late 1975, to 172 in 1981, and to 148 at the end of 1986;[9] the Certification Officer's report for 1986 does, however, provide income and expenditure details for some 328 employers' associations, indicating the existence of at least 180 reasonably well known, but unlisted, associations. The essence of the general decline in the number of employers' associations through time has been described in the following terms:

> For the most part . . . the reduction has resulted from the winding-up of small provincially based employers organisations or from the amalgamation of the local primary organisations which make up some of the large national employers organisations such as the Engineering Employers Federation, the National Federation of Building Trade Employers, and the British Printing Industries Federation. There have been few reductions in the number of national employers organisations. Indeed, the only major casualties in recent years have been in iron and steel and in shipbuilding.[10]

The 1977–8 workplace industrial-relations survey (conducted at the University of Warwick), of some 970 manufacturing-sector establishments, reported that (i) some 75 per cent of establishments (covering 72 per cent of employees) stated that they were members of an employers' organization (although it was noted that some of these responses may have been referring to membership of trade associations, rather than membership of employers' associations), but (ii) only the Engineering Employers Federation, the British Printing Industries Federation, the British Textile Employers Association, and the Chemical Industries Association had more than 50 per cent of the establishments in any one industrial order in membership.[11] The 1970s and 1980s in Britain have seen a strong and sustained movement away from multi-employer, industry-level bargaining, to bargaining on a single-employer basis at the plant and company levels (see Chapter 5). This major change in the structure of collective bargaining has had important consequences for the membership of individual employers' associations. Since the early 1970s, a substantial number of relatively large-sized firms have formally withdrawn from membership of employers' associations, or else retained their membership but without being a party to the wage negotiations conducted by the associations. For example, Chrysler withdrew from the Engineering Employers Federation in 1970 on the stated grounds that the federation was becoming too small-firm orientated, while the early 1970s saw the entire Unilever group, Cadbury/Schweppes, Kelloggs, HP, Golden Wonder, Ross, and Beecham pull out of the Joint Industrial Council for the food-manufacturing industry.[12] More recently, Reed Corrugated Cases, which in the early 1980s employed some 4,200 workers in fourteen manufacturing plants in the UK, withdrew in 1982 from the national agreement for fibreboard packaging, which is negotiated by the British Fibreboard Packaging Employers Association with SOGAT and GMBATU.[13] Among the major reasons for this decision were the increasing difficulties of agreeing an employers negotiating mandate and the delays in concluding national settlements.

The Engineering Employers Federation has been particularly prominent in the 1980s in attempting to retain its membership by proposing changes in the nature of their national wage agreement. In November 1983, for example, responding to members' feelings that too many changes had been imposed from above by the national agreement (e.g. the move to the 39-hour week in November 1981), the Federation proposed changes to the method and timing of implementation of nationally agreed terms and conditions. Specifically, they proposed that, first, any item agreed nationally which changes working conditions should only be implemented on domestic settlement dates (as was the case with national minimum pay rates in the years 1979–83) and, second, even on the due domestic settlement date there should be no obligation to implement any changes until (union) concessions had been made in return which enabled the company to offset the resulting costs. A joint working party was set up early in 1984 to consider these proposals, and in August 1987 it was announced that a reduction in the length of the working week (from 39 to 37.5 hours) had been negotiated in return for a union willingness to discuss more flexible working arrangements and practices.

More generally, employers' associations have sought to broaden the range of advisory and consultancy services they offer so as to – in conjunction with the traditional functions of operating disputes procedures and representation of employer interests in the political sphere – avoid further membership losses, particularly among larger firms.[14] The 1984 workplace industrial relations survey did, however, find that the use of employers' associations to settle pay and conditions disputes declined quite substantially in the years 1980–4.[15]

In general, it has been observed that:

> The establishment of associations along industry lines generally preceded the formation of central employers associations. At the central level the creation of overarching bodies for broad representational, political and legislative purposes lagged behind the rise of national trade union centres by roughly ten to twenty years.[16]

In Britain, the Confederation of British Industry (CBI) was only created in 1965 with the merger of the British Employers Confederation, the Federation of British Industries, and the National Association of British Manufacturers;[17] its creation at this time being clearly related to the introduction of a comprehensive incomes policy. As the leading employer spokesman and representative body in Britain, the CBI is essentially the counterpart to the TUC in the sense of representation on advisory bodies and committees. In 1966, for example, the CBI was represented on some 57 government bodies (its three predecessors were represented on 32 in 1958),[18] while in the 1970s it became the employer representative on all the leading tripartite bodies (e.g. ACAS, the Health and Safety Commission, MSC) created in those years. The available literature on the CBI has generally tended to make the following sorts of points about the organization.[19] First, the relatively long-standing organizational membership of the CBI is from the manufacturing sector (although the nationalized industries are also members), so that its capacity to speak for, and influence, establishments in non-manufacturing areas of activity is relatively limited.[20] However, the recession of the 1980s, which has particularly affected the manufacturing sector, has resulted in membership losses for the CBI which have led to attempts to increase membership in the finance and retailing sectors. Second, the industrial-relations views and positions of the CBI appear to have been most influenced by the relatively large, highly unionized manufacturing organizations amongst its membership. The result is that, on the one hand, proposals advanced by the CBI tend to be essentially collectivist or pluralist in nature, although (predictably) with an orientation towards shifting the balance of bargaining power away from unions and towards employers.[21] The more right-wing Institute of Directors, on the other hand, places much more emphasis on individualized 'employee relations' than does the CBI. Third, existing discussions of the feasibility of establishing corporatist labour-market arrangements in Britain have invariably argued that the CBI is less capable of ensuring the fulfilment of commitments by its membership than the TUC.[22] Fourth, few commentators are likely to disagree violently with the general conclusion of Grant and Marsh that: 'the CBI has little consistent direct influence over the policies pursued by Government. This is not to say that the CBI is not able to influence considerably a particular piece of legislation.'[23] Finally, there is no doubt that the CBI has enjoyed considerably less influence under the Thatcher administration than it expected to have at the time of the Conservative Government's election in 1979.

Larger industrial and corporate developments and industrial relations

It has been argued that certain major industrial-relations changes in organizations in Britain in the 1970s were not so much the result of industrial-relations specific adjustments by management (to contain and institutionalize union power at the shop-floor level) prompted by the recommendations of the Donovan Commission, but rather derived more from larger industrial and corporate-level developments. Specifically, they were a management response to (i) increased levels of industrial concentration and merger activity, (ii) changes in the organization and structure of individual corporations, and (iii) the development of more extensive and sophisticated systems of financial and budgetary control.[24] In this section we seek to provide some details of these larger developments and to highlight some of the more specific industrial-relations consequences of them.

The increase in the aggregate level of industrial concentration in Britain over the course of the century is well documented. Prais, for instance, has estimated the share of the 100 largest firms in manufacturing net output to have been 22 per cent in 1924, 34 per cent in 1935, 22 per cent in 1949, 27 per cent in 1953, 37 per cent in 1963, and 41 per cent in 1970.[25] Furthermore, Hannah[26] has shown that the share of the 100 largest firms increased rapidly in both the 1920s and 1960s, which were both periods of intense merger activity, while the fall in concentration during the 1930s and 1940s coincided with periods of low merger activity. This particular study was one of the many examined in the extensive literature review by Curry and George, which concluded that 'when all the facts and arguments have been assembled it is difficult to escape the conclusion that mergers have been the dominant factor in increasing concentration.'[27] The major peaks in the extent of merger activity have been the 1920s, the late 1960s, and the early 1970s; whereas more recent years have witnessed fewer mergers, although 'the average size of acquisition has been much larger in real terms since 1984 than in the early 1970s'.[28] Table 4.1 sets out some recent figures on the extent of merger activity, distinguishing between: (i) the acquisition of independent companies by parent groups (the most typically discussed); (ii) the sale of subsidiaries between parent groups; and (iii) management buy-outs (whereby the management of a company acquires the business by which they are employed).

Table 4.1 Acquisitions, divestments, and buy-outs, 1969–85 and 1986 (to third quarter)

Year	*Acquisition of independent industrial companies*			*Sales of subsidiaries between industrial parent groups*			*Management buy-outs*		
	No.	*£m*	*Avge.*	*No.*	*£m*	*Avge.*	*No.*	*£m*	*Avge.*
1969	742	961	1.30	102	100	0.98			
1970	608	954	1.57	179	126	0.70			
1971	620	745	1.20	264	166	0.63			
1972	931	2,337	2.51	272	185	0.68			
1973	951	1,057	1.11	254	247	0.97			
1974	367	459	1.25	137	49	0.36			
1975	200	221	1.11	115	70	0.61			
1976	242	348	1.44	111	100	0.90			
1977	372	730	1.96	109	94	0.86	13		
1978	441	977	2.22	126	163	1.29	23		
1979	414	1,438	3.47	117	186	1.59	52	26	0.50
1980	368	1,265	3.44	101	210	2.08	107	50	0.47
1981	327	882	2.70	125	262	2.10	124	114	0.92
1982	296	1,373	4.64	164	804	4.90	170	265	1.56
1983	302	1,783	5.90	142	436	3.07	205	315	1.54
1984	396	4,253	10.74	170	1,121	6.59	210	255	1.21
1985	339	6,281	18.53	134	793	5.92	229	1,176	5.02
1986/Q3	349	10,000	28.65	93	914	9.83	201	944	4.70

Source: Brian Chiplin and Mike Wright (1987), *The Logic of Mergers*, Hobart Paper 107, p. 17, London: IEA.

Industrial economists have examined the impact of merger activity on a number of aspects of subsequent corporate performance (e.g. profits and productivity), but comprehensive and systematic empirical studies of the impact on industrial-relations structure, process, and outcome remain conspicuous by their absence. However, an essentially conceptual paper by Geroski and Knight points out that mergers, in increasing both average firm-size and product-market concentration levels, can have various favourable and unfavourable implications for the bargaining power of unions, although on balance they believe that the result will generally be to alter relative bargaining power in favour of employers.[29] Specifically they contend that the growth in firm size from mergers reduces the control capacity of management, but that this effect has been more than offset by organizational changes designed to restore control. The most important of these organizational changes has been the growth of the multidivisional (or M-form) organization which Hannah has described as the most significant and widespread post-war development in management.[30] Channon's study of 100 large companies, for example, found that by 1950 only 13 per cent of them had a multidivisional structure, but by 1960 the figure had risen to 30 per cent and by 1970 to 72 per cent.[31]

There is, in fact, a substantial theoretical and empirical literature on the reasons for, and effects of, the development of the M-form organizational structure. Chandler, for example, has suggested that the M-form was developed in order to deal with increased organizational complexity (which resulted from a growth in firm size and diversification into new lines of business).[32] Williamson, however, has argued that the M-form, compared with the centralized (or U-form) organization, will be more profitable due to having more effective internal control systems which can (i) motivate the behaviour of divisional managers to be more in line with central management goals and (ii) allocate cash flows towards the more high-yield areas of the organization.[33] The development of the M-form organization has particularly important implications for the extent and nature of accounting information and control systems.[34] As early as 1936, accountants had greater representation on the boards of directors of British companies than any other professional group,[35] but in the late 1960s and early 1970s, when there was so much merger activity and movement towards the M-form organization, it was hardly coincidental to find a much more extensive and intensive adoption and use of sophisticated accountancy techniques within companies.[36] According to Batstone, this increased importance of management-accounting and financial-control techniques, which were largely procedural in nature and outcome orientated, militated against the serious consideration of industrial-relations matters at senior management level – although, more generally, these corporate-level developments of the late 1960s and early 1970s did produce an increased trend towards specialization within the management hierarchy of organizations, one particular manifestation of which was the growth in the personnel-management function during the 1970s.[37] (The latter will be considered in more detail later in this chapter.) One obvious implication of the view that the structures, processes, and outcomes of collective bargaining and industrial relations are much influenced by larger inter- and intra-corporate developments, is that industrial-relations researchers need to draw upon the insights of, and indeed be actively involved in, research with industrial economists and organization theorists and researchers. In order to illustrate this proposition in a little more detail, the next section takes a look at some of the methodologies, concepts, and findings of organization researchers that can be, and indeed in some cases have been, utilized by industrial-relations researchers.

Some insights from the organization-research literature

There currently exist a number of detailed categorizations and discussions of the substantial and heterogeneous body of literature that is labelled organization theory.[38] There is no attempt made here to discuss this literature systematically along such lines; rather, a brief review is made of various organization theories' treatment of the concepts of power and conflict, both of which are of central importance to industrial-relations researchers.[39]

The early managerial theories of organizations, which were concerned to elaborate the principles of 'the one best way to manage', essentially ignored the subject of conflict in organizations. The criticisms of these theories involved a recognition of the fact that conflict was to some extent inevitable in organizations and was not automatically an undesirable phenomenon for all organizational members. However, the popular contingency theories of the late 1960s and early 1970s were still basically apolitical, rational-decision-based models, albeit they rejected the view that there was one best way to manage and argued the need for an appropriate fit between structures and the particular environmental and technological context of the organization. In more recent years, a number of scholars have increasingly come to conceive of organizations as essentially political coalitions – in which divergent interests and aims, power, and conflict are among the most important influences shaping the nature of the decision-making processes. These theories have moved beyond the early French and Raven conception of the bases of individual power (i.e. reward power, punishment power, expert power, legitimate power, and referrent power),[40] towards systematically examining the determinants of departmental or sub-unit power within the management hierarchy of firms. In general, these discussions have tended to adopt a resource-dependency approach to power, focusing 'either on the dependence of the organization as a whole or of other subunits on the particular resources or certainty provided by other social actors within the organization.'[41] As we shall see in the next section, this view of the nature of intra-management power can be used to help explain developments in the personnel-management function within organizations. More generally, a recognition of significant differences in the aims and power-bases of the various parts of management which necessitate a considerable volume of intra-management bargaining has major implications, as we shall see in this and other chapters, for individual matters such as, for example: (i) the level of priority accorded to industrial relations matters in general in senior management decision-making circles; (ii) the extent of the specialist personnel management input to strategic decision-making processes; (iii) the content of personnel policies at a particular point in time and through time; and (iv) variation in attitudes (positive or negative) towards unions and collective-bargaining arrangements in general.

The current interest in viewing organizations as political systems does not lack rivals in either the theoretical or more practitioner-orientated literature. Specifically, views of the organization as essentially co-operative and unitary systems still exist, having come down from the human-relations movement of the 1930s, through the organization development and change models of the 1970s (with their emphasis on inter-personal trust, openness, and communciations), to the more popular emphases of the present time on the importance of creating an organizational culture which reflects the views of senior management. Table 4.2 sets out the eight principles for excellence in company performance that are contained in the most well-known of these recent 'popular' books on organizational culture.

There have been a number of criticisms of the methodology and substantive findings of Peters and Waterman; typical criticisms have included the claim of selective perception among the managers interviewed, the use of a limited range of performance indices, and the fact that a number of the companies concerned have subsequently experienced performance difficulties.[42] However, for present purposes, what is important about the content or message of their work is the strong emphasis placed on the role of senior management in shaping individual employees' values (to conform with those of the organizational culture) through the use of symbolism (i.e. not through facts but via rituals and myths). This perspective does have some *theoretical* basis in recent treatments of management's use of symbolic action to manipulate values,[43] and

Table 4.2 Eight principles of company excellence in performance

1. A bias for action: a preference for doing something – anything – rather than sending a question through cycles of analyses and committee reports.
2. Staying close to the customer – learning his preferences and catering to them.
3. Autonomy and entrepreneurship – breaking the corporation into small companies and encouraging them to think independently and competitively.
4. Productivity through people – creating in all employees the awareness that their best efforts are essential and that they will share in the rewards of the company's success.
5. Hands-on, value-driven – insisting that executives keep in touch with the firm's essential business.
6. Stick to the knitting – remaining with the business the company knows best.
7. Simple form, lean staff – few administrative layers, few people at the upper levels.
8. Simultaneous loose–tight properties – fostering a climate where there is a dedication to the central values of the company combined with tolerance for all employees who accept those values.

Source: T. J. Peters and R. H. Waterman (1982), *In Search of Excellence*, New York: Harper & Row.

indeed has some obvious linkages with some of the relatively early discussions of the nature of the psychological contract. Barnard, for example, argued that the extent of the authority of management is a function of employees' perceptions of the acceptable limits of such authority.[44]

As a control strategy, the attempt to align organizational and individual employee values through the creation of an organizational culture is likely to be related to, and indeed grounded in, the existence of relatively well developed internal labour-market arrangements, which themselves have been viewed as the latest stage in the evolution of management-control processes over the course of time (i.e. hierarchical control through technical control to bureaucratic control).[45] This radical view of the rationale for internal labour-market arrangements, which are essentially a set of administrative rules and procedures that involve the pricing and allocation of labour being determined inside (as opposed to outside) the firm,[46] needs to be placed alongside other explanations of their emergence. The more economics-orientated explanation views them as more efficient solutions to problems of management in complex environments,[47] while the institutional school of thought tends to make reference to a combination of factors – namely, skill specificity, on the job training, custom, and unionization.[48] A major task which has still to be systematically confronted by industrial-relations and organizational researchers is to demonstrate the extent and nature of the impact of relatively well-developed internal labour-market arrangements on measures of organizational performance and effectiveness, both directly and indirectly via the effect on industrial-relations performance.

The popular management, 'in search of excellence' type of literature appears to be a return to the 'one best way to manage' notion and, as such, clearly diverges from the theoretical literature on competitive strategies which still tends to involve essentially a contingency approach.[49] Furthermore, in recent years, organizational scholars, particularly industrial sociologists in Europe, have demonstrated that systematic differences exist between the organizational arrangements of firms in different countries – although they are in the same industries and are matched in terms of variables such as size and technology.[50] In one such study it was reported that there was 'much more extensive occupational specialisation outside the core production area' in British than in German plants, a finding held to be associated with relatively strong notions of 'professionalism' in British industry which, in turn, derived from differences in the post-school vocational education systems of the two countries.[51] For present purposes, the important point about the above finding is that the personnel-management function is one of the non-production specialist areas of management that has sought to enhance its status in recent decades by increasingly emphasising its professional approach and orientation. Accordingly, it is to an examination of this function that we now turn.

The status and determinants of the personnel-management function

In Britain, the growth of the personnel-management function is typically viewed as having been disproportionately concentrated in the years of the Second World War and in the 1970s. To document such growth (or indeed stagnation or decline) in any given period of time one can look to a variety of possible measures. The most obvious of these measures is the subjective views of personnel managers. And here we find, for example, that the 1977/8 workplace industrial-relations survey of manufacturing establishments (the Warwick Survey) reported that fully 82 per cent of the personnel respondents stated that their role had become more, or much more, important in the years 1972–7.[52] This sort of evidence however, is inadequate by itself, as it will undoubtedly be influenced by initial levels of expectation of the function's members and needs – to be accompanied, at the least, by information on other management functions' perceptions of personnel management. The 1984 workplace industrial relations survey certainly noted some divergences between the responses of personnel managers and those of works managers on the matter of the changing influence of personnel management.[53]

Another possible measure of change is that of membership of the Institute of Personnel Management (IPM). The membership of the Institute grew by some 270 per cent in the war years, 1939–45, by 90 per cent between 1969 and 1979, and by March 1987 totalled some 31,118 individuals, with an increase of some 54 per cent having occurred since 1979. These figures are unlikely to be systematically biased through time, so that they do constitute a useful pointer to periods of particularly significant change – although at any one point in time they do substantially under-count the total number of practising personnel managers in the country. The fact that all personnel managers are not members of the IPM has led to a distinction being drawn between 'insiders and outsiders' in personnel management (i.e. non-personnel and personnel specialists respectively),[54] a dichotomy that has been more recently refined into a typology comprising the mobile professional, the late professional, the local specialist, the general manager, and the part-timer.[55] A third possible measure of the changing position of the personnel function would be the nature of relative salary movements. And here some figures extracted from the annual *New Earnings Survey* for the average gross weekly earnings of personnel managers (male only) in 1979 and 1985 revealed the following picture: (i) they were 95 per cent of those of marketing and sales managers in 1979 (98 per cent in 1985); (ii) 109 per cent of those of local government general administrators in 1979 (118 per cent in 1985); and (iii) 115 per cent of those of accountants in 1979 (123 per cent in 1985). These calculations are designed to illustrate the potential value of more systematic examinations of this particular data source, although such 'raw' figures do not control for possible differences in the personal and labour-market characteristics of the groups of individuals concerned. The annual salary survey conducted by the IPM reported that a personnel director had average annual earnings of £38,929 in 1986 (£33,456 in 1985), while a senior personnel officer received on average £13,915 in 1986 (£13,252 in 1985), but unfortunately this data source did not make comparisons with other management functions in the same organizations.

One of the expectations of the *Donovan Commission Report* was that a general move away from multi-employer, industry-level, collective-bargaining arrangements would raise the priority that boards of directors attached to industrial-relations matters which would, in turn, result in the more explicit design and development of company personnel policies. Winkler's study of some nineteen private-sector organizations in the early 1970s certainly found little indication of the sort of board-level attitudes hoped for by the Donovan Commission, as strategies (conscious or unconscious) of 'industrial-relations avoidance' were very much in evidence.[56] Nevertheless, it appeared from the results of the Warwick survey that the specialist representation of personnel management on boards had increased over the course of the 1970s.[57] This representation was anything but randomly distributed across establishments in the manufacturing sector, however, being significantly associated with establishment characteristics such as large size, multi-plant status, foreign ownership, and relatively high levels of union density and industrial action.[58] Moreover, such survey evidence can obviously tell us little about the impact and effectiveness of personnel's presence on boards in influencing the outcome of intra-management discussions and negotiations on strategic and other matters. However, the 1984 workplace industrial-relations survey is important in revealing not only the fact that the level of specialist personnel management representation at board level changed little in the years 1980–4 (i.e. 42–3 per cent) but, rather more interestingly, that such representation was only loosely related to the extent of the personnel function's development at the establishment level;[59] no significant relationship existed between specialist personnel representation at the board level and the presence of a professional personnel manager at the establishment level. On the latter matter it is important to note that the extent of qualifications of members of personnel departments has been proposed as a measure of the effectiveness of the function, but the 1984 survey found that:

> In the great majority of workplaces the senior person dealing with personnel and industrial relations matters was someone with general management responsibilities. Specialist personnel or industrial relations managers were present in 15 per cent of workplaces in 1984, the same proportion as in 1980. They remained more common in larger workplaces and less common in the private services sector than elsewhere. They were also more common in foreign owned workplaces and those that used advanced technology. But personnel specialists increasingly had relevant experience and formal qualifications for their work. The proportion reporting that they had relevant formal qualifications rose from 49 per cent in 1980 to 58 per cent in 1984. More of

them had degrees of some kind and more had relevant degrees. Specialists were also more likely to have support staff in 1984 than before.[60]

The non-random distribution of full-time and qualified personnel managers across establishments was revealed in a detailed analysis of the 1980 workplace industrial-relations survey results;[61] such individuals were disproportionately associated with larger establishments, multi-establishment organizations, foreign-owned firms, and those with a relatively high proportion of non-manual employees and relatively high levels of industrial action. In addition to both specialist board-level representation and the level of staffing and qualifications of members of the personnel function, at the establishment level (and other levels within the organization), a final possible measure of the status and authority of the personnel function is the extent and nature of its input to major decision-making processes within the organization. Here it is relevant to note that (i) only some 8 per cent of the 150 strategic decisions examined by researchers at Bradford University were personnel ones,[62] (ii) only 24 per cent of personnel respondents in the 1977 Warwick survey stated that personnel and industrial relations considerations were important in decisions on fixed capital investment,[63] and (iii) the 1984 workplace industrial relations survey revealed the relatively limited involvement of personnel management in the introduction of technical (as opposed to organizational) change. As the latter study put it: 'Clearly, it was rare for the personnel department to have established a positive role for itself as expert on all the human implications of the management of major change.'[64]

If one moves away from *measures* of the changing status and authority of the personnel management function to consider the relevant *determinants* of such change, it is necessary to consider Batstone's contention that the major relevant factor was the changing nature of management control systems which, in turn, produced an increased division of labour within the management hierarchy of organizations; 'an increase in personnel specialists . . . is to be accounted for in terms broadly comparable with those which would explain a simultaneous growth in accounting specialists in the firm.'[65] The general value of this perspective is that it emphasizes the fact that the personnel-management function is an 'open system' within the organization at large, and hence changes in its resources, authority, and influence will be governed by both the 'intra-management politics' of the decision-making processes and the larger issues of organizational structure and strategy.

However, there are a number of specific weaknesses in the particular argument presented by Batstone. The first is that he does not actually demonstrate the existence of a relationship between, on the one hand, changes in the personnel function and changes in other management functions and, on the other, larger control systems at the level of the individual organization. The case he makes is essentially a negative one – namely, the relatively high levels of statistical significance of the two variables, large establishment size and multi-establishment status (which he calls the 'organizational rationale') in a multivariate investigation (undertaken by other researchers) of the presence (or not) of a specialist personnel director. Admittedly, the statistical significance of these two particular variables inevitably poses problems of interpretation in studies of a number of industrial-relations phenomena, because their influence is unlikely to reflect a single, self-contained hypothesis or underlying behavioural relationship (recall here the discussion in Chapter 3 of the relationship between large establishment size and the level of union membership). However, it is, to say the least, highly questionable to go to the extreme that Batstone does in suggesting that the statistical significance of these two variables reflects the existence of underlying relationships with absolutely no industrial-relations-specific content to them. Finally, Batstone is incorrect when he interprets the line of causation between the development of the personnel function (as indicated by, for example, a specialist personnel director) and the level of industrial conflict at the individual-establishment level in a cross-section survey as running from the former to the latter; this he justifies on the *ad hoc* grounds of increased bureaucracy leading to poorer communications and longer procedural delays.[66] The correct relationship is in fact the other way round, with relatively high levels of industrial conflict leading to a relatively well-developed personnel management function at the level of the individual organization at any one point in time. This particular empirical relationship follows logically from an application of the 'resource dependency power' theories of organization researchers (which we briefly touched on in the previous section) to the task of identifying the major determinants of changes in the status and authority of the personnel function.

The essence of this 'resource dependency power' approach involves the treatment of the personnel management function as a 'boundary spanning' unit designed to insulate the technical core of the organization from sources of environmental uncertainty. The particular sources of environmental uncertainty that are relevant to the personnel function are: (i) tight labour market conditions;

(ii) substantial government intervention (via legislation and regulations) in the individual and collective employment relationship; and (iii) organizational and behavioural manifestations of 'union power'. It is these three sets of environmental conditions which significantly shape the extent and nature of the resources, activities, and influence of the personnel function at any one point in time and over time, with the presence of one or more of these conditions always characterizing particular periods of time in which the personnel function has enjoyed relative gains within the management hierarchy of firms. There have been virtually no systematic empirical examinations of the relative strength of these particular influences on the changing power-position of personnel departments through the course of time using longitudinal firm-level data in either Britain or the United States. However, as indicated earlier in this section, analysis of cross-sectional survey data has revealed: (i) the non-randomly distributed nature of the development of the personnel function at the establishment level at a particular point in time (e.g. as measured by the presence or not of a specialist personnel director, and by the presence or not of a full-time, qualified personnel mamager); (ii) the significance of 'union power' specific variables (e.g. the levels of union density and industrial conflict) in accounting for the revealed pattern, as well as the influence of other organizational correlates (e.g. large establishment size) which are likely to be proxying, at least to some extent, the effects of union power and/or employment legislation. In addition to the findings of these particular studies based on multi-variate analysis, the 1984 workplace industrial relations survey also identifies labour-market conditions (i.e. the rate of redundancies) and industrial-relations legislation as important general influences on personnel management in the early 1980s, with certain specific effects being most apparent in establishments that recognized unions for the purposes of collective bargaining.[67]

The fact that the power basis of personnel management is essentially exogenous to the function's own control has a number of adverse implications for its longer-term growth and development. First, it is likely that the function's power will be highly variable through time (e.g. moving up and down as the extent of union power changes) and, second, in successfully coping with a particular source of environmental uncertainty (e.g. adopting procedures to institutionalize and regularize the demands of employment legislation), the function paradoxically reduces the extent of its own power within the management hierarchy. Furthermore, it is far from clear that personnel's gains from external (to the organization) sources of uncertainty in particular periods of time are an adequate basis for longer-term development in the face of other management functions' doubts about the particular worth and contribution of the personnel function to the effective performance of the organization at large. Indeed, in Drucker's view, 'the constant worry of all personnel administrators is their inability to prove that they are making a contribution to the enterprise'.[68] From the 1970s there has been: (i) an extensive debate within the personnel management community of a number of countries concerning both the feasibility and desirability of the personnel function becoming more 'bottom line' orientated (this has been very much associated with a movement away from the welfare origins of the function to becoming more 'professional' in orientation); (ii) considerable researcher (and practitioner) interest in developing a set of measures for evaluating the performance of the personnel function. However, most of the proposed indices of performance have potential limitations, in that single measures, such as employee turnover and absence rates, are not fully under the control of the function and do not capture the full range of their activities, while composite measures (e.g. employee-costs/value-added) lack a clear rationale for the inclusion and weighting of individual items.[69]

The latest proposed response to the belief that the personnel management function has suffered from a relative lack of role/goal clarity[70] comes in the largely US-dominated literature on 'strategic human resource management'.[71] According to Hendry and Pettigrew there are basically four elements involved in this particular term:[72] (i) the use of planning; (ii) a coherent approach to the design and management of personnel systems based on an employment policy and manpower strategy (often underpinned by a philosophy); (iii) a matching of human-resource-management activities and policies to some explicit business strategy; and (iv) seeing the people of the organization as a 'strategic resource' for achieving 'competitive advantage'. The basic thrust of the strategic human-resource-management literature, which is highly descriptive and prescriptive in nature, is that the personnel function needs to adopt a more proactive role in organizations by assuming central responsibility for augmenting investment in the 'human capital' of the organization – which, in terms of Tyson and Fells' three models of personnel management, means a move from both the 'clerk of works' and 'contract managers' models to the 'architect model'.[73]

The most recent work on the personnel-management function in Britain has involved a mixture of general, conceptual discussions, case studies of individual organizations, and the gathering and analysis of survey data. This work has very largely been concerned with a number of relatively long-standing issues of interest and concern to the personnel-management function, namely: (i) the importance and activities of the corporate-level personnel department compared to the more decentralized, establishment-level function; (ii) the relative balance of personnel activities as between line and staff management; (iii) the relative clarity of personnel objectives; and (iv) attempts to measure the outputs, as opposed to inputs, of the personnel department. Two of the more important substantive and methodological advances in this more recent work have been: first, the obtaining of perceptual data on the contribution of the personnel function from members of other management functions in the organization (and not just exclusively from personnel management respondents); second, the extension of studies of the function into the public sector. In fact, the personnel management function was only established in parts of the public sector (i.e. local government and the health service) in the 1970s (and, as such, was not an outgrowth of the earlier, welfare tradition or function). However, one recent study has suggested that, despite this late development (and other inter-sectoral differences in organizational and industrial relations arrangements), the similarities between public- and private-sector personnel management are very considerable, with any observable differences being essentially a function of differences in larger control systems.[74] Moreover, it is in the public sector in recent years that some of the most interesting developments in personnel management have occurred, particularly in relation to the age-old question of the balance of personnel activities between line and staff management. An important component of Edwards' approach at BL and McGregor's at BSC and the Coal Board was to decentralize personnel activities in favour of line management, while the Cassells report on personnel management in the Civil Service in the early 1980s also favoured a shift in authority towards individual departments and line management.[75]

The determinants of the mix and priorities of personnel policies

According to Gospel, it is useful when discussing the labour-management strategies of employers to distinguish between: (i) work relations which involve the way in which technology and social processes are organized at work; (ii) employment relations which are concerned with the form of job structure, job tenure, and employment benefits attached to jobs in the organization; and (iii) industrial relations defined as covering collective relations centred around the institution of collective bargaining.[76] These sub-categories of labour-management, personnel, or human-resource-management policies and practices obviously overlap a great deal in practice – hence, changes in one are likely to set off changes in the other two, with consistent one-way lines of causation being difficult to identify in practice. In this section I do, however, attempt to provide some analytical content to the general suggestions (noted already in this and earlier chapters) that managers are, first, raising the priority they attach to employment relations relative to industrial relations and, second, are re-defining their view of the 'desirable outcomes' of collective-bargaining arrangements.

There has, in fact, been remarkably little in the way of conceptual or empirical work designed to explain the mix or content of the personnel policies of organizations at a particular point in time. One of the few contributions in this regard is a conceptual paper by Murray and Dimick which, first of all, classified individual personnel policies as being concerned with: (i) the capability of employees (e.g. recruitment, selection, performance appraisal, training, and development), and (ii) the motivation of employees (e.g. compensation, job design, employee participation); and then went on to identify (iii) the incentives for policy adoption (e.g. labour-market pressures, government legislation and regulations, external reference groups, and the values of senior management), and (iv) the enabling conditions for policy adoption (e,g, organization size, organization slack and technology).[77] On the basis of this conceptual framework they concluded that:

> A combination of economic conditions, pressure from powerful outsiders, and the advocacy of positive reference groups will give rise to perception of personnel problems and will also identify the general area of policy in which the initiative should be taken. Organisational slack, size and technology strongly influence perceived affordability of the initiatives being considered. If the costs of not acting are clear and large, policies and programs will be seen as more affordable than if that were not the case. Given the willingness to meet the costs, the perceived benefit of various alternatives will be shaped by a combination of technically predictable outcomes and the values of key decision-makers, based on their reference groups and unique personal backgrounds.[78]

The authors went beyond this general conclusion to advance a number of specific, *a priori* hypotheses, such as the following: (i) motivation policies are primarily influenced by technology or slack; (ii) positive reference groups are the primary source of alternatives for performance motivation and social concerns policies;

(iii) pressures from the labour market and from the unions will generally encourage an emphasis on extrinsic motivation policies; and (iv) the attitudes, values, and beliefs of key decision-makers will be relatively more influential in generating performance-motivation policies. It is most unfortunate that these and other hypotheses outlined in this paper have not been the subject of any detailed, systematic, empirical analysis in either Britain or elsewhere.

In recent years, the considerable general discussion about the extent and nature of the relationship between overall business strategy (and performance) and the content of personnel policies and practices at a point in time and through the course of time (i.e the strategic human-resource-management perspective) has led to an interest in the use of portfolio analysis, which has long been a favoured analytical technique in the subject area of business policy and strategy. Specifically, a number of British academics have suggested that the Boston Consulting Group's taxonomy of the relative performance and prospects of different parts of the M-form organization (i.e. 'cash-cow', 'star', 'dog') constitutes a useful framework for understanding the nature of personnel policies and practices.[78] A second analytical tool of considerable potential value for understanding the nature of changes in management priorities in work relations, employment relations, and industrial relations through time is product, or organizational, life-cycle theory. This body of theory typically postulates a four-stage model of start-up, growth, maturity, and decline. Table 4.3 suggests some of the priority concerns of management in different areas of personnel or human resource management at these different stages.

It is the contents of the bottom row of Table 4.3 ('labour/employee relations') that are of particular interest here. One of the relatively strong-standing criticisms of British industrial relations arrangements has been the lack of predictability of behaviour and outcomes associated with collective bargaining arrangements;[80] and, in the relatively full employment/union growth years of the 1970s, both government and management sought improvements here through a process of intensified, procedural regulation. Rational management-control strategies (to maximize the achievement of general business objectives) were viewed as ones of collaboration with (rather than opposition to) unions, whose individual components included: (i) the encouragement of union membership (and support for the closed shop), (ii) encouragement of membership participation in unions, (iii) encouragement of inter-union co-operation, (iv) the institutionalization of irreducible

Table 4.3 Critical human-resource activities at different organizational or business-unit stages

Human resource functions	Life-cycle stages: *Introduction*	*Growth*	*Maturity*	*Decline*
Recruitment, selection, and staffing	Attract best technical/ professional talent	Recruit adequate numbers and mix of qualified workers. Management succession planning. Manage rapid internal labour market movements	Encourage sufficient turnover to minimize lay-offs and provide new openings. Encourage mobility as reorganization shifts jobs around	Plan and implement workforce reductions and reallocations
Compensation and benefits	Meet or exceed labour-market rates to attract needed talent	Meet external-market but consider internal-equity effects. Establish formal compensation structures	Control compensation	Tighter cost control
Employee training and development	Define future skill requirements and begin establishing career ladders	Mould effective management team through management development and organization development	Maintain flexibility and skills of an ageing workforce	Implement retraining and career consulting services
Labour/employee relations	Set basic employee relations philosophy and organization	Maintain labour peace and employee motivation and morale	Control labour costs and maintain labour peace. Improve productivity	Improve productivity and achieve flexibility in work rules. Negotiate job security and employment adjustment policies

Source: Thomas A. Kochan and Thomas A. Barocci (1985), *Human Resource Management and Industrial Relations*, p. 105, Boston: Little Brown & Co.

conflict, (v) minimization of areas of avoidable conflict, (vi) maximization of areas of common interest, (vii) reduction of the power of strategic groups, and (viii) the development of effective control systems.[81] In the 1980s, however, increased product-market competition (particularly from foreign sources), a general reduction in the length of product life-cycles, and the fact that unionized, collective-bargaining arrangements are disproportionately associated with older industries (in the mature or declining stages of the organizational life-cyle), led management to emphasize and seek not so much *stability* and *predictability*, but rather *flexibility*, in terms of what constitutes 'good' employee and industrial relations.

The motor-vehicle-manufacturing industry constitutes an excellent illustrative example here, given that:

> Heightened international competition has brought pressure for cost reduction, rapid technological change and improvements in product quality. At the same time, rapid prospective advances in productivity and moderate forecasts for growth in sales point to an overall employment decline.[82]

Moreover, the appropriate industrial-relations strategy for this industry has been held to be one which involves labour accepting:

> Increased work-rule flexibility and moderation in compensation, linking it closely to firm performance. In exchange, management would provide workers with greater employment security and more information on production and technological change, and would help to sustain institutions giving labor direct participation in decision-making.[83]

The British component of this particular industry study certainly indicated that more flexible work practices had accompanied the introduction of new technology and products (e.g. the Metro line at Longbridge), but found relatively little evidence of a coherent industrial-relations strategy along the above lines.[84] It was, however, suggested that the changes in work practices and productivity which had been achieved were influenced by changes in management's own practices, which raises the subject of 'management style' in industrial relations, the subject of the next section.

The issue of management style in industrial relations

Organization researchers have long held that management assumptions about the nature of individual employees on the job needs,

Table 4.4 Management styles towards employee relations

Title	*Description*	*Most likely to occur in these circumstances*	*Expected role of central personnel management*
Traditional	Labour is viewed as a factor of production, and employee subordination is assumed to be part of the 'natural order' of the employment relationship. Fear of outside union interference. Unionization opposed or unions kept at arm's length.	Small owner-managed companies (or franchise operations). Product markets often highly competitive, with the firm having a low share leading to emphasis on cost-control and low profit margins.	For personnel specialists.
Sophisticated human relations	Employees (excluding short-term contract or sub-contract labour) viewed as the company's most valuable resource. Above-average pay. Internal labour-market structures with promotion ladders are common with periodic attitude surveys used to harness employees' views. Emphasis is placed on flexible reward structures, employee appraisal systems linked to merit awards, internal grievance, disciplinary and consultative procedures, and extensive networks and methods of communication. The aim is to inculcate employee loyalty, commitment and dependency. As a by-product, these companies seek to make it unnecessary or unattractive for staff to unionize.	American-owned, single-industry, large, financially successful firms with a high market share in growth industries (electronics/finance sector).	Strong central personnel departments developing policies to be adopted in all areas of the company.
Consultative	Similar to the sophisticated human resource companies except that unions are recognized. The attempt is made to build 'constructive' relationships with the trade unions and incorporate them into the organizational fabric. Broad-ranging discussions are held with extensive information provided to the unions on a whole range of decisions and plans, including aspects of strategic management, but the 'right of last say' rests with management. Emphasis is also placed on techniques designed to enhance individual employee commitment to the firm and the need to change (share option schemes, profit	British/Japanese-owned single-industry companies which are large and economically successful, often with a high market share. Companies with relatively low labour costs (process industries) often adopt this style.	Central personnel departments produce policy guidelines or precepts providing advice and central direction when required.

	sharing, briefing or cascade information systems, joint working parties, quality or productivity circles/councils).		
Constitutional	Somewhat similar to the traditionalists in basic value structures but unions have been recognized for some time and accepted as inevitable. Employee relations policies centre on the need for stability, control, and the institutionalization of conflict. Management prerogatives are defended through highly specific collective agreements, and careful attention is paid to the administration of agreements at the point of production. The importance of management control is emphasized, with the aim of minimizing or neutralizing union constraints on both operational (line) and strategic (corporate) management.	Single-industry companies with mass production or large-batch production requiring a large unit of operation. Labour costs form a significant proportion of total costs. Product-market conditions are often highly competitive.	Relatively strong emphasis on the central personnel auditing/control function.
Opportunistic	The approach to employee relations is pragmatic. Trade unions are recognized in some or all parts of the business, often inherited with company acquisition. Employee relations are viewed as the responsibility of operational management at unit and/or division level. The importance attached to employee-relations policies changes in the light of circumstances. When union power is high and product and labour markets buoyant, or when legislative needs dictate, negotiation and consultation is emphasized. Fashionable employee-relations techniques are adopted over short periods as panaceas. When union power is low, or product markets become unfavourable, or major technical change threatens existing practices, unions are 'rolled back', and management seeks to regain its prerogatives. There can be marked differences of approach between establishments or divisions and between various levels in the hierarchy.	Most common in conglomerate multi-product companies which grew by acquisition and diversification, especially in the engineering and heavy manufacturing industries with long traditions of unionization.	Relatively weak central personnel departments with personnel specialists at operating-unit level having a fire-fighting role, reacting to union claims and the impact of labour legislation. The personnel function tends to have a chequered history: sometimes strong, sometimes weak.

Source: J. Purcell and A. Gray (1986), 'Corporate personnel departments and the management of industrial relations: two case studies in ambiguity', *Journal of Management Studies*, March, pp. 214–15.

attitudes, and behaviour will condition the nature of working arrangements and practices. This position is most explicit in the work of Douglas McGregor, who contrasts the managerial perceptions about the nature of employees' needs and attitudes towards work – which underpin his dichotomy between theory X and theory Y.[85] The traditional dichotomy in the industrial-relations literature was that between management adopting a *unitarist* and *pluralist* frame of reference which was held to shape their attitudes (and hence policies and practices) towards (i) the institution of unionism and (ii) the nature of industrial conflict (i.e. was it inevitable and acceptable, at least to some extent?). However, Fox's addition of a radical frame of reference – with (i) its stress on external-to-the-organization sources of power and control structures, and (ii) an emphasis on the differing extent of the discretion, status, and trust accorded to individual employees by management – produced a taxonomy of patterns of management–employee (as opposed to management–union) relations, consisting of traditional, classical conflict, sophisticated modern, standard modern, sophisticated paternalist, and continuous challenge.[86] Subsequent commentators have made a number of significant adaptations and changes to Fox's treatment of management style, as indicated by the contents of Table 4.4.

Existing discussions of differences in the 'style of management' appear to suggest that it is an intervening (as opposed to independent) variable, capable of providing considerable explanatory and predictive power in relation to certain industrial-relations phenomena – such as attitudes towards unions and industrial conflict, the content and mix of personnel policies, the nature of organization culture, and larger control systems in the organization. For this to be the case, it will be necessary to be able to: (i) readily classify particular organizations that conform to these categories; (ii) identify the relevant determinants of these differences in style; and (iii) indicate that these style differences, *ceteris paribus*, make a significant, independent contribution towards explaining any observed variation in particular industrial-relations structures, processes, and outcomes. In fact, the only systematic, empirical research that has been conducted to date has been for item (i) above, with a rather pessimistic set of findings being reported.[87] Specifically, Deaton listed the following five ideal types of management style:

1. *Paternalists* who do not recognize trade unions and show little formality in terms of procedures or the development of an industrial-relations function. They do however, consult and inform the workforce.

2. *Anti-union* employers who are similar to paternalists but without providing information or channels of communication. Clocking on of the workers is likely to be a feature of this group.
3. *Sophisticated paternalists* who do not recognize trade unions, but use consultative committees. They have formal procedures, a developed management structure, and a high degree of training. They use job evaluation but not payment by results, and do not belong to an employers' association.
4. *Sophisticated moderns* are similar to sophisticated paternalists but do recognize trade unions and support the closed shop. The range of bargaining is not, however, extensive.
5. *Standard moderns* recognize trade unions and give high importance to bargaining. However, management training, information giving, and consultation do not feature strongly. This group will tend to be characterized by PBR (payment-by-results), clocking-on and membership of an employers' association.

The resulting analysis (based on information contained in the 1980 workplace industrial-relations survey) showed only limited ability to identify and distinguish these categories of management style according to the listed indicators, a fact which led to the conclusion that 'if there is no pattern on such simple matters as what sort of pay system to employ or on whether or not to belong to an employers' association, it is not clear what the concept of a distinct pattern can signify.'[88] Admittedly, Gowler and Legge have, on the basis of some rather limited data, pointed to a consistency between the image of the employee presented to the public (in the annual reports of companies) and the industrial-relations style of management of organizations,[89] but, more generally, the validity and value of differences in management style in industrial relations still remains to be established by systematic, empirical research.

Some final observations

In this final section I comment briefly on two particular subject areas, one of which has been the subject of increased research attention in recent years and the other which has been virtually ignored by industrial-relations researchers, at least in Britain. The first subject area is that of managerial unionism, which was the logical, research extension of the interest in the relative growth of white-collar unionization in the 1970s. There is now a steadily accumulating body of knowledge in this area as a result of a number of general discussions of the factors that have stimulated management interest in creating and joining unions,[90] analyses of the characteristics of managers who are union members,[91] and detailed histories of changes in the orientation of individual managerial unions through the course of time.[92] This is an important line of research to be pursued in the future, given the relative growth of managerial/professional employees as a proportion of the total workforce (i.e. from some 4.4 per cent of the workforce in 1911 to nearly 14 per cent by 1980),[93] and the current interest of certain leading organizations in Britain (e.g. ICI) in seeking to lapse or decertify union recognition arrangements for their managerial employees so as to be able to treat them on more of an individualized basis.

A subject still awaiting systematic research in Britain is the management side of the process of wage bargaining. In the previous chapter I referred to the recent upsurge of interest among labour economists in modelling the nature of union objectives and demands in wage bargaining. Unfortunately, there has been no research counterpart on the management side of the collective bargaining process. Admittedly, 'insider–outsider' theories of wage determination emphasize the importance of the financial performance of organizations, but more empirically-informed treatments of individual matters – such as the determinants of management wage targets in bargaining and the nature of management adjustments to the fact of increased labour costs (resulting from negotiated wage increases) – are features of the US literature[94] which have yet to be replicated, let alone developed and refined, in Britain. This major deficiency in the literature clearly constitutes an opening for some important collaborative research between industrial-relations researchers and economists.

Chapter five

The essence of collective bargaining and bargaining structure

The industrial relations systems of both Britain and the United States are based on collective bargaining, with such arrangements being the major mechanism of union–management interaction for establishing and regulating the terms and conditions of employment. However, some academics in the United States have argued that the study of industrial relations, at least in that national system, must move beyond its traditional preoccupation with collective bargaining to investigate the nature of decisions and practices initiated at other (i.e. corporate and workplace) levels within individual organizations, which impact on employment related matters and hence interact with (in a positive or negative fashion) the decisions taken at the collective-bargaining level of analysis.[1] In this chapter I introduce the subject of collective bargaining by considering its essential nature, the extent of its coverage, and some of the major criticisms that have been made of its performance and impact. The majority of the chapter, however, is concerned with bargaining structure or, more specifically, the level at which collective bargaining is conducted. The concept of bargaining structure is, in fact, treated as the major intervening variable in any industrial-relations system based on collective bargaining, in that it is hypothesized to influence the outcomes of the collective bargaining process but is, at the same time, itself influenced or determined by features of the environmental context and by the organizational characteristics of both unions and management. The discussion here will be concerned with both the relevant determinants and effects of bargaining structure, the latter being particularly important in view of the present Conservative Government's recent criticism of national-level bargaining arrangements.

The basic nature of collective bargaining

A number of economists continue to view employee demands for the services of trade unions (as bargaining agents) as deriving from the inherent imbalance of power involved in individual wage bargaining.[2] This perspective can be criticized: first, for ignoring any possible employer interest in the establishment of collective bargaining arrangements; and, second, for conceiving of collective bargaining as being little more than a process of wage bargaining conducted at discrete intervals of time.

On the first point, Barbash has argued that the inherent conflict of interest (at least to some extent) between employees and employers in organizations (i.e. due to differing aims and authority relationships) means that the worth of collective bargaining, as a means of establishing and regulating the terms and conditions of employment, can only be judged in relation to possible alternative mechanisms (for establishing and regulating employment conditions), such as informal work group arrangements, government legislation, and unilateral human-resource management.[3] In Barbash's view, management may well find that collective bargaining is the most desirable mechanism, because of its (i) relatively limited transaction costs, (ii) relatively greater potential for 'shocking' management into improving labour utilization practices, and (iii) provision of more workable arrangements for the due process of grievances and dissent. In addition to this *a priori* argument, the historical record in Britain reveals the existence of a considerable employer role in the establishment of collective bargaining arrangements – particularly in relatively labour intensive industries characterized by piecework payment systems.[4] The strength of the positive relationship between collective bargaining coverage and the extent of payment by results working has also been documented in more contemporary data sources.[5]

Second, Flanders has, in an extensive criticism of the Webbs's treatment of the subject, demonstrated that collective bargaining is more than simply the collective equivalent and counterpart to individual wage bargaining, by emphasizing its role in regulating (and not simply establishing at periodic points in time) the terms and conditions of employment.[6] The nature of the argument he advanced was strongly influenced by Chamberlain's view of collective bargaining as involving: (i) a marketing function which fixes the basic substantive terms of the wage–effort relationship; (ii) an industrial government function which is a system of industrial jurisprudence whereby the procedural conditions under which employees operate are established and administered; and (iii) a method of management by which the views of employees and trade unions are represented in decision-making processes whose outcomes will have implications for their particular interests and concerns.[7]

The latter two essentially procedural functions, which impact on management (rather than market) relationships, have provided the basis for arguments concerning collective bargaining's contribution to 'industrial democracy',[8] and are also central to what Freeman and Medoff have termed the 'collective voice/institutional response' face of unionism;[9] this particular face (as opposed to the monopoly one) of unionism can, they argue, produce relatively favourable economic benefits for employees, management, and society at large.

The extent of collective bargaining coverage in Britain

The growth (or decline) of collective bargaining in any national system of industrial relations over time can be indicated by the changing proportion of employees covered by collective agreements. Unfortunately, such data are not available for Britain on a systematic and comprehensive basis prior to the 1970s,[10] although Table 5.1 does set out the relevant data from the *New Earnings Survey* in more recent years.

Table 5.1 The extent of collective bargaining coverage, all industries/services, 1973, 1978, and 1985 (in percentages)

	1973	*1978*	*1985*
Full-time manual men	83.2	78.3	70.6
Full-time non-manual men	70.4	59.5	56.1
Full-time manual women	71.7	70.9	61.9
Full-time non-manual women	64.8	66.7	64.7

Source: New Earnings Survey, relevant years.

There are a number of important points to bear in mind when considering the meaning, value, and implications of these figures. First, these are likely to be very much *upper level* figures for the extent of collective bargaining coverage in that they are responses to questions about collective agreements which affect the *pay* and conditions of employment of employees, both directly and *indirectly*. The point here is that the contents of collective agreements in Britain have traditionally been disproportionately concerned with wages–hours matters, while the particular question(s) asked here picks up both the direct and indirect coverage of collective bargaining. The latter can, for example, involve firms who do not recognize unions for collective-bargaining purposes, but whose management sets the pay and conditions of their employees by reference to the contents of collective agreements. This particular phenomenon, as well as the relatively limited extent of union security arrangements in recognized bargaining units, explains why these figures are considerably above those for the level of union density in these particular years (Chapter 3). Furthermore, these figures are based on employer responses which can be influenced by particular factors and considerations at the time, such as the existence and strength of incomes-policy constraints. Such influences may help to explain some of the 'odd' movements in these figures. For example, a fall can be observed in the extent of collective bargaining coverage for men workers, particularly non-manuals, between 1973 and 1978 – which were, in fact, years that witnessed a substantial increase in the overall levels of union membership and density in Britain (see Chapter 3).

The various limitations and weaknesses of these figures should not, however, obscure the fact that they generally suggest that the extent of collective bargaining coverage in Britain is relatively high by comparative standards. This fact is of considerable significance in that, despite numerous public statements having been made in favour of collective bargaining since the Royal Commission on Labour of 1891–4, the extent of tangible public-policy support for the institution of collective bargaining has historically been relatively limited (the government's traditional encouragement of public-sector unionization and the Fair Wages Resolutions of 1891, 1909, and 1946 – covering government contractors – constituting the most notable exceptions here): for example, statutory union-recognition provisions having only operated in the years 1971–4 and 1976–80. Furthermore, the institution of collective bargaining in Britain has never been short of critics; the next section therefore considers the nature of some of the leading criticisms that have been made of it.

Some criticisms of collective bargaining

One of the most well-known criticisms of collective bargaining comes from individuals who adopt essentially a unitarist frame of reference within individual organizations. The essence of their argument is that, first, a union presence and collective bargaining arrangements are unnecessary in that they only arise from a management failure to meet the on-the-job needs of their employees, and, second, the inevitable result will be conflict (particularly of an inter-role nature) within the organization which is both unnecessary and undesirable from the point of view of all concerned. In short, to those individuals who view organizations as essentially co-operative and unitary systems (with a single objective and focus of loyalty and authority), collective bargaining introduces a third party (i.e. the union) element into the basic employer–individual-employee relationship that is both unnecessary and counter-productive; this particular line of criticism, is not, of course, unique to the collective-bargaining arrangements of Britain. A second source of criticism of collective bargaining that transcends national systems of industrial relations comes from radical scholars. The essence of this criticism is that collective-bargaining arrangements operate to reinforce the *status quo* by not challenging the larger structures of ownership and control in society at large. Collective bargaining may be portrayed (by pluralists) as an instrument contributing towards an approximate power balance between organized interest groups in society, but in practice it has the effect of: (i) producing only marginal improvements in the terms and conditions of employment (i.e. largely wages–hours matters); (ii) lowering rank-and-file expectations with regard to what is 'realistically negotiable', and hence limiting the extent of challenge to the scope of managerial prerogative; (iii) making industrial conflict more manageable through the processes of procedural regulation; and (iv) limiting the development of a cohesive working class with a genuine trade-union consciousness orientated towards larger political and economic change.[11]

The leading advocates and supporters of collective bargaining are pluralists, given the basic view that they take of the nature of society in general, and business organizations in particular. In making this statement it must, however, be recognized that, first, the pluralist school of thought contains various shades of opinion,[12] and, second, the environment in which collective bargaining takes place, and indeed the institution itself, has been anything but a constant through the course of time. The result is that certain pluralists have in fact made particular criticisms of particular aspects of collective-bargaining arrangements at particular points in time. The nature of these various criticisms can usefully be discussed by reference to the traditional commitment of unions in Britain to the principle of 'voluntary collective bargaining'.

The traditional system of industrial relations in Britain (i.e. 1920s–50s approximately) was characterized, as we saw in Chapter 2, by the relative absence of labour law which reflected a conscious desire on the part of unions (and to some extent management) to avoid legislation which would bring them within the jurisdiction of the ordinary courts of law. This anti-court (as opposed to anti-government) position of the unions has been viewed as the essential feature of the 'voluntary system of collective bargaining' in Britain,[13] a system which at least one commentator viewed as being relatively mature, flexible, and responsible.[14] The term 'responsible' needs to be viewed in the light of the traditional conception of the 'public or social interest' in industrial relations, which was a procedural one, namely that of minimizing the level of strike activity, with a 'good' or 'responsible' system of industrial relations being held to be one that was relatively strike free; in Britain the tangible public-policy expression of this view was the relatively early establishment of voluntary third-party conciliation and arbitration facilities. However, there has always been controversy surrounding the content and use of the notion of the social or public interest in industrial relations. For example, some radical scholars have suggested that the term can easily be manipulated by the government of the day to serve its own self-interested ends in the industrial relations arena.[15] Pluralists obviously regard some level of strike activity as inevitable and acceptable, but stress that such conflict should be 'functional' in the sense of being kept within the bounds of what is socially tolerable and acceptable. However, issues of judgement inevitably arise here because the concept of the 'optimal' level of strike activity for society at large is one that has essentially no empirical content. The result is that some pluralists have criticized collective bargaining for being 'too strike-prone' in particular systems in particular periods of time. Such pluralist criticisms in both Britain and the United States have frequently involved the general contention that the power or leverage of the strike weapon has risen through time as a result of the increased interdependency of the economy.[16] Moreover, as the pattern or distribution of strike activity has exhibited some change through time, particular reservations have often been expressed in both Britain and the United States about the acceptability of strike activity in the *public* sector. The contention typically put forward here is that the strike performs more of a political, as opposed to economic, function in the public sector because the costs are largely borne by third parties rather than by those directly involved in the immediate area of dispute.[17] Furthermore, in recent years, a number of pluralists have increasingly characterized the British and US systems of collective bargaining as being overly 'adversarial' in nature.[18] The essence of this criticism is that the attitudes and tactics of the parties involved in collective bargaining have overwhelmingly been those of 'distributive' (i.e. fixed-sum game) bargaining, with the result that the extent of 'integrative' (i.e. varying-sum game) bargaining, or joint problem-solving, has been relatively limited; these two sub-processes of bargaining will be discussed more fully in the next chapter.

Pluralist criticisms of the performance (as opposed to the principle) of collective-bargaining arrangements in both Britain and the United States have moved beyond the original procedural concern to a preoccupation with the substantive outcomes of the processes of bargaining from the late 1960s. In effect, from this time onwards, a second element or component was introduced into the concept or notion of the 'public or social interest' in industrial relations – namely the desire to minimize the level of wage settlements so as to limit their contribution to the overall level of price inflation. This social interest in the substantive outcomes of collective bargaining received tangible expression in the operation of incomes policy in Britain in the years 1965–79, which raised the possibility of some degree of conflict with the original public concern about minimizing the level of strike activity.[19] A number of pluralists have been particularly prominent in arguing that collective bargaining in Britain took inadequate account of the public interest in having a relatively low rate of inflation,[20] and pluralists have certainly been well to the forefront in advocating particular reforms to the system of collective bargaining designed to minimize wage inflationary pressures.[21]

To date we have discussed a number of criticisms of collective bargaining that essentially transcend the particular institutional arrangements of any one national system. There have inevitably been suggestions, however, that certain costs and problems of collective bargaining have been both more extensive and intensive in Britain than in other national systems.[22] The absence of directly legally enforceable collective agreements in Britain, for example, has led one leading management spokesman to refer to:

> The debilitating and costly tradition of leaving the honouring of agreements to the discretion of individual members rather than establishing some form of control over them. . . . In short, on this issue the unions don't deliver. The result is a less predictable situation than in other countries.[23]

In addition to the lack of legally enforceable collective agreements, the relatively early development of the system, the extent of union legal immunities, and the decentralized nature of the union movement have all been cited as sources of overly 'adversarial' collective bargaining in Britain, whose processes and outcomes have adversely affected Britain's overall level of economic performance. In Chapter 7 I review some of the empirical evidence that is relevant to the validity and strength of such criticisms.

The basic concept of bargaining structure

The concept of bargaining structure is a multi-dimensional one, widely defined in Britain as comprising (i) bargaining levels, (ii) bargaining units, (iii) bargaining forms (i.e. the degree of formality of an agreement), and (iv) bargaining scope.[24] In practice, however, researcher, practitioner, and policy-maker discussion has overwhelmingly concentrated on the particular dimension of bargaining levels. This approach will be followed in the remainder of this chapter, although I begin here by briefly referring to some arguments and findings concerning the other dimensions of bargaining structure.

The limited discussion of the particular subject of bargaining *units* has overwhelmingly taken place in, first, studies of the nature of management-control systems in individual organizations and, seond, in examinations of third-party, decision-making processes during the years (i.e. 1971–4 and 1976–80) when statutory union-recognition provisions operated in Britain. For example, discussions of management-control strategies have considered various ways in which management may seek to reduce the power of strategically placed workgroups. The various strategies utilized by management in individual organizations have included the breaking up of the group(s), isolating it or redrawing the boundaries of bargaining units to produce larger units in which the power of the strategic group is diluted.[25] (This latter strategy is invariably discussed with reference to the position of the toolroom workers at BL in the 1970s.) In the two periods of time in which statutory-recognition provisions have operated in Britain, the relevant third-party, decision-making bodies (i.e. the CIR and ACAS, respectively) have outlined the various factors and considerations that influenced their decisions on the nature of 'appropriate' bargaining units.[26] Although ACAS was influenced to some extent by the CIR's approach to the definition of bargaining units, it continually experienced the problem of trying to reconcile employer and union arguments in favour of wider and more narrowly defined units, respectively.[27] (The importance of these arguments followed from the fact that unions were less likely to achieve recognition in cases involving relatively large-sized bargaining units.)

The scope of collective bargaining in Britain has traditionally been relatively narrow. Indeed, in the late 1960s, Flanders critically commented that:

> One of the striking contemporary features of British collective bargaining, compared say with collective bargaining in the United States, is the poverty of its subject matter, the limited range of substantive issues regulated by written and formally signed agreements. The principal subjects remain wages and working hours . . . Holidays with pay in the 'thirties and provisions for a guaranteed week in the 'forties have been the only new subjects introduced into the mainstream of collective bargaining since the first world war. Rarely are fringe benefits or contentious issues like union security and job security, not to speak of many other working conditions, brought within the realm of formal joint regulations.[28]

The 1970s witnessed a considerable broadening of the scope of collective bargaining as a result of environmental changes (e.g. the increased incidence of redundancies), the passage of individual pieces of legislation (e.g. the Health and Safety at Work Act 1974), and the general move towards single-employer bargaining levels. Indeed, some empirical studies of the extent of the 'frontier of control' documented the considerable inter-establishment (and inter-industry) variation in the scope of collective bargaining; and discussed in general, qualitative terms some of the factors that appear to have been responsible for such variation.[29] However, the relative absence of written, legally enforceable, collective agreements of multi-year duration in Britain (and, conversely, the relative importance of 'custom and practice') have limited the capacity of industrial-relations researchers to follow US researchers in using index-scoring techniques to systematically examine the nature, and determinants, of variation in the non-wage outcomes of collective bargaining;[30] these particular studies in the US have revealed, for example, that high-wage industries tend to have, on average, relatively favourable (to the union) non-wage provisions, and that the various non-wage sub-categories of provisions are also positively and significantly inter-related. The rise in unemployment in Britain (and in western Europe more generally) from the late 1970s, has led to considerable bargaining activity concerning reductions in the length of the working week,[31] although, more generally, the 1984 workplace industrial-relations survey revealed a considerable decline in the extent of negotiation over non-pay matters for both manuals and non-manuals in the years 1980–4;[32]

this decline was particularly marked at the workplace level and in the private-services sector. As to bargaining forms, there have been discussions of the various advantages and disadvantages, to both unions and management, of increasing the degree of formality of collective agreements and procedural arrangements.[33] The 1970s in fact saw a considerable increase in the degree of formality of agreements, and associated procedural arrangements; the growth in the extent of *written* disciplinary procedures, for example, being well documented.[34] However, multi-year-duration collective agreements still remain rare in Britain – in contrast to the position in the United States – while individual company interest (e.g. Ford UK) in trying to produce legally enforceable agreements have had virtually no impact on the mainstream of bargaining activity.[35]

As a component of bargaining structure, it is the level of bargaining which has been so central to discussions and analyses of the 'problems' and 'necessary reforms' of British industrial relations.[36] For example, the Donovan Commission (1965–8) saw private-sector industrial relations as stemming in large measure from a mismatch of bargaining structures, and recommended that there should be a substantial, voluntary-based movement towards single-employer bargaining structures at the plant and company level. And, as mentioned earlier, a number of senior members of the present Conservative Government made strong statements in 1986–7 that were highly critical of the continued maintenance of 'national' (i.e. industry and company level) bargaining arrangements.

The belief underlying these sorts of judgements and reform recommendations is that there is a single, best form of bargaining structure for the system of industrial relations as a whole. In fact, as we hope to show in the course of this chapter, there is no 'universalist', best-practice bargaining structure for any system of industrial relations as a whole. Instead, the most appropriate form of bargaining structure for any individual union–management relationship is ultimately a *contingency*-based concept or decision, depending on (i) the particular operating environment of the relationship, (ii) the particular industrial-relations needs and priorities of the parties concerned, and (iii) their organizational characteristics.

In advancing this general line of argument, it is readily acknowledged that substantial deficiencies exist in our research-based knowledge concerning both the relevant determinants and outcomes of different levels of bargaining. As we shall see, for example, we have considerable knowledge and understanding of the relevant factors that lead some union–management relationships to favour the establishment and maintenance of multi-employer, industry-level bargaining arrangements. In contrast we have considerably less understanding of the reasons that lead some relationships to bargain at the company level, while others prefer to bargain at the level of the individual plant in multi-establishment companies. Similarly, there is considerable disagreement about the relative importance of bargaining structure, *ceteris paribus*, in shaping bargaining outcomes both within and across national systems of industrial relations. Indeed, Phelps Brown has suggested that the wage outcomes of multi-employer and single-employer bargaining structures (at least at the level of national systems of industrial relations) may be rather less divergent than might be expected, due to the existence of informal arrangements, such as 'pattern bargaining' in a system of ostensibly single-employer bargaining arrangements;[37] such informal practices are not, however, always easy to identify and control for in research studies.

Staying with the traditional industry-level arrangements

The system of collective bargaining in Britain had its origins in the latter years of the nineteenth century, when the limited amount of bargaining that occurred was essentially on a district or local-area basis. This geographical-based structure was levelled up to that of industry in the first two decades of the present century. The prime movers in this change were, first, employers in the high-wage districts of the country who saw industry-level collective bargaining as a means of ensuring that their competitive position would not be undermined by employers in the low-wage districts. The second agent of change was the Government, which established compulsory arbitration bodies to award wage increases in line with cost-of-living movements during the years of the First World War, and these boards found it administratively convenient to promulgate awards on an industry-wide basis. This industry-based bargaining structure was a key component of the traditional system of industrial relations in Britain that operated with considerable success until well into the 1950s.

It was these industry-level bargaining arrangements which, as mentioned earlier, the Donovan Commission saw as having become increasingly irrelevant in the 1960s as a consequence of changes in the organizational characteristics of the unions, most notably as a result of the 'attack from below', which involved shop stewards engaging in fractional, workplace-level bargaining. Nevertheless, some individual union–management relationships have elected to stay with the traditional industry-level arrangements, a fact indicated by the contents of Table 5.2.

Table 5.2 Percentage of full-time employees whose pay was affected by various types of collective agreements: all industries/services, 1985

Type of employee	*Type of agreement*			
	National plus supplementary agreement	*National only agreement*	*Company district or local agreement only*	*No collective agreement*
Male manuals	19.3	37.6	13.7	29.4
Male non-manuals	8.4	37.9	9.8	43.9
Female manuals	17.0	32.2	12.8	38.1
Female non-manuals	8.3	50.3	6.2	35.3

Source: New Earnings Survey 1985, Part F, Department of Employment, January 1986, Tables 190–91.

The contents of Table 5.2 indicate the continued existence of traditional industry-level bargaining arrangements, either by themselves or in conjunction with supplementary agreements, although some findings from the 1984 workplace industrial-relations survey clearly indicate that the nature of these latter arrangements is generally more supplementary than national-level bargaining.[38] The *New Earnings Survey* for 1985 allows us to identify the major industries that remain relatively highly committed to the traditional national-only bargaining arrangements, and here we find that the following sort of picture emerges: woollen and worsted industry (43.8 per cent of male manuals covered by a national agreement only); footwear (65.8 per cent of male manuals); general construction and demolition work (56.7 per cent of male manuals); and food retailing (43.5 per cent of male manuals). These sorts of industries have a number of features in common. Specifically, they are industries characterized by: (i) relatively small firm size; (ii) highly competitive product markets; (iii) a relatively labour-intensive production process; and (iv) in many cases, have a location pattern involving considerable regional or spatial concentration.

As mentioned earlier, bargaining structure is an intervening variable which, if it is to work effectively (however defined), must be closely aligned with the organizational characteristics of the parties concerned and with the environmental context in which they exist and operate. The four characteristics above are ones that naturally incline the parties concerned to favour industry- or national-level bargaining structures.[39] For example, employers in highly competitive product markets have relatively limited ability to absorb wage increases, through passing them on to consumers in the form of price increases. The result is a strong desire to take wages out of competition by setting a floor to wage competition in the industry, a desire best attained by industry-level collective bargaining. A similar employer motivation exists in relatively labour-intensive industries, while the fact of spatial concentration tends to favour industry-level collective bargaining because the workforces of geographically concentrated industries are subject to relatively little variation in local labour-market pressures and hence it is possible to establish and maintain a reasonably meaningful industry-wide wage structure. Furthermore, a small, average plant size favours multi-employer, industry-level bargaining – because of the limited ability of such organizations to pay, and because the relatively limited development of specialist management functions (i.e. a personnel management function) within such organizations is a severe limitation on their ability to negotiate directly and individually with unions.

Over and above these particular private-sector industries, national or industry-level collective bargaining remains of major importance in the *public sector*. There has been, however, some notable movement away from the totally dominant position of national-level bargaining in different parts of the public sector in recent years. For example, the 1983 Water Act (which abolished the National Water Council) resulted in the five national negotiating bodies covering pay and conditions in the industry being wound up. The Government was in favour of completely abolishing national pay bargaining in the newly re-organized industry. However, some national arrangements were retained, with four new national negotiating bodies (for manuals, craft, staff, chief and senior officers) being created. Their constitutions limit them to deal with pay and main conditions of service, with some items (e.g. subsistence allowances) being negotiated at the individual-employer level; staff can also no longer take grading appeals to national level. Moreover, individual water authorities can withdraw from the national agreements after giving 12 months' notice of their intention to do so. The Thames Water Authority gave notice of withdrawal from the senior officers JNC in 1985 (followed by four other authorities) and now sets pay separately for senior staff, while late in 1986 it announced its intention to withdraw from the other three national bodies on the stated grounds that it did not have sufficient influence in the annual negotiations with the Water

Authorities Association, and would like greater independence to negotiate local incentive schemes with more emphasis on customer service. More recently (in anticipation of privatization of the industry) the water industry employers, as a group, have come out in favour of ending national-level negotiations.

There have, in fact, been earlier recommendations for, and actual moves towards, more decentralized collective bargaining in some parts of the public sector. The McCarthy review of industrial relations in the NHS in 1976, for example, contained a recommendation in favour of more bargaining being conducted at the regional level,[40] while a report by the National Board for Prices and Incomes in 1967 recommended that payment by results or bonus schemes be extensively adopted in local government in order to improve productivity and ameliorate the low pay problem there.[41] The implementation of this recommendation, at least for male manual workers, has resulted in bonus schemes constituting the most important element of authority-level bargaining in local government; the 1982 *New Earnings Survey*, for example, indicated that PBR schemes accounted for nearly 16 per cent of the pay of full-time manual men in local government (nearly twice the comparable figure for the workforce as a whole), while some 70 per cent of such employees in local authorities were covered by such arrangements (compared to a figure of 45 per cent for the workforce as a whole).[42] Moreover, early in 1987, local-authority employers engaged in a major restructuring exercise for manual workers – in which the issues of regrading, equal pay for work of equal value, and flexible working arrangements were all involved. Local authority employers do not currently appear to favour a move towards regional bargaining (as desired by the Government), although some recent consultative documents have argued that the number and scope of national agreements should be reduced. More generally, the *New Earnings Survey* for 1985 indicated that for some 50 listed national agreements in the public sector covering male employees, nearly a third of them (N = 16) involved more than 33 per cent of the relevant workforce being affected by supplementary bargaining; the comparable figure for women employees was 4 agreements out of 21 in 1985. The most (least) important areas of supplementary bargaining in the public sector in 1985 are indicated by the contents of Table 5.3.

The most recent proposed and/or actual moves towards decentralized bargaining in the public sector have been the following: (i) since the passage of the Transport Act 1985, national bargaining has been abolished in the National Bus Company, the municipal undertakings, and Passenger Transport Executives (a national

Table 5.3 Percentage of employees in the public sector covered by a national agreement but also affected by a supplementary agreement

National agreement/percentage affected by supplementary agreement	
Most affected	*Percentage*
BSC – iron and steel and pig iron manufacture	75.8 (male manuals) 75.6 (male non-manuals)
Omnibus industry: national council undertakings	85.2 (male manuals)
British Shipbuilders – shipbuilding and ship repairing	52.6 (male manuals)
Road passenger transport: municipal undertakings NJIC	50.2 (male manuals)
Water service staffs NJC	49.3 (male non-manuals)
Water service NJIC – non-craftsmen	48.8 (male manuals)
Least affected	
Coalmining – surface workers	0.0 (male manuals)
British Rail – railway workshops	0.3 (male manuals)
London Regional Transport – road passenger transport, drivers and conductors	0.0 (male manuals)
British Rail – footplate staff	0.0 (male manuals)
Civil Service – administration group (clerical grades)	0.2 (male non-manuals)
Post Office – clerical and executives	0.4 (male non-manuals)

Source: New Earnings Survey 1985, Part F, Department of Employment, January 1986, Table 187.

forum still exists for municipal buses, but pay bargaining is now conducted at the individual company level); (ii) at BR, negotiations for the wholly-owned subsidiary, British Rail Engineering Ltd, are conducted separately; (iii) in the non-industrial civil service there has been the break-up of multi-union bargaining (only four unions negotiated together in 1987), and (iv) in late 1988 the management of British Rail announced its intention to do away with national-level, collective-bargaining arrangements.

The move to single-employer bargaining: plant or company?

From the late 1970s there has been a considerable number of industrial-relations surveys conducted by a variety of institutions and individuals in Britain, all of which agree on the general trend away from multi-employer, industry-level bargaining, to single employer bargaining structures. However, they have tended to yield rather different findings on the matter of the relative extent and tendency towards plant-level, as opposed to company-level bargaining.[43] Furthermore, in recent years, a number of individual companies have frequently changed their bargaining structures in quite different directions. For example, Reed Corrugated Cases moved directly to a company-level bargaining structure,[44] following withdrawal from multi-employer, industry-level arrangements, while Pilkington (which has frequently been cited as a classic example of corporate-level, centralized, collective bargaining) moved to a system of decentralized, plant-level negotiations in 1984;[45] in that year, 59 separate sets of pay negotiations occurred throughout the company, whereas in 1970 more than 80 per cent of the company's employees (in 32 different locations throughout the UK) had been covered by the outcomes of five company-level negotiating committees.

In moving beyond the details of individual company-centred changes to provide a more general, system-wide perspective on the relative important of plant-level, as opposed to company-level, bargaining structures, the most sizeable and comprehensive set of evidence undoubtedly comes from a comparison of the two workplace industrial relations surveys conducted in 1980 and 1984. Table 5.4 sets out the major findings from these sources.

Table 5.4 Most important levels of bargaining influencing pay increases in private manufacturing and private services, separately

	Manual workers		*Non-manual workers*	
	1980	*1984*	*1980*	*1984*
Private manufacturing				
National/regional	41	40	18	19
Company/divisional	15	20	29	36
Plant-establishment	41	38	49	42
Private services				
National/regional	57	54	43	36
Company/divisional	28	33	36	52
Establishment	9	11	7	11

Source: Neil Millward and Mark Stevens (1986), *British Workplace Industrial Relations 1980–1984*, pp. 232 and 238, Aldershot: Gower.

The contents of Table 5.4 suggest that in the manufacturing sector there was a movement towards company-level wage bargaining for both manuals and non-manuals in the early 1980s, although only the latter constituted a statistically significant change. Similarly, in the services sector, company-level bargaining appeared to be of growing importance for non-manuals, although this gain was at the expense of industry-level bargaining, whereas in the manufacturing sector, the company-level gain had been more at the expense of plant-level negotiations.

Earlier I argued that industrial-relations reseachers now have considerable ability to understand the relevant factors that lead an organization to favour multi-employer, industry-level bargaining over single-employer bargaining structures. In contrast, the extent of our knowledge and understanding of the major forces that lead organizations to make a choice between plant- and company-level bargaining is very much less. Bodies like the CIR[46] have certainly produced useful check-lists of the various pros and cons of company- and plant-level bargaining, and individual company examples have highlighted one or two of the more obvious relevant influences. For example, it has been suggested that:

> Within single employer bargaining structures, companies with a number of geographically dispersed plants varying in size, product range and production process and especially if there are site-based productivity schemes will incline towards decentralised, workplace bargaining. On the other hand, companies with a small number of plants or sites clustered in a particular area, limited developed autonomy in plant management, and a high degree of interdependence in production between plants, will generally retain central control of the bargaining process.[47]

These sorts of general observations undoubtedly have a considerable amount of intuitive appeal, although one must acknowledge the fact that the strength of their influence has not been formally tested and substantiated in any satisfactory multivariate statistical analyses based on sizeable and representative data sets. There are arguably two major (quite different) reasons for the extent of our relatively limited knowledge about the relevant factors that shape the outcome of the decision to bargain at the plant as opposed to the company level. The first view would suggest that such a decision is ultimately a function of the particular history and traditions of individual organizations, with a resulting inherent limited ability to generalize across organizations. The second possible explanation of our limited ability to understand the nature of this particular decision or choice is that the vast majority of our surveys have been establishment- or plant-based ones. As a result, we lack the necessary information on company-level characteristics that is (arguably) essential to fully identify the relevant influences in this particular decision-making process. These two explanations, or interpretations, obviously have quite different implications for our ability to more fully understand this particular phenomenenon in the future.

There are two further qualifications or caveats to be made regarding the extent of our knowledge about the nature of contemporary bargaining structures in Britain. The first concerns the extent to which a plant-based bargaining structure in a multi-plant organization actually means that the results, or outcomes, of these ostensibly separate negotiations are uninfluenced by guidelines, advice and ultimately, financial control from the higher, corporate levels of the organization. A number of case studies reveal a diversity of practice in this matter, but with some attempt typically being made by management, albeit in different ways, to find a strategy which balances elements of both centralization and decentralization. For example, a study by Kinnie found that the 'federated' organization had formal plant bargaining – but with central co-ordination of these arrangements through guidlines and the provision of personnel services – while in the case of the organization referred to as 'autarky' there was informal plant bargaining but with strong financial control exercised centrally.[48] Furthermore, any general tendency to equate a plant-level bargaining structure with a pattern of outcomes labelled as 'separate' and 'independent' seems highly questionable, given that the 1984 workplace industrial relations survey reported a great deal of consultation with higher-level management both prior to and during the course of plant-level wage negotiations in the manufacturing sector, particularly in the case of negotiations for manual employees.[49]

The second point to note is that our information on bargaining structures is overwhelmingly for negotiations over wage matters, broadly defined. At the present time we have much less knowledge about the levels at which bargaining occurs within organizations over non-pay items, and the major determining factors involved in these particular decisions. For example, it would be useful to know if the emergence of non-pay, company-wide issues (such as pensions) have actually been an important internal, administrative stimulus in the move to company-wide bargaining structures over wages. Indeed, the whole question of the degree of synchronization and interdependence of bargaining subjects by bargaining levels remains almost untouched as an area of research.

Priority bargaining outcomes and bargaining structure

As well as the environmental context of the individual relationship and the organizational characteristics of the parties concerned, another set of potential influences on the choice of bargaining structure is the particular industrial-relations aims, objectives, and priorities of the parties concerned. This issue of the relative priority attached to different industrial-relations outcomes, or objectives, is not only of relevance to unions and management, but also involves the 'social' or 'public' interest in industrial relations outcomes. In other words, the priority concerns of 'the public interest' in industrial relations (e.g. minimize strike frequency, minimize the level of wage inflation, etc.), as interpreted by the Government of the day, will obviously influence views of what is the most suitable bargaining structure for the system of industrial relations as a whole. However, the problem here for unions, management, and the Government of the day is that there is arguably no one single bargaining structure capable of yielding all of the advantages and none of the disadvantages frequently sought after in a system of industrial relations. In short, choices and tradeoffs have to be made between the different outcomes of different bargaining structures by all concerned.

As a starting point for illustrating this proposition, one can consider Clegg's cross-national study of industrial-relations systems – which viewed bargaining structure as a major determinant of certain system outcomes.[50] Specifically, Clegg saw (as noted in Chapter 1) the level of bargaining as an important determinant of, for example, the extent of union democracy and the extent of strike frequency – with more decentralized, plant-based structures generally being associated with more democratic unions and a higher strike frequency. These observed relationships immediately pose a sharp choice for the public interest in industrial relations in that it would appear that there is no one form of bargaining structure capable of producing both democratic unions and a relatively low level of strike frequency at the same time. There may also be a trade-off between the different dimensions of strike activity, in that an industry-level bargaining structure may produce relatively few strikes but those that do occur are likely to be large, relatively drawn-out affairs. The result may well be a substantial number of working days lost through strike activity, so that again the social interest in industrial relations is likely to have to make a choice as regards which particular aspect of strike activity is most damaging for the economy at large and which therefore needs to be minimized.

In relation to bargaining structure, choices and trade-offs also have to be made by unions and management when considering the different outcomes of different structures. For example, relatively centralized, national-level bargaining structures often tend to be associated with relatively high overall levels of workforce unionization; but such structures tend, at the same time, to limit the scope of joint regulation to essentially wages/hours matters. The result is that the union movement is likely to require additional, complementary mechanisms to collective bargaining in order to try and exert some influence over non-wage/hours issues. The unions also need to consider the fact that in systems of more centralized bargaining structures, it is easier to evolve tripartite decision-making structures and for the union movement to both *offer* and *deliver* some measure of wage restraint in return for favourable industrial-relations and social-welfare legislation. For unions relatively centralized bargaining structures also offer the potential advantage of producing a more unified, 'solidaristic' union movement in that there will not be the sizeable variation in bargaining outcomes that stem from the substantial differences in union power that are apparent in decentralized bargaining systems. Turning to the management side, the available research on union relative-wage effects tends to suggest that the size of such effects are considerably less under more centralized bargaining arrangements. Gregory and Thomson, for example, reported that, for Britain:

> In the manual male grouping as a whole . . . for both the 1973 and 1978 surveys there is a gradient of returns with the national only agreement having the least favourable return to collective agreement coverage, the national plus supplementary the middle position and the company, district and local the most favourable.[51]

However, this apparent advantage to management needs to be seen in the light of the fact that productivity clawbacks, or *quid pro quos*, for such increases are much more capable of being negotiated and brought about under decentralized, plant-level bargaining structures; the latter point was certainly well illustrated by the nature and outcomes of the productivity bargaining movement in Britain in the 1960s.

In short, it appears that none of the parties with a stake or interest in industrial relations can expect to find a bargaining structure that delivers them nothing but unmixed blessings. This sort of conclusion is clearly 'at odds' with the present Government's view of bargaining structure, and it is to their criticism of national-level bargaining arrangements that we turn in the next section.

The Government criticism of national-level pay bargaining

The present Conservative Government's criticism of national pay bargaining is perfectly consistent with their general view of the weaknesses of the labour market (i.e. the need for more flexibility and reduced costs) and with other measures previously taken – such as the repeal of Schedule 11 of the Employment Protection Act 1975 and rescinding of the Fair Wages Resolution of 1946 (both of which sought to limit the widespread adoption of industry-wide, collectively bargained wages). In criticizing national bargaining arrangements, the Government is talking about *both* industry-level and company-level bargaining, with their favoured bargaining structures being those at the individual-plant/establishment or regional levels. The sort of bargaining arrangements favoured by the Government are those associated with companies such as British Aerospace, Hoover, and, more recently, Shell Oil and Brace Bros. – where there are very definite regional or plant differences in wage-settlement levels, based on factors such as local pay rates, local costs, and plant profitability. The essence of the Government's criticism is that national-level bargaining is a wage transmission mechanism between regions which (i) limits the extent of inter-regional variation in earnings levels, (ii) makes such earnings levels relatively unresponsive to regional (and local) labour-market pressures, and (iii) involves a loss of jobs in high unemployment regions, as their wage levels are set artificially high due to reflecting the influences of low unemployment regions such as the south-east of England.[52] The sort of position which the Government is trying to change is where, for example, male unemployment rates in the Northern region and the South East were some 22.6 and 11.3 per cent respectively in the mid-1980s, but male manual hourly earnings in the two regions were £3.50 and £3.59 respectively.

The immediate reactions to the Government's case against national pay bargaining have ranged from indifference and scepticism to outright criticism and hostility. For example, the CBI's major review of pay in the 1980s makes virtually no mention of the subject,[53] while the TUC argued that the Government's case exaggerates both the extent of national pay-bargaining arrangements and their role in determining actual pay rates.[54] However, with the Conservative Government being in a third consecutive term of office, it is likely that tangible moves to break up national bargaining arrangements in the public sector will be one of their more immediate industrial-relations priorities. Indeed, regional pay bargaining was one of the issues discussed by a union(s)–Treasury working party set up after the Civil Service dispute of early to mid-1987 (in which the Government imposed a pay settlement), and some recent pay offers in the NHS (e.g. for speech therapists) have opened up the possibility of health authorities negotiating local variations in pay, while in the private sector the National

Westminster Bank introduced in 1987 a much greater element of spatial variation in its pay structure.[55]

A full and comprehensive assessment of the Government's case needs to examine the numerical extent of national pay bargaining, the extent of pay variation associated with such arrangements, and the impact of such arrangements as a source of inter-regional earnings differentials. This task cannot be undertaken here, although what can be presented is some evidence concerning: (i) inter-regional variation in the nature of bargaining structures; and (ii) the size of wage differentials between workers covered by collective bargaining arrangements in Scotland and the South of England, and their relationship to the extent of national bargaining in Scotland.[56] The evidence concerning the first matter is set out in Table 5.5.

Table 5.5 (which is based on the 1980 workplace industrial-relations survey) reveals the generally limited extent of regional/district-level bargaining arrangements in all areas of the country and the relatively low level of collective-bargaining coverage in the southern regions of Britain. For present purposes, however, particular attention should be paid to the figures in columns (i) and (iii), which are the categories of bargaining that have been singled out for criticism by the Government. And here we find that the northern regions of the country have relatively high levels of national/industry-wide bargaining, although inter-regional differences in the extent of company (all plants) level bargaining arrangements (as with single-plant bargaining) are relatively small. Indeed, there does not appear to be a 'North–South' difference in the nature of bargaining structures of anything like the order of magnitude that some commentators have claimed to be the case.[57]

Turning now to the matter of wage differentials, some information contained in the annual *New Earnings Surveys* for 1973 and 1978 indicated that, for all industries, the average hourly earnings of male workers covered by collective bargaining arrangements in Scotland were some 9 per cent and 7 per cent below that in the South of England in 1973 and 1978 respectively. The largest sized negative differentials for Scotland were in transport and communications, and business services, while the most sizeable, positive differential was in the metals and chemicals industry. However, the results of correlation analysis did not find that industries (and socio-economic groupings) with relatively high levels of national (or at least industry-wide) pay bargaining had the least-sized wage differentials (between Scotland and southern England), which is the relationship that should be apparent according to the Government's argument. Furthermore, although

Table 5.5 Coverage by collective agreement (manual workers) in Scotland and selected other areas, 1980

	Percentage covered by:[a]						
Area[a]	*(i) National/ industry-wide*	*(ii) Regional/ district*	*(iii) Company: all plants*	*(iv) Company: some plants*	*(v) Single plant*	*(vi) Other miscellaneous*	*(vii) No agreement*
Scotland	42.5	4.4	12.3	3.6	22.1	1.5	13.5
Development regions	40.9	1.4	14.9	4.2	24.7	2.3	11.7
Southern regions	30.4	2.9	13.8	5.0	22.9	0.9	24.2
Other regions	31.9	1.8	15.7	4.9	33.0	1.3	11.4

Source: P. B. Beaumont and R. I. D. Harris (1988) 'The government case against national pay bargaining: an analysis for Scotland', in D. McCrone (ed.), *Yearbook of Scottish Government 1988*, Edinburgh: Edinburgh University Press.

Notes

[a] Development regions = North, North West, and Wales;
Southern regions = South East, East Anglia, and the South West.
Other regions = Yorks-Humberside, East and West Midlands.

[b] Respondents were asked to choose the *most* important type of bargaining agreement. Hence, other (different types of) agreements might also feature for some groups of workers.

it was clear that real earnings levels in Scotland and the South East of England had moved closely together over the period 1974–86, the extent of this relationship did not appear to be systematically related to the extent of national bargaining arrangements at the industry level. It is to be hoped that this sort of work can be taken further by, for example, an analysis of data in the *New Earnings Survey* for 1985 (which like that for 1973 and 1978 has information on collective bargaining coverage) so as to make a more informed input into any policy making discussions and decisions concerning the desirability of moves towards plant and/or regional bargaining arrangements.

Conclusions

The vast majority of this chapter has discussed bargaining structure as a major intervening variable in the collective-bargaining-based system of industrial relations in Britain. The chapter began, however, with a general introduction to the institution of collective bargaining, and in the following chapter this subject is pursued in more detail through a discussion of issues such as the processes of bargaining, strike activity, and the nature of bargaining power.

Chapter six

Collective bargaining processes, conflict, and power

Negotiations and bargaining activity in general

At the present time, the social-science research community (broadly defined) is showing an unprecedented level of interest in the subject of negotiation and bargaining activity. For example, economists' explanations of the unemployment–inflation trade-off are now frequently based on bargaining models,[1] political scientists are actively involved in the development of coalition theory,[2] legal researchers are increasingly studying civil-law judgments from a bargaining-mediation perspective,[3] while organization theorists (as we saw in Chapter 4) have largely abandoned the rational decision-making paradigm in favour of conceptualizations based on sectional interest groups, coalitions, and intra-management bargaining activities centred around notions of resource-dependency-based power.[4] This upsurge of research interest is a reflection of, and response to, society-wide changes. Dunlop, for instance, has argued that the extent of both market and government regulation has declined in importance relative to the usage of negotiation to resolve inter-group conflicts in western societies in more recent times.[5] Indeed, it has been suggested that any inter-personal or inter-group relationship is ultimately a bargaining-based one, if:

1. At least two parties are involved.
2. The parties have a conflict of interest with respect to one or more different issues.
3. Regardless of the existence of prior experience or acquaintance with one another, the parties are at least temporarily joined together in a special kind of voluntary relationship.
4. Activity in the relationship concerns: (a) the division or exchange of one or more specific resources and/or (b) the resolution of one or more intangible issues among the parties or among those whom they represent.

5. The activity usually involves the presentation of demands or proposals by one party, evaluations of these by the other, and concessions and counterproposals. The activity is thus sequential rather than simultaneous.[6]

The general trend towards increased negotiation activity within societies is certainly not one that is favoured by all individuals. Indeed the very term 'Thatcherism' is often defined as a rejection of decision-making processes involving negotiations and agreement by consensus,[7] while the major academic criticism of this society-wide trend towards negotiation is contained in the recent work of Olson, which argues that a proliferation of narrow sectional interest groups exercising power through the processes of negotiation will increasingly distort the operation of market forces, thus causing the society concerned to stagnate and decline in terms of economic performance.[8]

At the individual-organization level, existing studies of the nature of managerial jobs have identified various roles, including that of a negotiator.[9] The relative importance of this particular role is alleged to have increased substantially in recent times, as a result of changes in organizational structures (particularly towards those designed to facilitate horizontal communication), and the relative growth of the service sector, and the professional/managerial component of the workforce.[10] The increased importance of negotiations within organizations (and in society at large) has led to the publication of a number of 'popular' books which offer guidelines for effective negotiations by managers and other individuals.[11] Table 6.1 sets out the approach recommended in one such publication.

The strategy and tactics recommended in such publications are invariably seen as being generally applicable to the universe of negotiating activities. For industrial-relations researchers there are potentially some analytical and practical gains from setting collective bargaining processes in the larger context of bargaining activities, particularly if one subscribes to the view that the central subject matter of industrial relations is the generation and resolution of conflict, with bargaining power being a key analytical concept for industrial-relations researchers to focus on.[12] Certainly, some useful insights have emerged, for example, from comparisons of the processes of conciliation–mediation employed in industrial relations with those in international negotiations.[13] However, in considering the universe of negotiating settings it is important to distinguish the particular sub-sets which are characterized by the following features: (i) the parties are not engaged in a one-off

Table 6.1 The essence of principled negotiations

Problem – Positional bargaining: which game should you play?		*Solution — Change the game: negotiate on the merits*
Soft	*Hard*	*Principled*
Participants are friends. The goal is agreement.	Participants are adversaries. The goal is victory.	Participants are problem solvers. The goal is a wise outcome reached efficiently and amicably.
Make concessions to cultivate the relationship.	Demand concessions as a condition of the relationship.	Separate the people from the problem.
Be soft on the people and the problem.	Be hard on the problem and the people.	Be soft on the people, hard on the problem.
Trust others.	Distrust others.	Proceed independent of trust.
Change your position easily.	Dig in to your position.	Focus on interest, not positions.
Make offers.	Make threats.	Explore interests.
Disclose your bottom line.	Mislead as to your bottom line.	Avoid having a bottom line.
Accept one-sided losses to reach agreement.	Demand one-sided gains as the price of agreement.	Invent options for mutual gain.
Search for the single answer: the one they will accept.	Search for the single answer: the one you will accept.	Develop multiple options to choose from: decide later.
Insist on agreement.	Insist on your position.	Insist on objective criteria.
Try to avoid a contest of will.	Try to win a contest of will.	Try to reach a result based on standards independent of will.
Yield to pressure.	Apply pressure.	Reason and be open to reasons; yield to principle, not pressure.

Source: Roger Fisher and William Ury (1983) *Getting to Yes*, p. 13, London: Hutchinson.

transaction and hence must continue to interact over the course of time (i.e. there is a mutual interest in the survival of the relationship); (ii) the issues being negotiated are multiple in nature; (iii) the different interests, and hence potential conflict, involved in the bargaining relationships are not simply inter-personal in nature, because the bargainers are organizational representatives (i.e. there is the likelihood of inter-role conflict); and (iv) the parties to the relationship have internal differences (in strategy, tactics, priorities, etc.) among their constituent members (i.e. there is a likelihood of intra-organizational conflict).

These four conditions clearly differentiate collective bargaining from the processes involved in many other negotiating settings. Accordingly, the next section concentrates solely on collective bargaining by examining various conceptual models (and associated empirical work) of the processes of bargaining.

Models of the collective-bargaining process

The various theories of the collective-bargaining process are, as we shall see, far from homogeneous in content, but they tend to have two features in common. First, they tend to reject any notion that the outcomes of bargaining are solely a function of environmental forces and, second, they seek to identify determinate solutions within the range of interdependency identified in early bilateral monopoly treatments of union–management wage bargaining.[14] In seeking to arrive at determinate solutions, a *deductive* approach has often been adopted which (i) makes certain assumptions about the nature of the bargaining process, and (ii) treats environmental conditions as essentially static parameters of the process. The most well known work along these lines is arguably Hicks's economic model of employer concession and union resistance curves[15] (which are strongly shaped by estimates of likely strike duration), and game-theory treatments of bargaining based on notions of rational, individual utility-maximization in situations of interdependency of choice and pay-off.[16] These deductive models have yielded some individual insights and propositions that have been developed in subsequent empirical work. For example, the Hicks model is frequently referred to in the recent work of some economists that offers explanations of strike activity in terms of information/communication failures (i.e. strikes are mistakes),[17] while game theory has been the basis of the individual hypothesis that negotiators (and arbitrators) will tend to arrive at 'split the difference' solutions.[18] More generally, however, industrial-relations researchers have tended to argue that the highly restrictive nature of the assumptions made in such work seriously limits their applicability to, and hence value in understanding, the majority of 'real world' collective bargaining situations. For example, Kochan has criticized the Hicks model on the grounds of its unreasonable assumptions concerning each party's knowledge of the other's goals and willingness to strike, its individual decision-making basis which ignores the collective aspects of negotiations, its overly static treatment of goals and concessions, and the fact that it is difficult to subject to systematic, empirical testing.[19]

In conceptual terms at least, industrial-relations researchers have been much more favourably disposed towards the inductive-theory-based bargaining treatments of behavioural scientists. One of the leading, early studies here is that of Douglas – which emphasized the interplay of representative and personal roles as the 'skilled' bargainers involved in 'successful' negotiations moved sequentially through three stages:[20] (i) the establishment of the bargaining range (mainly inter-role processes); (ii) the reconnoitering of the bargaining range (mainly inter-personal processes); and (iii) the precipitation of the decision-making crisis (mainly inter-role processes). This sequential stage process, which is similar to various treatments of intergroup problem-solving,[21] is now a regular feature of textbook discussions of the processes involved in collective bargaining.[22] The most widely referenced and quoted behavioural study of collective bargaining, however, is undoubtedly that of Walton and McKersie.[23] This particular piece of work emphasized the essentially mixed-motive nature of collective-bargaining relationships, with inter- and intra-party relationships rarely being either totally competitive or totally co-operative in nature. Indeed, they identified the following four sub-processes involved in most bargaining relationships:

1. *Distributive* bargaining, which involves conflict – with one party seeking to achieve gains at the expense of the other. In this particular sub-process a key determinant of the processes involved and outcomes achieved will be relative bargaining power, as influenced by the likelihood and costs of strike action.
2. *Integrative* bargaining, which seeks to ensure mutual gains in areas where the parties have common interests. This particular joint problem-solving orientation will be influenced by factors such as the willingness of the parties to share information and the level of trust between them.
3. *Attitudinal* structuring, which involves attempts to establish and maintain a desired, longer-term working relationship between the two parties. The parties' preferences for different patterns of relationships here (i.e. some position along the distributive–integrative spectrum) are viewed as a function of overall strategic considerations, contextual factors, and the personalities and social beliefs of the leading representatives of the two parties.

4. *Intra-organizational* bargaining, which involves the process of reconciling and accommodating different interests within each of the individual parties involved in the bargaining relationship. The nature of these processes will be shaped by factors such as the authority and solidarity of the negotiating teams.

The second, major, conceptual contribution of Walton and McKersie was in relation to the bargaining-zone concept, where they emphasized the role and importance of strategies and tactics by, for example, party A in shaping party B's perceptions of the needs, intentions, and coercive capacity of A – although the objective determinants of, for example, A's coercive capacity were unchanged. The result of their approach in this regard has been two-fold. First, most contemporary discussions of the concept of bargaining power view it as very much a perceptual or subjective-based concept,[24] which involves considerably more than, for example, the objective costs of any strike action. Second, many existing discussions of the collective-bargaining process make substantial use of the contract-zone notion, in which the key concepts are the resistance points (i.e. bottom line positions) and target points (i.e. preferred settlement positions) of the parties, with the essence of the negotiating process being held to be that of (i) identifying the other party's resistance point (without revealing one's own), and (ii) influencing the other party to move from its initial resistance point to ensure an overlap of the two points in the positive contract zone – a move which significantly raises the probability of a settlement being achieved without recourse to strike action.[25]

The subsequent empirical testing and refinement of the work of Walton and McKersie has been somewhat disappointing in nature, because researchers have overwhelmingly concentrated on only one particular sub-process (i.e. integrative bargaining), and, even then, have very largely tended to examine the relevant determinants in non-fieldwork-based settings.[26] Admittedly, there are some exceptions to this statement – such as the work of Peterson and Tracy[27] and some studies of the operation of joint health and safety committees.[28] The former study, for example, suggested that integrative bargaining and attitudinal structuring were more interrelated than was suggested by Walton and McKersie, while the former work has indicated that unions in these particular joint structures tend to use a mixture of distributive and integrative bargaining strategies and tactics. However, the vast majority of empirical studies of the Walton and McKersie work have been conducted in laboratory settings: indeed, there is now a very substantial volume of laboratory-based studies of the processes of bargaining more generally. This laboratory-based research, which has tended to involve essentially four experimental paradigms, namely the distribution game, the game of economic exchange, the role-playing debate and the substitution debate,[29] has examined a number of individual hypotheses and issues, such as: (i) the nature of the behavioural response to concessions made by the other party; (ii) the effectiveness of threats in altering the motivation of the other party; and (iii) the effect of differing systems of communication in altering the relative balance of inter-personal and inter-role (or party) considerations in the negotiating relationship.[30] However, a number of industrial-relations researchers have questioned both the internal and external validity of the findings that have emerged from this particular stream of research;[31] among the particular concerns and criticisms here are the use of undergraduate student subjects, the relative absence of constituency pressures on the negotiators, and the possibility that subject behaviour may be influenced by the experimenters and/or their research goals.

Students (broadly defined) of collective bargaining (and indeed of bargaining more generally) usually subscribe to the view that negotiating skills and techniques can, at least to some extent, be usefully acquired through the processes of training – as indicated by the increasing use of case studies and collective-bargaining games in classroom sessions. However, as Strauss and Driscoll indicate, there are the following important differences between real and simulated bargaining relationships:[32]

1. The game is a one-time event; bargaining involves continuing interactions over the years.
2. The game rewards distortion and dishonesty; practitioners value their reputation for honesty and keeping their word.
3. Game players represent only themselves; real bargainers represent constituencies.
4. The game emphasizes the ritualistic elements of bargaining; real bargainers see beyond this.
5. The game rarely lasts more than 8–12 hours; real bargaining takes much longer with marathon all-night sessions being common.
6. Game players play for fun, slight momentary glory, and possibly a few points in a final grade (or even just because that's what the instructor tells them to do); for professional negotiators the stakes are much, much higher.

Table 6.2 Examples of organizational development (OD) interventions

Focus of intervention	*Example*	*Description*
Analysing operations	Survey feedback	Members of an organization or department express their attitudes (usually anonymously by questionnaire) about their jobs and organization. The information is used as the basis for general discussion and review.
	Role analysis	Job holders examine the expectations which significant others (e.g. their bosses, subordinates, work colleagues) have of them in their roles. By comparing these to their own priorities and the expectations of key 'role senders', conflicts and ambiguities can be resolved.
Employee performances	Performance counselling	The priorities of the job are reviewed by the employee and his/her immediate supervisor. The adequacy of back-up resources are also considered. Specific objectives are agreed, and, at a suitable future date, are reviewed in a further joint planning session.
	Job re-design	The design of jobs is examined, to explore the extent to which they meet psychological criteria. This process and the re-design of jobs it may lead to, is conducted in a participative way.
Interpersonal relations	Team-process review	Time is made available for the members of a working group to discuss the group's performance and modes of operation. The objective is to bring difficulties into the open so that group members can collaborate in the development of more effective strategies.
	Intergroup interventions	Members of two interdependent groups meet to review the expectations they each have of the other, and the stereotype views that may have developed. Real and imagined differences are distinguished and, normally with the help of a 'third party', appropriate action is planned.

Table 6.2 – continued

Focus of intervention	*Example*	*Description*
Personal styles and values	Life planning	Individuals work on a series of tasks designed to help them reflect on their past, present, and future. They are encouraged to distinguish between their 'superficial' and 'overriding' purposes (i.e. necessary trivia and crises) and their 'sustaining' purposes in life.
	Sensitivity training	An unstructured group meeting when, with the help of an experienced trainer, participants have the opportunity to examine the impact of their interpersonal styles and to explore the efficacy of new social skills and attitudes.

Source: Frank Blackler and Sylvia Shimmin (1984) *Applying Psychology in Organisations*, pp. 98–9, London: Methuen.

The conflict potential of collective bargaining and organization development

The existence of collective-bargaining arrangements is one (but not the only) formal reflection of the divergent interests, and hence potential conflict, between individual employees and management within their organization of employment. Such arrangements by definition involve trade-union representation (and hence introduce a new institutional interest), with the result that any subsequent conflict can involve and result from inter-organizational, interpersonal, intra-organizational, and procedural sources. This multifaceted conflict potential of collective bargaining needs to be placed in the larger context of organizational development (OD) and change initiatives, given that 'OD has looked upon conflict resolution as its special province'.[32] According to French and Bell, organization development, as a behavioural science concept, can be defined as:

> A long range effort to improve an organisation's problem-solving and renewal processes, particularly through a more effective and collaborative management of organisation culture – with special emphasis on the culture of formal work teams – with the assistance of a change agent or catalyst, and the use of the theory

and technology of applied behavioural science, including action research.[34]

Table 6.2 lists some of the most well-known types of organizational development interventions.

There are numerous discussions of the limitations of existing organizational-development and change models,[35] but two criticisms of particular interest here are (i) the general lack of attention given to the role of unions[36] and (ii) their general beliefs, assumptions and orientations concerning the nature of conflict (i.e. it is essentially due to misunderstandings and personality differences) which can be resolved through increased trust, openness, and communications at the face-to-face level, with little recognition of the existence (much less value) of bargaining, political, or power activities and considerations.[37] Nevertheless, the most well-known, large-scale OD exercises in Britain have involved companies with unions and collective bargaining arrangements (e.g. Shell and ICI), with management perceptions of particular industrial-relations difficulties and problems having been one of the factors responsible for the original interventions.[38] The much dicussed OD exercise at Shell, for example, was initiated and carried through by senior management and focused on changing individual values and attitudes – with the major instruments involved being job re-design projects, more participation-orientated management, new contractual relations with shop-floor employees (i.e. salaried-staff status being exchanged for the elimination of certain restrictive practices), and the building of a new refinery according to the principles of socio-technical systems theory.[39] The relatively limited longer-term impact of these changes was largely the result of intra-management resistance and opposition which was itself a function of the way the change process was introduced (i.e. exclusively 'top down' in nature) and orientated (i.e. individual- rather than group-focused).[40] This particular experience, together with the earlier-noted general limitations of OD interventions, would seem to suggest that OD-based, conflict-resolution techniques (even at their best) are likely to have only limited applicability to the all-important distributive sub-process of collective bargaining.[41]

Multiple manifestations of conflict and collective bargaining

Organization theorists have discussed the nature of intra-organizational conflict in terms of a conceptual framework involving conflict episodes or events, namely latency, feeling, perception, manifestation, and aftermath.[42] In this section we are solely concerned with the manifestation stage or episode of conflict, a concentration stimulated by theoretical arguments to the effect that the introduction of collective-bargaining arrangements into an unorganized labour market will have the effect of reducing individual manifestations of conflict, notably labour quits and turnover.[43] Indeed, industrial-relations researchers have given particular attention to the questions of whether various hypothesized manifestations of individual conflict (e.g. absence) and collective conflict (e.g. strikes) are related in a positive (i.e. a complementary, additive relationship) or negative (i.e. a substitute) manner. However, the resulting body of research often involves poorly articulated theoretical frameworks (i.e. the view that a relatively homogeneous stock of discontent underlies these various manifestations of conflict), a relatively narrow focus (i.e. a concentration essentially on strikes and absence), and unsatisfactory data bases (i.e. single-industry studies or highly aggregated inter-industry level data). As Kelly and Nicholson put it: 'it is the methodologically poorer studies which have supported a general inverse strikes–absenteeism relationship, while the better studies have found no clear cut relationship.'[44] In fact, the results of Kelly and Nicholson's own plant-level-based study did not support any notion that the different manifestations of collective conflict were interchangeable, nor that individual and collective manifestations of conflict were alternative outcomes of the same processes. Their findings also provided only limited support for the alternative hypothesis of significant, positive interrelationships between individual and collective manifestations of conflict. The inappropriateness of treating industrial conflict as essentially a homogeneous phenomenon was further reinforced by some of the findings of Edwards and Scullion's plant-based investigation which concluded that:

> the notion of alternative forms of conflict is not robust enough to stand up to detailed scrutiny. If it is used to point out, for example, that conflict cannot be equated with strikes then it is unobjectionable but correspondingly unilluminating. When it is rendered in a precise form it faces severe difficulties, of which perhaps the most basic is the assumption that behaviour which is labelled as, say, absenteeism has the same meaning in different settings. A related difficulty is that it is assumed that individual actions can usefully be described as forms of conflict. We have stressed, by contrast, the way in which activities are constituted as aspects of conflict by different forms of organisation of the labour process. Attention to the labour process provides a

grounded explanation of why particular actions occur in some settings and of how they relate to a notion of conflict.[45]

The increased availability of survey information in Britain has, however, improved our appreciation of the relative role and significance of strikes within the larger category of collective forms of industrial conflict. For example, both the 1980 and 1984 workplace industrial-relations surveys have revealed that overtime bans/restrictions and work-to-rules were the most frequent forms of non-strike action, with the 1980 survey explicitly stating that: 'less than one half of the establishments affected by any type of industrial action were affected by a strike which would come within the definition used for the official records.'[46] Moreover, studies of individual sectors of employment, such as local government, have revealed that work to rules/withdrawal of co-operation on the part of non-manual workers can substantially exceed the number of instances of strike action.[47]

It is strikes, however, that have been far and away the most extensively researched manifestation of collective industrial conflict. Indeed, there is a massive volume of strike literature for both Britain and other countries – a situation which Feuille and Wheeler cynically (but certainly not inaccurately) attribute to the operation of Gresham's law of social-science research[48] (i.e. the presence of low-cost and readily available data on one subject drives out the collection of high-cost and hard-to-obtain data on others). Fortunately, however, only a relatively small sub-set of individual issues and themes dominate this literature. These are the particular matters discussed in the next section. However, before turning to this material, it is useful to appreciate the general position that the majority of industrial-relations researchers have adopted towards strike activity, which is essentially as follows: (i) the right to strike is an essential feature of genuine collective bargaining; (ii) it is the credibility and strength of the threat to strike, rather than the actual carrying out of the threat, which is the really important dimension of union power; (iii) strikes are not pathological in nature so that some level of strike activity is both inevitable and acceptable; (iv) the quality of industrial relations cannot be measured or judged solely with reference to the level of strike activity; and (v) the social or public interest in industrial relations does not justify the elimination of strikes, but rather the establishment of conflict resolution procedures capable of yielding acceptable (as opposed to totally satisfactory) outcomes to all parties concerned over a given period of time. It is these particular beliefs or values that frequently separate such researchers from colleagues in economics and organization behaviour.

The major issues and themes in strike-related research

One of the recurring themes in the British strike literature concerns the accuracy of the officially produced strike statistics. In Britain, the exclusion of political strikes and inclusion of only those others which lasted at least a day and involved at least ten workers (unless the total number of days lost was 100 or more, in which case a strike not meeting the basic criteria would also be counted), means, by definition, that the Department of Employment statistics are not a full count of all strikes which occur in a given period of time. However, questions have inevitably been raised: first, about how many smaller strikes fall outside the coverage of the official figures and, second, how many strikes which meet the criteria for inclusion are not in fact 'picked up' by the official figures, due to the voluntary reporting procedures involved. On the latter matter, Creigh, drawing on the work of Kelly and Nicholson and Edwards, has suggested that the Department of Employment figures record about 70 per cent of all eligible stoppages and nearly all (i.e. 97 per cent) of the total number of working days lost in stoppages, with those that go unrecorded being small, short stoppages near the reporting threshold.[49] However, some controversy still surrounds this issue – with a recent study of twenty-five companies revealing relatively unsystematic collection and reporting procedures for industrial disputes in Britain.[50]

There are considerable differences between countries, in: (i) the definitions of officially recorded strikes (e.g. include or not political strikes, the particular reporting threshold in terms of numbers involved and length of time); (ii) the way in which the number of workers involved in strikes is calculated (e.g. include or not those indirectly involved); and (iii) the method by which strikes are identified for recording purposes (i.e. most countries have voluntary reporting procedures, the basis of which can vary considerably in nature).[51] Furthermore, an individual country may change the basis of its officially recorded strike statistics over time. In the US, for example, only those stoppages which last one day (or shift) and involve 1,000 workers have been counted since 1982, whereas prior to that date all strikes which lasted a full day (or shift) and involved six or more workers were counted; this change has been estimated to have reduced the recorded number of working days lost by 30–40 per cent. As a result, comparisons of the level of strike activity across countries always have to confront the issue and problem of whether 'like is being compared with like'.[52] In general, the particular dimension of strike activity which is held to be most suitable and appropriate for cross-country comparisons is that of working days lost. This is because a relatively small number of individually large stoppages tends to account for a relatively high proportion of the total number of working days lost through strike activity in most years in individual countries, and 'major disputes will generally be noticed and recorded in all countries whatever the system for compiling work stoppage statistics'.[53] In Britain, for instance, the Department of Employment has indicated that nearly half (i.e. 46 per cent) of all working days lost in the years 1960–79 were due to 64 large strikes.[54] In the years 1969–78, Britain had an average of 472 working days lost a year per 1,000 employees (a figure exceeded by 8 other OECD countries), while in 1979–83, working days lost per 1,000 employees in the UK averaged 500, which ranked it eleventh out of 16 countries (for which reasonably complete data were available) – being below Italy (1,190), Spain (970), Canada (750), Ireland (730), and Australia (590), but above, for example, France (120), West Germany (10), Japan (20), and Sweden (250).[55] In 1982–6 the UK average annual figure was 420 days lost per 1,000 employees (i.e approximately half a working day per employee per year), a figure exceeded by Italy, New Zealand, Greece, Finland, Spain, and Canada.[56] (For the years 1977–86 the UK was a little above the middle-ranked position among OECD countries.)

There currently exists a quite substantial number of 'international' strike studies, although the approach and orientation of individual studies which make up this particular body of literature tend to differ in a number of important respects. Some studies, for example, have highlighted the differing patterns of stoppage activity between countries (in matters such as size and duration) and have sought to relate these to differences in the nature of industrial-relations procedures and bargaining structure (e.g. greater strike frequency in more decentralized bargaining systems).[57] A second approach has involved the estimation of time-series regression models for a number of countries, in which unemployment and inflation have been key individual variables,[58] although certain political variables (e.g. labour-socialist parties in power in certain periods of time) have been increasingly included.[59] A third approach has involved detailed studies of individual countries: Ingham, for example, sought to account for differences in strike activity between Britain and Sweden in terms of the relative strength of employers' associations which, in turn, were related to differences in matters such as product-market concentration and the level of product specialization.[60] Finally, there have been some attempts to develop general theories or explanations of strike activity that transcend national systems of industrial relations. Kerr and Siegel, for example, have offered an explanation of the ranking of individual industries in strike activity across countries in terms of the physical/social location of workers in society and the (employee self-selection) process whereby individual employee and industry characteristics are matched together,[61] while Korpi and Shalev have presented an explanation of inter-country variation in aggregate strike activity in terms of class demands, which arise in the process of production, being met through either the political or industrial spheres of activity.[62]

A third issue or theme in the research literature on strike activity has concerned the nature of media presentation and discussion of such activity, with this particular subject being much more extensively researched and examined in Britain than in most other countries. This particular research orientation mirrors the media's preoccupation with strikes[63] (relative to other industrial-relations issues and developments), with researcher studies of individual strikes having suggested that the dominant value or normative premise of the resulting newspaper coverage is invariably support for non-disruption to the status quo.[64] The Glasgow University Media Group appear to have gone a stage further than this in arguing that television coverage (both BBC and ITV) of strikes conveys the impression that such 'problems' are ultimately the fault of the workforce.[65]

The nature of media coverage of strikes in the public sector is particularly important, because (i) the industry- or national-level bargaining structure of the public sector makes for relatively sizeable, 'highly visible' strikes, and (ii) the outcome of public sector strikes has been held to be strongly influenced by whether public opinion is relatively well disposed (or not) towards the strikers' cause.[66]

There have been a number of general discussions of the tactical dilemmas faced by public-sector unions in trying to ensure that their industrial action effectively exerts pressure on management (and ultimately on the Government), but at the same time does not cause them to lose the support and backing of other union members and the public at large;[67] the result has often been the use of selective industrial action (as in the Civil Service dispute in 1981 and the NHS one in 1982) in an attempt to achieve some balance between, or reconciliation of, these two potentially conflicting objectives. However, the various instances of national-level industrial action in the public sector since the late 1970s have seen both unions and researchers making numerous critical comments concerning the role of media coverage in adversely conveying the essentials of the unions' side of the dispute(s) to the public at large. This criticism was apparent during the so-called 'winter of discontent' in 1978–9,[68] but reached its high-water mark during the miners' strike of 1984–5. During this dispute, the National Coal Board spent a record amount of £4,566,000 on newspaper advertisements alone[69] which, with a media generally hostile to the miners' case,[70] undoubtedly helped account for the fact that opinion polls reported that public sympathy for the miners in 1984 (i.e. 26 per cent) was very much less than had been the case in the dispute of 1974 (i.e. 52 per cent).[71] The larger context of this media coverage issue is, of course, the changed party politics of Fleet Street, as its ownership has become more concentrated over time: in the 1945 election, for example, four national dailies (which accounted for almost 35 per cent of sales) supported the Labour Party, whereas in 1983 only the *Daily Mirror* (with 22 per cent of sales) recommended a Labour vote, as against six newspapers (accounting for 75 per cent of circulation) that were pro-Conservative.[72]

The extent of the costs involved in strike action to the various parties concerned has been extensively discussed, although conceptual treatments of the subject have far outweighed (in both numerical and quality terms) the extent of systematic empirical research. The existence of different patterns of strike activity across national systems of industrial relations has led to some debate and disagreement among commentators as to the relative costs of such differing patterns. The Donovan Commission, for example, was very much concerned with a relatively large number of small-sized, short-duration strikes which was held to be a relatively high cost pattern of activity – due to the inability of management to predict their occurrence and take offsetting action (e.g. build up inventories, contract out work).[73] In contrast, other individuals have claimed that a pattern of sizeable and long-duration strikes is the relatively high-cost one, because such strikes generate a disproportionate number of 'negative externalities' for other plants and industries (i.e. as suppliers and customers) not involved in the immediate area of dispute.[74] This sort of disagreement about which is the most important dimension (in terms of the relative costs to the economy at large) of strike activity (e.g. frequency, total working days lost, duration, etc.) is important in view of the fact that business-cycle models of strikes (to be discussed shortly) have had much greater success in accounting for inter-temporal variation in strike frequency than they have had in attempting to identify the determinants of, for example, strike duration. There have, in fact, been a number of studies which have developed composite indexes of strike activity,[75] although the construction (i.e. the relative weighting of the individual components) and interpretation (i.e. if the individual components are moving in quite divergent ways) of such indexes is not always a straightforward matter.

The most well-known conceptual treatment of the determinants of the economic (i.e. output) costs of strike action still remains that of Chamberlain and Schilling, who argued that the impact of a strike will depend upon three basic factors:[76] (i) the ability of consumers of the products of, and suppliers of the raw materials to, strike-affected establishments, to switch their orders and supplies to alternative firms or industries; (ii) the level of stocks which the strike-affected establishment's consumers and suppliers are able to run down and build up, respectively, during the stoppage; and (iii) the 'necessity' of the product concerned. This framework of analysis could be utilized to argue the case that public-sector strikes will be relatively high-cost ones – i.e. much of the output of the public sector consists of services (rather than goods) which are by definition non-storable, and for which there are limited, short run alternative sources of supply (the public sector being a monopoly producer in many areas of activity). However, the third factor in the above framework (i.e. the necessity of the product concerned) is arguably the most important, but, at the same time, is likely to be a source of considerable disagreement in inter-personal judgements concerning individual products and services. Certainly, the necessity of all public sector goods and services to all individuals should not be over-emphasized, in view of (i) the relatively long duration of many public-sector strikes in Britain, which seems somewhat inconsistent with allegations of their highly damaging impact, and (ii) the fact that, at least in many cases, these strikes disrupt rather than completely eliminate the short-run supply of public sector services[77] (for instance, army personnel frequently being used to maintain a certain level of provision).

The number of comprehensive and systematic empirical studies of the various costs of strikes is relatively limited in Britain and, indeed, in other countries. Admittedly there have been some studies of the costs of various National Emergency Disputes in the United States, which have generally suggested that much of the 'emergency' impact of these strikes is more rhetorical than real.[78] However, the quantitative examination of the dock strikes of 1967, 1970, and 1972 in Britain,[79] which concluded that they caused a reduction in trade flows which was not made good within the quarter in which they occurred and there was little sign that any reduction in trade was recovered by increased trade in quarters after the strikes or by anticipatory trading in advance of them, constitutes one of the very few examples of work along these lines. Indeed, it is clearly a difficult (some would say impossible) task to produce an aggregate, quantitative summary statement of the costs of individual strikes. The various quantitative and qualitative, short-term and long-term, costs and gains to the individual parties concerned is well illustrated by the detailed study of the 1980 national steel strike, which, having posed the question 'who won the strike?', produced the list of gains and losses for the various parties concerned.[80] This is set out in Table 6.3.

In view of the contents of the Table 6.3, it was not surprising that this study concluded that: 'in many ways the Government, more than either unions or management, were the winners of the strike'.[81] More generally, the evidence on the economic costs of strikes is limited,[82] although many industrial-relations researchers would probably still subscribe to Knowles's general suggestion that (i) the direct production loss of most strikes is small, and (ii) the sizeable loss due to a few large strikes can often be subsequently recovered.[83] The belief that the availability of social-welfare payments were influential in lengthening the duration of strikes in Britain in the 1970s led to a number of studies concerned with how employees finance themselves during the course of strikes.[84] The information from such studies is often used by the media to suggest that individual employees always lose (in wage terms) from strike action. However, this argument, which shows that the income loss of employees during a strike is not fully compensated for by the difference between the employer's final (pre-strike) wage offer and the wage settlement at the end of the strike, involves the questionable assumption that the various wage settlements reached in an individual union–management relationship over a given period of time are discrete, self-contained episodes, with a strike in one settlement-round having no implications for the size of subsequent wage settlements; in short, there is no recognition of the fact that a strike may constitute something of an 'investment' good.

In Britain, various studies of the basic pattern of strike activity have revealed a mixture of change and continuity over the course of time. The most recent studies are for the years 1946–73 and 1960–79, with the elements of change revealed including: (i) the substantially reduced proportion of all strikes accounted for by the coalmining industry (e.g. 59 per cent of all strikes in 1960, but only 4 per cent in 1970), (ii) the increased proportion of wage-related stoppages, and the increased proportion of longer-duration strikes in the 1970s, with the elements of continuity including the essential

Table 6.3 A check-list of gains and losses to the various parties in the 1980 steel strike

The unions (largely the Iron and Steel Trades Confederation)	*Management*	*The Government*
(i) Short term gains	(i) Gains included:	(i) Gains included:
(a) national wage offer improved from 2 per cent to 11 per cent	(a) some resulting procedural changes in collective bargaining which meant that wage increases could, to some extent, be based on the criterion of local productivity	(a) the creation of an example of wage restraint in the public sector
(b) effective resistance to management's plan to completely change bargaining from national to local level	(b) this procedural change, as a means of reducing labour costs, improved the corporation's image with the Government	(b) the picketing involved and the original (later reversed on appeal) legal decision that the strike was a political one aided the passage of the 1980 and 1982 Employment Acts which substantially narrowed the definition of a trade dispute
(c) improved inter-union relationships	(c) the moves towards joint union bargaining	
(ii) longer term gains, more doubtful:	(d) a reduced workforce size and changed working practices	
(a) industrial restructuring proceeded with employment and union membership losses	(ii) However, management's handling of the negotiations reduced their credibility	
(b) acceptance of management's wage offer in 1981 wage round (i.e. only a 3 per cent average annual wage increase) and delay to the introduction of 39 hour week		

Source: Compiled from Jean Hartley, John Kelly, and Nigel Nicholson (1983) *Steel Stike*, p. 165–7, London: Batsford.

stability of the industrial distribution of strike activity and the fact that the typical British strike remains a relatively small-sized and short-length affair.[85] Indeed, as Edwards has stressed:

> While there are obvious contrasts between the 1960s and the 1970s, the predominance of the small-scale, short and work-place-based stoppage has remained impressive. . . . the extremely short strike still dominates the strike picture in terms of the number of stoppages. What has changed, of course, is the

> significance of the official national strike. But in purely quantitative terms this type of strike has continued to play a small role. This is not to deny the importance of changes which have taken place, but it is essential to keep two forms of analysis separate. The first picks up various interesting developments, such as the 'post-Donovan' strike or the role of union officials in a few notable disputes, and discusses their changing significance. The second examines the broad pattern of strikes. The first should not be used as a substitute for the second.[86]

It has been observed that the extent of strike activity in Britain is disproportionately associated with a relatively small number of industries. For example, Durcan, McCarthy, and Redman reported that the eight most strike-prone industries (including motor vehicles, iron and steel, and shipbuilding) accounted for 56 per cent of all stoppages, 77 per cent of workers involved, and 71 per cent of days lost in the years 1949–73, although they only employed some 17 per cent of the total workforce.[87] More recently, this 'disproportionate concentration' relationship has been taken a stage further with a Department of Employment study which reported that only 5 per cent of manufacturing plants had experienced any stoppages over a 3-year period of time, and with only a small proportion of these accounting for nearly two-thirds of all days lost in the manufacturing sector.[88] This particular finding, however, has been subject to criticism on the basis of some survey evidence,[89] and certainly the 1984 workplace industrial-relations survey reported that the proportion of establishments experiencing a strike (among either the manual or non-manual workforce) was some 19 per cent in that year (15 per cent in 1980).[90]

There have been various attempts to account for the nature of inter-industry variation in strike activity. As mentioned earlier, one of the most ambitious of these studies was that by Kerr and Siegel which, on the basis of data from a number of countries, argued that inter-industry variation in strike activity could be accounted for by the extent of the social and physical location (and integration) of the workers in society at large, and the particular characteristics (psychological profile) of workers attracted to particular, individual industries. However, this explanation is difficult to test and evaluate formally, faces difficulty in accounting for changes in industry rankings (in strike activity) over time, and really offers little insight into the position of the medium strike-prone group of industries (i.e. it is very much an end-of-spectrum orientated explanation). There have been some general, qualitative discussions of the relatively strike-prone industries (which emphasize the role of factors such as fragmented bargaining arrangements and fluctuating earnings),[91] some detailed, individual industry studies (particularly of cars and coalmining),[92] and some quantitative attempts to identify the relevant determinants of inter-industry variation in strike activity. In the latter category of studies, Shorey, for example, found that strike frequency was significantly related to the proportion of women workers, the proportion of workers on piecework arrangements, average firm size, the rate of change of productivity, the rate of change of the capital stock, and certain earnings indices;[93] these were generally positive relationships, except in the case of women workers where an inverse relationship was involved. This particular study was, however, based on relatively few observations (i.e. 33 manufacturing industries), with the individual hypotheses tested being rather *ad hoc* in nature, although a subsequent, more disaggregated inter-industry study (i.e. 120 manufacturing-sector industry orders) revealed that strike activity was significantly associated with the labour intensity of production, the level of overtime working, the proportion of workers under payment-by-results schemes, the degree of industrial concentration, and the proportion of small-plant employment;[94] all relationships were positive except for the latter variable.

The increased availability of establishment-level survey data from the late 1970s has permitted a number of studies of inter-establishment variation in strike activity. One of the most recent of these utilized the 1980 workplace industrial relations survey to examine the occurrence (or not) of: (i) any industrial action; (ii) short strikes; and (iii) long strikes – with a theoretical framework that grouped a sizeable number of variables into the sub-vectors of frictional, organizational, incentive, and size influences.[95] The statistically significant relationships which emerged included the following:

(i) The probability of industrial action was positively related to payment-by-results working, multi-unionism, union recognition, the presence of shop stewards, the proportion of manual employees who are union members, and establishment size; but was negatively related to overall organization size and single-establishment status.
(ii) Longer strikes were positively associated with payment by results, union recognition, the presence of formal procedures, high union membership, and engineering industry status – and negatively related to shift working.
(iii) Shorter strikes were less likely in single, independent establishments, but were positively related to the proportion of manual

employees, payment-by-results working, and the presence of shop stewards.

The general direction in which research is moving in this particular sub-set of the strike literature is a desirable one – namely, away from the previous heavy concentration on analysis of strike frequency at the industry level, particularly for the manufacturing sector. Moreover, as the level of analysis has come closer to that where collective bargaining is actually conducted, it is apparent that some of the more popular, widely alleged influences (e.g. the nature of technology) have not in fact proved to be statistically significant. Indeed, Edwards's plant-based, manufacturing-sector study, for example, yielded very few significant relationships relative to the number of variables tested.[96] Furthermore, a number of important conceptual and statistical issues still surround certain of the significant, empirical relationships that have emerged in such work. For example, the significant, positive relationship with establishment size could be due to a number of different (underlying) behavioural relationships,[97] few of which can be directly examined on the basis of the existing survey data. The precise nature or shape of the relationship with establishment size is also an issue; is it a smooth, continuous relationship or is there a significant break or discontinuity in the relationship at a particular level of size? There is also the question of the nature of both the behavioural and empirical relationship between establishment and overall organization size with regard to strike activity which still requires considerable investigation. Finally, the nature of the relationship between foreign ownership and strike activity has been extensively discussed and examined. However, in view of the more broad-ranging interest in the role and influence of foreign-ownership status in the British system of industrial relations, we will discuss this subject in some detail in a subsequent section of this chapter. Table 6.4 sets out some recent strike figures for Britain.

In most systems of industrial relations the level of strike activity has exhibited considerable variability over the course of time. In Britain there has certainly been considerable discussion of the changed strike position of the 1980s compared to that of the previous decade: for example, the 1,330 strikes recorded by the Department of Employment in 1980 was the smallest number recorded in any year since 1942, while the number of working days lost through industrial action in 1986 was the lowest for 23 years. More generally, the question of how (and why) the level of strike activity has moved through the course of time has accounted for a larger proportion of the existing strike literature in Britain (and

Table 6.4 Strikes in Britain: annual averages for the 1960–9, 1970–9, and 1980–7

	Frequency	*Workers involved (thousands)*	*Working days lost per thousand employees*
1960–9 (annual average)	2,446	1,357	157
1970–9 (annual average)	2,598	1,616	569
1980–7 (annual average)	1,201	1,607	371

Source: D. Metcalf (1988) 'Water notes dry up', Centre for Labour Economics, LSE, Discussion Paper no. 314, July, p. 42.

elsewhere) than any other single issue or question. It has long been observed that the level of strike activity is positively related to short-run, business-cyle movements (i.e. rising in the upswing, and falling in the downswing of the cycle) while, over the longer term, those proponents of, what Cronin has labelled, 'modernization theory',[98] have argued that the level of industrial conflict should decline in advanced industrialized societies, due to, among other things, the increased 'maturity' of collective bargaining arrangements; needless to say, this thesis – of, for example, Ross and Hartmann[99] – has been subject to a great deal of critical comment.[100] However, the overwhelmingly favoured methodology at the present time – which is the estimation of time-series, multiple-regression models for the system as a whole, in which economic variables play a central explanatory role – very largely developed out of the work of Ashenfelter and Johnson in the United States in the late 1960s.[101] The micro-foundation of their work was a bargaining model which involved management, the union leadership, and the union rank and file — with the latter having some desired level of wage increase to which they felt entitled. If the level of wage increase desired by the rank and file was not met by management's offer, then the union leader could either accept the lower offer or call a strike. The effect of the latter, which was held to be the option generally favoured by the union leadership, would be to lower rank-and-file wage expectations over the course of the strike – with the result that the union leadership could then safely settle with management. In essence, strike action was viewed by Ashenfelter and Johnson as an equilibrating mechanism designed to align rank-and-file wage expectations with what the firm was prepared to pay. This underlying theoretical framework has been subject to considerable criticism (e.g. almost a 'conspiracy' theory of union leadership),[102] but certainly the estimation side of Ashenfelter and Johnson's work has stimulated many subsequent studies. Pencavel, for example, sought to account for variation in strike frequency in Britain,[103] using quarterly data for the years 1950–67, by estimating a trend-cycle model whose variables included a time trend, unemployment, a moving average of real-wage change, profits, quarterly seasonal dummies, and 'political' variables (i.e. incomes policy in operation and the Labour Party in office). The variables were generally statistically significant and correctly signed with a reasonably high overall level of explanatory power being achieved; the political variables were only significant when introduced in an interaction form. There have been similar studies in Britain and elsewhere,[104] although the level of criticism of the basic approach has increased substantially in recent years.[105] Among the leading individual criticisms of this line of research are the following:

1. These bargaining theory, macro-level estimation models have overwhelmingly sought to explain variation in strike frequency. And when the same models are used to try and account for variation in other dimensions of strike activity, such as strike duration, their overall level of explanatory power falls dramatically.
2. The models appear to be unstable in that the level of explanatory power achieved, even for strike frequency alone, appears to be satisfactory only for particular periods of time. The fact that such models appear to work reasonably well for certain periods of time but over- or under-predict when the data series is lengthened (backwards or forwards), has led to the suggestion that specific models need to be developed for specific periods of time.
3. A good deal of the overall explanatory power of the models comes from non-substantive, control variables, such as the time-trend and seasonal-dummy variables; no clearly specified, underlying behavioural relationships appear to account for the significance of these variables.
4. The models often appear to involve aggregation bias in that individual variables which perform reasonably well at the aggregate level are frequently insignificant and/or enter with odd signs when used to examine variation in strike frequency in the individual industries that make up the aggregate data set; the explanatory power of the models appears to be highly sensitive to the industrial composition of the dependent variable.

5. The underlying framework of the analysis is dominated by a wage bargaining focus.
6. The 'distance' between the theoretical and empirical constructs is so great that the proxy variables which are statistically significant are capable of numerous, often contradictory, interpretations.

It is possible to identify two basic lines of reaction against aggregate, time-series, economic models of strike activity. The first tends to reject the value of this level of analysis, arguing that what is required is well-grounded studies of strikes and conflict at the micro-level where they actually occur. This could involve studies of strikes 'in the context of the struggle for control as a whole'[106] in individual establishments, or more individual-employee-based explanations which draw on the insights of various disciplines.[107] The second line of response accepts the value of the aggregate level of analysis but utilizes a rather different underlying theoretical framework. This could take the form of rejecting the relevance of a single, all-encompassing model over an extended period of time, and estimating separate models for particular periods of time in which certain unique (time-specific) variables are especially emphasized. Alternatively, one could still continue to rely on a single model, but one which is very different to the bargaining-theory-based approach of economists. The leading study in this regard is arguably that of Shorter and Tilly, which views industrial conflict as essentially political in nature and hence closely related to wider, society-level struggles for power.[108] In their study of industrial conflict in France over the years 1830–1968 they emphasize, for example, that: (i) the timing of strikes has frequently been related to political occurrences; (ii) large-scale and brief strikes are often political demonstrations; and (iii) there has been a general relationship between major strike movements and the changing political party position. The comparative study by Korpi and Shalev also seeks to interpret strikes in relation to larger political arrangements and developments.[109]

Some key determinants of the structure and process of collective bargaining

As indicated in the previous section, a number of studies of both inter-industry and inter-establishment variation in strike activity have revealed a significant, positive relationship with establishment size. Indeed, 'large establishment size' has undoubtedly been the independent variable which has been most extensively investigated in British industrial-relations research. In addition to its role in strike studies, this variable has been shown to be a major determinant of: aspects of union organization (e.g. positive relationships with the level of union membership, collective bargaining coverage, and well-developed shop-steward systems); aspects of management organization (e.g. the presence of a specialist industrial-relations director); the nature of bargaining structure (e.g. a positive relationship with single-employer bargaining structures); the presence of particular institutional arrangements (e.g. a positive relationship with the presence of a joint health and safety committee); and to be positively associated with certain outcome measures such as the level of wages. In view of these (and other) relationships it is hardly surprising that a number of commentators have highlighted the trend towards a smaller, average plant size in Britain (i.e. the mean size of manufacturing-sector establishments was 92 in 1963, 86 in 1970, 64 in 1977, 61 in 1979, and 59 in 1981)[110] as having important implications for the future shape of industrial-relations arrangements.

However, as has been emphasized in this chapter (and other previous ones), it needs to be recognized, first, that any statistical association with establishment size may be due to a variety of underlying, behavioural relationships which can rarely be differentiated between on the basis of the available data. Second, the exact basis on which 'large size' has been defined and measured has varied considerably between individual studies, which tends to complicate any precise comparison of results. Third, only a relatively small number of studies have investigated in any detail the precise nature of the underlying relationship with size and the phenomenon in question; does, for example, strike activity increase proportionately with size?[111] Fourth, not all of the hypothesized relationships (e.g. the level of industrial accidents) with large size have been empirically confirmed. This may be due to the fact that certain offsetting action (according to contingency theory) taken by management has effectively prevented a possible relationship (or one which was apparent in an earlier period of time) being an empirical reality in the particular time period which was the subject of the study.[112] Finally, it needs to be recognized that some conceptual discussions of certain relationships which allegedly flow from large plant size appear to involve more than the effect of size *per se*. For example, the above average level of non-pecuniary job dissatisfaction which is alleged to characterize large plants is frequently held to be the result of a combination of poor communications and a relatively regimented working environment with a high degree of individual task specialization. The latter would appear to be more of a technology (than a size) effect, which means that the nature of technology needs to be fully controlled for in studies concerned with the effect of size, *ceteris paribus*; unfortunately, such controls have not always been present in the studies which have been conducted.

The nature of technology was in fact one of the key determinants of the content of the web of rules in Dunlop's original exposition of the systems model of industrial relations. However, it has been organization theorists and industrial sociologists whose research has traditionally been most concerned with the influence of technology. The nature of technology was one of the key determinants of organizational structure in the contingency-theory attacks of the 1960s on the 'one-best-way-to-manage' school of thought,[13] while Blauner's well-known study postulated an inverted U-curve relationship between worker alienation and the nature of technology[114] (i.e. craft, machine-tending, mass and process production). Blauner's work, together with Woodward's observation that industrial relations appeared to be less satisfactory in organizations with large batch and mass production (compared to organizations with either unit and small batch or process production), which she speculated may be due to wider spans of control, a lower proportion of skilled workers, a tendency towards more formal management, more dependence on staff specialists, and more formalized internal communications,[115] stimulated some studies by industrial-relations researchers on the relationship between strike activity and the nature of technology. In general, such studies have not identified the strong, positive relationship between strike activity and large batch/mass production that was hypothesized to exist;[116] such studies, however, have often failed to distinguish between all strikes and unofficial, 'wildcat' strikes – the latter ones being those most likely to be associated with the nature of technology. The limited extent, and narrowly focused body, of industrial-relations research on technology in the 1960s and 1970s is now all but forgotten in the current upsurge of research activity on the subject of new technology. The more recent work on this subject, which has been stimulated by the increased practical application of micro-electronics technology and Braverman's deskilling hypothesis,[117] will be considered in Chapter 9.

In more recent years, industrial-relations researchers in Britain have paid increased attention to the subject of large-organization, as opposed to large-establishment, size. This re-orientation of interest is a pragmatic response to the occurrence of the merger process (see Chapter 4) which has produced a situation whereby:

> Much of the classic heartland of British industry is exceptionally dominated by a small number of enterprises. In shipbuilding and marine engineering, for example, the five largest enterprises shared three-quarters of the employees in the industry, while in vehicles seven enterprises each with 20,000 workers employed 57.4 per cent of the industry's employees in 1978. In electrical engineering, six enterprises each with over 20,000 workers employed 37 per cent of the employees in the industry.[118]

Moreover, with a number of studies indicating how industrial-relations structures and behaviour at the plant level are strongly shaped by higher-level, decision-making processes concerning investment matters and product policy,[119] the study of the effect of large-organization size, *ceteris paribus*, on the structures, processes, and outcomes of industrial relations (at the establishment level) will clearly gather momentum, particularly as survey-data sets begin to gather information for corporate and divisional levels, as well as for the individual-establishment level. Indeed, one existing study has already revealed some separate company, as distinct from plant, size effects on strike activity, the level of unionization and the specialization of industrial-relations management.[120] Organization size is only currently being researched as a major determinant of industrial-relations structure, processes, and outcomes – whereas foreign ownership, as well as establishment size, has been a focus of industrial-relations research in Britain for some considerable time. Moreover, with some 16 per cent of manufacturing employment accounted for by foreign owned firms at the present time,[121] it is hardly surprising that a good deal of industrial-relations research will continue to concentrate on this particular subject.

Foreign ownership and multinational companies (MNCs)

Trade unions in Britain have traditionally expressed a number of worries, concerns and criticisms of the operation of foreign-owned firms. The major points made in this regard have essentially been the following ones:[122]

1. Foreign-owned firms tend to ignore the traditional industrial-relations conventions and practices of Britain. Specifically it has been contended that a relatively high proportion of them are non-union establishments, with the unionized ones tending not to join employers' associations or be parties to multi-employer, industry-level, collective-bargaining arrangements. (The latter

criticism has obviously receded with the general movement towards single employer bargaining structures from the 1970s.) Conversely, they will import employment practices (e.g. quality circles) developed in their own country which can conflict with, and undermine, traditional, collective-bargaining arrangements.

2. Foreign-owned firms can undermine the effectiveness of any industrial action in Britain by switching production to 'less militant' plants in other countries.
3. In wage bargaining, the capacity to pay of foreign-owned establishments cannot be readily and meaningfully identified, due to the use of sophisticated (internal) transfer-pricing arrangements.
4. It is difficult to identify and gain access to the real source of decision-making authority in such organizations, particularly in proposed redundancy situations.
5. The larger global strategies of such organizations will not involve a strong and sustained employment commitment to any one country, with the result that host countries like Britain are vulnerable to plant closures and employment run-downs, with the procedures contained in national legislation (e.g. for joint consultation over redundancies) having little capacity to affect such decisions.
6. The capacity of foreign-owned firms to play the governments of potential and actual host countries off against each other can result in considerable behind-the-scenes pressures being exerted by governments on union leaders to 'behave responsibly in the national interest'.

The union response to such fears and problems can take a variety of forms. One approach is to seek national-level legislation and associated arrangements (e.g. codes of practice) which contain individual provisions specifically orientated towards multi- or trans-national corporations. A number of the provisions of the ACAS Code of Practice on information disclosure for collective bargaining purposes (1977), for example, appear to have such an orientation, and certainly some of the leading union claims under Sections 17–21 of the Employment Protection Act 1975 have involved multinational firms (e.g. *British Timken* v. *AUEW and EETPU* 85/3). Second, such legal and administrative regulation can be sought from organizations, agencies, and bodies whose remit and authority transcends that of a single country. The most well-known initiatives in this regard include the International Labour Organization's Code of Practice (1977), and the guidelines of the Organization for Economic Co-operation and Development (1976). There are also various harmonization directives of the

European Economic Community[123] (e.g. joint procedures for handling redundancies, employee rights in a takeover situation) which are relevant – although not exclusively directed at multinational organizations – but the draft 'Vredeling' Directive (first proposed in 1980) which deals with employee rights to information and consultation is primarily concerned with such firms.[124] The industrial-relations section of the guidelines produced by the OECD, for example, cover some eight items – namely, the right to union representation, the provision of facilities and disclosure of information, standards of employment, employment and training of the local labour force, notice of employment reductions, non-discriminatory employment policies, access to centres of decision-making authority, and the non-use of threats to change operations between countries. These guidelines, which are not legally enforceable (the same with those of the ILO), were reviewed in 1979 and 1984, with some procedural, but no substantive, changes resulting;[125] between these two reviews the Trade Union Advisory Committee to the OECD brought some eighteen cases of alleged infringements of the guidelines to the attention of the relevant committee.[126] There has been no overall systematic study of the impact of these guidlines, although there have been a number of discussions of major cases of infringement (e.g. those involving the Badger company in Belgium and the Hertz corporation in Denmark) and the issues raised by them.[127]

There have, of course, been various initiatives taken by individual unions in an attempt to develop some form of collective-bargaining arrangements across national systems. For example, shop stewards involved in strike action have on occasions visited subsidiaries of multinational firms in other countries in an attempt to prevent production switching, officers from individual unions have met to exchange information on the collective-bargaining issues and problems involved in dealing with particular organizations, but the most well-publicized initiatives have involved the work of the International Metal Workers Federation, and the International Federation of Chemical and General Workers Unions, in establishing councils and international committees for leading multinational companies; for example, world auto councils were first set up by the former organization in 1966. There have been numerous discussions of the difficulties that such councils and committees face in attempting to develop integrated and co-ordinated collective-bargaining arrangements;[128] differences in bargaining structure and legal restrictions on secondary industrial action being among the most frequently mentioned difficulties. Moreover, the programme of research conducted at the Wharton

School in the 1970s has largely discounted union claims concerning the extent and depth of international collective-bargaining arrangements and activities.[129]

In the 1970s, the stream of industrial-relations research in Britain concerned with the influence of foreign ownership, overwhelmingly consisted of, first, case studies of the degree of centralization/decentralization in industrial-relations decision-making within individual organizations and, second, studies of the comparative levels of strike activity of foreign- and domestically-owned establishments; the less than adequate data sets utilized in the latter studies, however, tended to produce a rather mixed set of results and findings.[130] The increased appearance of sizeable survey data sets from the late 1970s, however, permitted a broader range of issues and hypotheses to be examined – with foreign owned firms being found to have, for example, relatively well-developed personnel-management functions and to favour single-employer bargaining structures.[131] One of the most recent survey-based studies, which covered some 143 enterprises, produced the following findings:[132]

1. There was little difference between foreign- and domestically-owned enterprises with regard to union recognition, the extent of collective bargaining, the use of formal dispute procedures, and the experience of industrial action.
2. Foreign-owned enterprises made more extensive use of human-resource management techniques in matters of employee communication and commitment (e.g. quality circles).
3. Foreign-owned firms devoted more resources to the personnel-management function at both the corporate and establishment levels than domestically-owned enterprises.
4. Corporate-level measures to monitor and control industrial-relations practices at the establishment level were more a feature of foreign-owned than British-owned enterprises.

This desirable tendency to look beyond the issue of strike activity in studies of the influence of foreign ownership on industrial relations practices is likely to continue in Britain in the future. Moreover, future studies are likely to pay increased attention to certain changes in the nature and composition of multinational investment in Britain and elsewhere. For example, as international joint ventures become increasingly important relative to wholly-owned subsidiaries in foreign investment streams, the personnel-management and industrial-relations practices, effects, and implications of the former type of organizations (which involve companies from two or more different countries) are likely to be an important area for future research; in particular, the integrated European market developments of the 1990s are likely to stimulate the establishment of such organizations. Furthermore, foreign-owned firms in Britain involve a considerable number of different countries of origin, whose potentially heterogeneous industrial-relations policies and practices need to be more fully reflected in the methodology and substantive content of research studies. Indeed, Enderwick has argued that both industrial-relations researchers and trade unions have an overly static conception of the foreign investment process as being dominated by large, US-based manufacturing enterprises with technically determined competitive advantages.[133]

This particular criticism has in some respects lost a good deal of its strength in the 1980s with the upsurge of research interest in Japanese management practices and employment policies. This particular re-orientation of research reflects the fact that the increasingly competitive product-market environment of the 1980s has produced very considerable British and US management interest in the subjects of organizational flexibility, corporate culture, and individual employee commitment to the organization – which are practices and arrangements very much associated with the leading Japanese companies. In his well-known book, William Ouchi contrasted Japanese and American organizations along the following lines:[134]

Japanese organizations	*American organizations*
Life-time employment	Short-term employment
Slow evaluation and promotion	Rapid evaluation and promotion
Non-specialized career paths	Specialized career paths
Implicit control mechanisms	Explicit control mechanisms
Collective decision-making	Individual decision-making
Collective responsibility	Individual responsibility
Holistic concern	Segmented concern

Ouchi went on to recommend the adoption of a Type Z organizational form (i.e. a modified American one) involving long-term employment, consensual decision-making, individual responsibility, slow evaluation and promotion, implicit informal control with explicit formalized measures, moderately specialized career paths, and a holistic concern. The above sort of characterization of the Japanese organization has, however, been subject to the criticism that (i) certain features and practices (e.g. life-time employment) are not as widespread or typical as alleged and

(ii) some features and practices have come about for rather different reasons than those given by Ouchi.[135] Nevertheless, recent studies of various national systems of industrial-relations have invariably suggested that the Japanese one responded most effectively to the various economic shocks of the late 1970s and early 1980s.[136] This fact has led to numerous discussions of the potential for adopting Japanese industrial-relations practices in other national systems,[137] with one such study suggesting that:

> Although culture undoubtedly played a role, recent research suggests that historical factors were a significant influence in the 1950s when much of the present Japanese system was put in place. Pivotal events in the period included the long strike at Nissan and the restructuring of the union movement which included a replacement of radical leadership. This historical perspective suggests that the industrial-relations system in Japan's auto industry comprises a set of institutions successfully introduced in a period of crisis and not strictly determined or bound by cultural traditions.[138]

A number of other studies have also suggested that the key features of the Japanese system of industrial relations, namely life-employment (for about one-third of the total workforce), the seniority wage system, the extensive use of bonus payments, enterprise unionism and synchronized annual wage bargaining, owe relatively little to cultural influences, being relatively recent pragmatic adaptations to constraints and problems.[139] However, in considering the potential for adoption of Japanese practices in Western systems of industrial relations, it has been argued that: (i) individual Japanese employment practices tend to be mutually reinforcing and may not be separable from other features of the total system; (ii) there is some disagreement about the particular lesson to be learned from Japan. To some individuals the Japanese example emphasizes the need to restore management's right to manage, whereas to others the basic message is to build co-operative structures and relationships at the level of the individual enterprise. In short:

> It is indicative of the unique character of the Japanese industrial-relations system and the difficulties Westerners have in understanding it that the Japanese experience is cited to support two opposing recommendations on how to make Western labor relations more competitive.[140]

The debate about the transferability of Japanese management and industrial-relations practices has inevitably resulted in studies of Japanese-owned subsidiaries operating in countries such as Britain and America. These studies have been particularly concerned with how many (and which) practices have been transferred, the response of the workforce to these arrangements, and the relative performance levels of these subsidiary operations; in Britain, for example, SP Tyres UK Ltd (owned by Sumitomo Rubber Industries Ltd) has converted the annual losses of about £20 million (at Dunlop Holdings PLC) in the early 1980s into a small profit in 1987, with 50 per cent more tyres being produced by 30 per cent fewer workers. Final offer (or pendulum) arbitration arrangements, which are an integral part of the controversial, single-union, no-strike package agreements of the EETPU in the 1980s, have acquired something of a reputation as a Japanese practice because of the fact that the first such agreement involved Toshiba Consumer Products in Plymouth in 1981; in fact, final-offer arbitration arrangements were pioneered in certain public-sector employment jurisdictions in the United States. The twenty-one single-union, no-strike agreements known to exist in mid to late 1986 (which involved some 5,000 union members),[141] include five Japanese companies, although to these can be added Nissan and Komatsu single-recognition agreements with the AEU. These package agreements – which typically include single-union recognition, equal conditions for manual and office staff, flexible work practices, an advisory board of elected staff representatives (not necessarily union members) empowered to discuss a wide range of matters, final-offer arbitration arrangements, and a union commitment to settle disputes without resort to industrial action – have been marketed by the EETPU in Japan as a set of arrangements that offers management something like the enterprise unionism which they are used to and favour; such agreements are obviously of interest to more than just Japanese management, as has been dramatically illustrated by Ford's decision not to go ahead with its plans for a £40 million components plant in Dundee because of difficulties in negotiating a single-union recognition agreement. More generally, however, the work of White and Trevor has suggested that: (i) Japanese subsidiaries in Britain are not characterized by distinctively Japanese employment practices; (ii) employees in such establishments report only average levels of job satisfaction, although (iii) the issues of recruitment and training in these subsidiaries were relatively high management priorities; and (iv) the distinctive profile of working practices in them consisted of an organized or orderly approach, an emphasis on detail, an overriding priority attached to quality, and a punctilious sense of discipline.[142] The general impression conveyed by this study is that of a pragmatic response by Japanese management to local conditions, with a resulting diversity of personnel management practices between the various Japanese organizations concerned; such themes will undoubtedly be pursued in future studies of Japanese subsidiaries operating in Britain. A related body of work is also likely to emerge on individual British organizations which have adopted some of the arrangements and practices favoured by Japanese companies.[143]

In this chapter, and others, we have had occasion to refer to the notion or concept of union power. The potential importance of this concept in shaping the outcomes of the collective-bargaining process follows from the inherent conflict of interests embedded in employment relationships, and the fact that the individual parties involved in such relationships are expected to try and achieve outcomes which largely reflect their self-interested aims. The concept of power has, of course, been of interest to more than simply industrial-relations researchers. Indeed, the work of political scientists has been particularly important in indicating that a concentration on the outcome of joint decision-making or bargaining processes in a potential conflict situation is a very narrow perspective to adopt on the notion of power in that it ignores two other important dimensions of power – namely (i) the use of power to exclude certain items from the actual processes of bargaining, and (ii) the use of power to limit perceptions of the reality of a conflict situation.[144] However, in the final section of this chapter we concentrate solely on the conceptual, as opposed to empirical, treatments of union power which have been developed by industrial-relations researchers, although some mention will also be made of the approach favoured by organization theorists.

The concept of union power

Even the concentration on only this single dimension of power has produced relatively limited agreement among industrial-relations researchers as to what constitutes and determines relative bargaining power. Some relatively early treatments of the subject did little more than list the potential determinants of bargaining power as (i) the tastes of workers and employers with respect to wages and hours bought and sold, (ii) market conditions, especially the degree and type of competition, and (iii) 'pure' bargaining power which involves the ability to obtain favourable bargains independently of market conditions.[145] This sort of approach has been subject to the criticism that 'power is determined by virtually everything', which makes the concept essentially an 'intellectual blunderbuss' with virtually no operational content.[146] Nevertheless, some industrial-relations researchers continue to draw distinctions between (i) primary or derived sources of power, which are exogenous to short-run union influence and control (e.g. the extent of product-market competition), and (ii) secondary sources of power which are subject to union control in the short run (e.g. particular bargaining strategies and tactics).[147]

The single treatment of power which still remains the most popular, conceptual one with industrial-relations researchers is that originally proposed by Chamberlain, and subsequently refined by him in conjunction with Kuhn.[148] The essence of this approach is that bargaining power is the capacity of a party to produce agreement on its own terms, with this capacity being based on the ratio of the opponents' costs of disagreeing on the party's terms to the opponents' costs of agreeing on those terms. The result is that the relative bargaining power of a union increases as management's costs of disagreement (with the union's demands) increase, or as management's costs of agreement with the union demands fall. Furthermore:

> Only if the difference to management between the cost of disagreement and agreement on labor's terms is proportionately greater than the difference to labor between the costs of disagreement and agreement on management's terms can one say that labor's bargaining power is greater than management's.[149]

Among the major specific points made in their treatment of the subject were the following: (i) bargaining power is very much a subjective concept because of the importance of tactical manipulation and influence; (ii) bargaining power is not invariant with respect to time; (iii) the relevant costs involved are a mixture of monetary and non-monetary ones; and (iv) bargaining power is a broader concept that simply the striking and resistance capacities of the parties.

The extent of subseqent conceptual and empirical refinements and developments of the approach of Chamberlain and Kuhn has been rather limited and disappointing. This is because many industrial-relations researchers have, at least implicitly, placed it within the control/sanction approach to power which treats bargaining power as the ability of parties to sanction or punish each other; bargaining power is, in short, a function of offensive and defensive capabilities. The result is that attempts to 'operationalize' the approach of Chamberlain and Kuhn have frequently involved little more than an identification of the factors (e.g. extent of plant interdependence, level of fixed costs, degree of brand preference) that shape the differing costs of strike action in different bargaining situations.

It is organization theorists who have arguably made much more of a substantive contribution to the development and refinement of the concept of power in bargaining theory. Although much of their work is laboratory-, as opposed to fieldwork-based, organization theorists have devoted considerable attention to the issues of motivation to bargain, and the cognitive and tactical components of bargaining power.[150] Moreover, in their conceptual and empirical examinations of inter-departmental (or intra-management) conflict within organizations, they have tended to pursue and develop a power-dependence approach (as mentioned in Chapter 4), which essentially holds that A has power over B to the extent that A controls resources which B values, and B has few alternative means of obtaining these resources.[151] Furthermore, as mentioned earlier in this chapter, organization theorists have developed the concept of conflict episodes proceeding from latency, feeling, perception, manifestation, and aftermath,[152] an approach which has stimulated some work along similar lines by industrial-relations researchers; Marchington's discussion of the four stages of power capacity, power realization, power testing and power outcomes at the work-group level is one such example.[153] Indeed, industrial-relations researchers, or at least some of them, appear to have become increasingly conscious of their rather limited contribution (compared to that of organization theorists) to the development of the concept of bargaining power. This fact is reflected in a recent overview paper which argued that a comprehensive theory of collective-bargaining power must address the specific issues of: the availability and control of resources; potential vs. enacted power; tactical uses of power; absolute, relative and total power; and the variability of power and power sources.[154]

Conclusions

The final section of this chapter has deliberately restricted itself to conceptual treatments of bargaining power. However, in the next chapter we are concerned with the outcomes of the collective bargaining process – i.e. the dependent variables in the model. In considering the findings of various studies, particular attention will be given to empirical treatments and representations of the concept of union power.

Chapter seven

Collective bargaining and the interaction with the environment

Some preliminary considerations

In Chapter 2 we discussed the influence of environmental forces on the structure, processes, and outcomes of collective bargaining, whereas here we acknowledge the fact that there is not a single, one-way line of causation between the environment and collective bargaining. This is because the outcomes of collective bargaining will, in turn, have an impact on the environment, via a relationship that Alton Craig has termed a 'feedback loop'.[1] The essence of the feedback-loop concept is that the outputs of the industrial-relations system (in, for example, period t) become inputs into the environment (in, for example, period t + 1), and subsequently through their effects on the environment flow back into the industrial-relations system (in, for example, period t + 2) as part of the continuing inputs. The nature of the feedback loop is potentially important in (i) shaping the nature of public-policy intervention in the industrial-relations system (to be discussed in Chapter 8), and (ii) effecting both the short-run and longer-run goal-attainment of employers which can, in turn, produce certain employer-adjustment processes that can have important implications for the future shape of the industrial-relations system. For example, in recent years researchers in both Britain and the United States have repeatedly stressed that the overall level of union density in the two systems is, and will continue to be, strongly determined by the attitudes and actions of individual employers towards the institution of unionism. However, it has to be conceded that the nature of both the short-run and longer-run processes of employer adjustment to the outcomes of collective bargaining remains essentially shrouded in mystery. Admittedly, the primary effect of unions operating via collective bargaining arrangements is held to be on wages, with economists discussing the nature of the employer-adjustment response in terms of a capital-for-labour substitution process, and industrial-relations researchers pointing to the possibility of a 'shock effect' whereby the employer makes, for example, changes in the nature of supervisory relations, and in intra-management structural arrangements and decision-making processes. But in both Britain and the United States there is a very real need for discussion along such lines to be much more informed by the results of systematic empirical research; both systems in fact urgently require a modern-day equivalent of the work of Slichter, Healy, and Livernash.[2]

In this chapter we examine the results of a number of studies which have looked at some of the larger environmental impacts of collective bargaining. The earlier part of this chapter is essentially concerned with macro-level impacts – such as the size of the union relative-wage effect, the influence of unions on the rate of money and real wage change, their effects on the distribution of national income between wages and profits and on the level and rate of growth of productivity. In considering the findings of such studies there are a number of important issues and considerations to bear in mind, some of which have been touched on in previous chapters. These include, first, the all-important question of whether the worth and value of collective bargaining arrangements in any system of political democracy can and should be exclusively, or even largely, assessed in an economic cost–benefit framework of analysis. Second, it needs to be recognized that the vast majority of these macro-impact type studies have been conducted by economists and, as Freeman and Medoff have emphasized, such researchers have overwhelmingly been concerned with the monopoly face of unionism.[3] In other words, there is something of a problem of balance in the existing research literature with studies of the alleged efficiency costs of unions far outnumbering studies of the potential benefits of unionism to society at large via the collective voice/institutional response face of unionism. Third, a number of studies of the impact of collective bargaining appear to interpret their findings as being overwhelmingly the result of union-side demands and behaviour, and thus appear to ignore the simple dictum that 'collective bargaining is a two-party process and that employer resistance is as much a part of the process as union demands';[4] as indicated in an earlier chapter, for example, attempts to model the nature of union demands in wage bargaining far outnumber any studies concerned with the nature of management demands in such bargaining. Finally, one needs to be aware of some of the major criticisms made by industrial-relations researchers of much of the macro-impact type of work conducted by economists. There are in fact two major lines of criticism of such work. The first is the argument that outcome-orientated studies of the union impact, or the average union effect, are essentially misplaced exercises because individual unions in a single national system differ to such a great extent in terms of their basic organizational practices and arrangements. The second criticism centres on studies which have sought to proxy 'union power' by the use of a single, objective measure such as the level of strike frequency or the overall level of union density. To many industrial relations researchers, union power is a complex, multi-dimensional concept which, as the concluding section of the previous chapter suggested, contains many subjective, situation-specific elements that cannot be adequately, much less fully, encapsulated by a single objective measure. It is in fact the inadequacy of 'the popular' proxies for union power that is mentioned at a number of points in this chapter.

The main portion of the chapter is followed by a focus on the individual organization, the importance of the latter level of analysis being due to the fact that the nature of the individual employer adjustment (or response) to the workings of collective bargaining will not simply be a function of macro-level impacts (e.g. the size of the union relative-wage effect) and influences (e.g. increasing product-market competition). There will, in fact, be a substantial contingency-based element in the nature of any such adjustment processes, so that it is essential to consider the following sorts of questions: (i) what is the evidence that 'good/poor' industrial relations performance is strongly related to 'good/poor' economic performance at the level of the individual organization? and (ii) what are the measures, and determinants, of a 'good collective bargaining relationship' at the level of the individual organization? These are questions which we hope to show require a great deal more research in Britain, and indeed in other national systems of industrial relations, in the future.

The size of the union relative-wage effect

The union relative-wage effect (variously referred to as the 'union mark-up' or 'wage gap') concerns the size of the wage advantage that unionized workers enjoy over non-unionized workers, everything else held constant. The earliest work along these lines in the United States estimated this effect indirectly, by comparing the average wage of more-organized groups of workers with the average wage of less-organized groups, with the revealed difference being attributed to the extent of unionization.[5] In more recent years, however, it has been possible to estimate this wage effect directly in the United States as a result of the availability of micro-data sets in which the unit of observation is either the individual employee or the individual establishment.[6] The available evidence for the United States suggests that the size of the union relative-wage effect has risen substantially through the course of time from some 10–15 per cent in the 1950s and 1960s to 25–30 per cent by the end of the 1970s.[7] The reasons for this rise through time are not entirely clear, although a macro-economic environment of high and rising unemployment has clearly played a part.[8] Furthermore, economists have argued that this large and rising union relative-wage effect goes a considerable way towards explaining the current extent of employer opposition to union organization in the United States.[9]

There are a number of both long-standing and more recent concerns with, not to say criticisms of, estimates of the size of the union relative-wage effect – which, essentially, transcend the institutional arrangements of particular national industrial-relations systems.[10] First, there is the problem posed by the fact that unions can potentially influence non-union wages, in either a positive or negative fashion. This may occur through normal market channels (i.e. changes in the relative demand for and supply of labour between the two sectors) or through the 'threat effect' which involves non-union employers seeking to minimize any threat of unionization among their employees by paying the relevant unionized rate; this effect causes empirical estimates of the union relative-wage effect to underestimate the extent of the full effect. A second issue has been the concern that existing estimates of the union relative-wage effect may contain an upward bias due to a failure to adequately control and account for other relevant wage determinants that are significantly correlated with the extent of unionization. The concern typically expressed here is that an element of the estimated effect may be essentially a 'compensating differential' deriving from a failure to fully account for differences in labour quality and working conditions between the unionized and non-unionized groups of workers – the union sector being held to have high-quality labour but poorer, non-pecuniary working conditions. A further line of criticism contends that there is not a single, straightforward line of causation from unions to higher wages, hence the union relative-wage effect cannot be appropriately estimated by an ordinary, least-squares, regression equation in which unionism is an exogenous variable; this is because the level of unionism is alleged to be as much a function of higher wages as a cause of them (hence a simultaneous estimating procedure is held to be essential). This particular criticism, however, has been subject to considerable counter-criticism on both theoretical and empirical grounds.[11] More recently, Lewis has argued that it is union status, rather than the extent of unionism, which is the critical variable that must be present in estimates of the union relative wage effect.[12]

This latter observation is particularly important in Britain in view of the fact that most studies of the union relative-wage effect, which have been based on *New Earnings Survey* data (for 1973 and 1978), have not in fact contained a union-status variable. These inter-industry studies, which tended to produce relatively high estimates (i.e. frequently 20–25 per cent) of the wage return associated with the extent of collective-bargaining coverage, have also been subject to a number of other critical comments.[13] Moreover, recent British studies which have used a different data source (e.g. the 1975 National Training Survey) to that of the *New Earnings Survey*, and included a union-status variable, have estimated a much smaller-sized, union wage gap of only some 8 per cent in the 1970s.[14] Some extensions to this latter piece of work have suggested that the union relative wage effect in Britain was some 5 per cent in the 1960s, 8 per cent in the 1970s, and 11 per cent in the early 1980s.[15] Most recently, economists in Britain have produced a number of estimates which indicate that the size of the union relative-wage effect is greater when closed-shop arrangements exist, and that more sizeable effects are apparent for women, black, unskilled, and disabled workers.[16]

The results of individual British and US studies are not always strictly comparable because, for example, the British studies have been much more narrowly confined to male workers in the manufacturing sector. In general, however, it would appear from the more recent work in the two systems that the union relative-wage effect in the US (i.e. 25–30 per cent) was considerably greater than that in Britain (i.e. 8 per cent) in the 1970s, despite the fact that the overall level of union organization in the former was relatively low (i.e. less than 25 per cent overall union density) and falling, whereas in the latter system it was relatively high (i.e. more than 50 per cent overall union density) and rising in those years. The 1970s certainly witnessed Britain moving much closer to the US system of industrial relations in the sense of being increasingly based on single-employer (i.e. plant and company level) bargaining structures, but there were (and remain) important institutional differences between the two systems which could have important implications for the respective sizes of the union relative-wage effect. These differences include the following:

1. The threat effect (mentioned earlier) can to some extent be institutionalized in a national system of industrial relations by the

passage of laws and regulations that require the payment of the going industry/collectively-bargained wage. Such institutionalization has been much more a feature of the British than the American system of industrial relations – with the Terms and Conditions of Employment Act 1959, Schedule 11 of the Employment Protection Act 1975, and the 1946 Fair Wages Resolution of the House of Commons all being operative in the former during the 1970s. The result is likely to be much less sizeable intra-industry, union-relative wage effects in Britain than in the United States.

2. Collective agreements in the US are legally enforceable and typically of some 2–3 years' duration – a structural feature of the system that makes collectively bargained wages considerably less cyclically sensitive than their non-union counterparts; the resulting ratchet effect is why the size of the union relative-wage effect in the US rises as unemployment increases. This structural explanation of an 'anti-cyclical-size-of-union/relative-wage effect' relationship would appear to have much less applicability in the more informal, open-ended collective-bargaining system of Britain – where there are annual negotiations whose results are not legally enforceable. Having said this, the point was made in Chapter 2 that wage freezes and cuts ('concession bargaining') have been much more a feature of US than British collective bargaining arrangements in the early 1980s.
3. The relatively high level of union security arrangements in collective agreements in the United States means that there is relatively little difference between the extent of unionization and that of collective-bargaining coverage. In Britain there is a considerable size difference between these two measures so that researchers who are concerned to estimate the size of the wage gap cannot use these two terms or measures interchangeably, as tends to be the practice in the United States.

Table 7.1 sets out the basic results of a recent multiple regression estimate of the size of the union wage gap in Britain in 1973 and 1978. These results, which were based on the *New Earnings Survey* returns for 1973 and 1978, indicate a much smaller relative wage effect from the union-status variable than that for the extent of collective bargaining coverage; recall here Lewis's argument that the former, rather than the latter, is the critical variable in such estimates. Indeed, these findings do not diverge greatly from Stewart's estimate of an 8 per cent wage gap attributable to union status in the 1970s (using the National Training Survey data) and hence further reinforce the belief that the size of the union relative-

Table 7.1 The union wage gap in Britain, 1973 and 1978

		Male manual manufacture	*Males (manual)*	*Female manual manufacture*	*Females (manual)*
Wage gap (union status variable)*	1973	2.46	4.15	4.78	7.00
	1978	2.16	3.83	5.33	7.10
Extent of collective bargaining coverage	1973	46.00	54.98	—	11.20
	1978	30.66	12.02	16.28	—

Source: P. B. Beaumont and R. I. D. Harris (1987) 'Collective bargaining and relative wages in Britain: some further evidence for the 1970s', Mimeographed paper, Department of Economics, Queen's University of Belfast.

*This variable was not an individual employee one, but an average of each case of three to five individual employees. (The nature of this data base suggests that the wage gap estimates here are lower limit ones.)

wage effect in Britain is considerably smaller than that which exists in the United States. This difference may, in turn, help explain why British employers are not currently displaying anything like the same extent of opposition to union organization that is the case with their counterparts in the United States. The latter difference is not, however, solely a function of this wage-gap phenomenon, as the discussion of Chapter 10 will indicate.

It is interesting to observe that a number of economists in Britain are now using the union relative-wage effect as a proxy for 'union power' or 'union militancy' in estimating equations of the determinants of real wage change, which are part of their overall framework for explaining the recent rise in unemployment. For example, in their well-known work on this subject, Layard and Nickell stated that:

> The union power variable which we use is worth commenting on because the use of some kind of proxy is inevitable. The one we use is a measure of the union/non-union mark-up, with some correction for skill composition. To be more precise, we run an industry cross-section regression of earnings on a number of factors including union coverage for every year of the sample. The series then consists of the union coverage coefficient for each year. This variable seems to us to represent a good *ex-post* measure of union activity which will reflect fluctuations in the autonomous use of power. For example, it rises strongly in the period 1968–72. This contrasts with the alternative variable

> which is sometimes favoured, namely union density. This seems to us to have a very limited theoretical pedigree as well as appearing to be highly unrobust once the sample period is extended beyond 1979. In fact, our experiments with this variable indicate that it is empirically more or less useless as a measure of union power.[17]

The results of their estimation work for the period of the early 1950s to the early 1980s suggest that the increase in the size of the trade-union mark-up since the 1960s has raised wage pressure by 3 or 4 percentage points and unemployment by 2–3 percentage points; the latter is a very much smaller effect than that obtained by Minford, who used union density as a proxy for union power.[18] In considering the use of the union mark-up as a proxy for union power in explanations of real wage and unemployment change, there are a number of points to bear in mind. First, the movement of this particular proxy is quite different from that of other frequently used proxies for union power – i.e. the former rose after 1979, whereas union density and strike frequency have fallen. Second, the explanation for the rise of the union relative-wage effect in an environment of high and rising unemployment (i.e. post 1979) in Britain always makes reference to the earlier work of Lewis in the United States (i.e. the ratchet effect), but without acknowledging that such a structural explanation does not, as we noted earlier, carry over in a straightforward manner to the British system; this is because of the fact that Britain does not have the 2–3-year-duration, legally enforceable, collective contracts that exist in the US. Third, when this basic framework of analysis has been applied in cross-country comparisons, the union mark-up has been the proxy for union power in Britain, whereas in other countries in the study it has been some measure of industrial conflict which has been used.[19] In view of the first point made above, this would appear to raise some questions about the comparability of the results which emerge.

Union power and money and real-wage change

In Britain it has been the empirical work of Hines that has been particularly prominent in stimulating discussions of the union role in independently (of the demand for labour) generating wage inflationary pressures. According to Hines, it was not the level of unionization, but rather the rate of change of unionization which was important in explaining the rate of change of money wages.[20]

The latter, rather than the former, variable was held to be a proxy for union power or union militancy, in that:

> When unions are being aggressive they simultaneously increase their membership and bid up wage rates. Suppose that when their membership increases unions feel stronger and become more intransigent in the wage bargain. Suppose further that, as union activity on the shop floor increases, the workers become more militant so that employers are left in no doubt that were strike action to be taken, it would effectively close down the business. Employers would then be more willing to concede wage increases. In such circumstances, union officials would regard a successful membership drive as a necessary accompaniment of success in the wage bargain. Therefore, when a union puts in a wage claim it would seek immediately *before* and *during* the period of negotiation to increase its bargaining power by increasing the proportion of the labour force over which it has direct control. Since it will be shown that the rate of change of unionisation is uncorrelated with the demand for labour [$\triangle$t] may be taken to be an index of cost push. It reflects the intensity of union activity which simultaneously manifests itself in wage claims and in the attitude to bargaining.[21]

The rate of change in money wages was regressed by Hines on the change in unionization for various time periods since 1893, while controlling for other factors (e.g. the level of unemployment and the rate of change in prices) – with a significant, positive relationship between them being apparent in the original aggregate-level study, and in a subsequent, more disaggregated one.[22] However, as the earlier quoted comment of Layard and Nickell indicated, there have been numerous criticisms on both conceptual and empirical grounds of the rate of change of unionization as a proxy for union power. For example, Purdy and Zis have argued that the quality and value of any proxy for union power in wage inflation studies should be assessed according to the following standards:[23]

(i) the degree of subjectivity involved in the construction of the proxy should be minimized;
(ii) the proxy should be sensitive to all the considerable annual variation in the degree of independent pressure brought to bear by the unions on the wage bargain;
(iii) the proxy should as far as possible be an unambiguous measure for union power which is not capable of other interpretations.

(iv) the proxy should be justified in terms of a reasonably well formulated theory of wage determination, rather than being introduced on essentially *ad hoc* grounds.

A good deal of the criticism of the rate of change of unionization as a proxy for union power in the Hines formulation has centred around points (ii) to (iv) above. For example, the fact that unionization changed little during the course of the 1960s (i.e. 44.2 per cent in 1960 and 45.3 per cent in 1969), a decade in which many individuals saw British industrial relations as beset with problems due to 'excessive union power', must cast some doubt on the (annual) sensitivity of this particular proxy. Second, Purdy and Zis have suggested that the observed relationship between the rate of change of unionization and the rate of change of money wages can be rationalized in quite different terms (i.e. emphasizing more the role of employer resistance to wage claims) to those advanced by Hines. Further criticisms of Hines include the claim that his model suffers from an omitted variable (i.e. the union relative-wage effect) problem, [24] and the fact that his empirical results are highly sensitive to the particular specification of variables, time periods studied, and data sources used.[25] The latter sort of criticism has also been made of the more recent work of McCallum, which uses the level of union density as a proxy for union militancy.[26] Finally, some more recent studies of wage inflation have found that the level of, rather than the changes in, unionization is the more robust empirical proxy.[27]

These criticisms of the rate of change of unionization and/or union density as a proxy for union power have resulted in the use of alternative proxies in wage-inflation studies. Some studies, for example, have utilized a measure of strike activity (most frequently strike frequency), which has made a statistically significant contribution to the explanation of wage inflation in Britain in certain periods of time.[28] However, the failure to replicate this relationship in other studies indicates that the statistical performance of a strike variable in wage equations is highly sensitive to the particular time period covered by individual studies.[29] In addition to this empirical criticism of strike frequency as a proxy for union power, there have been a number of conceptual reservations expressed about its use for such a purpose. For example, strike frequency may not be positively related to the concept of union power if it is the threat to strike, rather than the actual carrying out of this threat on a frequent basis, that is the major determinant of the strength of a union's negotiating position. Certainly, the work of Bacharach and Lawler has suggested that the actual use of coercive tactics, as opposed to the threat to use them, results in a decrease in the power of the party that used the tactic.[30] Furthermore, the use of strike frequency as a proxy for union power ignores both the other dimensions of strike activity and the non-strike forms of industrial action.

Finally, all of these wage-inflation studies (regardless of the particular proxy for union power used) implicitly assume that unions will use (on all occasions) their potential bargaining power to the fullest extent possible. In other words, they view enacted power as always being equal to potential power. This is an extremely powerful assumption to make, being quite different from (i) many conceptual discussions of bargaining power,[31] and (ii) Reder's argument that unions deliberately hold power in reserve, in that:

> The power of a union organization over wages lies not in what it has achieved but in what it can achieve in order to protect its interests . . . The idea that unions hold power in reserve may be conveniently rationalized by the hypothesis that, in the wage field at least, they are 'satisficing' rather than 'optimizing'. When union wage achievements are sufficient currently to satisfy the members, the leaders let well enough alone, rather than push further, and devote their time and resources to other objectives (including a quiet life). By not seeking all they can get without causing unemployment among the present members, union leaders reduce the risk of strikes; they also avoid creating antagonism among employers which may lead to vindictive countermoves if circumstances change, and finally they create a 'reservoir' of potential wage hikes they can obtain when and if the members press for them.[32]

The exceptionally high-strike-activity and wage-inflation years of 1969–70 in a number of European countries have been viewed as ones in which such reserves of union power were extensively drawn upon. These particular years (labelled 'the hinge' by Phelps Brown) were the all-important crossover point between the very different economic environments of the 1960s and 1970s. Table 7.2 provides some indication of the differing nature of the economic environment of these two decades in Britain.

The exceptional circumstances of the late 1960s and early 1970s have been the subject of a number of comparative studies, with the relatively high level of earnings increase being variously attributed to: (i) monetary overspill; (ii) a union reaction to the slow-down in the rise of real incomes in the previous 3 years; and (iii) fundamental shifts in the attitudes and expectations of individual

Table 7.2 Some features of the economic environment in Britain, 1960s and 1970s

Decade	*Union mark-up*	*Unemployment*	*Share of profits in net domestic income*	*Annual rate of earnings inflation*	*Annual rate of growth of sterling (M3)*
1960s	5	1.9	13	7	6
1970s	8	4.2	8	16	12

Source: David Metcalf, 'Unions and Pay' (1984) *The Economic Review*, September, p. 26.

employees concerning the size of appropriate pay increases.[33] These particular years were associated with the start of a considerable squeeze of the profit share in Britain, and it is to the subject of income distribution that we now turn.

Union power, income distribution, and the profit share

The impact of unions on both the distribution of earnings and the functional division of income between wages and profits is a subject area in which a number of very strong, but very different, points of view have been expressed. For example, some individual commentators have suggested that unions can do little to alter the relative size of factor shares as these are essentially historical constants, while others have argued that unions tend to increase the inequality of earnings distribution. These two potential union effects are brought together in Phelps Brown's well known claim that:

> Collective bargaining today is not between labour and capital, or employees and management, for the distribution of the products of particular industries between pay and profit, but between different groups of employees, for the distribution of the national product between them one with another, and between them as a whole and the inactive population.[34]

The most detailed and systematic empirical work on earnings distribution has been conducted in the United States, where Freeman and Medoff have shown that, on balance, the effect of unions is to reduce the inequality of the wage structure.[35] The extent and quality of the available evidence is very much less in Britain, although one recent study has reported that the extent of collective bargaining coverage appears to (i) narrow the pay structure by occupation and race, but (ii) increase the dispersion of pay across industries.[36] As to the functional division of income between wages and profits, the available time-series evidence indicates that the size of the labour share has tended to rise in most advanced industrialized economies over the course of this century (i.e. employee compensation as a percentage of national income typically rising from 55–65 per cent in earlier years and to 70–80 per cent by the 1960s),[37] but with this overall rise often being disproportionately concentrated in relatively short periods of time. In Britain, for instance, most of the movement in favour of the labour share occurred in and around the two wartime periods and in the years since the late 1960s[38]; in contrast, other periods of time (e.g. 1950–68) saw little change in the relative size of factor shares. Table 7.3 presents some profit-share (i.e. net operating surplus divided by net value-added) figures for selected countries in more recent years.

Table 7.3 The profit share for selected countries in recent years

	USA		*Germany*		*UK*		*Canada*		*Sweden*	
	(a)	*(b)*	*(a)*	*(b)*	*(a)*	*(b)*	*(a)*	*(b)*	*(a)*	*(b)*
1960	19.1	22.7	34.7	35.3	25.8	24.9	27.2	28.0		
1968	21.9	23.2	30.6	31.0	17.6	21.8	25.7	28.3	21.1	22.2
1973	18.6	20.0	23.4	24.1	19.7	22.2	27.6	29.8	18.0	23.6
1974	15.0	18.4	21.9	22.5	12.8	15.7	29.0	30.2	23.8	24.8
1975	17.5	21.8	19.6	20.7	8.9	11.9	25.3	26.9	19.3	21.1
1976	19.1	23.1	21.3	22.8	10.1	15.1	23.4	26.5	9.8	15.6
1977	19.8	23.4	20.4	22.3	16.3	20.7	21.0	26.2	3.2	11.2
1978	19.2	22.9	20.0	22.5	16.7	21.3	22.8	28.0	3.4	12.1
1979	16.5	21.2	20.3	23.2	11.5	20.2	26.1	32.4	10.9	17.7
1980	12.8	20.1	16.2	20.2	8.8	20.3	26.6	33.5	12.0	18.6
1981	13.6	23.1	14.6	18.7	8.7	22.6	24.3	30.0	9.3	18.1
1982	10.3	18.1	16.1	19.7	11.8	26.2	12.2	26.0	12.2	19.8
1983		18.6	19.5	22.4	15.3	29.8	16.0	29.0	20.8	25.5
1984						32.8	22.3	32.7		

Source: OECD Economic Outlook, Historical Statistics 1960–84 (1986), OECD: Paris, p. 74–5.

(a) = manufacturing only
(b) = manufacturing plus transport and communication

It was quite widely argued that the fall in the profit share in the manufacturing sector in Britain in the period from the late 1960s to the early 1970s was due to a conjunction of circumstances – namely, intensified product-market competition (from international sources) and the enhanced wage demands of trade unions.[39] However, in these essentially qualitative discussions of the role or influence of union power, the line of argument is basically circular in nature – i.e. the effect of union power is to reduce the size of the profit share, with the exertion of union power being shown by the reduced size of the profit share. More generally, Burkitt and Bowers have emphasized the limited extent of systematic research in this subject area in that 'no UK study of income distribution has yet related changes in relative shares to an objective measure of some aspects of union strength.[40]

One of the few British studies along the lines favoured by Burkitt and Bowers was a recent examination of some of the determinants of the wage and salary share at the inter-industry level of analysis.[41] This particular study was primarily concerned with the relationship between the level of product market concentration and the size of the wage share, according to Kalecki's 'degree-of-monopoly' theory of functional income distribution.[42] However, in view of the possibility that unions can to some extent offset the effects of the degree of product market monopoly,[43] Cowling and Molho's estimating equations contained a number of the traditional proxies for union power (i.e. the level of union density, the extent of collective bargaining coverage, strike frequency, and the number of working days lost through strikes) – although the authors were, in contrast to many economists, quite explicit about some of the potential limitations of these proxies. Among their findings was the fact that the level of union density was significantly and positively related to the size of the salary share at the individual-industry level for 1968 (although the unionization variable used was not exclusively a white-collar one), but the much less robust relationships between the various proxies for union power and the wage share for the years 1968 and 1973 suggest that a good deal more research is still required in this area before anything like reasonably firm conclusions can be reached. In the US, some studies of the movement of the wage share in individual industries over the course of time have reported positive relationships with the level of union density and strike frequency,[44] while the work of Freeman and Medoff indicates that the effect of unions is generally to lower the level of profitability, particularly in the more concentrated sectors of the economy.[45] In Britain, studies of the union impact on profits along the lines of Freeman and Medoff are, to say the least, few in number – although (i) work based on the 1984 workplace industrial relations survey has yielded a negative relationship between unionization and the (management) reported financial performance levels of establishments, and (ii) in a study of 145 manufacturing firms in the mid-1980s, union recognition was found to be associated with a below-mean, profit-to-sales ratio.[46]

Unions, prodictivity, and organizational change

There has been a long-standing debate over the non-wage (as opposed to the wage) induced inefficiencies of trade unions and collective bargaining in a number of national systems of industrial relations. This debate has revolved around the question of the extent to which trade union structures, attitudes, and behaviour have reduced or constrained management's ability to introduce technical (and organizational) changes designed to improve the effectiveness and efficiency of their organizations.

This debate among industrial-relations practitioners and researchers involves a particular view of the nature of union power – namely, that such power is essentially *negative* or reactive in nature, being manifested outside of (as well as inside) formal joint negotiating structures and processes in the form of various types of restrictive practices,[47] which are a source of X-inefficiency[48] (as are strikes), whereas 'excessive' union wage increases are held to cause allocative inefficiency (through producing too high a capital-to-labour ratio in the unionized sector).

The above debate has been nowhere more prominent than in the case of Britain. Indeed, the restrictive attitudes and behaviour of unions have figured prominently in some discussions of the causes of industrial decline of the country at large.[49] The *a priori* case that has typically been made in this regard makes reference to: (i) the relatively early establishment of the British industrial-relations system; (ii) the relatively high level of union-density and collective-bargaining coverage; (iii) the relative prevalence of craft and general unionism; and (iv) the limited influence of national unions at the level of the individual workplace.[50] Those commentators who hold the view that unions have had such an adverse effect in Britain then proceed from this *a priori* basis to cite a variety of evidence and supportive studies. The leading example of *indirect* evidence to this effect is the extent of productivity bargaining that occurred in the 1960s,[51] when approximately a quarter of the workforce was estimated to be operating under some form of productivity-bargaining arrangements by the end of that decade. The use of such evidence for this purpose does, however, have to confront the fact that productivity bargaining was a permissible exception to the wage norm(s) of the incomes policy that operated in the years 1965–70, with the likely result that many of these bargains existed more in name than in substance.

The available direct evidence on this subject can be divided into two basic groups, that which contains an explicit comparative dimension and that which is for Britain alone. Under the first sub-heading one can find a number of historical case studies of the relatively slow adoption and diffusion of particular (technical) innovations in individual industries (e.g. textiles and steel) in Britain compared to that in other countries.[52] A second set of relevant studies (of varying degrees of sophistication) have involved attempts to estimate the residual contribution of restrictive practices (and strikes) to observable productivity differentials between British plants and comparable establishments in other countries, once allowance is made for the effects of differences in product mix, scale of production and the age of the capital stock; the most well-known study along these lines is undoubtedly that undertaken by Pratten.[53] As to the British specific evidence, there are a number of existing statistical studies, including a Department of Employment Research Paper which documented a significant, negative correlation between the extent of collective-bargaining coverage and the growth in labour productivity at the industry level.[54] In addition, Pencavel identified a negative relationship between the level of union density and output levels in the coal-mining industry in the early years of this century,[55] while Caves reported a positive correlation between 'poor industrial relations' (as proxied by the incidence of strikes) and excessive inventories at the industry level.[56] Finally, there are various surveys of management respondents which report perceptions of the extent and effects of union restrictive attitudes and behaviour. For example, one such survey by Wenban-Smith in the early 1980s, which obtained responses from some fifty firms, stated that 'nearly a third reported that restrictive practices or other industrial relations problems were preventing them, at least to some extent, from achieving an optimal workforce size'.[57]

Those individuals who do not believe that union restrictive practices are sufficiently sizeable and widespread enough to have made a significant contribution to the relatively poor performance of the British economy can respond (and indeed have) to the above sort of evidence in a number of ways. The first, and most obvious, form of response has been to criticize the quality of the above evidence.[58] This could take the form of questioning the generalizability (and strength) of historical single-industry studies of technical diffusion (with their inferential line of argument) and/or the adequacy of 'controls' for other relevant determinants of productivity differentials in cross-country, plant-based studies. A second category of response has been to argue the case that there are considerably more important causes (that union restrictive attitudes and practices) of the relatively poor performance of the British economy; for example, the Williams study stresses the key roles of poor marketing and inadequate financial institutions.[59] On a more positive note, advocates of this view can point to a number of recent surveys of management respondents which report that unions are not perceived to be a particularly powerful constraint on the introduction of both organizational and technical changes designed to improve efficiency and effectiveness. For example, a survey by Edwards in 1984 of some 230 relatively large-sized manufacturing plants reported that union restrictions and overmanning were the important constraint on non-capacity working in only 15 per cent of the establishments that actually reported internal constraints on such working;[60] this figure represented only 3 per cent of the full number of sample establishments. Essentially similar, supportive findings emerge from: (i) a recent survey in the mechanical engineering industry;[61] (ii) the companion volume (on technical and organizational change) to the 1984 workplace industrial relations survey;[62] and (iii) a cross-country study (involving firms in France, West Germany, and Britain) of technical change.[63] In all of these surveys, the management respondents generally reported that unions were a relatively minor constraint on the introduction of change.

However, the value of any survey of management's perceptions of unions as a constraint on change (regardess of whether they report unions to be a significant or insignificant constraint) needs to be seen in the light of a recent study of inter-personal and inter-organization variation in such perceptions.[64] The results indicated that respondents from relatively large-sized establishments, from manufacturing-sector establishments, from establishments where new technology was viewed as having had a relatively substantial impact on the organization, and respondents who were middle-level managers, who were members of the personnel-management function, and who had held a relatively large number of positions in the organization, all tended to view unions as a relatively greater constraint on change. Accordingly, samples that score relatively high (low) on these particular organization and individual-respondent attributes, relative to the population(s) of organizations and individual managers at large, are likely, *ceteris paribus*, to report unions as relatively more (less) of a constraint on change. The result is that for such surveys to be of any real value (in the sense of generating population estimates) their sampling frames must not only be representative of all establishments, but also representative of the management hierarchy of the individual establishments concerned.

In the United States, the debate about the extent and nature of the union impact on productivity (as opposed to organizational change and effectiveness, more generally) has been moved on to a much higher plane by the work of Freeman and Medoff.[65] Unions can, in principle, adversely affect the level of productivity through restrictive practices, but also have the potential to raise it, through: (i) the relative wage effect leading to an increased substitution of capital for labour (admittedly this gain would come at the cost of allocative inefficiency) and the employment of better quality workers (in terms of their human capital content); (ii) providing the institutional basis (a voice mechanism) for the expression and resolution of worker grievances which acts to lower the level of labour turnover; and (iii) a 'shock effect' which results in management introducing more effective personnel policies and structures and more detailed arrangements for closely monitoring the nature of work performance. The approach of Freeman and Medoff is essentially to introduce the level of union density as a variable in estimates of the production function, with the findings generally pointing to a higher level of productivity in unionized establishments. The nature of their analysis does not always permit a precise identification of the routes through which this effect occurs (e.g. they rarely have measures of the actual performance of grievance procedures) and they qualify their results (particularly on the growth of productivity through time) by emphasizing that a favourable union effect is likely to be highly contingent upon the existence of 'good industrial relations'; the latter term is not always clearly defined, although they appear to view it as being associated with (i) an effectively functioning grievance procedure and (ii) the nature of the attitudinal climate between unions and management. It has to be said that this is the most controversial finding in their book, with the nature of their analysis being subject to some criticism,[66] and a number of subsequent studies producing rather different results;[67] the latter, in particular, highlights the need for more direct examinations of the routes through which such productivity impacts can occur.

In Britain, work along the lines of Freeman and Medoff is only in its relative infancy. However, the nature of the existing work and findings to date can be noted as follows:[68]

(i) A number of industry- and company-based studies have found unionization to be associated with lower productivity, or else no significant relationship is observed.
(ii) The much improved productivity performance of the British manufacturing sector in the 1980s (i.e. averaging a 6 per cent increase per year, which is more than double the rate of the previous 20 years) – which we noted in Chapter 2 – has been

associated with changes in the industrial relations system: namely, increased work rates, increased competition, and decentralization of bargaining arrangements. The existence of a less adversarial, more co-operative (i.e. integrative bargaining) based system of industrial relations, however, is more questionable, which raises questions about whether such increases can be maintained in the future.

(iii) At least one recent study by economists has sought to move beyond simply looking at the relationship between productivity and unionization by including a variety of other industrial-relations variables (e.g. scope of bargaining, sophistication of union, extent of eligibility and participation in share ownership schemes, specialist personnel director, etc.) in their estimating equations.[69] These various industrial-relations variables were found to have different relationships with productivity, although the nature of the behavioural processes and relevant lines of causation underlying a number of them were far from clear-cut in nature.

To date I have considered some of the widely alleged effects of the operation of collective-bargaining arrangements on the labour market and larger economic environment of Britain. In this task I have highlighted some of the conceptual and empirical weaknesses of existing studies which have utilized proxies for union power, and pointed to the relatively limited extent and quality of evidence on certain important matters in Britain compared to the position in the United States. To round off this macro-section it is useful to consider briefly the results of some comparative labour-market research which has included Britain in the countries studied.

First, as indicated in Chapter 2, the work on the degree of corporatism of labour-market arrangements has inevitably accorded Britain a relatively low ranking. In this regard, there continues to be much interest and debate among economists concerning the favourable macro-economic performance effects of differing labour-market structures. However, even studies which argue that certain forms of decentralized structures can, as an alternative to high corporatism, yield favourable macro-performance effects, tend to find Britain relatively lacking in this regard. Bruno and Sachs, for example, report the UK as low on corporatism but high on nominal-wage responsiveness.[70] In short, Britain has neither the advantage of Denmark (high corporatism) nor the advantage of the US (low nominal-wage responsiveness). Second, the 1980s have seen economists actively discussing the role of labour-market flexibility, with many commentators viewing the superior economic performance of the US and Japan relative to European countries, such as Britain, as being due to more flexible labour-market arrangements at the aggregate, sectoral, and firm levels.[71] In such studies, however, there is, first, considerable controversy about the particular features or aspects of labour-market operation which need to be considered. Second, questions have been raised about the appropriateness of certain statistical measures of flexibility: for example, not all economists would accept that the coefficient of variation is the ideal statistical measure of wage or labour-market flexibility. Third, one study of the nature (and changes in) various dimensions of the wage structure of six European countries in the 1970s has usefully indicated some interesting differences between Britain and the other countries concerned.[72] For example, in Britain the extent of pay dispersion among manual workers was particularly noticeable, the manual/non-manual wage differential was particularly narrow, while the biggest change in the wage structure of Britain in the 1970s was the reduction in the wage differential between men and women.

In the introduction to this chapter it was argued that the nature of individual employer adjustment to the workings of collective bargaining will not be simply a function of the impact of such institutional arrangements on the aggregate economic environment of Britain. In other words, it would seem unrealistic to assume that all employers (as individual decision-making units) would perceive of, and respond to, the workings of collective bargaining as though they were a perfect microcosm of the average or overall impact of the institution. One would expect considerable inter-employer variation in such matters, as a result of variation in the quality of the individual collective-bargaining relationship and in the level of individual organizational performance and effectiveness. In short, any feedback loop from (i) the impact of the industrial relations system on, for example, the economic environment to (ii) the industrial relations system, will involve a mixture of both macro- and micro-level considerations. Accordingly, in the remainder of this chapter we concentrate on some of the micro-level considerations that are of particular relevance in shaping the nature of individual employer adjustments to collective bargaining.

Industrial relations and economic performance at the individual-organization level

In Britain there have been virtually no systematic studies of the nature of the inter-relationships between (i) measures of industrial-relations performance and (ii) measures of economic performance, based on sizeable and representative survey data at the level of the individual corporation or establishment. Admittedly the 1980 workplace industrial-relations survey pointed to a number of potentially interesting relationships in this area.[73] It was indicated, for example, that the general climate of industrial relations was reported to be less favourable (i) where little information on the financial circumstances of the establishment was provided to employee representatives, and (ii) where formal procedures were held to be unsatisfactory and disciplinary fines had been imposed. The same survey also suggested that management reports of the overall quality of industrial relations appeared to be influenced by the occurrence (or not) of industrial action among manual workers in the previous 12 months, while in establishments that did not recognize trade unions for collective-bargaining purposes, management tended to report a relatively favourable industrial-relations climate and relatively better financial performance. Unfortunately, industrial-relations researchers have made little attempt to draw together such interrelationships in a conceptual framework (which, for example, specifies relevant lines of causation) which can be tested using multivariate statistical analysis. In addition to undertaking such analysis on the basis of the 1980 and 1984 workplace industrial relations surveys, it would be useful to conduct an industrial-relations and economic-performance analysis or audit of individual establishments that make up one of the large, multi-establishment (M-form) organizations discussed in Chapter 4.

As an indication of the potential value of such work, one can usefully consider the approach and findings of some recent research conducted in the United States.[74] Although this research acknowledged that 'no well-developed theory or set of propositions exists that relates variations in plant-level industrial relations outcomes obtained under collective bargaining to productivity or any other measures of organisational effectiveness',[75] it offered a number of preliminary hypotheses concerning the effects of conflict management systems on the level of organizational effectiveness. First, it suggested that relatively high levels of negotiation and grievance activity can entail considerable costs in terms of time and resources which might otherwise have been used for training, problem solving, and organization development exercises designed to improve effectiveness. Second, a substantial volume of grievance and disciplinary actions may indicate the existence of a deep-seated, generally poor-quality working relationship between unions and management. Third, the nature of the attitudes and behaviour involved in such distributive bargaining activities may not be self contained, but rather may adversely affect other areas of union–management interaction in which there is considerable potential for a joint problem-solving approach. These hypotheses which were concerned with the impact of conflict management systems, as well as those to do with the effect of individual-employee attitudes and behaviour, were tested by correlation and regression-analysis of plant-level data, with (i) strong interrelationships existing between the various individual measures of industrial-relations performance and (ii) some relationships being apparent between a number of these measures and some for the economic performance of the individual plant. For example, grievance and disciplinary action rates were found to be strongly interrelated, both measures were also positively related to absenteeism rates, while the rate of disciplinary actions was significantly related to the direct level of labour efficiency in the plant.

The most important aspects of this work were, first, the attempt to provide an *a priori* specification of the underlying behavioural relationships between industrial relations and economic performance at the individual plant level, and, second, the use of performance measures that were not simply subjective, perceptual-based constructs. The fact that these studies did not involve a longitudinal research design did, however, limit the capacity to precisely delineate lines of causation and feedback, as opposed to identifying associations and interrelationships. Furthermore, the work only examined a relatively limited range of economic performance measures. The particular measures used (e.g. product quality, direct-labour efficiency) are certainly not unimportant, although they do fall well short of the concept of 'organizational effectiveness' as traditionally discussed by organization theorists. Admittedly there are some difficulties for industrial-relations researchers wishing to pursue this particular line of study, because 'there is disagreement about what properties or dimensions are encompassed by the concept of effectiveness. There is disagreement about who does or should set the criteria to be employed in assessing effectiveness.'[76]

The existing literature on the subject of organizational effectiveness contains a mixture of studies that have used single and multiple measures of effectiveness, with an individual researcher's choice of measures being a function of pragmatic (i.e. what data is available?) and theoretical considerations. Scott, for example, has suggested that a researcher who favours a rational, systems view of organizations will emphasize measures of productivity or efficiency, whereas a natural-systems perspective inclines one to be concerned with participants' satisfaction, profitability, and survival, while an open-systems view of organizations will lead researchers to be interested in matters such as adaptability/flexibility and maximization of bargaining position.[77] It is obviously tempting to recommend that researchers should take as wide a range of measures of effectiveness as possible, although problems will obviously occur here if there is an absence of systematic and consistent relationships between the various measures across organizations; this would lead to the researcher having to make subjective assessments as to their relative importance. Such measurement difficulties concerning the concept of organizational effectiveness are obviously greater the more heterogeneous is the sample of organizations involved; it would therefore seem sensible at this stage to try and build up this line of research from studies of individual plants in individual multi-plant companies, where a reasonably common set of effectiveness measures can be derived from some degree of uniformity in ownership, technology, and product-market environment.

The US studies of the relationship between industrial relations and economic performance at the plant level, which we have discussed here, have explicitly argued that the level of grievance activity constitutes a useful proxy for the overall quality of an individual union–management relationship. This is one of the specific themes pursued in the next section, where we consider the all-important question of how one measures the quality of industrial relations at the level of the individual organization.

The quality of individual collective bargaining relationships

In outlining a conceptual framework for the study of collective bargaining, Kochan observed that:

> One of the purposes of an analytical framework is to facilitate evaluation of the performance of a social system. How then, can the performance of a collective bargaining system be evaluated? How do we know when it has been performing effectively? When is it in need of reform, readjustment, or rehabilitation? These questions, with a few exceptions, have not been systematically addressed by collective bargaining researchers in the past. Instead, it has been argued that collective bargaining has too many diverse and conflicting interests, is too dynamic and situation specific, or simply too complex an institution to conform to some social scientists' conception of 'good or bad' or 'effective or ineffective'.[78]

The above indicates that there has traditionally been relatively little research explicitly designed to measure and explain variation in the quality of individual collective-bargaining relationships in either the United States or Britain. Industrial-relations researchers have often done little more than argue that the quality of a collective-bargaining relationship cannot be fully and adequately assessed by reference to a single, 'universalist' measure; this argument frequently involves criticism of the use of some measure of strike activity, which tends to be the single measure of effective performance favoured by the media and policy makers. Furthermore, it appears that few organizations have attempted to formally evaluate the workings and performance of their collective-bargaining relationship(s), since personnel managers, when questioned on this matter, frequently tend to 'equate quality with the degree of personal rapport between management and union representatives in different plants of their organization'.[79]

Admittedly in the United States there have been some relatively long-standing attempts to classify the nature of collective bargaining relationships along a spectrum of conflict and co-operation. For example, Harbison and Coleman have categorized collective-bargaining relationships under such headings as open conflict, armed truce, working harmony, and union–management co-operation.[80] This sort of work, which strongly influenced Walton and McKersie's concept of attitudinal structuring, tends to be centrally concerned with the motivational orientation and action tendencies between unions and management which reflect beliefs about legitimacy and feelings of trust.[81] For instance, the major distinguishing characteristics of Harbison and Coleman's 'armed truce' category of collective-bargaining relationships are:

(i) a feeling on the part of management that unions and collective bargaining are at best necessary evils in modern industrial society;
(ii) a conviction on the part of the labour leadership involved that the union's main job is to challenge and protest managerial actions;
(iii) basic disagreement between the parties over the appropriate scope of collective bargaining and the matters which should properly be subject to joint determination;
(iv) rivalry between management and the union for the loyalty of workers.
(v) a frank admission on the part of both parties that settlements of major differences in collective bargaining are made on the

basis of the relative power positions of the company *vis-à-vis* the union.

(vi) a mutual desire to work out an orderly method of containing conflict and compromising differences by living together under the terms of a collective bargaining contract.

These types of classifications of collective bargaining relationships have usually been based on a small number of relatively well-known examples, hence they have a certain amount of intuitive appeal. However, their obvious limitations include the tendency to ignore the influence of external (to the organization) environmental forces and the fact that some of their major distinguishing characteristics are not easily amenable to being measured and tested in an inter-organization study. Undoubtedly, the most interesting and impressive study of the quality of union–management relationships at the individual-plant level still remains the one conducted by Derber and his colleagues in the United States.[82] This particular piece of work examined the satisfaction of both union and management representatives with regard to productive efficiency, earnings, job security, due process, union participation, and the overall psychological climate of the relationship. To these self-interest-based measures of performance were added a number of socially derived criteria, namely the avoidance of work stoppages, the avoidance of third-party intervention, grievance settlement without arbitration, equitable earnings, and steady employment. The major significance of this work lies in its use of multiple evaluative criteria assessed from the particular perspective of the various parties involved (admittedly individual employees are not included here), with important questions being raised about (i) the ability to adequately match and align theoretical and empirical constructs in evaluations of collective bargaining, and (ii) the direction and strength of the interrelationships between multiple evaluative measures at the individual plant level.

In more recent years, one can identify certain more positive research attempts to evaluate the quality of individual collective-bargaining relationships. The first line of research, which is concerned to identify the measures and determinants of a relatively well-functioning grievance procedure, has been stimulated by: (i) the long-standing view (in a number of countries) that the performance of the grievance procedure is a useful proxy for the overall quality of an individual union–management relationship;[83] and (ii) the various empirical findings of Freeman and Medoff (e.g. unionized relationships have relatively low levels of labour turnover), which they interpret as being due to unions performing a 'voice' function in the workplace – this voice effect is rarely, however, directly tested in the work of Freeman and Medoff. As a result, in the United States there have been a number of recent attempts to specify more clearly the measures (and determinants) of the performance of grievance procedures, with the key measures of performance typically identified being grievance rates, speed of settlement, level of settlement, usage of arbitration, and equity of settlement.[84] However, as these various measures are not always strongly intercorrelated,[85] it would not appear to be a completely straightforward exercise to produce an overall measure of the performance of individual grievance procedures in inter-organization studies which can, in turn, constitute a proxy for the overall quality of union–management relationships.

The second stream of research, which has involved contributions from Britain and North America,[86] has sought to develop measures of the climate of industrial relations at the level of individual organizations. The concept of the industrial-relations climate has been held to constitute an intervening variable between structure and behaviour which can be measured by scales concerned with union–management co-operation, aggression, apathy, hostility, union support, joint-participation, trust, goal identification, fairness, and power balance.[87]

At this stage, research on the climate of industrial relations is only its relative infancy, with most existing studies being restricted to examinations of the validity and reliability of the particular scales used. However, as such work develops on both an intra- and inter-organizational basis, it is to be expected that researchers will explicitly examine issues such as the internal and external determinants of variation in the industrial-relations climate and the mechanisms which perpetuate or bring about change in this climate over the course of time.

Conclusions

In this particular chapter I have examined some of the widely alleged effects of collective bargaining on the economic environment of the system as a whole and on that of the individual organization. The existing evidence concerning such effects is frequently deficient in both quantity and quality, but it is this sort of evidence – together with (i) wider economic changes (e.g. increased product-market competition), (ii) non-industrial-relations-specific changes at the organizational level (e.g. mergers and changes in organizational structures), and (iii) the larger value and belief systems of key individuals – which will strongly shape the nature of responses and adjustments to collective bargaining on the part of both employers and policy-makers. The nature of possible employer responses (in the short and longer term) will be considered in both Chapters 9 and 10. Meanwhile, Chapter 8 will consider the response of policy-makers.

Chapter eight

The changing role of the State in the industrial-relations system

A preliminary overview

Prior to the 1960s, research on the role of the State (i.e. Government, the judiciary, Parliament, the police, and the military) in industrial relations within pluralist democratic systems overwhelmingly concentrated on Government and the judiciary, and covered a relatively narrow range of subjects: namely, industrial-relations legislation, judicial decisions, and conciliation and arbitration procedures. This focus was understandable because of the limited role of Government in both the economic and industrial-relations systems, which was itself a function of the following beliefs and assumptions: (i) economic systems were essentially stable, equilibrating ones; (ii) any macro-economic problems were due to short-run, technical failures in the fine tuning of Keynesian aggregate demand policies; (iii) the outputs of the industrial-relations system had relatively little in the way of adverse implications for larger economic performance (except in wartime settings); and (iv) Government could only legitimately concern itself with the level of strike activity through giving tangible expression (e.g. provision of conciliation and arbitration facilities) to 'the social or public interest' in industrial relations which was exclusively concerned with the processes of the industrial relations system (i.e. a 'good' industrial-relations system was one that was relatively strike-free).

However, from the late 1960s, it has become apparent that Government is very much a pro-active organization with distinct, self-interested aims which it is seeking to achieve in the industrial-relations arena. This changed role of Government is very largely the result of: (i) the inherent stagflation tendencies from the late 1960s; (ii) the increased interdependence of the world economy (which subjected individual systems to periodic external shocks in the 1970s); and (iii) the relative growth of public-sector employment (and union membership) in the 1970s. The particular aims which Government has increasingly sought to achieve in the industrial-relations system from the late 1960s very largely reflect its general concern with effective macro-economic management; recall here the previous chapter's discussion of the concept of a feedback loop from industrial-relations outputs to the economic environment. The result was an increased Government concern with the outcomes (as opposed to the processes) of the industrial-relations system, which received tangible expression in the first generation of incomes policies (largely unilaterally introduced by Government) and the subsequent establishment of corporatist (or political-bargaining) arrangements in the Europe of the 1970s.

As mentioned in previous chapters, a number of economists have pointed to the relatively favourable macro-economic performance results and implications of relatively well-developed, corporatist, labour-market arrangements in cross-country studies. However, despite such favourable results, in the Europe of the 1980s we find that only some corporatist arrangements remain well-established (e.g. Norway and Austria), whereas others have decayed and declined (e.g. Italy and the UK), and yet a third group appear to be experiencing considerable internal strains and problems (e.g. Sweden). It is certainly not newly established corporatist arrangements which are catching the eye in the 1980s in Europe, but rather those 'dualist' tendencies (to use Goldthorpe's term) which involve increased areas of economic life being opened up to the influence of market forces – as evidenced by reductions in public expenditure and public sector employment, the increased growth of flexible working arrangements, and the encouragement of the small-business sector.

These changing tendencies in the role of the State in industrial relations have, first, produced considerable researcher interest in the reasons why the 1980s have seen something of a Government backlash against the desirability of having corporatist labour-market arrangements. The failure of top union leaders to deliver wage restraint, the excessive costs of union-demanded *quid pro quos* for their involvement in tripartite structures, the relative growth of public-sector union membership, the success and influence of Japan as an example, the difficulty of establishing and maintaining corporatist arrangements in the absence of certain structural and historical prerequisties, have all been mentioned in this regard.[1] Second, researchers have raised the question of whether Government-intiated changes – for example, the removal of a commitment to full employment together with attempts to reduce unionization levels and increase labour-market flexibility in a decentralized system of industrial relations – can produce levels of economic performance comparable to, or better than, those in corporatist economies.[2] Third, within Britain, there have been discussions of the reasons why the Thatcher Government has departed so substantially from the practice of previous Conservative Governments of consulting extensively with the trade-union movement.[3] This change, together with the sharp break with the State traditions of incomes policy and intervention (at the ministerial level) in major labour–management disputes, has led to the Thatcher Government being frequently referred to as 'neo-*laissez-faire*'. Indeed, one commentator on the position of Europe in the 1980s in general, has commented that:

> The major tendency at the present time is the expansion of those areas of industrial relations in which market relations, rather than institutional mediation, predominate, and also the increasing de-regulation of labour relations. Thatcherist neo-liberalism is the ideological mouthpiece of this tendency.[4]

However, this neo-liberalist, or neo-*laissez-faire*, label has to be viewed in the light of the fact that:

> The Thatcher Government has embraced the principle of free market forces in preference to voluntary collective bargaining as the best method of organizing a labor market. In consequence, the government has begun to play a more active role in labor market policy.[5]

The Thatcher Government has, in fact, been highly interventionist in the labour market, as witnessed by, for example: the volume of industrial-relations legislation passed; the use of the public sector to set a leadership by example model in relation to certain desired industrial-relations developments; and the passage of numerous measures and regulations that are not solely industrial-relations orientated, but which nevertheless have important implications for the industrial-relations system. (Labour-market training schemes and encouragement of the small-firm sector are leading examples of the latter type of initiatives.) The approach of the Thatcher Government in the industrial relations arena is in fact very different to that of the Reagan Administration in the US, with the latter adopting much less of a pro-active strategy;[6] budgetary cuts and administrative appointments unfavourable to the unions have been very much the Reagan approach, rather than legislative and public-sector management-led initiatives along the Thatcher Government lines. Moreover, with some of the major potential effects on the industrial-relations system coming from initiatives of the Thatcher Government that are not exclusively, or even mainly, industrial-relations-centred, there is a very real need for industrial researchers to widen their agendas and to be concerned with certain subject areas that they have traditionally left to academics from other disciplines and fields of study: for example, training measures in the past have been almost the exclusive research prerogative of labour economists.

More generally, industrial-relations researchers have become more interested in, and contributed towards, discussions of the theory(s) of the State, which was previously a subject area essentially dominated by political scientists. Traditionally, the major political-science perspectives on the State have been, first, the liberal-democratic one – in which the State is perceived 'as an autonomous complex of institutions, politically neutral and external to structurally-determined social forces. It is, then, 'up for grabs', to be 'captured' by elected regimes and used as an instrument for their own specific political purposes.'[7] This pluralist perspective, arguably the one adopted by most industrial-relations researchers, actually focuses on the political system, rather than the State as the major agent of policy formation. The alternative view is, of course, the marxist one – which sees the state as the tool of the ruling class, designed to assist both the processes of capital accumulation and capital legitimation, with the structure and functions of the State being overwhelmingly shaped by the global (economic and political) requirements of capital; there are, in fact, numerous variants of marxist thought here, some of which stress the economic functions which the State performs for capitalism (i.e. reproduction of the capitalist economy) whereas others primarily emphasize the importance of its political functions (i.e. maintain political stability). Both the pluralist and marxist approaches view the State as essentially a reactive mechanism to pressure generated within civil society, whereas some more recent discussions by industrial-relations reseachers[8] have argued that the State is not simply a captive of class forces, economic forces, or of the capitalist mode of production. In short, the State has some degree of relative autonomy, although, at the same time, it is not a completely independent, homogeneous, or all-powerful force – due to facing internal divisions, the constraints of history, contradictory demands from (internally) heterogeneous capital and labour groups, and from having to deal with crisis situations in which historically-approved, incremental measures do not always provide the answers. Unfortunately, such conceptual discussions have only yielded a small number of reasonably specific, potentially testable hypotheses to date. For example, the following claims have been put forward: (i) crisis situations (e.g. war periods, major economic depressions) increase the capacity for relatively autonomous action by the State; (ii) the existing history of State intervention in industrial relations strongly facilitates (constrains) new complementary (non-complementary) forms of State intervention; and (iii) the weaker the executive arm of the State, the more likely it is that the individual components of the State will pursue potentially conflicting aims, which limits the emergence of a long-run, coherent policy in industrial relations. Accordingly, a major task for industrial-relations researchers in the future, perhaps in conjunction with political-science colleagues, is to add to this list of hypotheses, which is urgently in need of expansion relative to the number pertaining to the union and management actors in the system.

In Chapter 2 we discussed the legislative role of Government in the system of industrial relations, while some other chapters have touched on certain aspects of public-sector industrial relations (such as the discussion in Chapter 5 on the nature of bargaining structure), and the basic concept of the public interest in industrial relations has also been previously discussed. This chapter will not duplicate the discussion of matters already examined in some detail, although it will provide more detailed information and coverage of a number of subjects which have been only briefly referred to in earlier chapters; this is consistent with the intention (stated in the preface to the book) to avoid an overly compartmentalized treatment of the field of study in which individual chapters provide very self-contained discussions of individual subjects and topics. The contents of this chapter are essentially concerned with third-party-dispute resolution procedures, incomes policy, and public-sector industrial relations. By focusing on these particular subjects we hope to reveal how Government's role in the system has changed through the course of time and how this process of change has raised the possibility of conflict between some individual functions of Government in the system of industrial relations.

Third-party dispute resolution procedures and the concern with process

A number of historical accounts of relatively early strikes in Britain (e.g. those involving merchant seamen in 1792 and 1815) indicate that conciliation activities were undertaken by prominent local individuals in the community, such as magistrates and senior naval officers.[9] Moreover, as collective-bargaining arrangements on a local area or district basis developed from the later half of the nineteenth century, the number of conciliation and arbitration boards (whose remit covered local areas in individual industries) increased in number. Sharp indicates that 64 such boards were known to exist in 1894, a total which rose to 162 by 1905, and to 325 in 1913.[10] However, for the system as a whole, it was the Conciliation Act 1896 and the Industrial Courts Act 1919 which placed voluntary conciliation and arbitration arrangements on a more formal basis. The essence of conciliation, which has always been the most favoured form of third-party dispute resolution in Britain, has been well summed up in the following terms:

> The conciliator helps the parties to communicate with each other more effectively. He can keep the temperature of the discussion down by confining it to the points at issue, and stating them in unemotive terms. When the parties lose their tempers with one another too easily to be able to talk face to face, he can go backwards and forwards between them. He may be able to devise proposals new in form or substance, which go some way to reconcile conflicting claims, or provide a rough compromise, or make it easier to give ground without losing face. He can save one side from trying to call the other's bluff when in fact it is not bluffing. Especially when both sides have stuck fast, thinking it a sign of weakness to be the first to climb down, he can get them to make concessions because he can tell each what the other will do in return, and can make what is given up appear as a favour to him, rather than a concession to the other side.[11]

These (and other) aspects of the conciliation role are usefully discussed in an ILO publication which lists the many sides of the conciliator as including discussion leader, alternative target or safety valve, communication link, prober, source of information and ideas, sounding board, protector, fail-safe device, stimulator, sympathizer, assessor or adviser, advocate, face-saver, coach, or trainer.[12] A number of the widely held beliefs and propositions about the conciliation (or mediation, as it is more commonly referred to in the US) process, which appear to transcend the institutional details of particular national systems of industrial relations, have been summarized as follows:[13]

1. Conciliators must be acceptable to the parties and perceived to be trustworthy.
2. Conciliation is at least partially an 'art' that must be learned

through experience, therefore experienced conciliators should be more effective than inexperienced ones.
3. The timing of conciliation efforts in the larger cycle of negotiations is crucial, as conciliation works best when the parties are under strong pressure to resolve their dispute,
4. The strategies conciliators employ will tend to vary over the course of the intervention process and over the different stages of the negotiation cycle. Initially the conciliator is likely to adopt a relatively passive strategy, but as the negotiations proceed the conciliator is increasingly likely to adopt a more active and assertive strategy aimed at changing the expectations of the parties and proposing possible compromise solutions.
5. Conciliator strategies vary considerably between individual conciliators.
6. Conciliators adopt different strategies according to the particular type or source(s) of conflict that is hindering a settlement.
7. Conciliation is more likely to resolve some types of conflict than others. In general, conciliation is held to be more likely to be successful in cases of relatively minor, less intense conflicts than in 'conflicts of principle' or in ones involving a negative contract zone.

These individual hypotheses have been most systematically and comprehensively examined in a public-sector-based study in the United States,[14] although one subsequent piece of work in Britain has investigated some of them.[15] The latter study reported that settlement outcomes, for example, were positively associated with employer requests for conciliation, experienced conciliators, and disputes concerning general wage claims and bonus payments, while situations where conciliation failed to achieve a settlement were characterized by disputes involving trade-union recognition, the size of the dispute, and the threat or occurrence of strike action. Although settlement or a reduced range of disagreement are the leading dependent variables employed in quantative studies of this type, most examinations of the workings of conciliation in Britain have overwhelmingly used the reported satisfaction of union and management users of conciliation as *the* (key) indicator of the effectiveness of the process.[16] The views of users of conciliation facilities need nevertheless to be placed in the larger context of the argument that such procedures constitute the tangible expression of the 'public or social interest' concern (in industrial relations) with minimizing the level of strike activity. However, the difficulties involved in estimating the size of the reduction in the costs of strike activity due to the operation of third-party-dispute resolution procedures, *ceteris paribus*, are, to say the least, very considerable.[17] Moreover, as the social or public interest in industrial relations has been redefined from the 1960s to include a concern with the outcomes (and not just the processes) of collective bargaining, and, as successive Governments have introduced wage-control or incomes policies (as an expression of this new concern), there has been considerable interest in the impact of the latter policies on the perceived independence, and hence usage, of third-party-dispute resolution procedures. In other words, there is the question of whether the two forms of Government intervention in the industrial-relations system (justified by the two separate elements of the public or social interest in industrial relations) may not be potentially in conflict with each other.

In Britain, the perceived independence of the Department of Employment conciliation function (which handled between 300 and 450 cases per year in the 1960s) was held to be compromised by the operation of incomes policy in the late 1960s and early 1970s; in 1970–2 the Conservative Government actually withheld conciliation services from disputes involving wage claims above the policy norm in those years. Indeed, the operation of a 'hard' incomes policy has been shown to have had a significant, negative relationship with the annual number of conciliation cases (particularly with the sub-set concerning wages) in the years 1961–74.[18] As a solution to this particular problem, the TUC and CBI reached an agreement to set up an independent conciliation and arbitration service in the early 1970s, but in practice this did not materialize, although the Advisory Conciliation and Arbitration Service (ACAS), with its tripartite council, assumed such a role when it was established in September 1974; ACAS was then placed on a statutory basis by the Employment Protection Act 1975 which repealed the Conciliation Act 1896 and parts of the Industrial Courts Act 1919. Table 8.1 indicates the annual size of the (collective) conciliation workload of ACAS in the years 1976–86.

The substantially changed labour-market environment from the late 1970s has been associated with a substantial decline in the number of conciliation requests received by ACAS; as Table 8.1 indicates, the number of requests has fallen by some 58 per cent in the years 1976–86. However, an examination of some of the basic characteristics of the requests for conciliation reveals a certain element of continuity over the course of time. For example, in 1976 some 57 per cent of the completed conciliation cases concerned pay and terms and conditions of employment, 21 per cent covered union-recognition claims, and 10 per cent were for discipline and dismissal matters; in 1986 the relevant figures for these three causes

Table 8.1 Annual conciliation workload of ACAS, 1976–86*

Year	*Requests for conciliation*	*Completed conciliation cases*
1976	3,460	2,851
1977	3,299	2,891
1978	3,338	2,706
1979	2,667	2,284
1980	2,091	1,910
1981	1,958	1,716
1982	1,865	1,634
1983	1,789	1,621
1984	1,569	1,448
1985	1,475	1,337
1986	1,457	1,323

Source: Relevant annual reports of ACAS.

*By way of comparison, the Department of Employment handled 866 conciliation cases in 1973.

of dispute were, respectively, 59 per cent, 14 per cent, and 13 per cent. Second, ACAS's figures for 'conciliation resulting in a settlement or progress towards a settlement' do not exhibit a great deal of year-to-year variation: in 1976 the reported figure was some 77 per cent, while in 1986 it was 84 per cent. It should be noted, however, that at least one study has raised some questions about the degree of success involved in the sub-set of cases labelled as involving 'progress towards a settlement' in these official figures.[19] Nevertheless, there does appear to have been something of a change in the major source of requests for conciliation: in 1976, for example, some 57 per cent came from unions and 24 per cent were joint requests, whereas in 1986 the union figure was 39 per cent and the joint figure 50 per cent. Finally, although there was a decline in the proportion of disciplinary procedures that provided for third-party intervention by ACAS in the years 1980–4, the use of ACAS in pay disputes rose (from 11 to 19 per cent of cases) in these same years.[20]

There has not been a great deal of substantive research on the factors associated with variation in the role and importance of conciliation facilities between different national systems of industrial relations, although it has been suggested that its importance is inversely related to the extent of legislation covering terms and conditions of employment.[21] However, Krislov's examination of the conciliation agencies of five different countries (including Britain) suggested that there was considerable discussion and debate concerning the following common issues in the 1970s and early 1980s:[22] (i) the administrative place of the agency; (ii) the reluctance of some parties to use conciliation; (iii) the curtailment of conciliation when an incomes policy is in operation; and (iv) the shifting of some of the costs from the general taxpayer to the parties. In addition to these issues, a significant matter that has confronted the conciliation services of a number of countries has been the concern that the short-term-settlement orientation (above all else) of traditional conciliation may be dealing only with the particular manifestations, rather than the underlying causes, of problems in individual high-conflict (low-trust), adversarial union–management relationships. This concern has produced arguments in favour of adopting a 'strategic' conciliation/mediation approach designed to create a more favourable environment within which unions and management can interact.[23] In the United States and certain provinces of Canada (e.g. Ontario) such strategic or preventative conciliation/mediation programmes have existed for a number of years. There is, for example, the 'Relations by Objectives' programme of the Federal Mediation and Conciliation Service in the US, which involves conciliators with expertise in the subjects of team-building and goal-setting working with union and management representatives to try and improve the overall quality of their collective bargaining relationship.[24]

In Britain, the Commission on Industrial Relations (CIR) sought in the early 1970s to stimulate industrial-relations reform along the lines of the recommendations in the Report of the Donovan Commission, although its role appeared in practice to be of only secondary importance relative to crises or traumas (e.g. the threat of plant closure) in stimulating actual attitude change and reform in individual union–management situations.[25] Currently, ACAS operates an advisory function, with more than a third of its workload being estimated (by individual ACAS officers) to arise out of prior conciliation contacts, which deals with a sizeable range of subjects; grievance procedures, disciplinary procedures, pay systems, and individual employee rights have accounted for much of its workload in recent years. The individual component of the work of the ACAS advisory function which comes closest to a preventative or strategic conciliation approach is the establishment of joint working parties, where 'the aim is to foster as far as possible a rational team approach to the solving of problems which yields results compatible with the objectives of both parties.'[26]

The ACAS annual report for 1981 indicated the existence of 74 joint working parties (a third of these having arisen from prior conciliation and another third having followed a diagnostic survey undertaken by the service), while the report for 1986 revealed the number of such parties to be 150. Although the turnover of key management or union personnel has been identified as a factor hindering the performance of such arrangements, the processes and outcomes of such joint problem-solving structures have not, as yet, been the subject of any detailed empirical research. Finally, it is relevant to note that the Work Research Unit (established as a branch of the Department of Employment in 1974) was transferred to ACAS in May 1985. This particular unit has traditionally been concerned with organizational change, quality of working life, and job-design issues, all of which have continued to figure prominently in their workload.

In Britain, compulsory arbitration arrangements have largely been confined to the two wartime periods, with voluntary arbitration being essentially the traditional, back-up stage to attempts to achieve a settlement via conciliation. Having said this, some dispute resolution procedures can provide for going straight to arbitration without a preliminary attempt at conciliation (i.e. 20–30 per cent of cases is often a figure cited by individual ACAS officers in this regard). The formal, system-wide basis of voluntary arbitration in Britain was provided by the Industrial Courts Act 1919 which created a permanent arbitration tribunal – the Industrial Court (renamed the Industrial Arbitration Board in 1971) – and provided for the appointment of *ad hoc* arbitrators and boards of arbitration; the non-industrial Civil Service was removed from the jurisdiction of the Industrial Court with the creation of a separate Civil Service arbitration tribunal in 1936. In the years 1939–59, for example, there was an annual average of some 50 awards by the Industrial Court, 35 by single arbitrators or boards of arbitration, 15 by the Civil Service arbitration tribunal, compared to an annual average of some 285 conciliated settlements in these years.[27] The relative absence of compulsory arbitration arrangements in Britain has meant that the alleged 'chilling' and 'narcotic' effects of such arrangements on the processes of collective bargaining have obviously not attracted anything like the research interest that has been accorded these matters in the United States.[28] Nevertheless, industrial-relations researchers in both systems have long been interested in the nature of the decision-making process involved in arbitration awards, in particular the extent to which arbitrators seek to fashion compromise solutions by splitting the difference between the positions of the parties in dispute; or else seek to produce acceptable or workable awards which reflect the arbitrator's judgement as to which party would have won if relative bargaining power had been the sole determinant of the outcome. However, beyond Sharp's examination of some early awards of the Industrial Court,[29] and a study of the awards of the Civil Service arbitration tribunal to the end of the

1950s,[30] empirical studies of the nature of arbitrator decision-making processes and the outcomes of awards are relatively few in Britain; as a consequence, the 'split the difference' notion, for example, is more an article of faith than a well-established empirical proposition.

At the present time, ACAS provides arbitration facilities under the terms of Section 3 of the Employment Protection Act 1975 by appointing individuals (typically academics) from a list of regular arbitrators; ACAS's own employees do not act as arbitrators. Table 8.2 sets out the arbitration case-load of ACAS for the years 1976–86.

Table 8.2 ACAS arbitration case-load, 1976–86*

Year	*Number of cases referred*
1976	323
1977	327
1978	421
1979	395
1980	322
1981	257
1982	251
1983	207
1984	202
1985	162
1986	184

Source: Relevant annual reports of ACAS.

*These figures are for both arbitration and mediation, although the former is overwhelmingly the major process involved (e.g. in 1986 there were only 10 cases involving mediation). The figures here exclude cases where ACAS assisted with private arbitration arrangements.

As the majority of arbitration cases arise out of unsuccessful, prior attempts at conciliation, it is not surprising to find here a substantial decline in the number of references to arbitration; however, the fall here (43 per cent) is less than that for the reduction in conciliation claims (58 per cent) over the same period of time. The vast majority of arbitration cases have involved single arbitrators (i.e. between 80 and 90 per cent of them), although there has been a change in the sources of dispute in these cases over the course of time. In 1976, for example, pay and terms and conditions of employment, and discipline and dismissals, were the two major sources of dispute, accounting for some 82 per cent and 10 per cent, respectively, of all arbitration cases, whereas in 1986 (although still the two major sources of dispute), the relevant figures were 60 per cent and 26 per cent, respectively.

The other body currently responsible for arbitration in Britain is the Central Arbitration Committee (CAC) which replaced the Industrial Arbitration Board, and was originally made responsible for ensuring the observance of certain provisions of the Employment Protection Act 1975: namely, Schedule 11 (extension of terms and conditions of employment), Sections 19–21 (disclosure of information for collective bargaining purposes), and Section 16 (observance of a recommendation for trade union recognition). The CAC was also empowered to ensure the observance of the Equal Pay Act, 1970. In the late 1970s, the CAC enjoyed a substantial workload, largely as a result of the number of claims under Schedule 11 and the Fair Wages Resolution of 1946 that sought to evade the restrictions of incomes policy in those years;[31] in the two years 1978–9, for example, the CAC made 826 awards under Schedule 11 and 514 under the Fair Wages Resolution. However, with the present Conservative Government operating without any formal, comprehensive incomes policy and having repealed both Schedule 11 and Section 16 of the Employment Protection Act 1975 and rescinded the Fair Wages Resolution of 1946, the arbitration workload of the CAC has fallen dramatically; in 1985, for example, there were only some 20 references to arbitration (16 of these concerning disclosure of information for collective bargaining purposes). The rather predictable result of this dramatic change was the CAC's call for the establishment of one organization as the focal point for all industrial arbitration,[32] although ACAS were less than enthusiastic about this proposal, arguing that there were advantages to maintaining the present flexibility of arbitration arrangements which derive from procedural differences between their practices and those of the CAC[33] (e.g. the CAC is required to publish its arbitration awards, whereas those of ACAS remain private to the parties).

In recent years there have been a number of significant developments in, and proposals concerning, arbitration arrangements in Britain. For example, the present Conservative Government have explicitly rejected the use of arbitration arrangements in a number of public-sector disputes, most notably in the Civil Service and NHS strikes of 1981 and 1982 respectively. In the latter strike, for instance, the Minister for Health at the time was strongly opposed to the use of arbitration – on the stated grounds that arbitrators are not ultimately accountable to the public at large and tend to try and fashion compromise solutions by splitting the difference between the positions of the two parties in dispute.[34] Furthermore, a Government report in the early 1980s, which examined 17 arbitration agreements in the public sector, recommended that in 11 of them the employers withdraw from and renegotiate the existing arrangements.[35] The essence of the recommended change was a move away from the right of unilateral reference to arbitration (traditionally much more of a feature of the public than the private sector), on the grounds that the existing arrangements: (i) encouraged irresponsibility among the parties (in that they had no responsibility for the final agreement and thus tended to hold to their original bargaining positions); (ii) favoured the union side; and (iii) were potentially inflationary in that they tended to undermine the effective operation of incomes policies and the system of cash limits. In the early 1980s, some banks also removed the unilateral right to arbitration in a number of procedural agreements in the finance sector.

As was seen in Chapter 6, the number and employee coverage of 'single-union-recognition/no-strike' package agreements is relatively limited in Britain at the present time. However, the final-offer arbitration procedures contained in these agreements have been a source of considerable interest to both industrial-relations researchers and practitioners: the Institute of Directors, for example, have advocated the use of final-offer arbitration arrangements in essential public services.[36] The essence of these procedures, which are historically associated with a number of public-sector jurisdictions in the United States, is that the arbitrator cannot make a compromise award, but rather must choose either the final offer of the employer or the final demand of the union; the belief underlying this practice is that it will mean greater potential costs for both parties in going to arbitration, so that the 'chilling' effect (i.e. little movement from the original bargaining positions) and 'narcotic' effect (i.e. repeated reference to arbitration over the course of time) on collective bargaining of conventional arbitration should be eliminated or substantially reduced. The operation of final-offer arbitration arrangements in certain parts of the public sector in the United States has been the subject of a good deal of research, with the available evidence providing some support for the alleged benefits of such arrangements on the process of collective bargaining.[37]

In Britain there has been some initial *a priori* scepticism about, not to say criticism of, the alleged virtues of such arrangements. The points typically made include a rejection of the view that conventional arbitration invariably involves compromise (i.e. split-the-difference) awards, and an emphasis on the difficulties of precisely identifying final offers and operating such arrangements in complicated, multiple-issue disputes.[38] In view of this general concern about the inflexibility of final-offer arbitration, it is interesting to note that when the final-offer arbitration arrangements were invoked in the Sanyo–EETPU agreement in 1985, some *ad hoc* flexibility was introduced into the procedures by the use of mediation, although the agreement did not formally provide for such usage. The limited presence of final-offer arbitration procedures in Britain at present has obviously restricted the amount of detailed empirical research undertaken, although some economists are likely to begin to follow their American counterparts in developing models of arbitrator behaviour under final-offer and conventional arrangements.[39] Indeed, some work along these lines has already been stimulated by Meade's view of arbitration as a potentially important vehicle of anti-inflation policy.[40] The essence of the Meade proposal is that, in the event of a dispute, either party could take the issue to a permanently established national arbitration court – which would be statutorily obliged to make an award on the basis of whether or not the rate of pay in dispute would constrain or encourage employment in that particular sector of the economy. A possible cooling-off period and sanctions for non-compliance with the court's awards are also discussed, but it has been the arbitrators' use of a single criterion (i.e. employment promotion) which has attracted most discussion. In effect, this 'not-quite-compulsory-arbitration' notion would essentially seem to involve a final-offer process (i.e. no capacity for compromise) in that the arbitrator has to make a straight choice between the employer offer and union demand, once the employment consequences of each are known. This proposal has already produced a number of critical responses by economists in Britain.[41] (which have generally questioned the validity of some of Meade's implicit assumptions about labour-market structure and union behaviour). It is interesting to note, however, that a greater use of disequilibrium quantity measures (as a means of injecting market criteria into the process) by arbitrators have also come in for recent discussion in other countries.[42]

As we have already noted, the broadening and expansion of the concept of the social or public interest in industrial relations – from a concern with the process of collective bargaining to a concern with the substantive outcomes of such bargaining – raised the possibility of some degree of conflict between these two constituent elements. This possibility appeared to have been realized, with the operation of incomes policy generally tending to undermine the perceived independence, and hence actual usage, of third-party-dispute resolution procedures (the experience of the CAC in the late 1970s being an interesting exceptional case in this regard). However, this individual cost of incomes policy may be viewed by the Government of the day as one worth paying, if the more general anticipated benefits of the policy were in fact realized. It is the larger record of incomes policy that we now consider.

Incomes policy and the concern with substantive outcomes

The substantial volume of literature on incomes policy in Britain and other countries has basically been concerned with the following matters: (i) the theoretical rationale for such policies; (ii) their form or manner of operations; (iii) the degree of effectiveness and success of such policies in practice and the methodological issues involved in evaluating such effects; and (iv) the practical problems encountered and possible changes or reforms to eliminate, or at least minimize, the future occurrence of such problems. These will be the issues or themes covered in the discussion of this section.

The positions that individual commentators adopt concerning the necessity and value of incomes policy are strongly shaped by their particular views with regard to the key determinants of money and real-wage change. In general, it is clear that the more institutional forces, particularly the role of unions (be it couched in terms of conflict over income shares, wage-leadership sectors, the level of real-wage aspirations, cost push effects, etc.), are held to be influential determinants of the extent and nature of wage-change, the more an individual is inclined to believe that there is some case for the use of incomes policy. From the 1960s, economists' discussions of the nature of wage-change have tended to evolve through a number of stages – from simple Phillips-curve relationships to expectations-augmented, Phillips-curve relationships and, more recently, into concepts and models of real-wage resistance.[43] These particular concepts, relationships, and models have figured prominently in discussions of the case both for and against the introduction of incomes policy. For example, advocates of the need for an incomes policy initially tended to argue that such a policy could produce a more acceptable inflation/unemployment trade-off by shifting the intercept term and/or slope of the Phillips curve, while subsequently it was argued to have the potential to (i) reduce inflationary expectations (thereby lowering the cost of controlling inflation in terms of the level of output and employment loss), and (ii) more closely align the level of union real-wage aspirations and targets with the productive capability of the economy. These same concepts could, of course, figure in arguments in which there was seen to be no case for having an incomes policy (e.g. a situation in which there was a stable, steeply-sloped Phillips-curve relationship – where traditional demand-management policies were held to be sufficient to produce an acceptable inflation–unemployment trade-off). Incomes policies in Britain have also had a number of secondary aims and rationales (such as that of reducing the extent of wage inequality) but, in general, the arguments for and against the introduction of such policies have tended to revolve around different views of the nature of the inflationary process. These differences of opinion have meant that the policy's rationale:

> As a means of controlling inflation, restraining union pushfulness, influencing inflation expectations, or producing permanent reductions in the unions' real wage target have all been criticised. Incomes policies have also been accused of distorting market signals, leading to a loss of efficiency in allocating resources . . . The essential point is that the case for incomes policy is based as much on the failure or inadequacy of the alternatives as on the policy's own particular merits. For its supporters, the hope has always been that the policies of tomorrow will be better than those of yesterday and today. For governments, moreover, the policy has the major virtue that it has an immediate visible impact, indicating that at least something is being done. In this sense the most convincing rationale for incomes policy is to be found more in the realm of political economy than of economics.[44]

The latter point made above receives some (but not overwhelming) support from the available opinion-poll evidence in Britain concerning the popularity of incomes policy with the public and electorate at large,[45] while a recent statistical study of the US experience has suggested that 'governments have been inclined to turn to an incomes policy when the popularity of the government is low'.[46] The provisions and associated administrative arrangements of incomes policy have varied a great deal, both between countries and within individual countries over the course of time. In cross-country comparisons, for example, the administrative basis of incomes policy has variously involved direct Government intervention, compulsory arbitration, employer co-ordination, bipartite co-operation between employers and trade unions, and tripartite co-operation between Government, employers, and the trade unions.[47] In particular, John Burton (writing as early as 1972) has aptly noted that Britain 'has gone through a veritable Kama Sutra of incomes-policy experiments and variations in the last couple of decades.'[48] He goes on to argue that the traditional 'soft–hard' dichotomy of incomes policy fails to reflect anything like the full variety of measures which have been used, and proposes a typology of incomes policy instruments which is as follows:[49]

1. Governmental exhortation for voluntary adherence to designated patterns of behaviour.
2. The surveillance, analysis, and public exposure of 'undesirable' wage and price movements.
3. Active governmental denunciations of non-co-operative behaviour.
4. Paradigmatic behaviour in the public sector.
5. The extraction of commitments to voluntary compliance.
6. Governmental intimidation and deterrence.
7. The use of legal powers and sanctions.

In Britain, incomes policies have typically been introduced in the circumstances of balance-of-payments difficulties, have initially involved short-term freezes on wages, and have generally been characterized by direct Government intervention and the use of statutory means of control. These particular policy characteristics have been held to be the result of Britain's relatively poor macro-economic performance in recent decades, the size of the public sector (where the centralized bargaining arrangements make for sizeable individual bargaining units whose settlements are highly visible), and the relatively decentralized nature of collective-bargaining structures in the private sector.[50] Table 8.3 sets out some basic information on the incomes policies of the 1970s in Britain.

In general, academic commentators in Britain have been far from impressed with the track record of incomes policies to date, with references typically being made to the following points: (i) such policies have not survived the course of time (typically being formally broken by strikes in the public sector): (ii) any short-run wage-restraint achieved by the policy has been offset (at least) by a wage explosion when the policy comes to an end; (iii) any stated objective of assisting lower-paid workers under such policies has not been achieved;[51] and (iv) some 'institutional costs' have occurred as a result of some impact on both the level of strike activity and the perceived independence of third-party-dispute resolution procedures.[52] However, it must be recognized that there are considerable difficulties involved in any estimation work concerned to identify the impact of incomes policy, *ceteris paribus*. According to Robinson and Mayhew, for example, 'precise quantification of incomes policy . . . cannot, in the present state of knowledge, be obtained. Assessments of the efficacy of incomes policy are therefore judgements rather than accurate measurements.'[53]

Table 8.3 Wage inflation and incomes policy in the 1970s in Britain

Incomes policy		*Changes in average weekly earnings (%)* (i) Prescribed by the policy	(ii) Actual
November 1972–April 1973	Freeze	0	1.8
April 1973–November 1973	£1 + 4% (£5 max)	6.7	10.3
November 1973–August 1974	£2.25 or 7% (£7 max) + 'threshold'	13.0	14.9
August 1974–August 1975	No limit	No limit	25.9
August 1975–August 1976	£6	10.4	14.3
August 1976–August 1977	5% (£2.50 min, £4 max)	4.5	7.3
August 1977–August 1978	10%	10.0	13.9

Source: Richard Layard (1986), *How To Beat Unemployment*, p. 128, Oxford: Oxford University Press.

The traditional approach of using policy on (policy off) dummy variables in wage equations to identify the impact of incomes policy has been substantially criticized for: (i) treating all policy episodes as relatively homogeneous in nature; (ii) treating the life-cycle of any one policy episode as relatively homogeneous in nature; (iii) assuming that the major impact of a policy episode is restricted essentially to the period of time in which the policy is operative; and (iv) possibly picking up the influence of other unidentified factors which are correlated with the policy years. Other criticisms include the fact that such estimation work makes no allowance for the effects of unions and management anticipating in their wage-bargaining the introduction of future wage controls.[54] There have been a number of responses to these sorts of methodological criticisms. For example, some more recent estimating work which still uses the dummy-variable approach does at least attempt to identify a potentially offsetting 'catch-up' or 'rebound' effect when the policy comes to an end.[55] There has also been some use made of simulation models (particularly in the US) which involve basic wage and price equations being estimated for non-policy periods, and their coefficients being used to generate predicated values of wage and price changes during subsequent policy periods; the difference between the actual and predicted values during the policy period being interpreted as the impact of the policy.[56] This particular approach, however, is difficult to utilize in economies (such as Britain) where some form of incomes policy has been a relatively regular feature of the environment over an extended period of time. One recent British study, which has criticized subjectively-derived dummy-variables to measure the strength of incomes policy, has also attempted to develop a more quantitative, continuous measure of incomes policy – based on real-wage pressure, the stringency of government attempts to apply the policy, and the overall response of the trade-union movement.[57] Finally, the results of one recent study in Britain appear to caution against judgements concerning the effect of incomes policy in general; the policies in 1975–7, for example, having 'led to a large deceleration in wage inflation, while the measured "catch up" effect is much smaller.'[58]

This finding concerning the differential impact of various periods of incomes policy is likely to encourage and stimulate further work on and discussion of the subject. Indeed, both economists and industrial-relations specialists still continue to discuss and debate the need for, and form of, a viable incomes policy in Britain, although (i) the present Conservative Government is the first administration not to have operated a formal, system-wide incomes policy in Britain in nearly 20 years, and (ii) incomes policies in the past in Britain have been anything but uniformly successful. This search for a new and better form of incomes policy in the future has been influenced by a number of factors. First, a belief that the economic circumstances of the past which have produced a need for an incomes policy are likely to continue to exist in the foreseeable future. Second, the view that there are no obviously superior policy alternatives to that of incomes policy. Third, the contention that the past failures of incomes policy are not inherent in the policy instrument, but rather have been due to issues and problems that are potentially capable of reform and remedy. In putting forward the latter sort of argument, reference is often made to the disruptive effects of external shocks to the economy, the non-complementary relationship between the operation of incomes policy and that of monetary policy in particular periods of time, the uneven incidence of the policy which has produced a backlash against it by particular groups of employees, and the relative loose specification (and monitoring) of 'exceptional' categories of workers entitled to wage increases above the general norm or limit laid down by the policy. In short, the belief is that the mistakes of the past are well known and need not necessarily be repeated in the future.

The result of this belief has been a substantial variety of proposals which are usefully surveyed by Blackaby in an aptly titled paper.[59] The individual proposals discussed by Blackaby are grouped under the following basic headings: (i) 'social contract' or concerted action proposals; (ii) traditional proposals for a norm with exceptions (e.g. a relativities board); (iii) the increased synchronization of pay settlements (or compression of the wage bargaining round); (iv) various proposals specifically concerned with the public sector (e.g. increased union co-ordination, synchronization of key settlement dates, amalgamation of individual review bodies, etc.); (v) alterations in the balance of bargaining power (e.g. a strike insurance fund for employers, more co-ordination among large companies in their pay-bargaining stance); (vi) tax-based incomes policies; and (vii) more radical proposals (e.g. Meade's not-quite-compulsory arbitration notion and Phelps Brown's idea of a central, tripartite consortium). At the present time it is tax-based incomes policy proposals which are most extensively discussed in Britain, although proposals along such lines are not particularly new; tax-based schemes to create rewards or penalties for parties complying, or not complying, with policy guidelines were widely discussed in the United States in the 1970s.[60] In Britain, the most well-known advocate of a tax-based incomes policy is undoubtedly Richard Layard, whose basic position is as follows:[61]

1. Conventional incomes policies have only worked for short periods of time. As a permanent policy-instrument they have the disadvantages that they suspend free collective bargaining, cannot adequately provide for the adjustment of wage differentials, and have more potential to affect wage settlements rather than actual pay levels.
2. Each year the Government should declare a norm for the growth of average hourly earnings. If earnings increase more than this figure, each enterprise would pay a tax on all its excess wage payments. (The tax rate should be a steep one.)
3. The presence of such a tax would influence the motivation and targets of both employers and unions in wage bargaining, with the result being a reduction in the degree of real-wage pressure at a given level of unemployment.
4. The tax should be confined to the private sector and the nationalized industries. However, its influence would be reflected in public-sector pay levels through the processes of comparability, etc.
5. The tax should come into effect immediately following the relatively short period of operation of a conventional incomes policy.

6. The tax should be levied at the level of the firm and, in the private sector, should cover only firms employing more than 100 workers. Pay would be defined as for PAYE. The firm would assess its own tax liability as for PAYE, and send in a cheque. The auditing of the scheme would only involve about 100 inspectors.
7. The tax would be part of the tax law, but the TUC and CBI would be consulted about the size of the wage norm.
8. The two potential costs of the tax-based policy explicitly mentioned by Layard are: the discouragement of productivity bargaining, and the penalties imposed on firms that are interested in upgrading the quality of their workforces.

Most of the responses to the Layard proposal, and discussions of tax-based incomes policies more generally, have focused on the potential problem areas of coverage, the passing on of the tax, and the administration of the tax,[62] although (arguably) the major difficulty will still concern the determination of an appropriate and acceptable wage norm which is inevitably much more of a political than an economic problem. The problem of application to the public sector has also been raised in relation to the Layard type of proposal. Moreover, the historical record indicates that the public sector has always been the major problem area in the administration of incomes policies in Britain – with virtually all periods of such policies having been formally broken by public-sector strikes and followed by wage explosions (e.g. 1969–70, 1972, 1974–5, and 1978–9), in which public-sector groups have been particularly prominent. In the light of such relationships, the next section of the chapter presents a discussion of the nature of public-sector industrial relations.[63]

Public-sector industrial relations

The analysis and recommendations of the Donovan Commission (1965–8) viewed the problems of British industrial relations as being very much problems of the private sector. This was because in the mid to late 1960s the public sector was an area of employment where authoritative, national-level, collective bargaining was subject to little challenge or threat from fractional bargaining or unofficial industrial action at the level of the individual workplace. At the same time, formal, comprehensive incomes policies were in their relative infancy in Britain, so that the wage outcomes of the public sector had not, as yet, been subject to any sustained and substantial 'attack from above'. The result was that the public sector hardly figured at all in the discussions of the desired direction(s) of reform in British industrial relations in the decade of the 1960s.

However, some 20 years after the report of the Donovan Commission, the position has changed to such an extent that most commentators now view any industrial-relations problems in Britain as being overwhelmingly centred in the public sector. In the 1980s, for example, it has been estimated that the proportion of working days lost through strikes in the public sector ranged from 43.7 per cent in 1981 to 88 per cent in 1984.[64] However, most commentators have taken a somewhat longer time-perspective, and viewed the whole of the 1970s as constituting a significant turning-point, or watershed, in public-sector industrial relations in Britain. Indeed, in the 1970s, one commentator observed some notable changes in 'the character' of unions – as indicated by increased strike activity and increased affiliations to the TUC – which were held to be overwhelmingly the result of perceived discriminatory treatment under incomes policies. Such changes in union attitudes and behaviour in the public sector have continued, and arguably increased, in the 1980s as a result of relative wage losses, although to this determinant of change has been added the facts and features of: (i) public-sector employment reductions; (ii) attempts to introduce private-sector employment practices into the public sector; and (iii) some government criticisms and attacks on public-sector union organization, facilities, and collective-bargaining arrangements. These causes of public-sector, industrial-relations change in the 1980s will hopefully be apparent as a result of the discussion in this section.

As a starting point, it is useful to identify a number of features that have traditionally differentiated public-sector from private-sector, industrial-relations arrangements in Britain.[74] Such a list would typically include the following: (i) the key role of the Government as a direct (or indirect) employer of labour; (ii) the relative remoteness of market (as opposed to political) forces; (iii) the relatively high level of unionization; (iv) the relative strength of national-level bargaining arrangements; and (v) the 'mixed', management-side (i.e. immediate, local employers and relevant central Government department) representation on a number of negotiating bodies in the public sector. In pointing to these (and other possible) differences between the public and private sectors, it is important, however, not to lose sight of certain important industrial-relations differences within the public sector itself. For example, in the case of the public corporations there is not the mixed, management-side representation on negotiating bodies that has existed in the case of education and the health service. Furthermore, in those parts of the public sector that have been taken relatively recently into public ownership from the private sector, there are likely to be important historical and traditional influences shaping contemporary structures and patterns of behaviour that differentiate them from the more long-standing parts of the public sector.

The public sector has long been the most highly unionized part of the economy, a fact attributed to the roles of employment concentration in large-sized establishments and the Government's encouragement of union membership there. This high level of union density is far from being overwhelmingly a manual-worker phenomenon, as union organization in the public sector extends well up the white collar employment hierarchy, reaching levels and positions that are relatively under-organized in the private sector. At the present time it is estimated that: (i) the level of union density in the public sector is some 81 per cent (compared to 38 per cent in the private sector); (ii) some 30 of the 88 unions affiliated to the TUC are solely or largely public-sector based; and (iii) some 44 per cent of the total TUC membership comes from public-sector unions.[65] Closely related to this high union density is the relatively high level of collective-bargaining coverage in the public sector. In 1978, for example, 90 per cent of male managers in the public sector had their pay determined by collective bargaining arrangements, whereas in the private sector the comparable figure was only 27 per cent.[66] Moreover, the public sector has long been the part of the industrial-relations system dominated by national or industry-level collective bargaining. However, as we saw in Chapter 5, there have been some recent changes in this regard – with the present Government being particularly keen to see further moves in the direction of more decentralized bargaining. As noted earlier in this chapter, the Government has also been highly critical of the operation of arbitration arrangements, and desires to see a move away from the right of unilateral access to arbitration facilities in the public sector. The most well publicized, not to say criticized, initiative of the Government in relation to public-sector unionization was the decision to ban or decertify trade unions at GCHQ at Cheltenham from March 1984. Following the House of Lords ruling in November 1984 in favour of the Government, the employee ballot results (announced in January 1985) showed that 58 per cent of those employees who voted (the turn-out figure was 66 per cent) were in favour of a staff association at GCHQ; the constitution of the resulting 'Government Communications Staff Federation' prohibits all forms of industrial action. The reaction of the unions is well known. Their offer of a no-strike agreement as a substitute for decertification was not accepted by the Government, protest stoppages occurred in the public sector (involving 120,000 working days lost in the quarter ending March 1984), the TUC temporarily withdrew from the NEDC, and the Council of Civil Service Unions took the case (unsuccessfully) to the European Court of Justice. The unions have also raised the question of whether this particular instance of union decertification will stimulate and encourage further moves along these lines. Most recently, changes in the contracts and methods of payment of senior management in British Rail have resulted in them being no longer represented by a union for collective-bargaining purposes. Furthermore, as noted in Chapter 3, the public sector has been very much to the forefront in the removal of closed-shop arrangements, the present edition of the Civil Service staff handbook no longer explicitly encourages employees to join a union, and the Civil Service national agreement on time off for trade-union duties has been extensively revised.

The present Conservative Government has frequently stated its opposition to the introduction of any sort of formal, comprehensive incomes policy. However, such statements need to be viewed in the light of frequent critical calls by Ministers for the exercise of 'responsible' wage behaviour and the Government's use of the cash-limits approach in the public sector. The essence of the latter has been: (i) the Government's *prior* announcement of a pay-provision figure for central Government services (i.e. 4 per cent in 1981–2, 3.5 per cent in 1982–3, 3 per cent in 1983–4, 3 per cent in 1984–5 – this practice was discontinued from 1985–6); (ii) strict limits in the Rate Support Grant and rate-capping for any overspending authorities in local government; and (iii) the use of external financing limits to constrain the spending of public corporations and the setting of performance targets for each of these industries.

A general review of pay movements in the public sector since 1979 reveals, first, that the rate of earnings increase in the public sector generally exceeded that in the private sector in 1979–80 and 1980–1. The relative gain of the public sector in 1979–81 should be seen in the light of the relative-wage movement against the public sector from the mid-1970s, and the resulting 'catch-up' awards of the Clegg Comparability Commission (which was abolished in August 1980). In contrast, in the four years 1981–2 to 1984–5, relative wage movements were against the public sector, whereas in 1985–6 there appeared to be rather less difference in the rate of earnings increase in the two sectors. Second, in any one year, the vast majority of public-sector wage settlements have exceeded the

Government's prior stated pay provisions, although the Government could clearly claim some degree of success in helping to bring down settlement levels in consecutive years: from a range of, for example, 13–20 per cent in 1981–2 to 4.5–6.5 per cent in 1984–5. Third, there was some notable variation in the size of wage settlements within the public sector itself: the size of settlements for the police (with their special indexation arrangements), for example, have consistently exceeded that of the public sector as a whole.

In the public sector at the present time, it is important to distinguish between groups whose pay is determined by a pay-review body, or by reference to a pay formula, and those where collective bargaining is still the determining factor. In the NHS at least 50 per cent of employees are currently covered by the recommendations of pay-review bodies, while in local government both the police and fire services now have their pay linked (albeit in different ways) to average-earnings movements. The majority of public-sector wage settlements are now concentrated in the months of April and July (the April concentration has been particularly encouraged by the TUC public services committee), and in the 1987 pay round we find that:[67]

(i) the range of settlements fell broadly in line with the range in the private sector, between 4.5 per cent and 7 per cent;
(ii) the review body groups received awards broadly in line with average earnings increases; 9.5 per cent for the nurses, 8.25 per cent for the doctors, and 4.7 per cent for the armed forces;
(iii) the indexation arrangements for police and firemen yielded 7.75 and 7.3 per cent respectively;
(iv) average earnings in the public sector were £197.30 per week in April 1987 compared to £199.60 per week in the private sector. (The average increase in 1986–7 was 6.9 per cent in the public sector, compared to 8.1 per cent in the private sector.)

Prior to 1985, major and even minor salary-structure adjustments were relatively few and far between in the public sector. However, in response to the increased bunching of white-collar staff at the top of salary structures in a number of areas of the public sector, and the Government's general desire to see pay related more closely to performance and market forces, 1985 witnessed merit- or performance-related pay proposals, such as in the case of the Civil Aviation Authority, where management proposed that the incremental structures for the majority of staff be replaced with a unified system of merit-based increases. Second, there was salary restructuring to alleviate pressure at the top; such restructuring occurred in some eight public-sector organizations in 1985. In the case of electricity supply, for example, management and higher-executive salary scales were restructured by deleting an increment at the bottom of the scale and adding a new one at the top. Third, there were special pay additions in 'hard-to-fill' vacancy areas – notably for secretarial staff in inner London, scientists at the Atomic Weapons Research Establishment at Aldermaston and the Royal Ordnance Factory at Burghfield, and insolvency staff at the Department of Trade – also discretionary payments for computer staffs and payments for GCHQ scientists.

Both the 1986 and 1987 pay rounds saw salary restructuring moves along these lines continuing in various parts of the public sector; the attempt here being to relate pay to 'merit', 'skills', and local labour-market conditions. For example, major restructuring developments in 1987 involved: professional, scientific, and technical Civil Servants; teachers; the NHS; local government groups; and staff at the Civil Aviation Authority, British Rail, Travellers Fare, London Transport, and the United Kingdom Atomic Energy Authority.[68] Obviously, questions (not to say criticisms) continue to surround such proposals in a sector where objective, quantifiable measures of output, and hence of performance, are so frequently lacking.

It was noted above that the present Government is strongly in favour of public sector pay being more closely related to the movement of market forces and measures of individual and organizational performance. The other side of this coin is the desire to significantly reduce the role of comparability in the wage-determination processes of the public sector; this is obviously related to the anti-national bargaining stance of the Government. Comparability has in fact been a major principle of pay determination in much of the public sector over a number of decades, with the commitment to comparability being most explicitly institutionalized in the case of the non-industrial Civil Service, where arrangements have come into frequent conflict with the operation of incomes policy and, subsequently, cash limits. The present Government's preference for arguments based on ability to pay and employee recruitment and retention figures in the Civil Service, was an important part of the background to the termination of its agreement with the national-staff side in 1981, and its willingness to accept a 21-week strike in order to keep down the size of the pay settlement in the Civil Service. The final settlement package included the establishment of the Megaw Committee of Enquiry into Civil Service pay, whose recommendations (in July 1982) downgraded, rather than eliminated, comparability as a factor in Civil Service pay determination.

The Government's desire to 'de-prioritize' comparability as a factor in wage determination is not confined to the Civil Service. Two tangible expressions, or indications, of their more general desire in this direction are: (i) their general reluctance to allow any further groups of public-sector employees to achieve 'special case' status through coverage by review bodies or indexation agreements; and (ii) the ending of a number of formal, intra-public-sector wage relationships, such as that between manual workers in local government and the NHS in 1980. It is important to emphasize here that the attack on the role and strength of the comparability principle in public-sector wage determination did not originate with the present Government. The National Board for Prices and Incomes which operated in the years 1965–70, for example, was a most outspoken critic of the strength of this particular influence in the public sector.[69] It is also relevant to note here the differing findings of two recent studies of the determinants of sectoral earnings in Britain. Some researchers at the National Institute of Economic and Social Research report that public corporations appear to lead other sectors, whereas work at the Centre for Labour Economics at LSE finds that it is the private sector which always constitutes the lead sector in earnings movements.[70] These differences indicate the sensitivity of estimation results to a particular model specification and the basic data source utilized. Moreover, a recent paper by Elliott and Murphy, which examines the relative pay of public and private sector employees for the years 1970–84, has argued that comparisons based on changes in average earnings can produce misleading impressions in that they fail to take account of influences such as changes in the age and occupational structures of the two sectors of employment.[71] Indeed, their adjusted figures suggest that the real relative wage loss of non-manual employees in central and local government was even greater over the period in question than a comparison of the 'raw' figures suggested. Finally, a recent study based on the wage data of the 1984 workplace industrial-relations survey revealed a 10 per cent wage premium to employees in nationalized industries, whereas for the rest of the public sector pay was some 15 per cent less.[72]

The 1970s was a decade in which there was considerable controversy concerning the growth of public-sector employment (and public expenditure) in Britain compared to that in previous periods of time and in other countries.[73] However, since 1979, a major facet or feature of change in the public sector has been the decline in employment there. In mid-1987 an estimated 6.4 million members

(25.7 per cent) of the total workforce were employed in the public sector – a figure comprising 1.0 million (4.0 per cent) in public corporations, 2.3 million (9.3 per cent) in central Government, and 3.1 million (12.3 per cent) in local authorities. Since 1981, public-sector employment has fallen (to mid-1987) by 11 per cent on a head-count basis, and by 15 per cent on a full-time-equivalent basis; excluding privatization of public corporations, the relevant reduction is of the order of 5–8 per cent. The level of public-sector employment is now at its lowest level since 1970, and Table 8.4 below sets out some more detailed figures for recent years.

Table 8.4 Employment changes, by sector, 1981–7

	000s	*% change*
Total employed labour force	+566	−2.3
Private sector	+1,380	+8.0
Public sector	−815	−11.3
Public corporations	−871	−46.7
General Government	+56	+1.1
Central Government	−107	−4.4
HM Forces	−15	−4.5
NHS	+5	+0.4
Other	−97	−11.0
Local authorities	+163	+5.6
Education	−32	+2.2
Social services	+48	+13.7
Police	+5	+2.7
Other	+78	+8.6

Source: M. Camley (1978), 'Employment in the public and private sectors 1981 to 1987', *Economic Trends*, no. 410, December, p. 98.

The present Government entered office with the explicit aim of reducing the size of the Civil Service from 732,000 to 630,000 posts by April 1984. In fact, the Government more than achieved this target, with the Civil Service being reduced by nearly 15 per cent by mid-1984 and, in November 1983, the Government announced its intention of seeking a further 6 per cent reduction of the Civil Service in the following four years (the manpower target for April 1988 was 590,400). It was estimated that only some 10 per cent of the reduction in the size of the Civil Service in 1979–84 had resulted from privatization (including contracting out), although it is generally felt that its proportionate contribution is likely to rise in the years 1984–8. The present Government's commitment to privatization has taken a number of forms. Selling off, in whole or part, has been the main strategy for the trading part of the public sector, with some sixteen major organizations having been privatized since 1979. In the service part of the public sector, the main policy has been to contract out to private companies those services previously performed by direct labour. The particular services targeted here for privatization are primarily cleaning, catering, laundry, and security services. In 1986 it was reported that some 16 per cent of local authorities had contracted out direct labour services to private contractors, while in the case of the NHS some available figures indicated the following basic position: the vast majority of competitive tenders have been for domestic services, with 29 per cent of these going to outside contractors, and with 5 per cent and 22 per cent of the smaller total number of tenders for catering and laundry services respectively going to outside contractors.[74] The recent Local Government Act is designed to ensure that local authorities seek tenders for refuse collection, street cleansing, building maintenance, ground maintenance, vehicle maintenance and catering, while the Government plans to privatize the British Steel Corporation, the electricity supply, and the water industry in the life of this Parliament.

Public-sector unions have expressed a number of worries and concerns about privatization, not the least of which has been the fear that their membership levels will plateau and then begin to decline. It is this particular fear that clearly influenced NALGO to pass a rule change to its constitution in 1984, allowing it to recruit members in the private sector (currently some 5 per cent of NALGO's membership is in the private sector). There have certainly been a number of well-publicized instances of local-level strike action against proposed privatization moves in the public sector, and in 1980–3 public sector employees were involved in nearly 50 per cent of all redundancy disputes (compared to 15 per cent in 1976–9) – although information provided by some of the key union officials involved in the early, large-scale privatization moves did not suggest any uniform pattern of substantial costs and losses to the unions concerned.[75] However, alongside these findings, it is important to note the recent critical review by the unions of the first 2 years of privatization in British Telecom. Among the union complaints and allegations were the following: (i) the fall in safety standards; (ii) the loss of more than 22,000 jobs since 1983, although BT engineers and technicians now work some 41 per cent more overtime than before privatization; (iii) the terms and conditions of remaining BT employees have worsened; and (iv) collective-bargaining structures have been undermined by decentralization, withdrawal of union recognition for managers, and the use of short-term contract staff. Such criticisms, although denied in a speech by

BT's chairman at the CBI conference in 1986, obviously formed an important part of the background to the 17-day BT dispute in January/February 1987.

Competitive tendering is only one (albeit the most controversial in nature) of the measures that the present Government has encouraged in its attempt to increase competitive pressures and efficiency in the public sector. Other well-known measures include the Rayner scrutinies and Financial Management Initiative in the Civil Service, the Griffiths Report recommendations and Resource Allocation Working Parties in the NHS, new systems of local government audit, more centralized control in the allocation of local authority funds, and the setting of performance targets for the individual public corporations. The whole thrust of the Government's approach is towards more decentralized, 'bottom-line' orientated management in the public sector. In summary, the new features of public-sector industrial relations in Britain in the 1980s (i.e. sizeable employment reductions, the replacement of traditional public-sector employment arrangements and practices with those drawn from the private sector, and the imposition of constraints on public-sector unionization) reflect the Government's views about the desirable means of macro-economic management (and the place of the public sector in this task) and, as such, are an excellent illustration of: (i) the major importance of political influences in public-sector industrial relations; and (ii) the fact that major impacts on industrial relations structures, processes and outcomes can result from decisions that are not exclusively, or even mainly, industrial-relations based.

Although individuals may disagree about the strength of the particular causes involved (e.g. reaction to incomes policy, changes in workforce composition, changes in the political complexion of union leadership, etc.) it was generally held that the changing nature of public-sector industrial relations in the 1970s derived from, or was at least most clearly manifested in, important changes in the character of the unions concerned. In essence, it was argued that employee representation bodies – particularly in the civil service, the NHS, and education sector – became increasingly less staff-association-like and, conversely, more union-like in their attitudes and behaviour during the course of the decade. This was indicated by a variety of actions that departed from traditional practice, most notably the increased occurrence of strikes and other forms of industrial action. The level of strike frequency in the public sector in the 1970s should certainly not be exaggerated, but there is no denying that it came increasingly to the forefront in discussions of the problems of British industrial relations. There are arguably three major reasons for the disproportionate amount of attention given to public-sector strikes in the decade of the 1970s (and subsequently). First, a number of national disputes involved groups of public-sector employees that had never previously been on strike (e.g. civil servants, firemen). Second, a considerable number of them were viewed as having constitutional overtones in that they were directed essentially against Government policy of the day; certainly, as we have already noted, virtually all episodes of incomes policy in Britain have been broken, at least formally, by public-sector strikes, with groups of public-sector employees spearheading the resulting 'pay explosions'. Third, these strikes have been alleged to be particularly high-cost ones, being especially harmful to the public at large and, in some cases, raising the possibility of threats to public health and safety.

Since the present Government came to power in 1979 there have been instances of national strike action in the public sector in virtually every year. These national-level actions have mainly concerned wage questions, although the miners' strike against pit closures in 1984–5 has been viewed as constituting the most direct challenge to overall Government strategy in the public sector. This particular dispute involved over 26 million working days lost, the highest in any industry since 1926 and, as a result, the total number of working days lost through strike activity in Britain was the second highest (after 1979) since the war; the strike was estimated to have affected the GDP of the country by 1.25 per cent – the major impact being felt through stock-building and imports.[76] There have been numerous discussions and analyses of the merits of the miners' case, the tactical errors made during the course of the dispute, and the larger implications for unions and management in the public sector.[77] There has also been much interest in the post-strike position in the industry – where certain key individuals have moved on, further pit closures have occurred, and disputes have continued to occur (for example, some 195 stoppages in the first 6 months of the 1986–7 financial year). Furthermore, the decision of the NUM in South Wales in September 1988 to reject the proposed framework of flexible 6-day working at the planned Margam pit has led British Coal to consider altering its rules on union recognition to allow the break-away Union of Democratic Mineworkers (UDM) to represent the workforce there. British Coal have also begun negotiating a 2-year productivity linked pay agreement with the UDM, but has refused to negotiate with the NUM until the latter recognize the UDM. The long-running teachers' disputes, both north and south of the border, have also been viewed as constituting important challenges to the Government's 'efficiency–flexibility' approach in the public sector, with the outcomes having significant public expenditure implications. The most obvious short-term outcome here has been the passage of the Teachers Pay Act 1987, which dismantled the Burnham Committee negotiating machinery and allowed the Secretary of State to impose his own settlement of some 16.4 per cent over 21 months (with new contracts of employment). This Act, which runs to 1990 (but can be extended) has, needless to say, not been well received by the major teaching unions; half-day strike rallies in selected centres occurred as protest measures both prior to and during the election campaign of mid-1987. However, the Secretary of State for Education has given an undertaking (in September 1988) to the National Union of Teachers to have a national pay-negotiating body in place by April 1990.

Major public-sector disputes in Britain have frequently been followed by calls from various organizations for the introduction of 'no-strike clauses' in 'essential services'. A report by the Centre for Policy Studies in the mid-1980s, for example, called for such restrictions to be introduced for the health service, the fire service, the gas, electricity, and water services, and for local authority workers responsible for burials and cremations.[78] The present Government was originally keen to proceed in this direction, although there has been little tangible outcome from discussions on this subject to date. This is presumably as a consequence of disagreements over the definition or scope of 'essential services' in the public sector, and over the desirability of institutionalizing compulsory arbitration arrangements in return for removing the right to strike.

As a 'second-best' alternative, the Government is likely to continue its present approach of encouraging the increased representation and status of 'non-militant' employee organizations in the public sector. The membership growth of the Royal College of Nursing in recent years (a 55 per cent increase in 1979–85) has certainly been well above that of its TUC rivals, COHSE and NUPE; while other 'alternative', non-TUC affiliated unions now exist in the coal industry, British Rail, education, the Civil Service, and local government. The most important of these are undoubtedly the Union of Democratic Mineworkers in Nottinghamshire and South Derbyshire, the Professional Association of Teachers (with its no-strike clause) and the Federated Union of Professional and Managerial Officers in local government (which favours the break-up of national bargaining there), all of which have been accorded national-level recognition status. Furthermore, the recent membership growth of the moderate Assistant Masters and

Mistresses Association has been such as to bring them close to being the second largest teachers' union in Britain.

The media have stressed that membership growth in the public sector in recent years is very much associated with the more moderate unions, whereas other commentators have made reference to the increased 'politicization' of public-sector unions in this same period. The latter has been observed in relation to ballots for political funds under the Trade Union Act 1984. The Institution of Professional Civil Servants is one of the latest unions to establish a political fund for the first time; some fifteen unions have done this, with a high proportion of these being in the public sector (including four in the Civil Service). Furthermore, both the Royal College of Nursing and the Royal College of Midwives balloted their membership in 1988 on the question of removing the non-industrial-action clause from their constitutions; the results, however, favoured the status quo. In addition, the frequent rhetoric about public-sector union co-ordination appears to have had some more tangible content in recent years. The Public Services Committee of the TUC (established in 1979) has sought to develop a common-core approach to collective bargaining – which, in 1984, for example, involved: (i) the negotiation of targets in excess of the Government's then current (i.e. 3 per cent) central Government service guideline; (ii) reductions in hours and overtime, 6 weeks annual holiday, and early retirement on adequate pensions; (iii) a minimum pay standard of two-thirds of average male earnings; and (iv) moves towards a common settlement date across the public services.

The present Conservative Government, which entered its third term of office following the June 1987 election, enjoys a reputation second to none of being 'anti-public-sector'. First, it has moved well beyond the approach of previous Governments of making *ad hoc* attempts to reduce wage and employment levels in the public sector, to actually questioning and constraining the institutional role of public-sector unions. Second, it is clearly trying to make the public sector more private-sector-like in many of its industrial relations arrangements and practices. The present Government is clearly committed to the following policies in the public sector: restraining public expenditure; further privatization moves; decentralizing collective bargaining; and extensive salary restructuring developments. These policies – when placed in the context of recent instances of industrial action, pressures for 'catch-ups' in public-sector pay, the reported difficulties of attracting and retaining qualified staff in certain parts of the public sector, and widespread complaints of low employee morale – certainly suggest the aptness of a recent report's conclusion that 'public-sector industrial relations are still in search of their identity, and the road to re-discovering it seems likely to be both long and rough.'[79]

Conclusions

If there is one clear message in this particular chapter it is the fact that, as the Government has increased the number and variety of forms of intervention in the industrial-relations system, it has become increasingly subject to the problems of inter-role conflict. For example, the Government in Britain (as in a number of other countries) has long acted as a model, or best-practice, employer – in the sense of establishing industrial-relations structures, procedures, and practices which, it is hoped, will constitute a role model that will be emulated in the private sector.[80] However, as the proportion of employment in the public sector has increased through time, and incomes policies have been utilized in an attempt to deal with the problems of stagflation, the Government has faced great difficulty in trying to achieve some sort of acceptable balance between its responsibilities for giving effect to the social or public interest in industrial relations and its responsibilities as an employer of labour. In the 1970s and 1980s Governments in Britain (of both political persuasions) have sought to resolve such inter-role conflicts by favouring the social or public interest at a particular point in time, but through the course of time this has meant that industrial-relations problems in Britain have become increasingly public-sector based, or centred – an outcome that has involved costs for both public-sector employees and the public at large.

One obvious effect of this situation has been the increased range of individuals who have become interested in the study of public-sector industrial relations in recent years. Specifically, from the late 1970s, a number of political scientists have made much more of a significant contribution to the study of public-sector industrial relations in Britain than in previous decades.[81] The contribution of these individuals tends, however, to be made in political-science or public-administration journals rather than in the specialist industrial-relations journals – a fact that students of industrial relations need to recognize in their reading on the subject. Finally, it is important to emphasize that these 'public-sector industrial relations problems' in the 1970s and 1980s are not unique to Britain.[82]

Chapter nine

Beyond collective bargaining

In Chapter 5 I outlined a number of the relatively long-standing criticisms of: (i) the institution of collective bargaining; and (ii) certain aspects of its operation, which have come from a wide variety of positions along the political spectrum – i.e. individuals with unitarist, pluralist, and radical frames of reference. Many of these criticisms essentially involved the view that 'there was too much collective bargaining' in the British system of industrial relations, whereas here I examine certain aspects of the increasingly popular, contemporary view that the industrial-relations system (some individuals here would favour the term 'employee-relations' system) of Britain is becoming much less of a collective-bargaining-based one. In other words, I now consider the question of whether there are significant on-going developments in the industrial-relations system of Britain, which are essentially occurring outside the formal processes of collective bargaining, with the result that the latter institutional arrangements are becoming much less the centrepiece of the system.

In one sense, such a change would appear to be an obvious fact of life in that, as we saw in Chapters 3 and 5, the proportion of the workforce who are union members and whose pay is determined by collective bargaining arrangements has declined in the 1980s. On the other hand, however, the available survey evidence does not indicate that the formal structural arrangements associated with collective bargaining have been removed by unilateral, management decision-making – at least, to any significant extent. There can nevertheless be important challenges to the central position of collective bargaining in the British system if, for example, there are: (i) significant attitude and behavioural changes associated with these unchanged structures; (ii) more and more decisions with an industrial relations content — or at least with important consequences for industrial-relations arrangements and practices – being made through non-collective bargaining channels or mechanisms;

and (iii) if certain arrangements and practices becoming more widespread which have the potential to substitute for, as opposed to complement, the operation of collective-bargaining arrangements.

The extent and nature of changes occurring along these lines is examined here through focusing on the following issues or themes: (i) collective-bargaining and 'integrative-bargaining' issues and subjects; (ii) collective-bargaining and strategic-level management decisions; (iii) collective bargaining and the motivation/commitment of individual employees; and (iv) collective bargaining and the human-resource management 'alternative'. The subject matter of this chapter will be ordered under these four sub-headings, with a brief, final section highlighting some of the major unresolved issues and debates in the broad subject area of employee involvement.

Collective bargaining and integrative bargaining issues

The normal collective-bargaining process (or 'distributive' bargaining in Walton and McKersie's terms) is typically held to be short-term orientated, concerned with subjects or issues in which unions and management have divergent or conflicting aims (at least to some extent), and which involves a limited mutual exchange of information relative to the extent of bluffing, threats, and the use of coercive tactics. This characterization of collective bargaining suggests that there may be certain subjects or issues (which affect the determination and regulation of the terms and conditions of employment) in any organization which may not be particularly well handled through the normal process of collective bargaining. A view to this effect, however, immediately raises two potentially contentious questions – first, which particular subjects fall into the latter category and, second, what are the alternative means to collective bargaining of dealing with them? – in other words, should it be a system-wide legal regulation, unilateral management decision-making, or some sort of consultation or problem-solving arrangements involving either groups of employees, or trade union and management representatives?

It is often argued that union–management consultative or joint problem-solving arrangements ('integrative' bargaining in Walton and McKersie's terms) is most appropriate in subject areas where: (i) there is limited conflict between the interests and aims of unions and management; and (ii) all workers in a particular bargaining unit do not attach a relatively high priority to the particular issue or subject concerned.[1] For example, Kochan has commented that:

> Safety and health had always been an issue of middle-range importance to American workers, yet not an issue of high enough priority to a sufficient number of union members that they were consistently willing to strike to achieve demands for safety improvements. This is partially a function of the high variance in the exposure of different workers in the same bargaining unit to unsafe or risky jobs or conditions. . . . A union's dilemma, therefore, is to find ways of responding to the health and safety problems of workers exposed to hazards, without relying on the threat of the strike to achieve its demands. One strategy has been to promote joint committees to study and monitor health and safety conditions in the plant.[2]

In Britain, voluntarily established joint health and safety committees have a long history stretching back to the early decades of this century. In particular, the factory inspectorate consistently sought to encourage the establishment of such committees, but the extent of progress in this regard was always relatively limited and uneven; the history of these committees constitutes an important exception to any view that employers have always been the driving force in favouring and establishing joint consultative arrangements. As late as 1969, for example, only some 27 per cent of plants examined by the inspectorate were found to have such joint committees, with considerable inter-industry variation (from a low of 8 per cent in clothing and footwear to 56 per cent in gas, electricity, and water) being apparent.[3] The eventual response to the limited, voluntary establishment of such committees was the passage of the Health and Safety at Work Act 1974; there had in fact been a number of previous calls (from both unions and the factory inspectorate) to provide a statutory basis for the establishment of joint health and safety committees.[4] Under the terms of the 1974 Act, it is union safety representatives, rather than joint health and safety committees, which have statutory rights pertaining to information and inspection, with the former individuals to be the major focus of union–management consultation over health and safety matters. The practical significance of the distinction between consultation and negotiation (a distinction that is often made in industrial-relations legislation in Britain) has frequently been questioned,[5] and certainly a substantial proportion of the (admittedly small volume of) research concerning the workings of union safety representatives has concentrated on this issue of whether they perform more of a consultation, as opposed to a negotiation, function;[6] in practice, it would appear that major determinants of this particular distinction are the individual safety representative's *perceptions* of both workforce and management interest in health and safety matters. As to joint health and safety committees, the available survey evidence indicates that the extent of their existence has increased quite considerably since the relevant provisions of the 1974 Act came into force late in 1978.[7] Interestingly, the existing research on these committees, both in Britain and the United States,[8] indicates that: (i) the attitudes and behaviour that are associated with their workings (particularly from the union side) are not those of purely or exclusively integrative bargaining bodies; (ii) it is difficult to objectively identify the impact of these committees' activities on the level of industrial accidents (much less on health) in individual workplaces, *ceteris paribus*; and (iii) self reported measures of committee effectiveness consistently tend to be associated with factors such as the presence of relatively senior-management representation on the committee.

The other well-known, relatively long-standing institutional arrangement in Britain which tends to be viewed as an integrative bargaining body is that of joint consultative committees. The general view taken towards such committees is that they: (i) have generally been favoured by management as a limited exercise in employee and union involvement which does not seriously threaten the extent of managerial prerogatives; (ii) give the appearance that management is interested in the concerns and viewpoints of employee representatives; (iii) may assist the process of implementing previously discussed changes; (iv) may lower the expectations of employee representatives as to what are realistic and feasible demands; and (v) may produce certain attitudinal and behavioural changes in the direction of increased co-operation which may, in turn, filter through into the processes of distributive bargaining.

However, it is widely acknowledged that the management interest in establishing and maintaining joint consultative committees has varied quite widely between different organizations at a single point in time and over the course of time. For example, Derber has argued that (at the level of individual organizations) 'where union organisation was weak or non-existent and management was human relations orientated . . . the consultative machinery became of prime import'[9], whereas a much more macro-level perspective on such committees views them as growing out of the joint production committees established (under Government encouragement) during the years of the Second World War. The latter view essentially sees the popularity of joint consultative committees in the 1940s and 1950s as one among a number of periods of time in which management was particularly interested in the subject of employee participation;[10] these periods of interest were due to the occurrence of increased manifestations of 'union power', with management seeking to devise structures designed to institutionalize and modify such manifestations.

The historical record in Britain tends to indicate that joint consultative committees are basically unstable structures, with much of this instability being inherent in the nature of the structures. The point here is that the activity levels of joint consultative committees (and even their formal existence) can easily decline or decay through the course of time if, in trying to remain strictly separate from distributive bargaining structures and activities, they ony deal with residual, relatively trivial subjects or issues. On the other hand, any attempt to maintain their life by increasing the range and importance of subjects they deal with is likely to set in motion a desire on the union side to break down the artificial (in their eyes) distinction between joint consultation and joint negotiation. In other words, increasingly important terms of reference for, or agenda items in, joint consultative committees are likely to make them *de facto* (distributive) bargaining bodies; this is very much the view taken of joint consultative committees as shop stewards became increasingly represented on them in the course of the 1960s. This 'highly sensitive' nature of joint consultative committees appears to be true of other integrative bargaining arrangements in both Britain and elsewhere. Indeed, Kochan and Dyer have suggested that for any joint problem-solving arrangement, or structure, to be successful and survive the test of time, it must overcome (a far from easy task) the following difficulties:[11]

1. Both parties must be able to see the change programmes as being instrumental to the attainment of goals valued by their respective organizations and/or constituents.
2. The internal political risks to union leaders and management officials must be overcome.
3. The programmes must produce tangible, positive results in the short run and must demonstrate a high probability of being able to continue to achieve valued goals in the future.
4. The initial stimulus or pressure to embark on the programmes must continue to be important, and the initial goals of the programmes must continue to be of high priority to the parties.
5. The gains or benefits from the initial programme must be equitably distributed among the workers and the employer.
6. The union must be perceived as being an instrumental force in achieving the goals or benefits of the programme, and the union

leaders must be protected from getting over-identified as part of management.
7. The change process must be successfully integrated with the formal structures and procedures of collective bargaining.

In Britain there has been considerable debate, not to say controversy, concerning the current status and future role of joint consultative committees.[12] There are, in fact, two quite separate issues involved in this debate – which are not always clearly distinguished in practice. The first issue is whether the extent of joint consultative committees has increased over the course of time, particularly in the 1970s. Second, whether the coverage, composition, and subject matter of joint consultative committees has become increasingly heterogeneous in nature through the course of time. The first point to make here is that the available survey evidence is simply not adequate to the task of telling us whether the extent of joint consultative committees grew, declined, or remained essentially stable in the years prior to the 1980s. This is because we do not have the relevant information from two comparable and nationally representative surveys conducted at two different points in time, nor do we have any panel data for a sample of organizations which contains such information over an extended period of time. The most that we can safely say under this particular heading is that the overall extent of joint consultative committees at the individual-establishment level was essentially the same (i.e. 34 per cent of all establishments) in 1980 and 1984.[13] This is, of course, not an unimportant finding – particularly in view of the Conservative Government's attempts to encourage the further development of such committees as a voluntary, uniquely British arrangement for employee involvement and participation which would minimize the impact of EEC proposed legislation in this area according to the draft Fifth Directive;[14] the latter has been strongly opposed by the Government and employer bodies in Britain.[15] Moreover, recent examinations of individual-organization, employee-involvement statements under Section 1 of the Employment Act 1982 (which will be discussed more fully later in this chapter) tend to find considerably more reference to communications arrangements and profit sharing schemes than to joint consultative committees.[16]

On the separate question as to whether the distribution, composition, and subject matter of joint consultative committees has become more heterogeneous in nature, we are on firmer grounds as regards the quality of evidence. And the answer to this question would appear to be 'yes'. In principle, those establishments which a contemporary survey found to have a current joint consultative committee, could consist of: (i) establishments which had only ever (in their history) had the one committee, which was long established; (ii) establishments which had only ever had the one committee, which was recently established; (iii) establishments which had (in their history) more than one committee, with the current one being long established; and (iv) establishments which had more than one committee, with the current one being recently established. This level of detailed distinction is rarely undertaken in survey work, although some analysis of survey data does indicate that older committees and more recently established ones are in establishments with quite different organizational characteristics.[17] Moreover, a recent analysis of the 1984 workplace survey data found that the existence of a joint consultative committee was not significantly related to either union or non-union status, indicating the existence of such committees in both sectors of employment.[18] The basic data contained in the 1984 survey also indicated some notable changes in the membership and subject matter of joint consultative committees in the years 1980–4;[19] for example, exclusive representation by trade union appointees declined, while pay and working conditions appeared to be less frequently discussed matters. Finally, Marchington has argued that 'the nature of joint consultation is more varied and complex than recent research would have us believe', with neither the revitalization or marginality views of joint consultation being fully and adequately able to capture the essence of these increasingly heterogeneous arrangements in recent times.[20]

If separate integrative bargaining arrangements sit rather uneasily alongside traditional distributive bargaining arrangements, what is the likelihood that the latter can increasingly involve a joint problem-solving approach that would reduce the need for the former type of (separate) arrangements? There is certainly no shortage of views to the effect that both British and US collective-bargaining practices have traditionally been 'too adversarial' in nature, with an increasingly integrated world economy (of intensified product market competition) necessitating a change in this regard. The position typically taken is that a more joint problem-solving approach in collective bargaining will require fundamental attitude and behavioural changes on the part of both management and unions in an overall context assisted by the nature of Government policy. Table 9.1 sets out one view (a US one) of the necessary changes in this regard.

Among those commentators who hold that collective bargaining increasingly needs to move in this sort of direction, it is possible to discern differences as to the likelihood that it will do so, and the

Table 9.1 Practices for competitiveness

Unions	Individualized treatment of companies by unions, in wages or working conditions or both. Concern for competitiveness of a particular company. Flexibility in order to provide greater efficiency.
Companies	Better relations with the rank and file (a union can't deliver employee commitment). Participative operational decisions. Delegation of responsibility and sharing information. Emphasis on employment security. Compensation system possesses variability as business conditions and/or performance alters (i.e. competitiveness requires a greater flexibility in compensation to reduce employment variability).
Government	Programmes for the displaced, when objective is re-employment, not only income support.

Source: D. Quinn Mills and Malcolm Lovell (1985), 'Enhancing competitiveness: the contribution of employee relations', in Bruce R. Scott and George C. Lodge (eds), *US Competitiveness in the World Economy*, p. 163, Boston, Mass.: Harvard Business School Press.

key factors that will be essential to assist in any such process of change. The most optimistic of views would be a general macro-level one which argues that the strength of environmental forces (e.g. increasingly competitive, integrated product markets) is such that this type of change must come about or the parties concerned will simply not survive. According to this view, high unemployment, and the threat of redundancies and plant closures will be environmental factors that pressure unions and employees into making such changes. The rather more pessimistic views would tend to suggest that such a change will, at least initially, be restricted to individual union–management relationships where certain key contingency factors are operative. As regards the latter view, an OD researcher, for example, is likely to stress the all-important role of a strong senior management commitment to this type of change in order to bring it about, while an industrial relations researcher is more likely to emphasize (i) the prior state of attitudinal structuring (or the overall state of the industrial relations climate) between the two parties, and (ii) the degree of consistency between senior-management statements and lower-level management actions as the important determinants of the emergence (or not) of a more joint problem-solving, collective-bargaining approach. More generally, it may be argued that, in any individual union–management situation, a one-step move from the 'old' to the 'new' collective-bargaining approach is unlikely to come about smoothly, so that an all-important task may be that of devising a set of mutually acceptable transitional arrangements and practices, perhaps along the lines of those discussed by Walton.[21]

Collective-bargaining and strategic-level management decisions

In Chapter 4 it was argued that some of the most powerful influences on the behaviour and outcomes of plant-level, collective-bargaining arrangements have been management decisions taken at the corporate (and divisional) level concerning matters such as investment strategy, product development, marketing strategy, sub-contracting, and technical change. These sorts of decisions may have important implications for industrial relations, but are not typically viewed by senior management as being industrial-relations-based ones, with the result that the extent of the input of the personnel function into the relevant decision-making processes appears to be relatively limited. Moreover, because these decisions are taken at corporate or divisional levels in M-form organizations, they are either not formally introduced into the collective bargaining process at all, or else are only introduced at a relatively late stage in the overall processes of joint decision-making; this means that collective bargaining can, at most, affect the implementation of changes (with the key decisions concerning matters such as the choice between options already having been made unilaterally by management).

The problem here for unions committed to collective-bargaining arrangements is that these particular subjects or issues are central to management's definition of their prerogatives, with this definition being difficult to challenge at the company or corporate level because of the limited union, organizational presence and depth at this particular level of decision-making. Admittedly, shop-steward-combine committees are often mentioned in this context, but these are not widely established and, where they do exist, have been viewed as 'nothing more than a recognition that trade union organisation has been ill-adapted to the oligopolistic structure of most industries and to the multiple-plant nature of the large firm.'[22]

Throughout the 1970s and 1980s, various statements and documents produced by the British trade-union movement have stressed the need for an increased range of 'trade-union rights' concerning access to information and decisions on strategic matters at the company level. If such rights were to be enacted by legislation, then two obvious questions which arise are: (i) what is to be the particular form of the joint decision-making arrangements to be established? and (ii) are the information and back-up services and facilities for trade union representatives sufficient to ensure that they can be fully involved in decisions over matters where they have had little prior experience and no specialist training? Lane has certainly raised a number of important question-marks concerning this latter capability.[23]

In relation to the former question, a proposed answer in the 1970s was that of worker or trade-union representation on the board of directors of companies. These particular years saw the terms 'industrial democracy' and 'worker or trade union directors' viewed as almost one and the same thing in Britain, a not surprising occurrence in view of: (i) Britain's entry into the EEC; (ii) the attempt to establish (particularly under French and German influence) more of a common, European-wide model of industrial relations (which involved an increased range of individual employee rights and a reduction in the extent of unilateral management decision-making); and (iii) the West German system of industrial relations (with its industrial unionism, corporatism, and co-determination arrangements) being widely viewed as the model system of arrangements for emulation by other countries. Indeed, such influences were not confined to Britain, as, in the period 1970–7, some eight European countries passed legislation to introduce worker directors on to boards for the first time, or to strengthen already existing legislation on this matter.[24] In Britain, in 1977, the Bullock Committee of Inquiry reported in favour of private-sector companies (with 2,000 plus employees) having single-tier boards consisting of an equal number of shareholder and employee representatives (the latter to be chosen through the unions), with a smaller number of independent members (i.e. the $2x + y$ formula); the idea of a two-tier board structure, as in West Germany, with employees represented on the supervisory (but not the managing) board was rejected in the report. The strength of industry's opposition to this report (which was, to some extent, reflected in the minority report of the committee) combined with the less than enthusiastic response of the union movement as a whole, inevitably meant that the Bullock Committee's proposals were not translated into legislative form.

However, some experiments with trade-union directors in Britain, most notably in the British Steel Corporation and the Post Office, have been useful in revealing the limited validity and strength of the two all-important assumptions made by advocates of the case for such directors, namely that: (i) the board is central to all pro-active, senior-management, decision-making processes concerning strategic issues; and (ii) trade union directors will disproportionately concentrate their concern and attention on strategic issues and subjects (such as marketing, product development, organization change, investment strategy, etc.) so that their input complements, rather than overlaps or duplicates, the subject coverage of collective bargaining. In fact, as Brannen's review of these experiments revealed:

> Even with the Post Office scheme . . . the areas where the worker directors were most active, personnel and industrial relations, were not seen by the rest of the board as crucial. The boardroom, moreover, is often not where decision-making takes place; both external constraints and the activities of internal management interest groups can limit the board's scope for decision. In addition, the full-time executive board members can operate to structure the nature of information and decisions coming to the board. . . . Worker directors of necessity enter into worlds already established in terms of both formal roles and processes, of custom and practice, of values and language. The social dynamics of those worlds strongly favour the encapsulation of worker directors within the pre-existing boardroom ethos and organisation, and within, though in a limited way, the pre-existing organisational categories of information and analysis.

The draft Fifth Directive, which would apply to all companies with over 1,000 employees (including subsidiaries) within the EEC, includes employee representation (between one-third and one-half of the non-executive directors) on either the supervisory board or the unitary management board among its four proposed systems of employee representation; the other three systems are employee representation on a supervisory board appointed through co-option, a company council of employee representatives only (with rights to information and consultation), and other company-level schemes negotiated through collective bargaining. The board-level representation option is arguably the least likely to come about in Britain, given the particular strength of employer opposition to it (despite the findings of the Post Office and BSC experiments), and the concern of many trade unions that it would draw them too far into the management function and thus compromise their traditional, independent collective-bargaining function. However, doubts still remain about the capacity of an exclusive reliance on collective bargaining, particularly in the absence of any enabling legislation, to bring about and maintain some measure of joint control of strategic matters, as is indicated by the following discussion of the particular case of technological change.

Collective bargaining and new technology as a strategic issue

The subject area of new technology is currently one attracting a great deal of attention from social-science researchers representing a wide variety of disciplinary backgrounds and particular fields of study. The leading individual themes or issues in the current research debate are basically similar to those contained in discussions of previous experiences of technological change – i.e. the impacts of technological change on unemployment, the skill content of jobs, control over the conduct of work, and centralization vs. decentralization in organizational structures and hierarchies. However, the potentially vast range of applications of innovations in microelectronics-based technology – which are generally associated with the management objectives of reduced operating costs, increased flexibility, improved product quality or service, and increased organization control and integration[26] – has resulted in a rapidly growing literature on the management of new technology, which has been categorized along the following lines.[27]

1. Technical literature describing the capacities of the available hardware and software systems.
2. Technical/organizational literature of a prescriptive nature outlining the steps that managers should follow in introducing new technology.
3. Organizational/technical literature of an analytical, diagnostic character which may be sub-divided into: (a) the 'handbook' type guides which emphasize the analytical techniques in identifying, choosing, planning, implementing, and controlling new office technology by management (heavily influenced by business-policy and management-science traditions); and (b) the social-participative emphasis on achieving a 'fit' between social and technological systems.
4. Optimistic, 'missionary' literature designed to convince readers of the need for technical innovation with the emphasis overwhelmingly on the benefits of such innovation.
5. Pessimistic-critical literature which tends to hold something of a technical deterministic perspective, with the focus being on the costs and negative consequences of technical change.
6. Organizational literature with a political perspective that rejects a determinist view of a universalist set of outcomes of technical innovation. The consequences of technical change are viewed as being strongly shaped by the micro-politics of particular settings, with a special emphasis on inter-personal, inter-departmental, and inter-hierarchical interest group differences which

have to be negotiated and resolved within individual organizational structures.

The latter perspective is especially associated with the work of a number of leading organization-behaviour researchers,[28] whereas students of industrial relations (broadly defined) have been particularly interested in: (i) locating technical change in the larger context of management control systems and examining the associated issues of (ii) the 'de-skilling' consequences of technical change (according to Braverman);[29] and (iii) the nature and effectiveness of the union response to the introduction and implementation of technical change. These three issues are discussed here, with, as a first step, Table 9.2 setting out one view of the nature of management-control systems.

Table 9.2 Four strategies of control in organization

Each strategy will utilize one or more of the features listed

1. *Personalized centralized control*
   (a) centralized decision-taking
   (b) direct supervision
   (c) personal leadership: founded upon ownership or charisma, or technical expertise
   (d) reward and punishment reinforce conformity to personal authority.

2. *Bureaucratic control*
   (a) breaking down of tasks into easily definable elements
   (b) formally specified methods, procedures and rules applied to the conduct of tasks
   (c) budgetary and standard cost-variance accounting controls
   (d) technology designed to limit variation in conduct of tasks, with respect to pace, sequence, and possibly physical methods
   (e) routine decision-taking delegated within prescribed limits
   (f) reward and punishment systems reinforce conformity to procedures and rules

3. *Output control*
   (a) jobs and units designed to be responsible for complete outputs
   (b) specification of output standards and targets
   (c) use of 'responsibility accounting' systems
   (d) delegation of decisions on operational matters: semi-autonomy
   (e) reward and punishment linked to attainment of output targets

4. *Cultural control*
   (a) development of strong identification with management goals
   (b) semi-autonomous working: few formal controls
   (c) strong emphasis on selection, training and development of personnel
   (d) rewards orientated towards security of tenure and career progression

Source: John Child (1984), *Organisation* 2nd edn, p. 159, London: Harper & Row.

As Child notes, technology – which he classifies as an individual feature of bureaucratic control – is often identified as a separate control strategy in its own right. Edwards, for example, views the control process as having evolved through the three stages of hierarchical, technical, and bureaucratic control.[30] Although lists (such as that in Table 9.2) of the features or components of individual management control strategies are commonplace, it is apparent that 'the term control is used in the organisational literature in a number of different ways, sometimes precisely, but usually very loosely'.[31] It has been argued that there are basically four major control issues facing any form of organization. The first issue ('control 1') is the co-ordination of different elements of a complex task performed by different individuals (the only control issue free of the exercise of power), the second issue ('control 2') involves the fact that any one individual can gain by exerting a below-average level of effort in a common task, while 'control 3' and 'control 4' involve, respectively, the slope of and position on the effort–reward relationship function or curve.[32]

The Braverman thesis concerning technological change, which more than any other single study was responsible for the revival of the labour-process debate,[33] is that it will inevitably result in a process of deskilling, a process which involves a number of sub-processes such as the exclusion of shop-floor workers from involvement in the design and planning of work, the increased fragmentation of the individual components of work, a redistribution of tasks in favour of lesser skilled employees and the general transformation of work away from the craft system to forms of labour control (as suggested by Frederick Taylor). There have been a number of *a priori* criticisms of the work of Braverman, such as his: (i) overly romanticized view of the nature of craft work; (ii) failure to discuss the possibility of employee opposition to deskilling; (iii) failure to recognize some of the inevitable/inherent contradictions involved in all control strategies; and (iv) assumption or belief that Taylor's principles of job organization were extensively implemented.[34] Furthermore, reviews of the available case-study evidence certainly do not universally support the view that deskilling is the inevitable result of technological change.[35] In fact, the existing empirical evidence tends to favour more a 'contingency-micropolitics', rather than a 'universalist-deterministic' view of the outcomes of the introduction of new technology.

It is frequently argued that the 'social interest' in industrial relations requires that the trade union movement of any country adopts a mode of response to technological change of either 'acceptance' or 'adjustment'.[36] These particular response patterns appear most likely to come about where: (i) the overall economic situation is relatively buoyant; (iii) only a relatively small proportion of jobs are likely to be lost; (iii) the change is perceived by the unions to be largely inevitable; and (iv) some form of *quid pro quo* can be obtained for the job loss involved.[37] It is factors (ii) and (iv) that would seem most amenable to some degree of influence and control in individual union–management relationships, so that the obvious question to pose is whether the union movement in Britain can utilize the traditional collective-bargaining mechanism to try and minimize job loss and extract certain valued *quid pro quos* for any adverse employment effects of the introduction of new technology.

The general approach of unions in Britain towards the introduction of new technology was much influenced by the framework agreement adopted by the 1979 meeting of the TUC, the major elements of which were as follows:[38]

1. Change must be by agreement: consultation with trade unions should begin prior to the decision to purchase, and status-quo provisions should operate until agreement is reached.
2. Procedures must be developed to cope with technical change which emphasize the central importance of collective bargaining.
3. Information relevant to decision-making should be available to union representatives or nominees prior to any decision being taken.
4. There must be agreement both on employment and output levels within the company. Guarantees of job security, redeployment, and relocation agreements must be achieved. In addition, enterprises should be committed to an expansion of output after technical change.
5. Company retraining commitments must be stepped up, with priority for those affected by new technology.
6. The working week should be reduced to 35 hours, systematic overtime should be eliminated and shift patterns altered.
7. The benefits of new technology must be distributed. Innovation must occasion improvements in terms and conditions of service.
8. Negotiators should seek influence over the design of equipment, and in particular should seek to control work or performance measurement through the new technology.
9. Stringent health and safety standards must be observed.
10. Procedures for reviewing progress, and study teams on the new technology should be established.

In the wake of these TUC 'guidelines', a number of individual unions have made statements in favour of (and outlined the elements of model or best practice) jointly negotiated new technology agreements. There has been a considerable amount of critical comment concerning this particular union approach in Britain. For example, some individuals have been opposed to the basic approach or principles which they embody[39] (viewing them as little more than an 'employers' charter'), while others have pointed to: (i) the limited and declining (through time) number of agreements actually negotiated; (ii) their uneven incidence[40] (i.e. a disproportionate concentration among a relatively small number of white-collar groups of employees and unions); and (iii) the fact that the provisions of actual agreements tend to depart quite considerably from the contents of the model agreements set out by individual unions. On the latter point, for instance, it has been commented that:

> Our survey of some 70 agreements bears out comments by trade union research departments and academics that the achievements – judged by the unions' own standards as laid out in the TUC congresses and union conferences and detailed in the model agreements and reports – are modest. Health and safety is the most strikingly precise of the issues agreed: the others, such as job security, consultation and disclosure, and sharing benefits, are usually either tentative or vague, and all depend heavily on the maintenance of considerable strength and vigilance on the part of the unions.[41]

Over and above the issue of negotiating separate, explicit new-technology agreements, a number of studies have pointed to limited union involvement and/or influence in the original management decision-making processes concerning the introduction of new technology.[42] This fact has been attributed to a variety of constraints on the activities and effectiveness of unions, namely: (i) the limited information made available to them by management; (ii) the limited internal information and technical resources of the unions as organizational entities; (iii) the basic nature of management decision-making processes concerning technical innovation (i.e. the level at which decisions are made, and the particular management functions involved); and (iv) the absence of statutory support for collective bargaining in this particular subject area.[43] These constraints reflect the facts that, first, the major, initial decisions concerning the introduction of new technology are corporate-level ones where formal joint negotiating structures are not well established. Second, decisions on technical change tend to be viewed by senior management as ones of management prerogative in which technical expertise is the all-important consideration and input. Third, although both the planning and implementation of new technology in individual organizations are likely to be heavily influenced by the 'micro-politics' of intra-management discussions and negotiations, our general review of the 'power' of the personnel management function (Chapter 4) does not suggest that personnel and industrial-relations considerations will figure strongly in these particular deliberations; a view certainly supported by some findings of the 1984 workplace industrial-relations survey.[44] These existing limitations on the voluntary collective-bargaining process could be interpreted as providing a strong case for the unions' seeking statutory assistance and support in this particular subject area. Legislative support and assistance for collective bargaining over technical change is particularly important in the Scandinavian countries, although the relevant legislation there is not exclusively about the issue of new technology (e.g. the 1977 Co-determination Act and the 1978 Work Environment Act in Sweden). A recent review of the Scandinavian experience in this area concluded that the unions there 'have been instrumental in highlighting the inter-relationship between legislation, the negotiation of collective agreements (and) state-sponsored support for trade union education and research.'[45] This legislation/collective-bargaining/union-training interrelationship is particularly important in having the potential to reduce the substantial variation in voluntary collective-bargaining outcomes that will inevitably be associated with new technology, as such variation has been associated with voluntary-bargaining outcomes for most subjects or issues in the past. In other words, the historical record of collective bargaining in Britain and elsewhere generally indicates that, for individual union–management relationships, relatively favourable (from the union point of view) bargaining outcomes over one issue tend to be positively interrelated with favourable outcomes for other issues. Indeed, Batstone and Gourlay have argued that 'other things being equal, the pattern of negotiation between management and unions over technical change will be broadly similar to the more general pattern of negotiation.'[46]

In short, it would appear that, in the absence of any system-wide legislation, the extent to which union involvement via voluntary collective bargaining will occur in relation to the introduction and application of new technology will be highly variable between individual union–management relationships, with the best predictor of relatively high involvement in relation to this particular subject area being the *prior* extent of the scope or subject coverage of collective bargaining in an individual union–management relationship. Finally, as regards research orientation, it has been suggested that more attention should be given to 'the new forms of work organisation that accompany technological change.'[47] This judgement about the position in Britain is highly consistent with a number of recent US arguments to the effect that: (i) too much existing research has been concerned solely with the alleged employment loss and deskilling effects of the physical hardware dimension of new technology; and (ii) a particular management strategy concerning new technology which is seeking to bring about accompanying changes in the larger systems of work organization (i.e. in the direction of more flexible organizational arrangements) may ultimately pose more significant challenges to the operation and effectiveness of traditional collective-bargaining arrangements than a more straightforward management strategy of using new technology for labour-cost minimization purposes.[48]

At the present time, trade-union attempts to increase the extent of their involvement in decision-making processes concerning strategic issues, or matters, face an awkward combination of: (i) management opposition to such involvement (i.e. a defence of traditional management prerogatives, largely on the grounds of technical expertise); and (ii) management interest in bringing about increased individual employee involvement in (and commitment to) issues of more immediate and direct relevance to the performance of both individual jobs and work groups; the latter issues are non-strategic in nature, with the relevant organizational arrangements being of a non-representative nature. These management orientations need to be seen in the context of, first, surveys of individual employees which generally indicate a desire for more involvement in subjects or issues concerned with their immediate work situation,[49] and, second, Fox's contention that representative arrangements – such as collective bargaining – are inherently incapable of altering the dynamics of a low trust/high conflict individual employee–management relationship or pattern.[50]

Collective bargaining and the motivation/commitment of individual employees

There are a number of pieces of evidence which indicate the current concern of management with the particular issue of individual employee motivation and commitment in individual organizations. For example, Edwards's recent survey of factory managers contains responses concerning aspects of labour-relations policy (i.e. importance and philosophy) which generally point to an 'individual employee/needs of the business' orientation or focus.'[51]

In short, utilizing Gospel's classification, these subjective responses appeared to suggest that 'industrial relations' (pivoting around the institution of collective bargaining) was receiving lesser priority from management relative to 'work relations' and 'employment relations' matters.[52] Second, the information contained in the 1984 workplace industrial relations survey on the subject of increased employee involvement initiatives in the years 1980–4 indicates that improved two-way communication between management and individual employees was a much more significant development (in a quantitative sense) than the extent of structural innovations (e.g. new joint consultative committees).[53] And, as mentioned earlier in this chapter, the emphasis on employee communication revealed by the 1984 survey is consistent with the nature of employee-involvement initiatives most frequently reported under the terms of Section 1 of the Employment Act 1982; this has since been consolidated as Section 235 and Schedule 7 Part V of the Companies Act 1985.

Section 1 of the Employment Act 1982, which applies to the annual reports of companies employing 250 or more people in the UK, obliges companies to publish a statement covering the steps taken during the year to introduce, maintain, or develop arrangements aimed at: (i) systematically providing employees with information on matters of concern to them as employees; (ii) consulting employees or their representatives on a regular basis so that employees' views can be taken into account in making decisions which are likely to affect their interests; (iii) encouraging the involvement of employees in the company's performance through an employees' share scheme or by some other means; and (iv) achieving a common awareness on the part of all employees of the financial and economic factors affecting the company's performance. Government ministers have made little secret of the fact that the employee-involvement information reported under these provisions will be an important resource for them in attempting to 'head off', or limit, any EEC-wide, statutory-based set of arrangements for employee involvement (i.e. the draft Fifth Directive). However, at least one assessment of Section 1 of the 1982 Act suggests that its impact on the extent and quality of employee–management communications has been relatively limited.[54] Indeed, there appears to be considerable divergence between official, Department of Employment assessments and those of outside researchers, as to: (i) the 'quality' of company reports under these regulations; and (ii) the larger significance of the initiatives which are reported.[55] In other words, there is considerable disagreement as to the extent to which these legislative requirements will be an important external agent of change in relation to employee-involvement initiatives broadly defined; the point to be emphasized here is that the 1982 legislation does *not* require initiatives to be undertaken, but, rather, only requires those which are undertaken to be reported.

In addition to the emphasis on employee communication, the term 'employee involvement' invariably has a financial element or dimension to it in current discussions in Britain. Discussions of employee involvement in (and hence identification with) the economic and financial performance of individual organizations are, of course, neither unique to the present period of time, nor to the British system of industrial relations. Indeed the so-called first wave of interest in employee participation in Britain in the late nineteenth and early twentieth century was very much associated with profit-sharing developments, particularly in the coal and gas industries.[56] However, the limited extent and staying power of this particular 'wave of innovation' in general, is revealed by an official, Ministry of Labour enquiry in the late 1920s, which reported that: (i) the number of firms (excluding co-operative societies) with profit-sharing schemes was 121 in 1910 and 308 in 1928; (ii) the number of employees entitled to participate in such schemes was 57,000 in 1910 and 222,000 in 1928 (the total workforce in the latter year was some 18–19 million); (iii) the number of profit-sharing schemes initiated in all industries was a small proportion of all firms in those industries; (iv) nearly 50 per cent of all schemes known to have been started had been discontinued; and (v) the gas industry was the exceptional case 'in which a large proportion of the principal company-owned undertakings have introduced schemes, comparatively few of these schemes have been discontinued, and a number have been in operation for twenty years or longer.'[57] A recent review of various forms of financial-participation arrangements in the US, Britain, West Germany, France, the Netherlands, Denmark, and Sweden concluded that there had been a marked growth in such arrangements from the early 1970s, with legislation having been important in encouraging and facilitating the increased presence of such forms of particpation.[58]

In Britain, employee share ownership has been encouraged by the provisions of the 1978 Finance Act; employers can put shares in the company into trust for their employees, for up to 10 per cent of their income (or £1,250, whichever is greater), and the money used to acquire these shares is subject to corporation tax relief. There are also two schemes which encourage the holding of employee share options, namely the savings related share-option scheme introduced in the 1980 Finance Act and the discretionary share-option scheme introduced in the 1984 Finance Act. Furthermore, the Government introduced tax concessions on profit-related pay in the Finance (No. 2) Act 1987; schemes registered with the Inland Revenue can exempt half of employees' profit-related pay from income tax (up to 20 per cent of total pay or £3,000, whichever is the lowest). In October 1987 there were 145 registered schemes, covering 26,411 employees, while in September 1988 there were 784 schemes for 107,300 employees.[59] In the original 1986 Green Paper (Cmnd 9835), which argued the case for encouraging profit-related pay, the major alleged benefits were held to be, first, a closer individual-employee-organization identification process and, second, a reduction in the variability of output and employment over the course of time. The latter, alleged macro-level benefits obviously owe a great deal to the work of Weitzman,[60] whose basic proposal has stimulated considerable Government, practitioner, and academic interest in the subject of profit-sharing in a number of countries in recent years.

The essence of Weitzman's argument is as follows:

> A profit-sharing system, where some part of a worker's pay is tied to the firm's profitability per employee, puts in place exactly the right incentives to resist unemployment and inflation. . . . The superiority of a profit-sharing system is that it has enough built-in flexibility to maintain full employment even when the economy is out of balance from some shock to the system. When part of a worker's pay is a share of profits, the company has an automatic inducement to take on more employees in good times and, what is probably more significant, to lay off fewer workers during bad times. . . . The key thing is not to get total worker pay down (it could even go up within reason), but to lower the base wage component relative to the profit-sharing component. The marginal cost of labor is approximately the base wage, more or less independent of the profit-sharing component.[61]

A number of economists have raised conceptual questions concerning the validity of Weitzman's all-important assumption that firms will regard the marginal cost of labour as being the base wage rather than the level of total remuneration per worker; if the latter is the relevant concept, the profit-sharing may make little difference to employment and inflation.[62] Furthermore, some recent empirical research has revealed: (i) a positive correlation between profit-sharing and other employee-involvement practices (particularly those concerning consultation) at the firm level;[63] (ii) a significant, positive relationship between profit-sharing and union recognition at the establishment level[104] (a relationship not favoured in the Weitzman proposal); and (iii) the absence of any significant relationship between profit-sharing and above-average (reported) financial performance at the individual establishment level.[65] However, despite the latter finding, it is clear that the extent and popularity of such arrangements are very much on the increase; the Department of Employment survey of employee-involvement practices in 1988 found that financial participation was the most frequently mentioned practice,[66] while the ACAS 'flexibility survey' of nearly 600 organizations in 1987 reported that more than 25 per cent had profit-sharing or share-option schemes, with a further 20 per cent planning to introduce them.[67]

The trend towards more 'employee relations' (and, conversely, less 'industrial relations', involving collective bargaining), as personified by recent developments in two-way communications and profit-sharing schemes (and much less extensive, although well publicized developments in quality circles and semi-autonomous workgroups) can be interpreted in two possible ways. The first is to view it as 'nothing particularly new', with many of the attitudes and assumptions embodied in management's current thinking being little more than a return to, and attempted revitalization of, the human-relations school of thought. Such a view of these current developments – as constituting little more than a 'neo-human-relations' movement – could claim, with some considerable justification, that the nature of current management initiatives tends to share with Elton Mayo's human relations approach the following sorts of key beliefs or assumptions: (i) major influences on worker attitudes and behaviour are located in the immediate working environment; (ii) the major influences on labour productivity are not exogenous to the control of individual organization; (iii) high job-satisfaction will lead to high labour-productivity; (iv) management has a more long-run orientated, non-emotive understanding of the real needs of workers than do individual employees themselves; (v) there is an essential harmony of interests between workers and managers; and (vi) a limited role for unions and collective bargaining means that any conflicts will be essentially inter-personal in nature and hence can be 'ironed out' by improved communications, etc.[68] The alternative interpretation is a more forward-looking one which sees the current developments as heralding a move towards human-resource management; indeed some journal articles in Britain are already beginning to label and categorize the individual developments discussed in this section (e.g. profit sharing schemes) under such a heading.[69] In Chapter 4 we briefly introduced the subject of strategic human-resource management, with its emphasis on the need for a relatively close integration of the process of employment and business planning in order for individual organizations to gain some element of competitive advantage. The points made there were that this essentially descriptive and prescriptive body of literature tends to revolve around a small number of well-known company examples. This is a perspective that should be borne in mind in the following, more general, discussion of the concept.

Collective bargaining and human-resource management

One view of the assumptions which distinguish human-resource management from personnel management in the academic literature (as opposed to organizational practice) is set out in Table 9.3. This emphasis on the fact that these are perspectives contained in the academic literature is all-important because, as Guest has aptly noted:

Table 9.3 Stereotypes of personnel management and human-resource management

	Personnel management	*Human-resource management*
Time and planning perspective	Short-term, reactive, *ad hoc*, marginal	Long-term, pro-active, strategic, integrated
Psychological contract	Compliance	Commitment
Control systems	External controls	Self-control
Employee-relations perspective	Pluralist, collective, low-trust	Unitarist, individual, high-trust
Preferred structures/ systems	Bureaucratic/ mechanistic, centralized, formal defined roles	Organic, devolved, flexible roles
Roles	Specialist/professional	Largely integrated into line management
Evaluation criteria	Cost-minimization	Maximum utilization (human-asset counting)

Source: David E. Guest (1987), 'Human resource management and industrial relations', *Journal of Management Studies* 24(5), September, p. 507.

> There is danger of confusing 'management thinkers' with management practitioners and assuming that because human resource management is being discussed it is also being practised. There is a risk that it will be 'talked' or 'written' into existence, independently of practice, and then, on the basis of a few cases, will be assumed to be practised.[70]

The recent 'popular' book by Leadbeater and Lloyd, for instance, certainly contains many more examples of what management says it is thinking about doing under the human-resource management heading than examples of what it has actually done to date in Britain;[71] the relatively recent union–management agreement at Ford UK (prior to the 1988 strike) which reduced the number of individual job classifications from 500 to 58 being a major exception in this regard.

The individual components of a sophisticated human-resource management system are typically held to be relatively well-developed, internal labour-market arrangements (in matters of promotion, training, and individual career development), flexible work-organization systems, contingent compensation practices (e.g. profit sharing), skills- or knowledge-based pay structures, high levels of individual-employee and workgroup participation in task-related decisions, and extensive internal-communications arrangements; it is typically conceded, however, that this is an idealized system with individual organizations in practice being unlikely to have all of these elements in place. Researchers from different disciplines and fields of study have focused on different aspects and implications of human-resource-management systems. For example, industrial-relations researchers (particularly in the United States) have been particularly interested in the potential 'union-substitution effects' of these policies.[72] In other words, such policies can be viewed as part of an organic, as opposed to mechanistic, management system,[73] the essence of which is a strong individual employee-organization identification process which, in turn, has the potential to limit the extent of employee job dissatisfaction – which existing research has shown to be a necessary, if not sufficient, condition for employees demanding union representation. In contrast, organization theorists have tended to produce rather broader, conceptual treatments of the relationship between business/competitive strategies and human-resource-management policies; these developments are an elaboration of some of the points touched on in Chapter 4. For example, one recent paper,[74] having identified (i) an innovation strategy designed to gain competitive advantage (i.e. develop products or services different from those of competitors); (ii) a quality-enhancement strategy (i.e. enhance product and/or service quality), and (iii) a cost reduction strategy (i.e. be a low-cost producer), went on to consider the patterns of employee-role behaviour and human-resource-management policies held to be associated with these particular business strategies. In this type of work there is virtually no reference to the attitudes, behaviour, and role of trade unions.

In both Britain and the US it has been argued that any adoption of comprehensive and integrated human-resource-management systems is likely to be disproportionately concentrated in organizations where exceptional opportunities for change exist. Guest, for example, has explicitly cited the special circumstances of the appointment of a new chief executive, the occurrence of a major crisis, and a greenfield-site location.[75] The importance of the latter factor as both an incentive for, and facilitator of, change in relation to human-resource-management systems has also been strongly emphasized in the relevant US literature. For example, Edward Lawler has argued that:

> New organizations simply have a number of advantages when it comes to creating high involvement systems. They can start with a congruent total system; they can select people who are compatible; no-one has a vested interest in the status quo; and it is possible to do the whole organisation at once so the participative island disease is avoided.[76]

In a subsequent publication, Lawler looked in some detail at the key characteristics of new-design plants in the US (which he estimates to number more than 200), such as employee selection, design of the physical layout, job design, pay system, organizational structure, and the approach to training, all of which are underpinned by an explicit management philosophy in favour of employee involvement.[77] An explicit management philosophy has certainly been associated with a number of well-known, new plants in Britain, as the contents of Table 9.4 illustrate.

In considering the likelihood of sophisticated human-resource-management policies being disproportionately concentrated in new plants in Britain, there are at least three points which should be borne in mind. First, analyses of both the 1980 and 1984 workplace industrial-relations surveys indicate that newly established plants (particularly in the manufacturing sector) are significantly and positively associated with non-union status.[78] Second, the work of urban and regional researchers indicates that the overall rate of new-plant formation has fallen significantly in the last 10–15

Table 9.4 Management philosophy at the new Pilkington plant at St Helens, Merseyside

(1)	Increased site commitment
(2)	Better co-operation between trade unions
(3)	Well-trained employees who fully understand their role in the works as a whole
(4)	Flexible employees – able to do a wide range of tasks
(5)	Management style based on openness and employee involvement
(6)	Push responsibility down the hierarchy
(7)	Remove status differences which cannot be justified
(8)	Simple, effective, easily understood reward system
(9)	Eliminate payment for overtime

Source: Derek Norman (1983), 'How a new plant made Pilkington reflect on its IR structure', *Personnel Management*, 15(8), August, p. 22.

years.[79] Finally, one needs to be quite precise about just what is meant by a 'greenfield site', as the conventional (if not always explicit) definition of this term (i.e. new, one part of a multi-plant organization, 'innovatory' employment practices, location outside major metropolitan centres) is considerably more specialized than the term 'new plant'.[80] However, existing case studies of four greenfield-site establishments in Britain have identified the following common features of work organization:[81]

(i) fewer tiers of management;
(ii) abolition of the roles of chargehands, foremen and conventional supervisors, with enhanced status of first-line managers;
(iii) minimization of status differences;
(iv) giving groups of employees joint responsibility for a range of tasks;
(v) dissemination of more information on work-related matters;
(vi) communication to and from employees directly, through group meetings, rather than through trade unions.

These particular organizational practices certainly point in the human-resource-management direction so that future research on this subject should particularly concentrate on greenfield sites, in order to identify: (i) the extent of such arrangements; (ii) any observable effects on organizational performance; (iii) any attempt to diffuse such practices to older plants in multi-establishment organizations; and (iv) the organizational outcomes of any observed diffusion to older plants.

If comprehensive, integrated, human-resource-management systems are disproportionately concentrated in greenfield sites and new plants, their system-wide implications in Britain would appear to be rather limited. Such a view, however, could be subject to the criticism that, first, the success of union attempts to achieve organization and recognition in new plants will have important implications for the future levels of overall union density in the system at large — i.e. the unions need to break out of the situation where their organization is disproportionately associated with older industries, companies, and plants. Second, even if the comprehensive human-resource-management systems do not spread or diffuse much beyond the special circumstances of new plants, it is still possible that some individual policies or components of these packages will be adopted elsewhere. In regard to the latter possibility, there are two empirical findings worthy of note at this stage. First, movements in the human-resource-management direction in individual organizations appear to require a combination of external (from the environmental) stimuli and internal (to the organization) facilitating changes. As regards the latter, for example, the work of Hendry, Pettigrew, and Sparrow indicates that thirteen of the twenty organizations they studied had experienced changes in their senior-management ranks.[82] Second, the Institute of Personnel Management's survey of human-resource-planning activities in some 245 organizations in 1988 indicates that the administration of these activities was mainly the responsibility of the personnel function, although the assessment of the implications of such activities for the organization was much less an exclusively, or even largely, a personnel-based responsibility; a joint responsibility with line management was much more the norm.[83]

Some unresolved issues and debates in the area of employee involvement

The existing literature on employee involvement initiatives, particularly in the United States, has tended to be dominated by behavioural scientists who have adopted very much a 'micro-level' focus in their work, with the concern being to identify factors and influences at the level of the individual organization which stimulate such initiatives, sustain them (or not) through the course of time, and assist (or hinder) the spread or diffusion of such initiatives within the rest of the organization and across to other organizations. Much of this literature has been influenced by the three-stage model of the processes of organization development and change (i.e. unfreezing, change, and refreezing) associated with the early work of Kurt Lewin,[84] with the only notable exceptions to this type of analysis coming from non-behavioural scientists who have emphasized the role of macro-level developments in product (e.g. increased competition) and labour markets (e.g. increased union power) in stimulating management interest in such innovations.[85] More recently, Cole has criticized this micro level, behavioural-science line of research in employee-involvement initiatives for: (i) ignoring influences external to individual organizations (with the exception of some economic variables); and (ii) producing a series of studies whose results and findings are frequently inconsistent and non-comparable.[86] Cole's own comparative analysis of the institutionalization of small group activities, in Japan, Sweden, and the United States in the period 1960–80, involves very much a macro-political perspective on organizational change which emphasizes the incentives in national labour-markets for management to innovate, the establishment of industry- or national-level employers' organizations to communicate the means and support the processes of change, and the attitudes of organized labour towards such changes.

The blend of, and consistency between, macro- and micro-level explanations of various phenomena has become a matter of increased interest, not to say concern, in a number of areas of social-science research in recent years. Against this larger background, Cole usefully emphasizes the need for researchers to look beyond the organization as the basic unit of analysis when considering the all-important question of factors that facilitate or hinder the process of diffusion both within and between organizations. In addition to this question about the appropriate level, or unit, of analysis, there are some major limitations and weaknesses in the available literature on the impact and effectiveness of employee-involvement initiatives. For example, the existing empirical literature in this subject area can be criticized for: (i) concentrating much more on 'reported successes' than on failures; (ii) involving evaluations of outcomes which are all too frequently conducted by the actual agents of change; (iii) the relative absence of longitudinal studies; (iv) most evaluations involving only self-reported, perceptual measures of change; and (v) the actual mechanisms through which enhanced employee involvement is held to impact on organizational outcomes being rarely explicitly identified and examined. On the latter point, Miller and Monge have recently identified.[87]

(1) Cognitive models of participation. These models hold that participation will lead to increases in productivity through bringing higher-quality information to decision-making processes and increasing the overall extent of knowledge at the

stage when decisions are implemented. The basic prediction of these models is that increases in individual employee productivity will only follow from participation in specific decisions that draw on the individual's expertise; working in a participative climate will not result in such an outcome.

(2) Affective models of participation. These suggest that working in a participative climate (as opposed to involvement in specific decisions where the individuals have specialist knowledge) will result in increased productivity, and that participation will disproportionately increase the job satisfaction of employees whose higher-order needs are not met in other aspects of the job.

(3) Contingency models of participation. These various models suggest that favourable employee responses to participation will be strongly influenced by the needs and personalities of particular employees, with some decisions being more appropriate for participation than others.

Their review of existing US studies on employee participation (i.e. broadly defined as joint decision-making) provided most support for the affective models which linked participative climate with the job satisfaction of employees. Some other notable findings from their review were: (i) only a minority of the studies identified in their original literature search contained quantifiable estimates of the relationship between participation in decision-making and satisfaction or productivity; (ii) the particular environment of the research (e.g. laboratory or field studies) influenced the outcomes observed; (iii) specific organizational factors (i.e. contingencies) influenced the effects of participation; and (iv) participation tends to impact more strongly on satisfaction than on productivity – this last finding was consistent with that of another relatively recent review of the US literature.[88] If one looks beyond the relevant US literature, we find that a multivariate statistical study of some forty firms in West Germany has identified a significant, positive relationship between employee participation and productivity,[89] while a longer-term field-work study of autonomous workgroups in an organization in Britain concluded that:

> Autonomous workgroups had specific rather than wide-ranging effects on employee attitudes and behaviour. Although implementation of this work design substantially enhanced intrinsic job satisfaction, it did not demonstrably affect job motivation, organisational commitment, mental health, work performance and voluntary labor turnover. At an organisational level,

implementation made productivity benefits possible because the autonomous work groups reduced indirect labor costs; a side effect was increased dismissals. Employees clearly appreciated the autonomous work system. On balance, managers did too, though clearly there were costs in terms of personal stress arising from the difficulties involved in managing and maintaining the system. Overall, the most striking aspect of these findings is the restricted range of effects on individual attitudes compared with the range predicted from the literature.[90]

The substantive findings from the latter two (non-US) studies are certainly worthy of attention, but it is above all their methodology and approach that is important for future research. They are exceptional and unusual studies in the non-US-based literature on employee involvement, a situation that will hopefully change over time as more atention is given to matters such as: (i) the development of indices of the degree of employee involvement; (ii) a clear, explicit specification of the mechanisms through which employee involvement is alleged to impact on employee attitudes and organizational outcomes; (iii) the use of objective outcome measures; and (iv) the gathering of longitudinal data. Only when a substantial number of studies with such features have been conducted will it be worthwhile even to contemplate the idea of undertaking a meta-analysis-based review of research in this particular subject area outside the US.

Chapter ten

Back to the future?

Introduction

If one stops the clock at any point in time to observe *any* national system of industrial relations, inevitably one will observe a mixture of stability and change. In other words, one will see the existence of relatively well-known and long-established structures and patterns of behaviour, but also the presence of 'new' arrangements and practices that have rarely existed before, or else have 'resurfaced' (in a more modern guise) from an earlier period of time, after an intervening period of years in which they were presumed to have essentially died away. To talk about the emergence of (or moves towards) a new system of industrial relations is to argue, first, that the latter, 'new' developments are becoming increasingly common or widespread and, second, to predict that at some stage in the not too distant future they will be of greater importance – in either a quantitative or qualitative sense – than the older, more long-standing features of the system. In speculating on the future shape of the British system of industrial relations, the following sorts of considerations and issues need to be continually borne in mind:

(1) The most representative picture of the system is provided by the results of surveys, such as the 1984 workplace industrial relations one. However, such survey evidence is overwhelmingly for industrial-relations stuctures, and therefore tells us relatively little about the extent and nature (if any) of attitudinal and behavioural change.
(2) The historical record tells us that changes in industrial relations are frequently concentrated in relatively short periods of time. For example, the normal weekly hours of male manual workers in all industries/services declined from 47.7 in 1920 to 40.5 in 1968, but this change was disproportionately concentrated in the years 1946–9 (47.7 to 44.7), 1960–2 (43.7 to 42.4), and 1964–6 (42.2 to 40.6).[1]

(3) A period of change in industrial relations can be almost immediately followed by a period of time that effectively reverses the original change. For example, 1914–20 saw a substantial narrowing of wage differentials, but the drastic widening of differentials that followed in 1920–4 saw almost a complete return to the pre-war position.[2] Furthermore, the 1970s and 1980s have continually illustrated the fact that legislation with significant (negative or positive) implications for union organization and behaviour which is introduced by one Government can be repealed by a subsequent administration.

(4) A careful monitoring of the media to ensure that one is familiar with up-to-date examples of change obviously exposes the commentator to the risk of identifying 'newsworthy', as opposed to 'representative' or 'typical', developments. Moreover, even here, judgements have to be made concerning the relative importance and significance of particular examples. For instance, in January 1987, 76 per cent of 600 manual employees at Tioxide Ltd approved the withdrawal of negotiating rights from five unions (*Financial Times*, 19 March 1987), while, in September 1987, unions failed to obtain representation rights for workers on the Docklands Light Railway in East London, where 43 employees were in favour of representation, 11 against, and 47 did not vote in the representation ballot (*The Times*, 3 September 1987); in the latter case, a second ballot (some 6 months later) produced a vote (105–13) in favour of union representation. The former type of occurrence is arguably the more costly and worrying of the two for the future size of the union movement in Britain, although at the present time it is likely that the latter is the more common of the two types of occurrence.

(5) The use of different data sources can yield rather different findings and conclusions on individual issues. For example, the ACAS survey in 1985 (which was heavily orientated towards larger-sized, unionized manufacturing-sector establishments) reported that 41 per cent of establishments still used 'last in, first out' as the most important criterion in redundancy selection,[3] whereas Income Data Services have claimed that 'the abundant evidence from industrial tribunals is that selection is a very lively issue indeed and criteria such as overall performance, and an individual's disciplinary and absence record, figure much more widely in arguments about redundancy than ACAS claims'.[4]

These sorts of issues and considerations inevitably raise problems for individual commentators seeking to predict the future shape of any national system of industrial relations.[5] The dangers of such exercises are that cautious predictions open one up to the potential criticism of 'stating the obvious', while the more ambitious one attempts to be, the greater the risk that subsequent developments will prove the predictions to be incorrect. Accordingly, in the remainder of this chapter we seek to identify and highlight some of the leading individual issues and questions that currently confront the various actors in the system, the answers to which will ultimately be among the major determinants of the extent and nature of any future change in the British system of industrial relations. This discussion is structured so as to cover the world of work, the Government, management, and the trade unions.

The world of work

Various employment forecasts to the mid-1990s suggest that (1) employment growth will favour part-time workers, women workers and the self-employed, and (2) employment growth will be disproportionately concentrated in the business and miscellaneous services sector.[6] For example, the Institute for Employment Research have recently forecast that the annual percentage change in employment for the whole economy will be 0.8 per cent in 1987–95, and −0.5 per cent for the manufacturing sector, but 2.6 per cent and 2.9 per cent for business services and miscellaneous services respectively.[7] Such forecasts can usefully be placed in the context of Robertson's four-sector view of the economy, namely:[8] (i) big industry (i.e. capital-intensive, highly-mechanized activities of production); (ii) big services (i.e. labour-intensive, commercial-service activities); (iii) small local enterprises (i.e. conventional small businesses plus a growing range of community businesses, associations, and activities); and (iv) the household and neighbourhood sector (i.e. conventional and newer forms of home-based paid and unpaid work). Although forecasting work suggests that job creation will continue to occur in the big-service sector into, at least, the middle of the next decade, Robertson is one of a number of a commentators who view the relative employment decline of sectors (i) and (ii) and, conversely, the relative growth of sectors (iii) and (iv) as *inevitable* facts of life.

Those advocates, such as Robertson and Handy,[9] of 'the work' (as opposed to 'employment') scenario obviously reject any view that 'full employment' (as the term was conventionally understood) can ever be returned to and maintained in western, industrialized societies, and economists in Britain are certainly highly sceptical of the possibility of such an outcome by the end of this decade. Metcalf, for example, has calculated that to reduce unemployment to two million by 1989 will require the creation of 1,163 jobs per day between 1984 and 1989 – a rate of new job creation far in excess of the post-war average in Britain.[10] This being said, there is no shortage of claims by economists that the current level of unemployment can be reduced, without adverse implications for the level of inflation, by means of a well-co-ordinated set of complementary policy instruments:[11] i.e. an internationally co-ordinated expansion of demand, policies to regulate the movement of real incomes, and micro-orientated policies concerned with work sharing, training, and the development of new products and processes.

The four-sector view of the economy, noted above, has already led to an increased interest among urban and regional researchers in the small, local-enterprise sector, and among sociologists in the household and neighbourhood sector. In contrast, industrial-relations researchers are likely to maintain their traditional concentration on the big-industry and big-services sectors which, according to the work scenario, are likely to be relatively declining areas of activity. However, developments in these individual sectors are unlikely to be self-contained in nature, so that the industrial-relations system, as conventionally defined and studied, will certainly feel the impact of reductions in the extent of (i) the division between home and work and (ii) between paid and unpaid labour. Indeed, one can go even further and argue that some of the more important implications for industrial relations in the future will not even be exclusively confined to the world of work, broadly defined. For example, some sociologists have stressed that the available evidence 'of the effects of consumption on people's perception of their political interest and identity is impressive.'[12]

Indeed, trends in consumption patterns (particularly the rise in home ownership, from 40 per cent in 1960 to 58 per cent in 1981), when taken in conjunction with trends in occupational structure and demography, are held by political scientists to be most favourable to the Conservative Party and least favourable to the Labour Party.[13] These perspectives, which are becoming increasingly apparent in the work of sociologists and political scientists, will need to be increasingly drawn upon by industrial-relations researchers in order to appreciate the fact that the nature of individual-employee attitudes and patterns of behaviour is not completely explicable in terms of a purely worker role, or in terms of exclusively workplace based, or centred, influences. In short, researchers will increasingly need to be concerned with the implications of facts such as: (i) 76 per cent of trade unionists owned their homes in 1988 (compared to 68 per cent of the general public) – a figure up from 60 per cent in 1983; and (ii) 23 per cent of trade unionists owned shares in 1988 (compared to 20 per cent of the general public) – a figure up from 7 per cent in 1979.[14]

Within the big-industry and big-services sectors – the traditional concentrations of industrial-relations researchers – the single word which is held to capture the essence of employment developments in the foreseeable future is flexibility. This being said, the term is in some danger of becoming 'all things to all people', with different individuals emphasizing different measures and causes of labour-market rigidity that need to be eliminated or minimized. In Britain, for example, individuals have variously cited excessive job-security guarantees, too high a level of industry and regional wage-floors, heavy reliance on employment as opposed to wage ajustments, and limited intra-organizational movement of workers between different job grades as major dimensions of labour-market inflexibility. These various perspectives have led to empirical research being conducted by individuals from a number of disciplines and backgrounds, with industrial-relations researchers in Britain paying particular attention to the notion of 'core' and 'periphery' groups of workers in individual organizations, which are increasingly characterized by numerical flexibility (e.g. part-time, limited-life employment contracts), functional flexibility (e.g. team-based working), and financial flexibility (e.g. contingent compensation practices).[15] A general management interest in moving in this sort of direction has been held to be stimulated and facilitated by changes in product-market conditions (e.g. increased competition and shorter product life-cycles), the sizeable potential range of application of new, micro-electronics-based technology, and by certain measures of Government encouragement (e.g. tax concessions for profit-related pay schemes). However, other researchers have made various criticisms of both the internal logic and empirical reality of the core-periphery-based notion of the flexible (numerical, functional, and financial) firm, arguing that:[16] (i) the extent of development and changes along these lines can easily be exaggerated in numerical terms; and (ii) it is questionable whether any individual changes observed have derived from a conscious, coherent management strategy in favour of this form of organization. Indeed, the essence of the debate and controversy very largely revolves around whether one views the flexibility developments of the 1980s as little more than a return to the relatively self-contained, productivity-bargaining experience of the 1960s, as opposed to viewing such developments as an integral part of larger structure and strategy moves towards an organic,[17] as opposed to mechanistic, management system. In reflecting on this debate, it is important to note the following facts and findings which have emerged from some recent studies:

(1) An analysis of the CBI wage data-bank for the manufacturing sector revealed that some two-thirds of bargaining groups made at least one productivity concession as part of a collective agreement in the years 1979-80–1985-6, with more than one-third of them making more than one concession in this period of time.[18]

(2) A study of negotiated and non-negotiated changes in working practices in over 200 manufacturing establishments reported that the extent of significant change was relatively limited, was relatively concentrated in the food, drink, and tobacco industries, and that most of the changes had been introduced without direct, formal negotiations.[19]

(3) A survey by ACAS of nearly 600 organizations produced a substantial range of findings on the extent of numerical, functional, and financial flexibility.[20] Among their leading findings were the following: 34 per cent of organizations had introduced flexibility between groups of craft workers in 1984–7; 25 per cent had in the same years introduced arrangements which allowed production workers to do routine maintenance work; 28 per cent had introduced shift working in 1984–7; 21 per cent had introduced payment systems which rewarded the acquisition of new skills; and 24 per cent had introduced systems which involved merit pay.

The *quid pro quo* for union agreement to management proposals for increasingly flexible work practices and arrangements has been argued to be information disclosure, employee participation, and job security. However, there has been little detailed discussion of the processes of such bargaining in order to see whether such outcomes have, in fact, been attained. Admittedly, some researchers have linked a management interest in achieving flexibility with the introduction of harmonization and single-status policies in certain cases,[21] but beyond this (generally limited) relationship we have only some survey and case-study work which suggests that: (i) employee and union opposition to flexibility changes is considerably less when they are linked with the introduction of new technology[22] (arguably due to the employee belief that this will enhance future job prospects); and (ii) particular organizational examples point to a greater union acceptance of a step-by-step negotiating approach – with, for example, interchangeability within job groupings and grades being more readily attained than flexibility between grades and groups. In addition to research on the processes of union–management negotiations over flexibility, industrial-relations researchers could usefully devote more attention to some of the intra-union implications of developments along these lines. This is because numerical, functional, and financial flexibility moves have the potential to increase the extent of variation in the terms and conditions of employment of members of individual unions, and to enhance the possibility of conflict between the different hierarchical levels of individual unions. For example, we noted in Chapter 3 that shop stewards depend more on management-provided resources than on external union-provided ones to carry out their basic tasks, and flexibility moves could well add significantly to the potential role-conflict of shop stewards by increasingly posing questions concerning their basic source of identity – employees in the individual plant or the larger union. The emergence of such intra-union difficulties would obviously have a number of implications for larger industrial-relations developments and, as such, would be worthy of considerable research attention in the future.

The present Government's record in industrial relations

A *Financial Times* publication prior to the mid-1987 general election suggested that, in reviewing the record of the first two Thatcher administrations, 'the most unequivocal success has been in the field of industrial relations';[23] the defeat of the NUM, the reduction in the number of strikes, the increased legal regulation of union activities, and enhanced union–employer co-operation being examples cited in support of this judgement. Furthermore, Kavanagh has assessed the overall record of the Government in the years 1979–85 as having 'fallen short of the hopes of the more radical free-market groups . . . [but] is one which has achieved substantial changes when viewed in comparison with other governments since 1951';[24] the industrial-relations area was viewed as one of these areas of substantial change. These two assessments provide the starting point for the discussion of this section, which considers the basic aims of the Thatcher Government in industrial relations, the successes and limitations of its approach, and the next steps it is proposing to take.

In the industrial-relations area, the Thatcher Government has essentially sought a reduction in the overall workforce level of unionization, an increase in the size of the non-union employment sector and, third, a more 'responsible' union movement, which the

Government views as being democratic in its internal decision-making processes, relatively dispute free, flexible in its response to organizational change, and restrained in its wage demands. In the light of these aims, the Thatcher Government can obviously point to a number of developments and indicators of 'success', notably: (i) the reduction in the size of the union movement by some 2.5–3 million members since 1979; (ii) the fact that the proportion of manual employees in private-sector establishments where unions were recognized fell from some 84 per cent to 70 per cent in the years 1980–4 (see Table 1.1); and (iii) the significant, positive relationship between the non-union status of private-sector establishments and newer, younger-aged establishments. Other 'favourable' developments in the Thatcher years which are frequently referred to include the relatively rapid increase in productivity, the decline in strike activity, and the increased use of pre-strike ballots (the Labour Party have stated their intention to retain the latter in some form or another).

More generally, however, a number of important question-marks still hang over the potential, longer-term success of the Thatcher programme in industrial relations. First, even supporters of the Thatcher approach have conceded that both high unemployment and the new restrictive legislative environment have had only a limited impact on the size of wage-bargaining outcomes, relative to the level of inflation.[25] Second, no comprehensive and coherent solutions have as yet been put in place for the many problems centred around the nature of pay-determination arrangements in the public sector. Indeed, as we saw in Chapter 8, the public sector has become increasingly the central problem-area in British industrial relations during the 1980s. Third, while the Thatcher Government has undoubtedly raised many important questions about the nature of the British industrial-relations system, the answers offered have not always found favour with a significant number of private-sector employers. For example, reference is frequently made to the fact that employers have responded with only limited enthusiasm to the Government lead, calls, and encouragement for: removing closed shops; moving away from national-level (industry and company) bargaining structures; and embracing profit-related pay arrangements. Finally, the aims and elements of the legislative programme appear to involve certain internal inconsistencies and questionable assumptions which may not, through time, produce the sort of outcomes the Government is seeking. For example, in previous chapters we have questioned the validity of the Government's belief that trade unions, being relatively democratic and strike-free, are complementary, as opposed to substitute, relationships. In addition, the Government's belief (as embodied in the strike ballot provisions of the 1984 Act) that strike action frequently results from a relatively militant, national union leadership has led to the suggestion that 'trade-union bureaucracies are a known quantity: cautious, fairly cohesive and well-integrated with the prevailing pattern of policies. The rank-and-file are something else . . . [and] Conservatives may yet rue the day they undermined the trade-union officials'.[26] Indeed, Kelly has argued that:

> One area in which some judgements can be made is the use of ballots in union decision making, specifically to test support for the closed shop, to decide on official strike action and on whether unions should retain political funds, and to elect voting members of union executives. The most eloquent proof of the failure of these measures to live up to their architects' expectations is the passage of the Employment Bill (1987) which undoes or amends previous legislation in all these areas. The reason it does so can be gleaned from data on the results of these four types of ballots. According to ACAS (1986) 77% of the pre-strike ballots held between 1984 and 1986 recorded support for industrial action, whilst 82% of the closed shop ballots up to the end of 1980 went in the unions' favour. All 38 unions with political funds voted overwhelmingly to retain them, and the ballots to elect union executives have failed to produce a widespread move to the right. It is almost certainly this pattern of results which has led the government to introduce further measures against trade unions[27]

The Employment Bill (1987) referred to in this quote, which became law in 1988, contains provisions which: (i) guarantee union members certain rights in relation to the powers of their union; (ii) require the election of general secretaries, presidents, and all members of union principal, executive committees by full postal ballots under independent scrutiny; (iii) remove the remaining statutory support for the closed shop; and (iv) provide for a commissioner to assist union members in enforcing certain statutory rights. Among the guaranteed rights for union members in relation to unions as organizational entities is the right not to be 'unjustifiably disciplined' by their union for a failure to take part in and support industrial action. It is this particular provision which a number of employer-representative organizations, notably the CBI and the EEF, have argued is inconsistent with, and hence has the potential to seriously undermine, the pre-strike ballot provisions of the 1984 Act. Other alleged inconsistencies in and between various

Government initiatives, which have produced outcomes rather different to those the Government were seeking, have been the following:[28] (i) the provisions of the Wages Act (1986) restrict wages councils to setting a single, minimum hourly-wage rate which, in the case of the retail sector, has led to higher wage rates as a result of the London rate being retained and spread to workers in other areas of the country; (ii) the competitive tendering initiatives concerning contract cleaning in the NHS have tended to promote national minimum-wage standards, as the special section (for companies with NHS cleaning contracts) of the Contract Cleaners and Maintenance Association has agreed to adhere to minimum conditions of employment not less favourable than the NHS terms; (iii) although the Government has sought to restrict the independent powers of the local authorities, there has been a 'municipalization' of training, with the local-government sector accounting for more than 15 per cent of YTS places and being centrally involved in the other major Government employment scheme, the Community Programme.

Finally, a useful indication of some of the Government's current thinking on industrial-relations matters is provided by the contents of the Employment Bill published in December 1988. This Bill should be seen against the background of (i) the Sex Discrimination Act (1986) – which came into force in November 1987 – which gives all employees, irrespective of gender, the right to retire at the same age; and (ii) the decision of the Employment Appeal Tribunal in *Hammersmith and Queen Charlotte's Special Health Authority* v. *Cato* which was followed by a Government announcement that it intended to introduce legislation equalizing the age limit for statutory redundancy pay for both men and women at 65, or the normal retirement age for the job where that is below 65 and non-discriminatory. This stated intention, which is designed to comply with relevant EEC obligations, is realized in the contents of the 1988 Bill, although the Bill also abolishes the Training Commission (a tripartite structure in which the unions were involved) and contains the following 'de-regulation' measures:[29]

(1) Exempts employers with fewer than twenty employees from the requirement of the Employment Protection Act 1978 to provide employees with particulars of the disciplinary procedures which apply to them.
(2) Limits the requirement of an employer to allow trade-union officials time off for trade-union duties.
(3) Increases from 6 months to 2 years the qualifying period of continuous employment which entitles an employee to be

given, on request, a written statement of the reasons for dismissal.

(4) Provides for regulations to be made to give an industrial-tribunal chairman the discretion, at the pre-hearing stage, to require a deposit of up to £150 from one party as a condition of proceeding further, if it is considered that the party's case has little reasonable prospect of success.

If one puts the stated aims and priorities of the Thatcher Government in the industrial relations area in the context of the larger operating environment of the 1980s, a number of commentators have suggested that, first, some of the Government's priority aims have not been achieved and, second, some of the developments which have occurred may be in the direction desired by the Government but do not solely, or even largely, derive from their particular initiatives and measures. In practice, one can discern four 'critical' perspectives on the industrial-relations achievements of the Thatcher Government, some of which we have already touched on in this section. The first perspective is that the falls in union membership and strike activity since 1979 are perfectly explicable in terms of the traditional, historical relationship that such measures have with the nature of business-cycle movements, and that such declines may not be politically sustainable over the longer term. Moreover, advocates of this view may also argue that it is distributional and compositional shifts and changes in the economy (i.e. the move to more of a white-collar, part-time, women, service-sector based workforce) – developments which pre-date the Thatcher Government being in office – that pose relatively more of a longer-term challenge to the future of workforce unionization (although the unions have successfully coped with such challenges in the past). A second perspective, which is of a very different nature to the first one, contends that the Thatcher Government's industrial-relations aims have not been fully realized because the Government has not gone far enough in pursuit of the logical implications of its own arguments and beliefs. This is frequently the sort of view taken by commentators sympathetic to the general approach of the Thatcher Government; a recent example of such a view is Matthews and Minford's assessment of the years 1979–87, which suggests that political considerations, rather than economic logic, have prevented the Government from imposing the full, necessary degreee of market discipline to lower unemployment.[30] A third perspective involves the contention that the individual industrial-relations measures of the Thatcher Government do not add up to a fully cohesive and coherent strategy; a number of internal inconsistencies in the beliefs and assumptions of the Government in industrial-relations matters was noted above. Indeed, Incomes Data Services have suggested that the Thatcher approach of seeking a wide range of changes in industrial relations has tended to inhibit any change in depth,[31] while a more general assessment of 'Thatcherism' is that it is 'more a matter of attitudes and instincts than a clearly thought-out political philosophy in which policies fit together within a coherent intellectual framework'.[32] The fourth, and final, 'critical' perspective is that the extent of change has been limited by the Thatcher Government's pro-active strategy being too far ahead of what individual managers in individual organizations feel is either desirable or feasible in the present circumstances. In other words, the Government's lead in industrial relations has not always been backed and matched by the actions of management. This particular perspective is one which is discussed further in the next section.

The individual employer position towards unions

Historically, the establishment of trade-union recognition arrangements (and union growth) in Britain was strongly associated with Government pressure (to this end) on employers' associations during the two wartime periods. However, as Britain has increasingly diverged from the European model of relatively centralized, formal bargaining structures in the 1970s and 1980s, employer attitudes and positions towards union recognition and the institution of collective bargaining are now much more *individual*-employer-specific in nature and, conversely, less capable of being influenced by any processes of employer-association/government interaction: for example, a recent cross-crountry study by Freeman has suggested that unionization levels in the 1980s have held up least well in decentralized bargaining systems.[33] As a consequence of this change, and others in the larger environment of the 1980s, industrial-relations researchers need seriously to question the extent to which employer attitudes and actions of the past will be a 'safe guide' to (or accurate predictor of) their attitudes and actions in the future. Indeed, there has been research interest in the question of whether employers are likely to make more use of their legal rights under the 1980s legislation than was the case under the Industrial Relations Act 1971; in fact, studies of the existing use of injunctions[34] suggest that the absolute numbers involved are not large (e.g. eighty in mid-1984 to mid-1989), with a heavy concentration of them in a relatively small number of industries (e.g. the printing, public services, and shipping/transport sectors).

More generally, the question has been posed as to whether there will be a general, adverse reaction by employers against the institutions of union recognition and collective bargaining, with the result that trade unions in Britain will increasingly begin to follow their American counterparts down a path of longer-term, secular decline in membership; in the US it is increased management opposition to unionism that is frequently identified as the leading, single cause of union membership decline in recent decades.[35] To assist this discussion, one can consider the following forms or types of possible management adverse reaction against the institutions of trade unionism and collective bargaining:[36]

(1) Different patterns of behaviour associated with existing joint structures. If management has lowered the priority it attaches to such negotiating or consultative bodies (as a result of a general reaction against union organization, as opposed to dissatisfaction with the specific workings of such bodies), this could be reflected in indicators such as less regular meetings, less well-attended meetings, significant changes of personnel, a reduction in the scope of the agenda, and less independent decision-making powers.
(2) The introduction of new structural arrangements and practices that emphasize an individual-employee/organization identification process, that has the potential (although not necessarily the conscious intention) to undermine the sense of individual-employee identification with the union; quality of working life innovations, quality circles, and direct forms of management communication with the workforce are often viewed as coming into this category.
(3) The appearance of strong and sustained management opposition to the granting of any new recognition arrangements for currently 'uncovered' groups of employees in partially unionized establishments.
(4) The lapsing or decertification of existing recognition (or closed shop) arrangements.
(5) The appearance of non-union establishments as an increased proportion of a given population of firms or establishments.

In terms of this schema, some of the more immediately apparent worries for unions concern points (3) and (5) above. Specifically, we find that newer establishments are more likely to be non-union ones, and that recent ACAS annual reports make reference to increased management opposition to establishing new recognition arrangements; both the 1985 and 1986 reports, for example, state that only one in three recognition claims involving conciliation resulted in some form of recognition being achieved (this is a fall of some 10 percentage points in the union success rate of the late 1970s).[37] However, both survey evidence (such as that from the 1984 workplace industrial relations survey) and practitioner comments suggests that there is currently relatively little in the way of activities under sub-heading (4) above – i.e. the de-recognition of unions (for example, only 5 of the 179 ACAS conciliation cases concerning recognition in 1986 were de-recognition cases).[38] In other words, it would appear that the example of Tioxide Ltd (cited earlier in this chapter) is anything but a typical case at the present time in Britain; the Labour Editor of the *Financial Times* has estimated that there were only some 40 known cases of union de-recognition in the years 1984–8, although the nature of some of the companies involved in these (e.g. ICI, British Rail) should arguably constitute something of a worry for the unions (i.e. this practice is far from being confined to small, poor-quality employment-standards organizations). As de-recognition of unions or removal of closed shops tends to be viewed as the most powerful indication of (to use the phrase in the popular management literature) 'macho-management', some commentators have drawn a number of comforting conclusions (from the relative absence of such activites) for the future of the trade-union movement in Britain. Such conclusions may be somewhat premature or misplaced, however, if one recognizes the following: (i) this particular form of management opposition to unions is likely to be a later-stage manifestation of opposition only tending to occur on a significant scale following an initial period of sustained union decline; (ii) de-recognition of unions is only a relatively small-sized contributor to the overall decline of union membership in the United States;[39] and (iii) the substantial decline of union membership in *individual organizations* can still occur in the absence of 'macho-management' initiatives along the de-recognition lines. The contents of Table 10.1 provide an illustrative example of the latter point.

In this particular corporation, which had over 20,000 employees in 1977, total employment in the corporation fell by 46 per cent in the years 1977–85, while the overall level of union density fell from 65 per cent to 52 per cent. The latter was not the result of any management de-recognition activities, but was the outcome of a severe internal readjustment and restructuring process (due to increased product-market competition, especially from abroad) which involved employment reductions being disproportionately concentrated in the older plants and companies of the corporation which, in turn, had relatively high proportions of manual employees

Table 10.1 Union density in a large corporation, by individual company, 1977 and 1985

Company number	Union density (1977)	Union density (1985)
1	86.0	70.5
2	8.8	0.0
3	28.8	30.3
4	26.1	17.0
5	41.0	35.8
6	50.5	54.0
7	59.9	68.6
8	51.2	50.3
9	0.0	0.0
10	69.1	61.2
11	79.2	83.9

Source: P. B. Beaumont (1987), 'Industrial restructuring and union density: the experience in one large corporation', *Employee Relations* 9(1), p. 15.

and lower-level staff grades who were the more highly unionized employee groups within the corporation; the rank order of individual companies (in terms of the level of union density) changed little in these years, but the previously close relationship between the level of union density and total employment numbers at the company level became a relatively weak one as a result of this internal restructuring process.

The majority of industrial relations commentators appear to believe that the extent and nature of management opposition to unions and collective bargaining in Britain will never reach the scale and proportions which are currently observed in the United States. Indeed, Kelly has claimed that 'of all the countries one could use to illustrate Britain's future, America is undoubtedly the worst and most inappropriate example'.[40] This sort of view can be based on three separate arguments. The first is the contention that, historically, US management has been much less well disposed towards the institution of trade unionism than their British counterparts because of fundamental differences in the larger value-systems of the two societies. Such an argument has a considerable amount of intuitive appeal, although it has to be said that there are frequently considerable weaknesses in its manner of presentation. This is because: (i) the argument can easily become basically circular in nature (i.e. the greater opposition of management to unions in the US has resulted in lower levels of unionization than in Britain and this greater management opposition is indicated by lower levels of unionization); (ii) studies of management value-systems across countries do not always ensure that like is being compared with like (e.g. are the establishments in the different countries selected for study essentially similar in size, product-market circumstances, etc.?); (iii) there is the inevitable problem of the extent to which the stated or reported attitudes and values of management, in the absence of information on operating circumstances and constraints at a particular point in time, are a good guide to actual patterns of behaviour (e.g. does the fact that British management is less vocal about operating on a union-free basis compared to their US counterparts necessarily mean that they will not take advantage of opportunities to do so?); and (iv) in the particular case of Britain, it should be recalled that, historically, the achievement of union-recognition arrangements has owed more to Government pressure on employers (via employers' associations) than to the latter's favourable attitudes. A second argument in support of the above view could be based on some of the evidence reviewed in Chapter 7 concerning the size of the union relative-wage effect in Britain and the United States. That is to say, if one viewed differences in management opposition to unions across national systems as largely a function of differences in the size of the union relative wage effect at any point in time, then the figures reported in Chapter 7 would certainly incline one to expect relatively more management opposition in the US; within a single national system, however, management opposition may grow if the size of the union relative-wage effect increases in relation to its historical basis. The third argument tends to focus more on the differing *ability*, as opposed to differences in the incentive, of employers to operate on a non-union basis in the US and Britain. The point here is that a considerable proportion of the decline in the level of union organization in the US appears to be associated with falling levels of union density in partially organized corporations that operate both union and non-union plants or establishments. This particular phenomenon (frequently referred to as 'double-breasting' in the US) has little counterpart in Britain at the present time due to the smaller geographical size of the economy, the absence of state-level 'right-to-work' legislation in a non-federal government structure, the more established practice of 'recognition by extension' in multi-establishment organizations and the existence of national-level legislation providing institutional rights (to consultation) for unions in redundancy situations. In short, it is more difficult for a firm to close a union plant and open a new one on a non-union basis in Britain than is the case in the US. Nevertheless, significant inter-regional differences in the level of union density do exist in Britain (i.e. much lower levels in southern regions which are not simply a function of their particular mix of industries/occupations) and attempts to establish non-union operations in some new merchant-banking ventures (e.g. Barclays, de Zoete Wedd) have led BIFU to take certain legal actions and to question the strength of the EEC Transfer of Undertakings regulations.

This third argument for not expecting the British unions to follow the same path of decline as their US counterparts seems a reasonably powerful one. Although, having said this, one should be aware that differences in the extent and nature of management opposition to unions in the two systems at the present time are not always as comforting to British unions as is often claimed to be the case. This is because the peak level of union density in the US was reached over 25 years ago, whereas the peak level in Britain was as recent as 1979, a difference that is likely to produce different levels and forms of management opposition to union organization in the two systems at any given point in time. Moreover, although it has been argued that the current employer interest in flexible organizational structures and practices is not primarily motivated by anti-union considerations,[41] one can envisage situations where an insufficient change (as perceived by employers) in union attitudes and behaviour, *vis-à-vis* flexibility demands, produces a more direct attack on the structures of unionism and collective bargaining. Given that increased product-market pressures for flexible working arrangements are common to both systems, it is therefore difficult to see how Britain can remain entirely free from the possibility of some of the latter-stage type of opposition (e.g. the Tioxide Ltd example).

The trade union response

The trade unions and the trade-union/Labour-Party relationship have faced a combination of short run and longer run problems and pressures for changes since 1979 which in total raise major question marks concerning whether traditional attitudes, structures, and patterns of behaviour can and should be maintained in the future. The most obvious problems for the Labour movement include the loss of nearly three million union members since 1979, the reduced trade union vote for the Labour Party, the expectation of a relatively high level of unemployment to at least the end of the decade, the return of the Conservative Party for a third successive term of office, the relative growth of the under-organized sectors of the labour market, and the intensity of integrated, product-market competition – pushing employers in the direction of flexible organizational structures and working practices. These developments have led a variety of observers to argue that: (i) the present problems facing the trade-union movement are not simply a function of high unemployment and the policies of the Thatcher Government; and (ii) for unions to survive there must be signifcant departures from 'traditional ways of doing things'.[42] Predictably, however, there is considerable variation in the nature of the changes, or reforms, that the unions are urged to pursue. For example, Handy urges the unions to adopt more of an adviser–advocacy role for individual employees,[43] Fogarty looks to the development of more sophisticated, 'integrative bargaining' arrangements at the corporate level,[44] while Hain is in favour of the unions trying 'to overcome their historic limitations by constructively politicising their activities, broadening their sectional interests into community-wide ones, mobilising public support, revitalising and democratising their structures to involve their members more effectively, and, most important, campaigning for industrial democracy as a step towards real workers control.'[45] The specific steps which Hain sees as essential for the emergence of a new, more politically conscious trade-union movement in Britain include: (i) the fuller and more active penetration of unilateral management decision-making processes at the corporate level; (ii) the pursuit of demands raised by the women's movement; (iii) a strengthening of workplace–community linkages; (iv) the building of wider alliances with reformist groups outside the Labour movement; (v) the development of alternative or counter-plans in relation to industrial policy; (vi) a movement towards industrial unionism; and (vii) a revitalization of union branch life and more union involvement in the Labour Party at the local level.

The nature of individual union responses to the decline of membership since 1979 has been grouped under the following headings:[46] (1) work for the return of a Labour Government and supportive legislation; (2) merge with other unions; (3) recruit new members in the fastest growing industries and among previously neglected groups; (4) improve services to members; and (5) change trade-union purposes. Under the first heading we find that the TUC–Labour Party Liaison Committee (established in 1972) has produced plans for increased union involvement in company-level decision-making processes, 'Trade Unions for a Labour Victory' organized the political funds ballots campaign, 'Trade Unions for Labour' contributed an estimated £5 million to the Labour Party's election fund in 1987, the GMB has sought to build closer relationships with constituency Labour parties, and there have been a number of union discussion documents concerning the shape of desirable, future industrial-relations legislation. However, a number of individuals have questioned the organizational capability of unions to successfully carry through some of the strategic-planning-level initiatives proposed by the TUC–Labour-Party Liaison Committee,[47] and stressed the very limited likelihood of future developments in the corporatist decision-making direction.[48] In various political-science periodicals and journals there has also been considerable discussion of the trade-union– Labour-Party relationship following the Conservative election victory in 1987. Robert Taylor, for example, has argued that there is a very real need to change the situation whereby some twenty of the twenty-nine seats on the Labour Party's National Executive are controlled by the union block votes, particularly in view of Neil Kinnock's desire to widen the franchise in the selection of Labour parliamentary candidates.[49] The Labour Party is currently seeking to increase individual union membership of the party, while, as mentioned in an earlier chapter, the unions are increasingly looking to Brussels – as opposed to Whitehall – for new, 'progressive' developments in employment legislation and regulations.

Second, we saw in Chapter 3 that there has been a substantial fall in the number of individual unions in Britain (as in other countries) over the course of time, with most of the large 'open' unions tending to grow through the processes of merger and amalgamation. This is a process which is expected to continue, with many viewing it as the major means by which individual unions can expect to grow in the future. Furthermore, the contents of Table 10.2 provide some illustrative examples of recent union initiatives under headings (3) and (4) which were outlined above.

The Unity Trust Bank plc, which was established and is owned by a large number of TUC unions and the Co-operative Bank, has been heavily involved in membership-benefits developments, while the 'Union Law' scheme, arranged between the TUC and the Law Society, which will provide special legal assistance to members of TUC-affiliated unions for personal and domestic matters, is scheduled to come into operation in Spring 1989. These individual union initiatives need to be viewed in the light of, first, some of the problems facing unions in attempting to develop a comprehensive range of consumer services for members. In addition to the obvious financial and resource costs involved for unions, some problems have been encountered in meeting the commercial criteria of financial companies. For example, the Prudential Insurance Company withdrew from offering a package of pensions, mortgage, and insurance advice to SOGAT members when their market research suggested that the take-up by the union's members of these services was unlikely to be more than 1 in 4. Second, recent

Table 10.2 Recent examples of individual union recruitment and membership services initiatives

Individual union	*Nature of initiative*	*Comment*
1. EETPU	'Moneywise' package adding a broad range of financial services to existing education training and legal aid facilities.	Membership take-up of mortgages, portable pensions, and savings-related schemes low in comparison to house, car, and accident insurance schemes.
2. UCATT	'Moneysavers' deal involving financial services (such as mortgages, insurance, personal pensions, and investment advice) and consumer discounts (e.g. bargain holidays, discounts on car hire and travellers' cheques).	
3. SOGAT	A £70,000 national recruitment campaign, with key areas identified including administration workers in the provincial press, magazine and book publishing and the fibreboard industry, with the recruitment literature directed specifically at women, part-timers, and ethnic minorities. (The immediate background here was declining union membership, and the level of sequestration and dispute benefit costs.)	Stated target is 10,000 new members over the next 12 months.
4. GMBATU	Recruitment in national growth industries, such as hotels and catering, the security industry, and the community programme, with the individual regions of the union setting their own local target areas (e.g. the Northern region focusing on the unemployed and self-employed).	Central to the campaign is the focus on 'fair laws and rights in employment' for individual employees. That is, the union is offering protection of individual employee rights in matters such as health and safety, and equal opportunities where collective bargaining arrangements may be difficult to establish.

Table 10.2 — continued

Individual union	*Nature of initiative*	*Comment*
5. USDAW	Encoraging shop stewards to devote more attention to the recruitment of part-time employees in the retail trade sector.	Stated target is to raise total membership numbers beyond the 400,000 level.

Source: Industrial Relations Review and Report, no. 385, 3 February 1987, pp. 2–14.

union recruitment campaigns among part-time, temporary, and women workers (e.g. by NALGO and the TGWU, as well as those listed above) need to be seen against the background of the findings of the 1984 workplace industrial relations survey which revealed, for example, that only 15 per cent (10 per cent) of establishments with no manual (non-manual) union members reported that there had been an attempt by unions to recruit members in the years 1979–84.[50] Finally, there has been much heated debate within the TUC as to the basic purposes of trade unions, specifically over the question of the degree of departure from traditional practice that is an 'acceptable level' of adjustment to the new product- and labour-market environments of the 1980s. This controversy has overwhelmingly centred around the single-recognition/strike-free agreements associated with the EETPU. As we have seen, the number (and membership coverage) of these package agreements is relatively small, but other unions – particularly those with a membership interest in the establishments concerned – have been highly critical of them as 'selling out' the principles of independent trade-unionism and setting up a cycle of inter-union competition which will produce a substantial reduction in the standards and levels of recognition agreements through the course of time. Admittedly a number of myths surround these agreements, in that single-recognition agreements are not a new phenomenon unique to the EETPU, and a union statement of intent to avoid or minimize industrial action is not a directly, legally enforceable contract, although one cannot deny the extent of hostility to these agreements on the part of other unions. Indeed, as noted in an earlier chapter, the EETPU was expelled from the TUC in September 1988; there are General Council concerns about other unions poaching members of the EETPU (e.g. both the TGWU and MSF have established 'holding branches' for this purpose in 1988); and there will still undoubtedly remain difficulties for TUC disputes committees (the changes agreed at the meeting of Congress in 1988, which were discussed in Chapter 3, notwithstanding) in trying to fashion a consistent and coherent body of 'case law' concerning the definition of a 'greenfield site' that is acceptable to all unions concerned. The importance of the latter task cannot, however, be over-estimated when it is recalled that: (i) newer plants are significantly more likely to be non-union ones; and (ii) if there is a natural home for the establishment and development of unilateral human-resource-management practices it is on greenfield sites.

One assessment of the annual meeting of the TUC in September 1987 was that 'while opposition to current and proposed trade union and employment law was reaffirmed almost as a matter of course, Congress placed higher priorities on information, education, on setting negotiating goals, and on discussing ways to reach out to unorganised workers.'[51] The new promotional video (*Building for the Future*), launched at the Congress, stressed the relevance of unions in modern society – through, for example, promoting equality for women at work. This is a major area for change and development in Britain and other countries given that, as one recent comparative study concluded:

> Equality in unions creates a special challenge, for unions have presented themselves to their members and to the public as significant agents of change and pillars of political and economic democracy. Yet on the sex-equality issue they have shown themselves to be reluctant in accepting women as equals in the organisations and have been only tardily responsive to women's needs in bargaining with employers.[52]

Feminist writings have urged the union movement to do away with their 'macho image' and move away from a narrow focus on workers' interests which 'obviously excludes women working in the family just as it excludes other groups who are not on the cash nexus . . . [and] also tends to disregard areas of life which are crucial in women's lives'.[53] This particular message has important implications for the future size of the union movement and for the nature of its role in social and community life, given that: (i) nearly 25 per cent of the TUC membership is made up of women (73 per cent of these being in public-sector unions); (ii) the one bright spot for the Labour Party in the trade union vote in 1987 was that 41 per cent of women trade-union members voted Labour (34 per cent in 1983) compared with 29 per cent of them who voted Conservative (34 per cent in 1983);[54] and (iii) one of the few positive occurrences and lessons for the unions to emerge from the miners' strike of 1984–5 was the emergence of a network of women's support groups (largely under the umbrella of the 'Women Against Pit Closures' organization) in the wider community.[55]

In Chapter 3 we noted that in late 1987 the General Council of the TUC initiated a general review of strategy and tactics in relation to union organization. This was an important development in the sense of recognizing the fact that not all of the current and future problems of union organization were attributable to high unemployment and the policies of the Conservative Government. The early stages of the review have seen the airing of a number of proposals similar to those discussed and undertaken in the United States: these include co-ordinated, multi-union organizing campaigns, campaigns concentrating on particular geographical areas, an increased role for the union confederation in organizing initiatives, an increased range of consumer benefits and services to union members, and the development of a union advisory/protective role for individual employees in situations where formal collective-bargaining arrangements are not established.[56] Although some individual unions have already been highly critical of any proposals perceived as likely to reduce their degree of autonomy (*vis-à-vis* the TUC) in the matter of membership recruitment, the emergence and implementation of any tangible proposals from this review exercise will be important developments to watch. This is because the major challenge facing the unions at present is whether new organizing developments by themselves can check and reverse the extent of the membership decline experienced since 1979 in the face of both an economic and political environment that is 'hostile' to membership recruitment. If this does in fact occur it will be: (i) a major departure from historical experience (where the record suggests that membership growth requires the co-existence of favourable economic conditions, supportive government measures, and new unions and recruitment strategies); and (ii) dramatic confirmation of the views of some academics that existing time-series-based studies of variation in union membership tend to be overly demand-side dominated and thus seriously underestimate the capacity of individual, growth-orientated unions to shape their own, and the larger movement's, destiny.

The TUC has also recently reviewed the subject area of trade-union education.[57] The main component of the TUC's educational programme (since legal rights to time off with pay to attend union education courses was introduced in 1975) has been the two-stage courses of 10 days' duration each (i.e. individuals attend 1 day a week for 10 weeks). The level of such course provision has, however, declined substantially from the late 1970s, with short courses of 1–3 days' duration being introduced in 1984 to try and offset this trend. The TUC review report instanced difficulties in obtaining paid release for representatives (and, indeed, increasing difficulties in obtaining volunteers to act as union representatives), argued the case for a wider definition of relevant trade union education (i.e. education 'in those issues which affect workers, employment, the operation of industry and the local and national economies'), and recommended that union representatives need at least 200 hours of training during their first 2 years.

In reflecting on the future of trade unions in Britain and other advanced industrialized economies, it is highly likely that: (i) the nature of individual members' attachment to the union movement will become increasingly heterogeneous in nature (i.e. varying from extensive joint decision-making at company level, through wages/hours-only collective bargaining, to legal assistance to individual members in unfair dismissal claims); and (ii) unions as organizational entities will increasingly have to confront choices and decisions, in a resource-scarce environment, that involve trade-off effects. The most obvious and important choice for individual unions, and the movement as a whole, will be that concerning the balance to be struck between recruitment of new members and the representation of existing members. The problem for the unions in a world of finite resources is the old fixed-sum-game problem – namely, that developments or improvements in the performance of one of these functions is likely to involve costs for the other one. Indeed, it has already been suggested, in evidence to the TUC Special Review Body, that any special recruitment campaigns (at least by the large general unions) will find it difficult to deliver sizeable membership gains over the course of time, given the existing workloads and priorities of national-level officers.[58]

In conclusion

There are two final issues and questions to be considered here. The first has to do with the recent appearance of a number of publications which have argued that the British trade unions, far from being in a state of crisis, have remained in a reasonably healthy position in the high-unemployment and restrictive-legislative environment of the 1980s. In support of this view, Kelly, for example, contends that the recent fall in union membership and density is less than in previous recessions, workplace organizational structures have rarely been removed by unilateral management actions, the finances of most unions are relatively satisfactory, employees who have remained in employment have enjoyed real wage increases, and the results of the political fund ballots were a triumph for the unions.[59] In addition, 'favourable reference' could also be made to the increase in the size of the union relative-wage effect in the 1980s and to the findings of opinion polls which suggest that the 'popularity' of unions is relatively high in the 1980s.

Arguments along these lines have been useful in emphasizing the need for researchers to: (i) be careful about using strong terms such as a 'union crisis'; (ii) distinguish carefully between short-term (cyclical) and longer-term (secular) causes of change; (iii) use multiple, as opposed to single, measures of change; and (iv) place the 1980's position in a longer-term historical context. These are valuable contributions, although it has to be said that such publications are themselves open to a certain amount of criticism. First, some of the arguments which they criticize are little more than 'straw-men' hypotheses. For example, they tend to be criticizing more the statements of politicians and the media, rather than the views of other researchers. Indeed, as argued in this chapter, the peak level of union density in Britain was reached less than a decade ago, so that a widespread lapsing and de-certification of closed shops and unions by management at the present time is hardly to be expected, and, as such, these researchers cannot claim to be investigating a 'serious hypothesis'. Second, these researchers are overwhelmingly concerned with the effects of high unemployment and the Conservative Government's legislation on the union movement – which are serious, but potentially cyclical problems for the unions if a change of government is not completely ruled out as a possibility in the future. In contrast, they pay much less attention to the role of product-market changes in stimulating changes in business strategies which are, arguably, more of a longer-term problem for a union movement heavily committed to traditional, collective-bargaining arrangements and practices. Third, they tend to ignore the fact that certain union short-term gains and advantages can potentially be a source of longer-term problems for the union movement itself. For example, a large, sustained increase in the size of the union relative-wage effect may be something of a mixed blessing for unions in the present environment, in that it is potentially an important source of increased management opposition to new and further union organization. Finally, they tend to imply that the relative stability of collective-bargaining arrangements is essentially due to the strength and depth of the union movement. In fact, the stability of such structures at the present time probably owes more to management action or inaction, which cannot necessarily be assumed to remain the norm in the future.

The second issue for consideration concerns the question of whether the British system of industrial relations is currently experiencing any major change and, if so, what is the essential nature of this change. Prior to the 1980s, the contemporary British system of industrial relations was seen as one strongly shaped by its deep, historical roots and influences – with individual instances of change and proposed reform being relatively small and self-contained. For example, the Donovan Commission looked to improved procedural regulation of the collective-bargaining system, the productivity bargaining experience of the 1960s was viewed as management taking more of an innovative, rather than a reactor, role in collective bargaining, and researchers argued that the increased role of statute law in the system in the 1970s called into question the appropriateness of viewing the collective-bargaining system as a 'voluntary' one.

In the 1980s, however, one has for the first time a Government in power which is actually questioning the value and desirability of the British system of industrial relations remaining a collective-bargaining based one. This questioning has led to a variety of views as to the currently evolving shape of the system. At one extreme, some commentators believe that the relative size of the non-union employment sector will increase, and that employee-relations practices in the unionized sector will increasingly have an individual-employee orientation and focus, while those who subscribe to the view that the system will remain basically a collective-bargaining one can be categorized into two groups: those who hold (or hope) that collective bargaining is and will become less adversarial in nature (i.e. more of an integrative, joint problem-solving process) and those who view the present situation as involving nothing more than a strong swing in bargaining power in favour of management, within the context of traditional collective-bargaining arrangements.

Admittedly, few researchers subscribe to the view that both human-resource-management practices and co-operative (integrative) bargaining practices are widespread phenomena at the present time. This being said, it is important to recognize that employers who are seeking more integrative collective bargaining but who do not achieve it, do not only have the option of removing collective-bargaining arrangements and substituting human-resource-management practices. They could also seek to increasingly circumvent collective bargaining by taking more and more decisions which have important implications for industrial relations at non-collective-bargaining (i.e. corporate and workplace) levels. This is something which has been argued to be occurring on a systematic basis in the US from the 1970s. In Britain, systematic moves in this direction, involving a coherent, long-run management strategy, are more difficult to discern, although undoubtedly a number of more piecemeal, *ad hoc* moves along these lines have occurred. Indeed, it is only if and when the nature of management strategy – whose outcome will be strongly shaped by the ongoing interaction between product-market circumstances and management value-systems – becomes clearer, that we will be able to see whether the British system of industrial relations remains one largely centred around the institution of collective bargaining.

Appendix

Teaching material

For busy teachers of industrial relations, the following questions are ones which I have found useful for exam and essay questions and for providing a focus for classroom discussions.

Chapter 1

Assess the contribution of Dunlop's systems approach to the development of industrial-relations theory.

'The growth of non-union firms poses a major challenge to the traditional approach of industrial-relations researchers'. Discuss.

Chapter 2

'All the current trends in the labour market suggest that union decline is an inevitable fact of life'. Discuss.

Consider the role of product-market competition in stimulating changes in organizational structures and the implications of such changes for union organization.

Is corporatism a feasible and desirable development in Britain?

'Both public-opinion polls and electoral results have particularly worrying implications for the future of trade unions in Britain'. Discuss.

What have been the major legislative trends in British industrial relations since the 1960s?

Chapter 3

'It is only shop stewards who have held out against the forces that have incorporated other levels of the trade union movement through the course of time'. Discuss.

Is it important for any government to obtain TUC backing in the administration of an incomes policy?

Change in industrial relations

Critically assess the state of our knowledge concerning the role orientation of shop stewards.

Are union mergers a good thing?

Is democracy a useful and meaningful concept to utilize in the study of trade unions?

'Research on union membership changes through the course of time has simply told us that unions are fair weather creatures'. Discuss.

What are the implications for unions of limited closed shop coverage?

Can economic analysis adequately explain the nature of union behaviour in wage bargaining?

Chapter 4

'The declining role of multi-employer, industry-level wage bargaining in Britain means that employers' associations have little contemporary impact on industrial relations'. Discuss.

Compare the relative strengths and weaknesses of the CBI and TUC as pressure groups in industrial relations.

What have been the industrial-relations effects of company mergers?

What have been the major measures and determinants of the changing position of the personnel function in organizations?

'Product life-cycle has major implications for the mix of personnel policies in unionized firms'. Discuss.

Critically assess the state of our knowledge concerning the concept of management style in industrial relations.

Chapter 5

'Collective bargaining is essentially a summation of the processes of individual bargaining'. Discuss.

What have been the major criticisms made of the institution of collective bargaining?

Is there one best bargaining structure for the system of industrial relations as a whole?

Assess the merits of the Government's case against national wage-bargaining arrangements.

Why do some organizations favour company-level bargaining structures, and others plant-level arrangements?

Chapter 6

Is collective bargaining in any way different from bargaining over other subjects?

Has the conceptual work of Walton and McKersie added substantially to our knowledge of the processes of collective bargaining?

What are the major limitations of existing OD and change models when applied to union–management situations?

What is the relationship between strikes and other forms of industrial conflict?

Have economic models of strike activity substantially added to our understanding of the causes of strikes?

'All public-sector strikes are particularly high-cost ones'. Discuss.

'It is the size of an overall organization, rather than the size of an individual plant, that is so important in shaping the structure and processes of collective bargaining'. Discuss.

What have been the major union fears of, and responses to, MNCs in host countries?

'Bargaining power is a major concept in industrial-relations research, but one which lacks an adequate empirical foundation'. Discuss.

Chapter 7

How does the size of the union relative-wage effect in Britain compare with that in the United States?

Has empirical research conclusively demonstrated a relationship between union power and inflation?

What does the historical record reveal about the impact of unions on the size of the wage share in Britain?

'We cannot ignore the fact that personnel managers, with their detailed knowledge of industrial relations, report that unions are a significant constraint on organizational change'. Discuss.

Is it possible to define and measure the concept of 'good industrial relations'?

Chapter 8

Is 'the State' anything more than simply the existing political party in office in terms of the implications for the industrial-relations system?

Are final-offer arbitration arrangements something that should be encouraged in the British system of industrial relations?

Change in industrial relations

Is the historical track record of incomes policies in Britain one of total failure?

'The short-term-settlement orientation of the conciliation process limits the capacity to deal with serious underlying union–management problems'. Discuss.

Is it possible and useful to talk of separate models of public- and private-sector industrial relations?

'The present Conservative Government enjoys a reputation second to none of being anti-public-sector'. Discuss.

Chapter 9

'Integrative-bargaining subjects should be a part of the normal collective-bargaining process rather than being dealt with by separate arrangements'. Discuss.

Have new-technology agreements been a success, from the union point of view, in Britain?

'It is not only the weakness of union organization at the corporate level in Britain that limits the extent of union influence over strategic management decisions'. Discuss.

'Profit sharing is the wave of the future for employee involvement in Britain'. Discuss.

Is human resource management essentially a greenfield-site phenomenon?

'All the indications are that management is thinking in terms of employee relations rather than collective bargaining at the present time in Britain'. Discuss.

Chapter 10

'Flexible organizational structures pose a major threat to collective bargaining as we know it'. Discuss.

'The one safe prediction about the future of work is that it will bear little relation to what it has been in the past'. Discuss.

'The future of the unions is in their own hands if they would only recognize this fact and make a greater commitment to organizing activities'. Discuss.

'A greater union identification with and commitment to the economic performance of individual organizations is essential for union survival'. Discuss.

Appendix

There are a number of case studies which I have found to be useful in illustrating some of the issues and arguments presented in these chapters. Some of the cases in the books by Hawkins,[1] Clegg, Kemp, and Legge (eds),[2] Tyson and Kakabadse (eds),[3] and Green[4] have proved especially helpful in this regard.

Notes and references

Chapter 1 Industrial relations as a field of study

1 See John R. Commons, *Institutional Economics: Its Place in the Political Economy*, New York, Macmillan, 1934.
2 S. and B. Webb, *The History of Trade Unionism 1666–1920*, London, Longman, 1920.
3 Clark Kerr, 'The intellectual role of the neorealists in labor economics', *Industrial Relations*, 22(2), Spring 1983, pp. 301–2.
4 ibid., p. 304.
5 Peter Cappelli, 'Theory construction in IR and some implications for research', *Industrial Relations*, 24(1), Winter 1985, p. 94.
6 For a useful, brief discussion of these terms, see Chris Clegg, Nigel Kemp, and Karen Legge (eds) *Case Studies in Organisational Behaviour*, London, Harper & Row, 1985, pp. 8–12.
7 See T. D. Jick, 'Mixing quantitative and qualitative methods: triangulation in action', *Administrative Science Quarterly*, 24, 1979, pp. 602–11.
8 See J. M. Beyer and H. M. Trice, 'The utilisation process: conceptual framework and synthesis of empirical findings', *Administrative Science Quarterly*, 27, 1982, pp. 591–622.
9 George Strauss and Peter Feuille, 'Industrial relations research: a critical analysis', *Industrial Relations*, 17, October 1978, pp. 259–77.
10 John T. Dunlop, *Industrial Relations Systems*, New York, Holt, Rinehart & Winston, 1950. See here, for example: A. Shirom, 'The labor relations system: a proposed conceptual framework', *Relations Industrielles*, 40(2), 1985, pp. 312–24; J. E. Goodman, J. Armstrong, J. Davies, and A. Wagner, *Rule Making and Industrial Peace: Industrial Relations in the Footwear Industry*, London, Croom Helm, 1977.
11 Dunlop, op. cit., p. 6.
12 See G. S. Bain and H. A. Clegg, 'A strategy for industrial relations research in Great Britain', *British Journal of Industrial Relations*, 12, March 1974, pp. 91–113.
13 Michael P. Jackson, *The Price of Coal*, London, Croom Helm, 1974.
14 John C. Anderson, 'Bargaining outcomes: an IR systems approach', *Industrial Relations*, 18(2), Spring 1974, pp. 127–43.

15 Thomas A. Kochan, Robert B. McKersie, and Peter Cappelli, 'Strategic choice and industrial relations theory', *Industrial Relations*, 23(3), Winter 1984, pp. 16–39.
16 See, for example, Gerald G. Somers (ed.), *Essays in Industrial Relations Theory*, Ames, IA, Iowa State Univeristy Press, 1969.
17 Hugh Clegg, *Trade Unionism Under Collective Bargaining*, Basil Blackwell, Oxford, 1976.
18 See, for example, Toby Wall, and Nigel Nicholson, 'Psychology's place in industrial relations', *Personnel Management*, 8(5), May 1976, pp. 22–5.
19 For recent exception, see A. Oswald, 'New research on the economics of trade unions and labour contracts', Discussion Paper no. 261, Centre for Labour Economics, LSE, November 1986.
20 For an interesting discussion of this subject, see David Marsden, *The End of Economic Man?*, Brighton, Wheatsheaf, 1986.
21 Richard B. Freeman and James L. Medoff, *What Do Unions Do?*, New York, Basic Books, 1986, pp. 3–25.
22 Everett M. Kassalow, 'Japan as an industrial relations model', *The Journal of Industrial Relations*, 25(2), June 1983, pp. 201–19.
23 John P. Windmuller, 'Model industrial relations systems', *Proceedings of the Industrial Relations Research Association*, December 1963.
24 Clark Kerr, John T. Dunlop, Frederick Harbison, and Charles A. Myers, *Industrialism and Industrial Man*, New York, Oxford University Press, 1964.
25 John T. Dunlop, Frederick H. Harbison, Clark Kerr, and Charles Myers, *Industrialism and Industrial Man Reconsidered*, Inter-University Study of Human Resources in National Development, New Jersey, Prentice Hall, 1975.
26 John Goldthorpe, 'The end of convergence: corporatist and dualist tendencies in modern western societies', in Bryan Roberts, Ruth Finnegan, and Duncan Gallie (eds), *New Approaches to Economic Life*, Manchester University Press, Manchester, 1985, pp. 132–44.
27 *ibid.*
28 Richard B. Peterson, 'Research design issues in comparative industrial relations', *Proceedings of the Industrial Relations Research Association*, December 1986.
29 See Solomon Barkin, (ed.), *Worker Militancy and Its Consequences 1965–1975*, New York, Praeger, 1975.
30 See Richard Edwards, Paolo Garonna, and Franz Todtling (eds), *Unions in Crisis and Beyond: Perspectives from Six Countries*, Dover, Auburn House, 1986.
31 Hervey Juris, Mark Thompson, and Wilbur Daniels (eds), *Industrial Relations in a Decade of Economic Change*, Madison-Wisconsin, IRRA, 1985.
32 Michael Poole, *Industrial Relations: Origins and Patterns of National Diversity*, London, Routledge & Kegan Paul, 1986.
33 Peterson, *op. cit.*, n. 28.

34 See, for example, Arndt Sorge and Malcolm Warner, *Comparative Factory Organization*, Aldershot, Gower, 1986.
35 See, for example, Robert J. Flanagan, David Soskice, and Lloyd Ulman, *Unionism, Economic Stabilisation and Incomes Policy*, Washington, Brookings Institution, 1983.
36 See, for example, R. Bean, *Comparative Industrial Relations*, London, Croom Helm, 1985, pp. 4–7.
37 See, William Foote Wyte, 'Framework for the analysis of industrial relations', *Industrial and Labor Relations Review*, 3(3), April 1950, pp. 393–401.
38 See, for example, E. J. Hobsbawn, 'Trade union history', *Economic History Review*, 20(2), August 1967.
39 Donald P. Schwab, and Larry L. Cummings, 'Theories of satisfaction and performance: a review', *Industrial Relations*, 9, October 1970, pp. 408–30.
40 V. Vroom, *Work and Motivation*, New York, John Wiley, 1964.
41 See Alan Fox, 'The meaning of work', in Geoff Esland and Graeme Salaman (eds), *The Politics of Work and Occupations*, Milton Keynes, Open University Press, 1986, pp. 139–91.
42 For a recent example, see the book review in *The Academy of Management Review*, 10(2), April 1985, p. 375.
43 See Andrew Thomson and Malcolm Warner (eds), *The Behavioural Sciences and Industrial Relations*, Aldershot, Gower, 1981.
44 Thomas A. Kochan, 'Collective bargaining and organizational behaviour research', in Barry M. Staw and Larry L. Cummings (eds), *Research in Organisational Behaviour*, Greenwich, JAI Press, 2, 1980, pp. 130–6.
45 Sylvia Shimmin and R. Singh, 'Industrial relations and organizational behaviour: a critical appraisal', in B. Barrett, E. Rhodes, and J. Bershon (eds), *Industrial Relations and the Wider Society*, London, Collier Macmillan, 1975, pp. 30–1.
46 A. Fox, *Beyond Contract: Work, Authority and Trust Relations*, London, Macmillan, 1974.
47 See the two articles on these subjects in *Industrial and Labor Relations Review*, 40(2), January 1987.
48 Harry C. Katz, Thomas A. Kochan, and Mark R. Weber, 'Assessing the effects of industrial relations systems and efforts to improve the quality of working life on organizational effectiveness', *Academy of Management Journal*, 28(3), September 1985, pp. 509–26.
49 For an example of such an American union reaction, see P. Payne, 'The consultants who coach the violators', *The Federationist*, 84, 1977, pp. 22–9.
50 Alan Fox, 'Industrial sociology and industrial relations', Donovan Commission Research Paper no. 3, London, HMSO, 1966.
51 Fox, *op. cit.*, pp. 297–8.
52 Daniel Quinn Mills, *Labor–Management Relations*, New York, McGraw Hill, 1978, Chapter 4.
53 Thomas A. Kochan, Harry C. Katz, and Robert B. McKersie, *The*

Transformation of American Industrial Relations, New York, Basic Books, 1986, Chapter 3.
54 Solomon Barkin, 'The curent unilateralist counterattack on unionism and collective bargaining', *Relations Industrielles*, 41(1), 1986, pp. 19–22.
55 David Deaton, 'Management and industrial relations', Unpublished report of the Workplace Industrial Relations Survey, December 1981, (mimeographed).
56 Neil Millward and Mark Stevens, *British Workplace Industrial Relations, 1980–1984*, Aldershot, Gower, 1986, pp. 1–17.
57 P. B. Beaumont, *The Decline of Trade Union Organisation*, London, Croom Helm, 1987, Chapter 5.
58 S. Fothergill and G. Gudgin, *Unequal Growth*, London, Heinemann, 1982, pp. 117–9; M. Beesley and P. Wilson, 'Government aid to the small firm since Bolton', in J. Stanworth, A. Westrip, D. Watkins, and J. Lewis (eds), *Perspectives on a Decade of Small Business Research*, Aldershot, Gower, 1982, pp. 181–99.
59 A. Rainnie, 'Small firms, big problems: the political economy of small businesses', *Capital and Class*, 25, Spring, pp. 140–68.
60 *MSC Labour Market Quarterly Report, Great Britain*, February 1987, p. 10.
61 D. J. Storey, 'Regional policy in a recession', *National Westminster Bank Quarterly Review*, November 1983, pp. 44–5.
62 P. B. Beaumont and L. Cairns, 'New towns: a centre of non-unionism?', *Employee Relations* 9(2), 1987.
63 P. B. Beaumont, 'Individual union success in obtaining recognition: some British evidence', *British Journal of Industrial Relations*, XXV(2), July 1987.
64 D. J. Storey, 'New firm formation, employment change and the small firm: the case of Cleveland county', *Urban Studies*, 18, 1981, pp. 335–45.
65 P. B. Beaumont and I. Rennie, 'Organisational culture and non-union status of small businesses', *Industrial Relations Journal*, 17(3), Autumn 1986, pp. 214–24.
66 M. F. R. Kets de Vries, 'The entrepreneurial personality: a person at the cross-roads', *Journal of Management Studies*, 14, 1977, pp. 53–5.
67 'Trade union towards the year 2000', *Industrial Relations Review and Report* no. 285, February 1987.
68 For a useful discussion, see R. L. Butchart, 'A new UK definition of the high technology industries', *Economic Trends* 400, February 1987, pp. 82–8.
69 *ibid.*, pp. 87–8.
70 P. B. Beaumont, 'Industrial relations policies in high technology firms', *New Technology, Work and Employment*, 1(2), Autumn 1986, pp. 152–9.
71 P. B. Beaumont and R. I. D. Harris, 'High technology industries, non-union status and human resource management policies: the

British picture', Department of Economics, Queen's University of Belfast, mimeographed paper, 1988.

Chapter 2 The larger environment of collective bargaining

1 Alan Fox, *History and Heritage*, London, Allen & Unwin, 1985, p. 432.
2 David Marquand, *The Unprincipled Society*, London, Fontana, 1988.
3 See, for example, *Midland Bank Review*, Summer 1987, p. 5.
4 See: D. Metcalf, 'On the measurement of employment and unemployment', *National Institute Economic Review*, no. 109, August 1984; and R. Layard and S. Nickell, 'The causes of British unemployment', *National Institute Economic Review*, February 1985.
5 *OECD Economic Outlook*, no. 41, December 1986, p. 27.
6 Layard and Nickell, *op. cit.*, n. 4.
7 Department of Employment, *Employment: The Challenge for the Nation*, 1985, pp. 13–4.
8 For a useful summary, see Ken Mayhew, 'Reforming the labour market', *Oxford Review of Economic Policy* 1(2), 1985, pp. 60–79.
9 See D. Metcalf, 'Labour market flexibility and jobs: a survey of evidence from OECD countries with special reference to Great Britain and Europe', Discussion Paper no. 254, Centre for Labour Economics, LSE, October 1986.
10 For a general overview see Dennis Kavanagh, *Thatcherism and British Politics: The End of Consensus?*, Oxford, Oxford University Press, 1987, Chapter 8.
11 OECD, *op. cit.*, n. 5, pp. 39 and 43.
12 A. A. Carruth and A. J. Oswald, 'Wage inflexibility in Britain', Discussion Paper no. 258, Centre for Labour Economics, LSE, October 1986, Table 3.
13 D. E. Cullen, 'Recent trends in collective bargaining in the US', Geneva, ILO, 1985 (mimeographed); see also, *Collective Bargaining: A Response to the Recession in Industrialised Market Economy Countries*, Geneva, ILO, 1984, Chapter 3.
14 D. Metcalf and S. Nickell, 'Will pay cuts bring more jobs?', *New Society*, 28 February 1985.
15 R. Layard and S. Nickell, 'The performance of the British labour market', Discussion Paper no. 249, Centre for Labour Economics, LSE, 1986, p. 41.
16 M. Gregory, P. Lobban, and A. Thomson, 'Bargaining structure, pay settlements and perceived pressures in manufacturing 1979–1984: further analysis from the CBI databank', *British Journal of Industrial Relations*, 24, 1986, p. 215–32.
17 D. G. Blanchflower and A. J. Oswald, 'Internal and external influences upon pay settlements: new survey evidence', Discussion Paper no. 275, Centre for Labour Economics, LSE, 1987, pp. 2–3.

18 D. Metcalf, 'Water notes dry up', Discussion Paper no. 314, Centre for Labour Economics, LSE, July 1988.
19 See, for example, Michael Fogarty with Douglas Brooks, *Trade Unions and British Industrial Development*, London, PSI Research Report, 1986, pp. 32–8.
20 Metcalf (1984), *op. cit.*, n. 18, p. 66.
21 Fogarty with Brooks, *op. cit.*, n. 19, p. 37.
22 *OECD Economic Outlook*, June 1987, p. 32.
23 Central Statistical Office, *op. cit.*, p. 107.
24 Charles Handy, *The Future of Work*, Oxford, Blackwell, 1984, p. 85.
25 See Handy, *op. cit.*, *passim*; also Michael Rose, *Re-working the Work Ethic*, London, Batsford, 1985, Chapter 7.
26 Colin Crouch, 'The future prospects for trade unions in western Europe', *Political Quarterly*, 57, 1986, pp. 6–7.
27 Fogarty with Brooks, *op. cit.*, n. 19, pp. 18–19.
28 Richard K. Brown, 'Attitudes to work, occupational identity and industrial change', in Bryan Roberts, Ruth Finnegan and Duncan Gallie (eds), *New Approaches to Economic Life*, Manchester, Manchester University Press, 1985, p. 462.
29 J. E. Thurman, 'Job satisfaction: an international overview', *International Labour Review*, 117(3), November–December, 1977, pp. 252–5.
30 For a particularly strong criticism of such findings, see Graeme Salaman, *Class and the Corporation*, Glasgow, Fontana, 1981, pp. 72–88.
31 Alan Fox, 'The meaning of work', in Geoff Esland and Graeme Salaman (eds), *The Politics of Work and Occupations*, Milton Keynes, Open University Press, 1980, pp. 91–139.
32 Thomas A. Kochan, *Collective Bargaining and Industrial Relations*, Homewood, Irwin, 1980, pp. 142–7 and pp. 373–7, respectively.
33 Brown in Roberts, Finnegan and Gallie (eds), *op. cit.*, n. 28, pp. 463–9.
34 See, for example, Henry Phelps Brown, *The Origins of Trade Union Power*, Oxford, Oxford University Press, 1986, pp. 111–12.
35 See D. R. Deaton and P. B. Beaumont, 'The determinants of bargaining structure: some large scale survey evidence for Britain', *British Journal of Industrial Relations*, XVIII, 1980, pp. 202–16.
36 For a useful review with some recent findings, see David Blanchflower, 'Wages and concentration in British manufacturing', *Applied Economics*, 18, 1986, pp. 1025–38.
37 P. K. Edwards, 'Managing labour relations through the recession', *Employee Relations*, 7(2), 1985, pp. 6–7.
38 Michael Chisholm, 'De-industrialisation and British regional policy', *Regional Studies*, 19(4), August 1985, p. 306.
39 For a useful diagrammed illustration, see Thomas A. Kochan, Robert B. McKersie, and Peter Cappelli, 'Strategic choice and industrial relations theory', *Industrial Relations*, XXIII, Winter 1984, p. 25.
40 See D. Quinn Mills and Malcolm Lovell, 'Enhancing competitiveness:

the contribution of employee relations', in Bruce R. Scott and George C. Lodge (eds), *US Competitiveness in the World Economy*, Boston, Mass., Harvard Business School Press, 1985.
41 John E. Kelly, *Scientific Management, Job Redesign and Work Performance*, London, Academic Press, 1982.
42 See, for example, Ralf Dahrendorf, *On Britain*, Chicago, Chicago University Press, 1982, pp. 65–78.
43 James E. Cronin, *Labour and Society in Britain, 1918–1979*, London, Batsford, 1984, p. 1.
44 See, for example, D. Lockwood, 'The sources of variation in working class images of society', *Sociological Review*, 14(3), 1966.
45 Howard Newby, C. Vogler, D. Rose, and G. Marshall, 'From class structure to class action: British working class politics in the 1980s', in Bryan Roberts, Ruth Finnegan and Duncan Gallie (eds), *op. cit.*, n. 28, p. 87.
46 R. E. Pahl, *Divisions of Labour*, Oxford, Blackwell, 1984.
47 Newby *et al.*, *op. cit.*, n. 45, p. 100.
48 See also Philip Bassett, *Strike Free*, London, Macmillan, 1986, pp. 31–40.
49 *New Statesman*, 10 July 1987, p. 10; *The Economist*, 18–24 July 1987; Robert Taylor, 'The trade union "problem" since 1960', in Ben Pimlott and Chris Cook (eds), *Trade Unions in British Politics*, London, Longman, 1982, p. 209.
50 Martin Harrop, 'Voting and the electorate', in Henry Drucker, Patrick Dunleavy, Andrew Gamble, and Gillian Peele (eds), *Developments in British Politics*, London, Macmillan, 1986, pp. 34–59.
51 Colin Crouch, *Trade Unions: The Logic of Collective Action*, Glasgow, Fontana, 1982, pp. 201–2.
52 *ibid.*, p. 190.
53 See D. Volker, 'NALGO affiliation to the TUC', *British Journal of Industrial Relations*, IV(1), March 1966, pp. 49–76.
54 Lewis Minkin, 'The British Labour Party and the trade unions: crisis and compact', *Industrial and Labor Relations Review*, 28(1), October 1974, pp. 25–8.
55 See Peter Jenkins, *The Battle of Downing Street*, London, Charles Knight, 1970.
56 Minkin, *op. cit.*, n. 54, p. 28.
57 K. Middlemas, *Politics in Industrial Society: The Experience of the British System Since 1911*, London, André Deutsch, 1979.
58 Rodney Lowe, 'Hours of labour: negotiating industrial legislation in Britain, 1919–39', *Economic History Review*, 35(2), August 1982, pp. 254–71.
59 See Colin Crouch, *The Politics of Industrial Relations*, Glasgow, Fontana, 1979, Chapter 8.
60 Lord Hailsham, *The Dilemma of Democracy*, London, Collins, 1978.
61 Leo Panitch, 'Trade unions and the capitalist state', *New Left Review* 125, January–February 1981.
62 Crouch (1979), *op. cit.*, n. 59, p. 187.

63 See, for example, A. W. J. Thomson, 'Trade unions and the corporate state in Britain', *Industrial and Labor Relations Review*, 33(1), October 1974, pp. 36–54.
64 See: D. Metcalf, 'Labour market flexibility and jobs: a survey of evidence from OECD countries with special reference to Great Britain and Europe', Discussion Paper no. 254, Centre for Labour Economics, LSE, October 1986, pp. 13–16; and C. R. Bean, P. R. G. Layard, and S. J. Nickell, 'The rise in unemployment: a multi-country study', *Economica*, 53, Supplement, 1986, pp. 16–17.
65 Lars Calmfors and John Driffill, 'Bargaining structure, corporatism and macroeconomic performance', *Economic Policy*, 6, April 1988.
66 See A. Newell and J. S. U. Symons, 'Corporatism, the laissez-faire and the rise in unemployment', Discussion Paper no. 260, Centre for Labour Economics, LSE, November 1986.
67 Calmfors and Driffill, *op. cit.*, n. 65.
68 Crouch (1986), *op. cit.*, n. 26, p. 10.
69 John H. Goldthorpe, 'The end of convergence: corporatist and dualist tendencies in modern western societies', in Roberts, Finnegan, and Gallie (eds), *op. cit.*, no. 28, pp. 132–50.
70 For some figures on the size of trade-union political funds see Michael Pinto-Duschinsky, 'Trends in British political funding 1979–1985', *Parliamentary Affairs*, 38(3), 1985, p. 342.
71 *New Statesman*, 10 July 1987, p. 10. Also *The Economist*, 18–24 July 1987.
72 See Michael Moran, *The Union of Post Office Workers: A Study in Political Sociology*, London, Macmillan, 1974.
73 Robert Worcester, 'Keeping tabs on tides in public opinion', *Personnel Management*, 16(10) October 1984, p. 53.
74 Kavanagh, *op. cit.*, n. 10, p. 169.
75 Lord Wedderburn, *The Worker and the Law*, Harmondsworth, Penguin, 3rd edn, 1986, p. 22.
76 *ibid.*, p. 18.
77 See Henry Phelps Brown, *The Origins of Trade Union Power*, Oxford, Oxford University Press, 1986, Chapter 3.
78 See F. A. Hayek, 'The trade unions and Britain's economic decline', in W. E. J. McCarthy (ed.), *Trade Unions*, Harmondsworth, Penguin, 2nd edn, 1985, pp. 357–64.
79 Lord Wedderburn, 'The new politics of labour law', in McCarthy (ed.), *op. cit.*, n. 78, pp. 497–532.
80 These terms are from O. Kahn-Freund, 'Industrial relations and the law–retrospect and prospect', *British Journal of Industrial Relations* 7(3), November 1969, pp. 302–4.
81 B. Hepple, 'Individual labour law', in G. S. Bain (ed.), *Industrial Relations in Britain*, Oxford, Blackwell, 1983, p. 393.
82 See, for example, Roy Lewis (ed.), *Labour Law in Britain*, Oxford, Blackwell, 1986.
83 For details see Wedderburn (1986), *op. cit.*, n. 75, pp. 79–82.

84 *ibid.*, pp. 83–5.
85 *ibid.*, pp. 86–91. See also Olga Aikin, 'Legal aftermath on the miners' strike', *Personnel Management*, 17(7), July 1985, pp. 24–7.
86 Linda Dickens, Michael Jones, Brian Weeks, and Moira Hart, *Dismissed*, Oxford, Blackwell, 1985. See also: Paul Lewis, 'Ten years of unfair dismissal legislation in Great Britain', *International Labour Review*, 121(6), November–December 1982, pp. 713–30; Kevin Williams, 'Unfair dismissals: myths and statistics', *Industrial Law Journal*, 12, 1983, pp. 157–65; and Steven Evans, John Goodman, and Leslie Hargreaves, 'Unfair dismissal law and changes in the role of trade unions and employers' associations', *Industrial Law Journal*, 14, 1985, pp. 91–108.
87 These figures are cited in Wedderburn, *op. cit.*, n. 75, pp. 251 and 259.
88 Dickens *et al.*, *op. cit.*, n. 86. See also R. W. Rideout, 'Unfair dismissal–tribunal or arbitration', *Industrial Law Journal*, 15, 1986, pp. 84–96.
89 R. Layard and S. Nickell, 'The performance of the British labour market', Discussion Paper no. 249, Centre for Labour Economics, LSE, September 1986, pp. 22–3.
90 *ibid.*, p. 24.
91 See, for example, A. Zabalza and P. Z. Tzannatos, 'The effect of Britain's anti-discriminatory legislation on relative pay and employment', *The Economic Journal*, 95, September 1985, pp. 679–99.
92 P. Z. Tzannatos and A. Zabalza, 'The anatomy of the rise of British female relative wages in the 1970s: evidence from the new earnings survey', *British Journal of Industrial Relations*, 22(2), July 1984, pp. 177–194.
93 For examples, see: W. W. Daniel and E. Stilgoe, *The Impact of Employment Protection Laws*, London, PSI no. 577, 1978; and Paul Willman and Howard Gospel, 'Disclosure of information: the CAC approach', *Industrial Law Journal*, 10, 1981, pp. 10–22.
94 W. W. Daniel, 'The United Kingdom', in Michael Cross (ed.), *Managing Workforce Reduction: An International Survey*, London, Croom Helm, 1985, p. 68.
95 Neil Millward and Mark Stevens, *British Workforce Industrial Relations 1980–1984*, Aldershot, Gower, 1986, pp. 160–3.
96 See, for example, William McCarthy, *Freedom at Work: Towards the Reform of Tory Employment Laws*, Fabian Society Tract no. 508, November 1985.
97 See Bob Hepple, 'Restructuring employment rights', *Industrial Law Journal*, 15, 1986, pp. 69–83.
98 Bob Hepple, 'The crisis in EEC labour law', *Industrial Law Journal*, 16, 1987, pp. 77–86.

Chapter 3 Trade unions as organizational entities and bargaining agents

1 John T. Dunlop, 'The development of labor organization: a theoretical framework', in Gordon F. Bloom, Herbert R. Northrup, and Richard L. Rowan (eds), *Readings in Labor Economics*, Homewood, Irwin, 1963, p. 59.
2 *ibid.*, pp. 64–5.
3 For Britain see, for example, H. Clegg, A. Fox, and A. F. Thompson, *A History of British Trade Unions Since 1889, vol. I: 1889–1910*, Oxford, Oxford University Press, 1964.
4 For useful summaries, see: Jonathan Zeitlin, 'From labour history to the history of industrial relations', *Economic History Review*, XL(2), 1987, pp. 159–84 and Jonathan Grossman and William T. Moye, 'Labor history in the 1970s: a question of identity', in Thomas A. Kochan, Daniel J. B. Mitchell, and Lee Dyer (eds), *Industrial Relations Research in the 1970s: Review and Appraisal*, Wisconsin, IRRA, 1982, pp. 283–310.
5 See E. J. Hobsbawm, *Labouring Men*, London, Weidenfeld & Nicholson, 1964, and E. P. Thompson, *The Making of the English Working Class*, Harmondsworth, Penguin, 1968.
6 Zeitlin, *op. cit.*, n. 4, p. 164.
7 *ibid.*, pp. 165–6.
8 See, for example, R. Price, *Masters, Unions and Men: Work Control in Building and the Rise of Labour, 1830–1914*, Cambridge, Cambridge University Press, 1980.
9 Zeitlin, *op. cit.*, n. 4, p. 178.
10 Richard Hyman, 'Trade unions, control and resistance', in Geoff Esland and Graeme Salaman (eds), *The Politics of Work and Occupations*, Milton Keynes, Open University Press, 1980, p. 320.
11 Calculated from the basic data contained in George Sayers Bain and Farouk Elsheikh, *Union Growth and the Business Cycle*, Oxford, Blackwell, 1976, pp. 134–44.
12 Henry Phelps Brown, *The Origins of Trade Union Power*, Oxford, Oxford University Press, 1986, pp. 284–9.
13 John P. Windmuller, 'Concentration trends in union structure: an international comparison', *Industrial and Labor Relations Review*, 35(1), October 1981, pp. 43–57.
14 P. Willman and T. Morris, 'The finances of British trade unions 1975–1986', Department of Employment Research Paper no. 62, London, 1987.
15 See H. A. Turner, *Trade Union Growth, Structure and Policy*, London, Allen & Unwin, 1962.
16 See, for example, H. A. Clegg, *The Changing System of Industrial Relations in Great Britain*, Oxford, Blackwell, 1979, pp. 186–94.
17 William Brown, Robert Ebsworth, and Michael Terry, 'Factors shaping shop steward organisation in Britain', *British Journal of Industrial Relations*, 16(2), July 1978.

18 J. D. M. Bell, *Industrial Unionism: A Critical Analysis*, Edinburgh, McNaughton & Gowenlock, 1949.
19 Royal Commission on Trade Unions and Employers Associations, 'The reduction of multi-unionism', in W. E. J. McCarthy (ed.), *Trade Unions*, Harmondsworth, Penguin, 1972, p. 148.
20 Arthur Marsh, *Trade Union Handbook*, Aldershot, Gower, 1979, p. 19. See also Peter J. Kalis, 'The effectiveness and utility of the disputes committee of the Trades Union Congress', *British Journal of Industrial Relations*, XVI(1), March 1978. p. 41–51.
21 *The Times*, 15 July 1987.
22 See, for example, Robert T. Buchanan, 'Mergers in British trade unions, 1949–79', *Industrial Relations Journal*, 12(3), May–June 1981, pp. 40–9.
23 Robert Taylor, *The Fifth Estate*, London, Pan Books, 1980, pp. 303–4.
24 *Financial Times*, 27 June 1985.
25 *Glasgow Herald*, 5 December 1986.
26 R. Undy, V. Ellis, W. E. J. McCarthy, and A. M. Halmos, 'Recent merger movements and future union structure', in W. E. J. McCarthy (ed.), *Trade Unions*, Harmondsworth, Penguin, 2nd edn, 1985, pp. 164–5.
27 V. L. Allen, *Trade Unions and the Government*, London, Longman, 1960, pp. 32–4.
28 *ibid.*, p. 40.
29 Timothy C. May, *Trade Unions and Pressure Group Politics*, Farnborough, Saxon House, 1975, pp. 68–76.
30 See, for example: G. A. Dorfman, *Wage Politics in Britain 1945–1967*, London, Charles Knight, 1974; and Warren H. Fishbein, *Wage Restraint by Consensus*, Boston, Routledge & Kegan Paul, 1984.
31 See Peter Gourevitch *et al.*, *Unions and Economic Crisis: Britain, West Germany and Sweden*, London, Allen & Unwin, 1984, especially pp. 46–64; and Robert J. Flanagan, David W. Soskice, and Lloyd Ulman, *Unionism, Economic Stabilisation and Incomes Policy*, Washington, Brookings, 1983, pp. 18–36.
32 See, for example, Gerald A. Dorfman, *British Trade Unionism Against the Trades Union Congress*, London, Macmillan, 1983.
33 Ross M. Martin, *TUC: The Growth of a Pressure Group 1868–1976*, Oxford, Clarendon Press, 1980, pp. 345–7.
34 Lewis Minkin, 'The British Labour Party and the trade unions: crisis and compact', *Industrial and Labour Relations Review*, 28(1), October 1974, p. 19.
35 Quoted in Taylor, *op. cit.*, n. 23, p. 80.
36 *ibid.*, pp. 87–8. See also J. W. Leopold and P. B. Beaumont, 'The local government committee of the TUC – a decade of activity', *Local Government Studies* 8(6), November/December 1982, pp. 49–68.
37 Arthur Marsh, *Managers and Shop Stewards*, London, Institute of Personnel Management, 1963, p. 11.

38 J. Hinton, *The First Shop Stewards Movement*, London, Allen & Unwin, 1973.
39 See, for example, Ian McLean, *The Legend of Red Clydeside*, Edinburgh, John Donald, 1983.
40 See W. E. J. McCarthy and S. R. Parker, 'Shop stewards and workshop relations', Research Paper no. 10, Royal Commission on Trade Unions and Employers Associations, London, HMSO, 1968.
41 See, for example: N. Nicholson, 'The role of the shop steward: an empirical case study', *Industrial Relations Journal*, 7(1), 1976, pp. 15–25; B. Partridge, 'The activities of shop stewards', *Industrial Relations Journal*, 8(4), 1977, pp. 28–42.
42 E. Batstone, I. Boraston, and S. Frankel, *Shop Stewards in Action*, Oxford, Blackwell, 1977.
43 See, for example: M. Marchington and R. Armstrong, 'Typologies of shop stewards: a reconsideration', *Industrial Relations Journal*, 14(3), Autumn 1983, pp. 34–48; P. Willman, 'Leadership and trade union principles: some problems of management sponsorship and independence', *Industrial Relations Journal*, 11(4), 1980, pp. 39–49.
44 L. R. Sayles, *The Behaviour of Industrial Work Groups: Prediction and Control*, New York, Wiley, 1958.
45 See, for example, Michael Rose, *Industrial Behaviour*, Harmondsworth, Penguin, 1978, pp. 195–200.
46 P. B. Beaumont, *Safety at Work and the Unions*, Beckenham, Croom Helm, 1983, pp. 95–120.
47 R. Hyman, 'The politics of workforce trade unionism', *Capital and Class*, 8, 1979, pp. 54–67; R. Hyman and A. Elgar, 'Job controls, the employers offensive and alternative strategies', *Capital and Class*, 15, 1981, pp. 115–49; Michael Terry, 'Shop stewards through expansion and recession', *Industrial Relations Journal*, 14(3), Autumn 1983, pp. 49–58.
48 Eric Batstone, *Working Order*, Oxford, Blackwell, 1984, Chapter 3. See also, C. Edwards and E. Heery, 'The incorporation of workplace trade unionism? Some evidence from the coal mining industry', *Sociology*, 19(3), August 1985, pp. 345–63, and the subsequent interchange in *Sociology*, August 1986, pp. 435–9.
49 William Brown, 'Britain's unions: new pressures and shifting loyalties', *Personnel Management*, 15(10), October 1983, p. 48–51.
50 Neil Millward and Mark Stevens, *British Workplace Industrial Relations, 1980–1984*, Aldershot, Gower, 1986, pp. 79–91 and 123–37.
51 See, for example, Arnold S. Tannenbaum, 'Unions', in J. G. March (ed.), *Handbook of Organisations*, Chicago, Rand-McNally, 1965, pp. 710–63.
52 John Child, Raymond Loveridge, and Malcolm Warner, 'Towards an organizational study of trade unions', *Sociology*, 7(2), February 1973, pp. 71–91.
53 On this point see the 'iron law of oligarchy' thesis in R. Michels, *Political Parties*, Glencoe, Illinois, Free Press, 1949.

54 R. Undy, V. Ellis, W. E. J. McCarthy, and A. M. Halmos, *Changes in Trade Unions*, London, Hutchinson, 1981, pp. 38–60.
55 Jean Hartley, John Kelly, and Nigel Nicholson, *Steel Strike*, London, Batsford, 1983, pp. 181–6.
56 John C. Anderson, 'Bargaining outcomes: an IR systems approach', *Industrial Relations*, 18(2), Spring 1979, pp. 127–43.
57 Myron Roomkin, 'Union structure, internal control and industrial strike activity', *Industrial and Labor Relations Review*, 29(2), January 1976, pp. 198–217.
58 J. Hemingway, *Conflict and Democracy: Studies in Trade Union Government*, Oxford, Clarendon Press, 1978.
59 Roderick Martin, 'Union democracy: an explanatory framework', in W. E. J. McCarthy (ed.), *Trade Unions*, Harmondsworth, Penguin, 2nd edn, 1985, pp. 239–40.
60 John C. Anderson, 'A comparative analysis of local union democracy', *Industrial Relations*, 17(3), October 1978, pp. 278–95.
61 George Strauss, 'Union government in the US: research past and future', *Industrial Relations* 16, May 1977, pp. 215–42.
62 Anderson, *op. cit.*, n. 56.
63 Nigel Nicholson, Gill Ursell, and Paul Blyton, *The Dynamics of White Collar Unionism*, London, Academic Press, 1981, p. 224.
64 Roger Undy and Roderick Martin, *Ballots and Trade Union Democracy*, Oxford, Blackwell, 1984, p. 59.
65 *ibid.*, pp. 209–10. See also Harry Urwin and Gregor Murray, 'Democracy and trade unions', *Industrial Relations Journal*, 14(4), Winter 1983, pp. 21–30.
66 Kenneth Walsh, 'The measurement of trade union membership in Ireland and the UK', *Industrial Relations Journal*, 16(1), Spring 1985, pp. 25–32.
67 Cited in *Industrial Relations Review and Report*, 417, 1 June 1988, p. 10.
68 R. Hyman, 'Wooing the working class', *New Socialist*, September/October 1983, pp. 41–3.
69 G. S. Bain and R. Price, 'Union growth: dimensions, determinants and destiny', in G. S. Bain (ed.), *Industrial Relations in Britain*, Oxford, Blackwell, 1983, p. 5; and A. Oswald and P. Turnbull, 'Pay and employment determination in Britain: what are labour contracts really like?', Discussion Paper no. 212, Centre for Labour Economics, LSE, February 1985.
70 For a summary of this largely US literature, see Richard N. Block and Steven L. Premack, 'The unionization process: a review of the literature', *Advances in Industrial and Labor Relations*, 1, 1983, Greenwich, JAI Press, pp. 33–43.
71 Irving Bernstein, 'The growth of American unions', *American Economic Review*, 44(3), June 1954, pp. 301–18.
72 Orley Ashenfelter and John H. Pencavel, 'American trade union growth: 1900–1960', *Quarterly Journal of Economics*, 83(3), August 1969, pp. 434–68.

73 G. S. Bain and Farouk Elsheikh, *Union Growth and the Business Cycle*, Oxford, Blackwell, 1976.
74 For a summary see Barry T. Hirsch and John T. Addison, *The Economic Analysis of Unions*, Boston, Allen & Unwin, 1986, pp. 52–7. See also P. Kumar and B. Dow, 'Econometric analysis of union membership growth in Canada, 1935–1981', *Relations Industrielles*, 41(2), 1986, pp. 236–53.
75 Alan Carruth and Richard Disney, 'Where have two million trade union members gone?', *Economica* 55(1), February 1988, pp. 1–19.
76 Bain and Price, *op. cit.*, n. 69, p. 32.
77 George Sayers Bain and Peter Elias, 'Trade union membership in Great Britain: an individual-level analysis', *British Journal of Industrial Relations*, 23(1), March 1985, pp. 85–6. See also Alison Booth, 'Estimating the probability of trade union membership: a study of men and women in Britain', *Economica*, 53, 1986, pp. 41–61.
78 P. B. Beaumont and R. I. D. Harris, 'Sub-systems of industrial relations: the spatial dimension in Britain', Occasional Paper no. 28, Department of Economics, Queens University of Belfast, June 1987.
79 Michael Poole, Roger Mansfield, Paul Frost, and Paul Blyton, 'Why managers join unions: evidence from Britain', *Industrial Relations* 22(3), Fall 1983, pp. 426–44.
80 P. B. Beaumont, *The Decline of Trade Union Organization*, Beckenham, Croom Helm, 1987, Chapter 3.
81 For a summary see G. S. Bain, D. Coates, and V. Ellis, *Social Stratification and Trade Unionism*, London, Heinemann, 1973, pp. 126–36.
82 R. Undy, V. Ellis, W. E. J. McCarthy, and A. M. Halmos, 'The role of union leadership in membership growth: further criticisms of Bain's theory', in W. E. J. McCarthy (ed.), *Trade Unions*, Harmondsworth, Penguin, 2nd edn, pp. 281–6.
83 See, for example, Nigel Nicholson, Gill Ursell, and Jackie Lubbock, 'Membership participation in a white collar union', *Industrial Relations*, 20(2), Spring 1981, pp. 162–78.
84 For a recent example, see J. W. Thacker and H. Rosen, 'Dynamics of employee reactance to company and union: dual allegiance revisited and expanded', *Relations Industrielles*, 41(1), 1986, pp. 128–42.
85 See Booth, *op. cit.*, n. 77, pp. 42–5. See also, Thomas A. Kochan and David E. Hellman, 'The effects of collective bargaining on economic and behavioural job outcomes', in R. Ehrenberg (ed.), *Research in Labor Economics*, Greenwich, JAI Press, 4, 1981, pp. 331–2.
86 John R. Commons, *The Economics of Collective Action*, Madison, University of Wisconsin Press, 1950.
87 Moncur Olson, *The Logic of Collective Agreement*, Cambridge, Mass., Harvard University Press, 1965. See also D. P. Kidd and A. J. Oswald, 'A dynamic model of trade union behaviour', Discussion Paper no. 259, Centre for Labour Economics, LSE, November 1986.
88 P. B. Beaumont, *The Decline of Trade Union Organisation*, Beckenham, Croom Helm, 1987, pp. 174–5.

89 See, for example, Stephen Dunn and John Gennard, *The Closed Shop in British Industry*, London, Macmillan, 1984.
90 W. W. Daniel and Neil Millward, *Workplace Industrial Relations in Britain*, London, Heinemann, 1983, Chapter 3, and W. E. J. McCarthy, *The Closed Shop in Britain*, Oxford, Blackwell, 1964.
91 *ibid.*, Chapter 4.
92 Dunn and Gennard, *op. cit.*, n. 89, p. 109.
93 W. Hood and R. D. Rees, 'Inter-industry wage levels in United Kingdom manufacturing', *Manchester School* XLII(2), June 1974, pp. 171–85.
94 D. Metcalf, 'Trade unions and economic performance: the British evidence', Discussion Paper no. 320, Centre for Labour Economics, LSE, August 1988, p. 3.
95 John T. Dunlop, *Wage Determination Under Trade Unions*, New York, Macmillan, 1944.
96 See, for example, Ken Mayhew, *Trade Unions and the Labour Market*, Oxford, Martin Robinson, 1983, pp. 74–7.
97 Lloyd Ulman, 'Marshall and Friedman on union strength', *Review of Economics and Statistics* 37(4), November 1955, pp. 384–404.
98 See Daniel J. B. Mitchell, 'The impact of collective bargaining on compensation in the public sector', in B. Aaron, J. R. Grodin, and J. L. Stern (eds), *Public Sector Bargaining*, Washington, Bureau of National Affairs, 1979, pp. 129–41. See also Hirsch and Addison, *op. cit.*, n. 74, pp. 145–7.
99 Arthur M. Ross, *Trade Union Wage Policy*, Berkeley, University of California Press, 1948.
100 Daniel J. B. Mitchell, 'Union wage policies: the Ross–Dunlop debate re-opened', *Industrial Relations*, 11, February 1972, pp. 46–61.
101 For useful discussions see Hirsch and Addison, *op. cit.*, n. 74, Chapter 2. See also: David Marsden, *The End of Economic Man?*, Brighton, Wheatsheaf Books, 1986, Chapter 2; and A. Oswald, 'New research on the economics of trade unions and labour contracts', Discussion Paper no. 261, Centre for Labour Economics, LSE, November 1986.
102 For some exceptions, see J. Dertouzos and J. Pencavel, 'Wage and employment determination under trade unionism: the international typographical union', *Journal of Political Economy*, 89(6), 1981, pp. 1,162–181; and A. Carruth, A. Oswald and L. Findlay, 'A test of a model of trade union behaviour: the coal and steel industries in Britain', Discussion Paper no. 238, Centre for Labour Economics, LSE, December 1985.
103 Marsden, *op. cit.*, n. 101, p. 63.
104 Oswald, *op. cit.*, n. 101, and A. Oswald and P. Turnbull, *op. cit.*, n. 69.
105 See, for example, Thomas A. Kochan, Harry C. Katz, and R. B. McKersie, *The Transformation of American Industrial Relations*, New York, Basic Books, 1986, Chapter 8.

Chapter 4 Management strategy, structures, and policies for industrial relations

1 See, for example, John Purcell and Roger Undy, 'Research into the management of employee relations at Templeton College, Oxford', *Employee Relations*, 8(5), 1986, p. 16.
2 J. Purcell, 'The management of industrial relations in the modern corporation: agenda for research', *British Journal of Industrial Relations* 22(1), March 1984.
3 For a useful summary, see R. Bean, *Comparative Industrial Relations*, Beckenham, Croom Helm, 1985, pp. 50–5.
4 John P. Windmuller, 'Employers associations in comparative perspective: organization, structure and administration', in John P. Windmuller and Alan Gladstone (eds), *Employers Associations and Industrial Relations: A Comparative Study*, Oxford, Clarendon Press, 1984, p. 1–2.
5 Henry Phelps Brown, *The Origins of Trade Union Power*, Oxford, Oxford University Press, 1986, p. 131.
6 R. J. Adams, 'A theory of employer attitudes and behaviour towards trade unions in western Europe and North America', in G. Dlugos and K. Weirermair (eds), *Management Under Differing Value Systems*, New York, de Gruyler, 1981.
7 Geoffrey K. Ingham, *Strikes and Industrial Conflict*, London, Macmillan, 1974.
8 Peter Jackson and Keith F. Sisson, 'Employers confederations in Sweden and the UK and the significance of industrial infrastructure', *British Journal of Industrial Relations*, XIV, 1976, pp. 306–23.
9 In addition to these listed numbers from reports of the Certification Officer see Keith Sisson, 'Employers organizations', in G. S. Bain (ed.), *Industrial Relations in Britain*, Oxford, Blackwell, 1983, p. 122.
10 *ibid.*
11 William Brown (ed.), *The Changing Contours of British Industrial Relations*, Oxford, Blackwell, 1981, p. 19.
12 P. B. Beaumont, A. W. J. Thomson, and M. B. Gregory, 'Bargaining structure', *Management Decision*, 18(3), 1980, p. 127.
13 *Industrial Relations Review and Report*, no. 316, 1984.
14 Sisson, *op. cit.*, n. 9, pp. 128–34.
15 Neil Millward and Mark Stevens, *British Workplace Industrial Relations 1980–1984*, Aldershot, Gower, 1986, p. 181.
16 Windmuller, *op. cit.*, n. 4, p. 3.
17 Wyn Grant and David Marsh, *The CBI*, London, Hodder & Stoughton, 1977, Chapter 2.
18 *ibid.*, pp. 125–6.
19 For a useful summary, see E. G. A. Armstrong, 'Employers associations in Great Britain', in John P. Windmuller and Alan Gladstone (eds), *Employers Associations and Industrial Relations: A Comparative Study*, Oxford, Clarendon Press, 1984, pp. 48–55.
20 Grant and Marsh, *op. cit.*, n. 17, p. 210.

21 For useful illustration, see D. R. Glynn, 'The last 14 years of incomes policy – a CBI perspective', *National Westminster Bank Quarterly Review*, November 1978.
22 See, for example, A. W. J. Thomson, 'Trade unions and the corporate state in Britain', *Industrial and Labour Relations Review* 33(1), October 1979, pp. 50–1.
23 Grant and Marsh, *op. cit.*, n. 17, pp. 213–14.
24 Eric Batstone, *Working Order*, Oxford, Blackwell, 1984, pp. 66–73.
25 S. J. Prais, *The Evolution of Giant Firms in Britain*, Cambridge, Cambridge University Press, 1976.
26 L. Hannah, *The Rise of the Corporate Economy*, London, Methuen, 1976.
27 B. Curry and K. D. George, 'Industrial concentration: a survey', *Journal of Industrial Economics* XXXI(3), March 1983, p. 247.
28 Brian Chiplin and Mike Wright, *The Logic of Mergers*, Hobart Paper 197, London, IEA, 1987, p. 14.
29 Paul Geroski and K. G. Knight, 'Corporate merger and collective bargaining in the UK', *Industrial Relations Journal* 15, 1984, pp. 51–60.
30 Hannah, *op. cit.*, n. 26, p. 152, (2nd edn).
31 D. F. Channon, *The Strategy and Structure of British Enterprise*, Cambridge, Harvard University Press, 1973, p. 67. See J. Cable and P. Steer, 'Internal organisation and profit: an empirical analysis of large UK companies', *Journal of Industrial Economics* XXVII(1), September 1978, pp. 13–30.
32 A. D. Chandler, *Strategy and Structure*, Cambridge, MIT Press, 1962.
33 O. E. Williamson, *Markets and Hierarchies*, New York, Free Press, 1975.
34 See Mahmoud A. Ezzamel, 'On the assessment of the performance effects of multidivisional structures: a synthesis', *Accounting and Business Research*, 61, Winter 1985, p. 23.
35 Hannah, *op. cit.*, n. 26, p. 81.
36 Batstone, *op. cit.*, n. 24, p. 70.
37 *ibid.*, pp. 60–1.
38 Jeffrey Pfeffer, *Organizations and Organization Theory*, Boston, Pitman, 1982, p. 3. See also Graham Astley and Andrew Van de Ven, 'Central perspectives and debates in organisation theory', *Administrative Science Quarterly*, 28, June 1983, pp. 245–73.
39 This discussion draws heavily on Thomas A. Kochan and Anil Verma, 'Negotiations in organizations: blending industrial relations and organizational behaviour approaches', in Max Bazerman and Roy Lewicki (eds), *Negotiating in Organizations*, Beverly Hills, Sage, 1983, pp. 15–16.
40 J. French and B. Raven, 'The bases of social power', in D. Cartwright (ed.), *Studies in Social Power*, Institute for Social Research, Ann Arbor, University of Michigan, 1959.
41 Jeffrey Pfeffer, *Power in Organizations*, Boston, Pitman, 1981, p. 101.

42 See, for example, Ian Mitroff, Susan Mohrman, and Geoffrey Little, *The Global Solution*, San Francisco, Jossey-Bass, 1987. Also see Michael Hitt and Duane Ireland, 'Peters and Waterman revisited: the unended quest for excellence', *Academy of Management Executive*, 1(2), May 1987, pp. 91–8.
43 J. Pfeffer, 'Management as symbolic action: the creation and maintenance of organizational paradigms', in L. L. Cummings and B. Staw (eds), *Research in Organizational Behaviour*, 3, Greenwich, JAI Press, 1981, pp. 1–52.
44 Chester Barnard, *The Functions of the Executive*, Cambridge, Harvard University Press, 1938.
45 Richard C. Edwards, *Contested Terrain: The Transformation of the Workplace in the Twentieth Century*, New York, Basic Books, 1979.
46 As to whether these arrangements should be termed market ones, see David Marsden, *The End of Economic Man?*, Brighton, Wheatsheaf Books, 1986, pp. 152–63.
47 See Williamson, *op. cit.*, n. 33.
48 Paul Osterman, 'Introduction: the nature and importance of internal labor markets', in Paul Osterman (ed.), *Internal Labor Markets*, Cambridge, Mass., MIT Press, 1984, p. 12.
49 See, for example, Michael Porter, *Competitive Strategy: Techniques for Analysing Industries and Competition*, New York, Free Press, 1980.
50 For useful summary, see Marsden, *op. cit.*, n. 46, p. 47–9.
51 J. Child, M. Fores, I. Glover, and P. Lawrence, 'A price to pay? Professionalism and work organization in Britain and West Germany', *Sociology*, 17(1), February 1983, pp. 63–78.
52 Brown, *op. cit.*, n. 11, p. 32.
53 Millward and Stevens, *op. cit.*, n. 15, pp. 41–61.
54 H. A. Clegg, *The Changing System of Industrial Relations in Great Britain*, Oxford, Blackwell, 1979, p. 127.
55 D. Guest and R. Horwood, 'Characteristics of the successful personnel manager', *Personnel Management*, May 1981, p. 30.
56 J. T. Winkler, 'The ghost at the bargaining table: directors and industrial relations', *British Journal of Industrial Relations*, 12, 1974, pp. 191–212.
57 Brown, *op. cit.*, n. 11, p. 32.
58 P. B. Beaumont and D. R. Deaton, 'Personnel management in the management hierarchy', *Management Decision*, 18(4), 1980, pp. 203–11.
59 Millward and Stevens, *op. cit.*, n. 15, pp. 34–6.
60 *ibid.*, p. 300.
61 P. B. Beaumont and D. R. Deaton, 'Correlates of specialisation and training among personnel managers in Britain', *Personnel Review*, 15(2), 1986, pp. 29–31.
62 David Hickson and Geoffrey Mallory, 'Scope for choice in strategic decision making and the trade union role', in A. Thomson and

M. Warner (eds), *The Behavioural Sciences and Industrial Relations*, Aldershot, Gower, 1981, pp. 47–60.
63 Brown, *op. cit.*, n. 11, pp. 40–2.
64 Millward and Stevens, *op. cit.*, n. 15, p, 47.
65 Batstone, *op. cit.*, n. 24, p. 36.
66 Eric Batstone, 'What have personnel managers done for industrial relations?', *Personnel Management*, June 1980, pp. 36–41.
67 Millward and Stevens, *op. cit.*, n. 15, pp. 25–51.
68 Peter Drucker, *The Practice of Management*, London, Pan Books, 1977, p. 331.
69 A. Tsui, 'Personnel department effectiveness: a tripartite approach', *Industrial Relations*, 23, 1984, pp. 184–97.
70 P. B. Beaumont, 'The perceived clarity of personnel objectives: some determinants', *Personnel Review*, 16(1), 1987, pp. 10–14.
71 See, for example, G. S. Odiorne, *Strategic Management of Human Resources*, San Fransisco, Jossey-Bass, 1984.
72 Chris Hendry and Andrew Pettigrew, 'The practice of strategic human resource management', *Personnel Review*, 15(5), 1986, p. 4.
73 Shaun Tyson and Alan Fell, *Evaluating the Personnel Function*, London, Hutchinson, 1986, Chapter 2.
74 Lesley Mackay, 'Personnel management in the public and private sectors', *Industrial Relations Journal*, 17(4), Winter 1986, pp. 394–20.
75 J. S. Cassells, *Review of Personnel Work in the Civil Service*, London, HMSO, 1983, pp. 38–9.
76 Howard F. Gospel, 'Managerial structures and strategies: an introduction', in Howard F. Gospel and Craig R. Littler (eds), *Managerial Strategies and Industrial Relations*, London, Heinemann, 1983, pp. 12–20.
77 V. V. Murray and D. E. Dimick, 'Contextual influences on personnel policies and programs: an explanatory model', *Academy of Management Review*, 3(4), October 1978, pp. 750–61.
78 *ibid.*, p. 757.
79 Hendry and Pettigrew, *op. cit.*, n. 72, p. 6.
80 For a summary see Michael Fogarty with Douglas Brooks, *Trade Unions and British Industrial Development*, London, PSI, 1986, Chapter 2.
81 John Purcell, 'A strategy for management control in industrial relations', in J. Purcell and R. Smith (eds), *The Control of Work*, London, Macmillan, 1979, pp. 27–57.
82 *The Future of the Automobile*, The Report of MIT's International Automobile Program, London, Counterpoint, 1985, pp. 218–19.
83 *ibid.*, p. 219.
84 *ibid.*, pp. 281–6.
85 Douglas McGregor, *The Human Side of the Enterprise*, New York, McGraw Hill, 1960.
86 Alan Fox, *Beyond Contract*, London, Faber, 1974, Chapter 7.
87 David Deaton, 'Management style and large scale survey evidence', *Industrial Relations Journal*, 16(2), Summer 1985, pp. 67–71.

88 *ibid.*, p. 71.
89 Dan Gowler and Karen Legge, 'Images of employees in company reports', *Personnel Review*, 15(5), 1986, pp. 1–18.
90 H. Gospel, 'European managerial unions: an early assessment', *Industrial Relations*, 17, 1978.
91 See, for example, M. Poole, R. Mansfield, P. Frost, and P. Blyton, 'Why managers join unions: evidence from Britain', *Industrial Relations*, 22(3), Fall 1983.
92 See, for example, Greg Bamber, *Militant Managers*, Aldershot, Gower, 1985.
93 Ed Snape and Greg Bamber, 'Analysing the employment relationship of managers and professional staff', in V. Hammond (ed.), *Current Research in Management*, London, Frances Pinter, 1985, p. 145.
94 T. A. Kochan, *Collective Bargaining and Industrial Relations*, Homewood, Illinois, Irwin, 1980, pp. 210–22 and pp. 330–5 respectively.

Chapter 5 The essence of collective bargaining and bargaining structure

1 Thomas A. Kochan, Harry C. Katz, and Robert B. McKersie, *The Transformation of American Industrial Relations*, New York, Basic Books, 1986.
2 See, for example, Brian Burkitt and David Bowers, *Trade Unions and the Economy*, London, Macmillan, 1979, Chapter 2.
3 Jack Barbash, 'The new industrial relations', *Proceedings of the Industrial Relations Research Association*, Spring 1986, pp. 528–33.
4 Allan Flanders, 'Collective bargaining', in Allan Flanders and H. A. Clegg (eds), *The System of Industrial Relations in Great Britain*, Oxford, Blackwell, 1954, pp. 260–72.
5 P. B. Beaumont and M. B. Gregory, 'The role of employers in collective bargaining in Britain', *Industrial Relations Journal*, 11(5), 1980, pp. 46–52.
6 A. Flanders, 'Collective bargaining: a theoretical analysis', *British Journal of Industrial Relations*, 6(1), March 1968, pp. 1–26.
7 N. W. Chamberlain, *Collective Bargaining*, New York, McGraw Hill, 1951, p. 121.
8 Hugh Clegg, *A New Approach to Industrial Democracy*, Oxford, Blackwell, 1960.
9 Richard B. Freeman and James L. Medoff, *What Do Unions Do?*, New York, Basic Books, 1984.
10 For some earlier figures see Allan Flanders, *Collective Bargaining: Prescription for Change*, London, Faber, 1967, pp. 13–14.
11 See, for example, Richard Hyman, *Industrial Relations: A Marxist Introduction*, London, Macmillan, 1974, and Alan Fox, *Man Mismanagement*, London, Hutchinson, 1974, Chapter 6.
12 This point is well illustrated in John E. Kelly, *Scientific Management,*

Job Redesign and Work Performance, London, Academic Press, 1982, Chapter 8.
13 Allan D. Flanders, 'The tradition of voluntarism', *British Journal of Industrial Relations*, 12(3), November 1974, pp. 352–70.
14 O. Kahn-Freund, 'Intergroup conflicts and their settlement', in Allan D. Flanders (ed.), *Collective Bargaining*, Harmondsworth, Penguin, 1969, pp. 59–85.
15 See, for example, Murray Edelman, *The Symbolic Uses of Politics*, Urbana, University of Illinois Press, 1967, pp. 134–8.
16 E. H. Phelps Brown, 'New wine in old bottles: reflections on the changed working of collective bargaining in Great Britain', *British Journal of Industrial Relations*, 11(3), November 1973, p. 333.
17 See, for example, Jack Stieber, 'Collective bargaining in the public sector', in Lloyd Ulman (ed.), *Challenges to Collective Bargaining*, Englewood Cliffs, New Jersey, Prentice Hall, 1967, pp. 79–83.
18 See, for example, Jack Barbash, 'Values in industrial relations: the case of the adversary principle', *Proceedings of the Industrial Relations Research Association*, Winter 1981, pp. 1–7.
19 See Robert J. Davies, 'Economic activity, incomes policy and strikes: a quantitative analysis', *British Journal of Industrial Relations*, 17, 1979, pp. 205–23.
20 Flanders (1967), *op. cit.*, n. 10, pp. 19–27.
21 See F. T. Blackaby, 'An array of proposals', in F. T. Blackaby (ed.), *The Future of Pay Bargaining*, London, Heinemann, 1980, pp. 64–91.
22 For a summary see Michael Fogarty with Douglas Brooks, *Trade Unions and British Industrial Development*, London, PSI, 1986, Chapter 2.
23 *Financial Times*, 17 January 1979.
24 Department of Employment Manpower Paper no. 5, *The Reform of Collective Bargaining at Plant and Company Level*, London, HMSO, 1971.
25 See, for example, John Purcell, 'A strategy for management control in industrial relations', in J. Purcell and R. Smith (ed.), *The Control of Work*, London, Macmillan, 1979, pp. 49–53.
26 CIR Study no. 5, *Trade Union Recognition: CIR Experience*, London, HMSO, 1974 and *ACAS Annual Report 1977*, pp. 45–51.
27 *ACAS Annual Report 1980*, pp. 81–2.
28 Flanders (1967) *op. cit.*, n. 10, p. 15.
29 See, for example, John Storey, *The Challenge to Management Control*, London, Kogan Page, 1980.
30 See, for example, Thomas A. Kochan and Richard N. Block, 'An inter-industry analysis of bargaining outcomes: preliminary evidence from two-digit industries', *Quarterly Journal of Economics*, 91(4), August 1977, pp. 431–53.
31 For a useful summary see Paul Blyton, 'The working time debate in western Europe', *Industrial Relations*, 26(2), Spring 1987, pp. 201–7.
32 Neil Millward and Mark Stevens, *British Workplace Industrial*

Relations 1980–1984, Aldershot, Gower, 1986, pp. 249–53.
33 See W. E. J. McCarthy, 'The role of shop stewards in British industrial relations', *Royal Commission on Trade Unions and Employers Associations*, Research Paper no. 1, London, HMSO, 1966. See also M. Terry, 'The inevitable growth of informality', *British Journal of Industrial Relations*, 15(1), March 1977, pp. 76–90.
34 W. W. Daniel and Neil Millward, *Workplace Industrial Relations in Britain*, London, Heinemann, 1983, pp. 163–5.
35 A. W. J. Thomson and S. R. Engleman, *The Industrial Relations Act*, London, Martin Robertson, 1975, pp. 134–7.
36 The next three sections of this chapter are very much based on P. B. Beaumont and A. W. J. Thomson, 'The structure of collective bargaining in Britain', in A. Bowey (ed.), *The Handbook of Salary and Wage Systems*, Aldershot, Gower, 3rd edn, 1987.
37 E. H. Phelps Brown, *The Economics of Labour*, New Haven, Yale University Press, 1962, pp. 172–3.
38 Millward and Stevens, *op. cit.*, n. 32, pp. 240–2.
39 D. R. Deaton and P. B. Beaumont, 'The determinants of bargaining structure: some large scale survey evidence for Britain', *British Journal of Industrial Relations*, 18(1), March 1980, pp. 202–16.
40 Lord McCarthy, *Making Whitley Work*, Department of Health and Social Security, London, HMSO, 1976.
41 National Board for Prices and Incomes Report no. 29, *The Pay and Conditions of Manual Workers in Local Authorities, the National Health Service, Gas and Water Supply*, Cmnd 3230, London, HMSO, 1967.
42 P. B. Beaumont and M. Ingham, 'Low pay, productivity and collective bargaining in local government in Britain', *Journal of Collective Negotiations*, 12(3), 1983, pp. 250–1.
43 John Purcell, 'The management of industrial relations in the modern corporation: agenda for research', *British Journal of Industrial Relations* 22(1), March 1983, pp. 7–8.
44 *Industrial Relations Review and Report*, no. 316, 1984.
45 *ibid*.
46 Commission on Industrial Relations, Report no. 85, *Industrial Relations in Multi-Plant Undertakings*, London, HMSO, 1974.
47 *Industrial Relations Review and Report*, no. 341, 1985, p. 3.
48 N. Kinnie, 'Single employer bargaining', *Industrial Relations Journal*, 14(3), Autumn 1983.
49 Millward and Stevens, *op. cit.*, n. 32, pp. 242–4.
50 H. A. Clegg, *Trade Unionism Under Collective Bargaining*, Oxford, Blackwell, 1976.
51 M. B. Gregory and A. W. J. Thomson, 'The coverage mark up, bargaining structure and earnings in Britain, 1973 and 1978', *British Journal of Industrial Relations*, 19(1), March 1981, p. 33.
52 See the statement of the Employment Minister cited in *IDS Report*, no. 495, April 1987. See also NEDC, 'Regional pay variations', mimeographed paper, 25 November 1986.

53 'Pay in the 1980s', *Memorandum by the CBI to NEDC*, 20 February 1987.
54 'National pay bargaining', *Memorandum by the TUC to NEDC*, 25 November 1986.
55 *The Times*, 14 and 24 August, 1987.
56 For full details see P. B. Beaumont and R. I. D. Harris, 'The government case against national pay bargaining: an analysis for Scotland', in D. McCrone (ed.), *Yearbook of Scottish Government 1988*, Edinburgh, Edinburgh University Press, 1988.
57 Howard Newby, C. Volger, D. Rose, and G. Marshall, 'From class structure to class action: British working class politics in the 1980s', in Bryan Roberts, Ruth Finnegan, and Duncan Gallie (eds), *New Approaches to Economic Life*, Manchester, Manchester University Press, 1985, p. 93.

Chapter 6 Collective bargaining processes, conflict, and power

1 See, for example, S. J. Nickell, 'A bargaining model of the Phillips Curve', Discussion Paper no. 130, Centre for Labour Economics, LSE, June 1982.
2 See, for example, A. Deswaan, *Coalition Theories and Cabinet Formations*, San Fransisco, Jossey-Bass, 1973.
3 James A. Wall and Lawrence F. Schiller, 'The judge off the bench: a mediator in the civil settlement negotiations', in Max H. Bazerman and Roy J. Lewicki (eds), *Negotiating in Organizations*, Beverly Hills, Sage Books, 1983, pp. 177–92.
4 H. Mintzberg, *Power In and Around Organizations*, Englewood Cliffs, New Jersey, Prentice-Hall, 1983.
5 John T. Dunlop, *Dispute Resolution: Negotiating and Consensus Building*, Dover, Mass., Auburn House, 1984, pp. 3–8.
6 J. Z. Rubin and B. R. Brown, *The Social Psychology of Bargaining and Negotiation*, New York, Academic Press, 1975.
7 Dennis Kavanagh, *Thatcherism and British Politics: The End of Consensus?*, Oxford, Oxford University Press, 1987, pp. 9–14.
8 M. Olson, *The Rise and Decline of Nations*, New Haven, Yale University Press, 1982.
9 H. Mintzberg, *The Nature of Managerial Work*, New York, Harper & Row, 1973.
10 Thomas A. Kochan and Max Bazerman, 'Macro determinants of the future of the study of negotiations in organizations', in R. J. Lewicki, B. H. Shepard, and M. H. Bazerman (eds), *Research in Negotiation in Organizations*, Greenwich, Conn, JAI Press, 1, 1986.
11 See, for example, Gavin Kennedy, John Benson, and John McMillan, *Managing Negotiations*, London, Hutchinson, 2nd edn, 1984.
12 See, respectively, C. J. Margerison, 'What do we mean by industrial relations? A behavioural science approach', *British Journal of*

Industrial Relations, 7(2), July 1969, pp. 273–86; and Gerald G. Somers, 'Bargaining power and industrial relations theory', in Gerald G. Somers (ed.), *Essays in Industrial Relations Theory*, Iowa, Aines, Iowa State University Press, 1969, pp. 39–54.

13 See, for example, Thomas A. Kochan, 'Step by step in the Middle East from the perspective of the labor mediation process', in Jeffrey A. Rubin (ed.), *Dynamics of Third Party Intervention*, New York, Praeger, 1981, pp. 122–35.

14 For a useful summary of this literature see S. B. Bacharach and E. J. Lawler, *Bargaining Power, Tactics and Outcomes*, San Francisco, Jossey-Bass, 1981, Chapter 1.

15 J. R. Hicks, *The Theory of Wages*, London, Macmillan, 2nd edn, 1963, Chapter 7.

16 See, for example, J. Pen, 'A general theory of bargaining', *American Economic Review*, March 1952; see also Howard Raiffa, 'A strike game', in Clark Kerr and Paul D. Standohar (eds), *Industrial Relations in a New Age*, San Francisco, Jossey-Bass, 1986, pp. 239–43.

17 Barry T. Hirsch and John T. Addison, *The Economic Analysis of Unions*, Boston, Allen & Unwin, 1986, pp. 79–86.

18 Daniel S. Hamermesh, 'Who wins in wage bargaining?', *Industrial and Labor Relations Review*, 26(4), July 1973, pp. 1146–9.

19 Thomas A. Kochan, *Collective Bargaining and Industrial Relations*, Homewood, Illinois, Irwin, 1980, p. 240.

20 A. Douglas, *Industrial Peacemaking*, New York, Columbia University Press, 1962.

21 See, for example, R. F. Bales and F. L. Strodtbeck, *Interaction Process Analysis: A Method for the Study of Small Groups*, Reading, Mass., Addison-Wesley, 1950.

22 See, for example, Derek Torrington and John Chapman, *Personnel Management*, London, Prentice Hall, 2nd edn, 1983, pp. 192–7.

23 R. E. Walton and R. B. McKersie, *A Behavioural Theory of Labor Negotiations*, New York, McGraw Hill, 1965.

24 See, for example, Bacharach and Lawler, *op. cit.*, n. 14, Chapter 1.

25 See, for example, Kochan, *op. cit.*, n. 19, pp. 243–4.

26 See, for example, Dean G. Pruitt, 'Achieving integrative agreements', in Bazerman and Lewicki (eds), *op. cit.*, n. 3, pp. 35–50.

27 R. B. Peterson and L. Tracy, 'Testing a behavioural theory model of labor negotiations', *Industrial Relations*, 16(1), February 1977, pp. 35–50. Admittedly this particular study has stimulated some similar work in other countries. See, for example, David Smith and Don Turkington, 'Problem solving in collective bargaining: a comparative study of union and management negotiators', *Industrial Relations Journal*, 13(4), Winter 1982, pp. 56–64.

28 See, for example, T. A. Kochan, L. Dyer, and D. B. Lipsky, *The Effectiveness of Union–Management Safety and Health Committees*, Kalamazoo, Michigan, Upjohn Institute for Employment Research, 1977.

29 Ian E. Morley, 'Behavioural studies of industrial bargaining', in G. M. Stephenson and C. J. Brotherton (eds), *Industrial Relations: A Social Psychological Approach*, Chichester, Wiley & Sons, 1979, pp. 220–2.
30 For a summary see *ibid.*, pp. 223–30.
31 Michael E. Gordon, Neal Schmitt, and Walter G. Schneider, 'Laboratory research on bargaining and negotiations: an evaluation', *Industrial Relations*, 23(2), Spring 1984, pp. 218–33. See, also Jeanne M. Brett and Tove Helland Hammer, 'Organizational behaviour and industrial relations', in Thomas A. Kochan, Daniel J. B. Mitchell, and Lee Dyer (eds), *Industrial Relations Research in the 1970s*, Madison, Wisconsin, IRRA, 1982, pp. 263–70.
32 George Strauss and James W. Driscoll, 'Collective bargaining games', *Exchange*, v, February 1980, pp. 19–20.
33 George Strauss, 'The study of conflict: hope for a new synthesis between industrial relations and organizational behaviour', *Proceedings of the Industrial Relations Research Association*, Winter 1976, Madison, Wisconsin, p. 331.
34 Wendell French and Cecil H. Bell, *Organization Development*, Englewood Cliffs, New Jersey, Prentice Hall, 2nd edn, 1978, p. 14.
35 See, for example, *ibid.*, Chapter 20. See aslo Cary L. Cooper (ed.), *Organizational Development in the UK and USA: A Joint Evaluation*, London, Macmillan, 1977.
36 E. F. Huse, *Organizational Development and Change*, St Paul, Minn., West Publishing Co., 1975, p. 65.
37 Strauss, *op. cit.*, n. 33, p. 332. See also T. A. Kochan and L. Dyer, 'A model of organizational change in the context of union–management relations', *Journal of Applied Behavioural Science*, 12, 1976, pp. 57–78.
38 Andrew Pettigrew, *The Awakening Giant: Continuity and Change in ICI*, Oxford, Blackwell, 1985, p. 345. See also C. J. Margerison, 'Industrial relations and organization development', *Industrial Relations Journal*, 5(3), Autumn 1974, pp. 18–26.
39 P. Hill, *Towards a New Philosophy of Management*, London, Gower, 1971.
40 F. Blackler and C. Brown, *Whatever Happened to Shell's New Philosophy of Management?* London, Saxon House, 1980.
41 Strauss, *op. cit.*, n. 33, pp. 332.
42 See L. R. Pondy, 'Organizational conflict: concepts and models', *Administrative Science Quarterly*, 17, 1967, pp. 296–320.
43 See, for example, C. C. Holt, 'Job search, Phillips wage relation and union influence: theory and evidence', in E. S. Phelps (ed.), *Microeconomic Foundations of Employment and Inflation Theory*, London, Macmillan, 1971.
44 John Kelly and Nigel Nicholson, 'Strikes and other forms of industrial action', *Industrial Relations Journal*, 11(5), November/December 1980, p. 22.
45 P. K. Edwards and Hugh Scullion, *The Social Organisation of Industrial Conflict*, Oxford, Blackwell, 1982, pp. 276–7.

46 W. W. Daniel and Neil Millward, *Workplace Industrial Relations in Britain*, London, Heinemann, 1983, p. 292.
47 M. Ingham, 'Industrial relations in British local government', *Industrial Relations Journal*, 16(1), Spring 1985.
48 Peter Feuille and Hoyt N. Wheeler, 'Will the real industrial conflict please stand up?'. in Jack Stieber, Robert B. McKersie, and D. Quinn Mills (eds), *US Industrial Relations 1950–1980: A Critical Assessment*, Madison, Wisconsin, IRRA, 1981, p. 258.
49 S. W. Creigh, 'Strikes in Britain: a selective annotated bibliography', *Quality of Working Life Journal*, 1(5), 1984, p. 4.
50 IMS Report no. 125, 'The measurement of industrial disputes in selected industries', cited in *Industrial Relations Review and Report* no. 389, 31 March 1987, pp. 14–15.
51 Michael P. Jackson, *Strikes*, Sussex, Wheatsheaf Books, 1987, Ch. 2.
52 See, for example, M. Fisher, *Measurement of Labour Disputes and Their Economic Effects*, Paris, OECD, 1973.
53 S. W. Creigh, N. Donaldson, and E. Hawthorn, 'Stoppage activity in OECD countries', *Department of Employment Gazette*, 88(11), November 1980, p. 1176.
54 'Large industrial stoppages, 1960–1979', *Department of Employment Gazette*, 88, 1980, pp. 994–9.
55 *Department of Employment Gazette* 93(4), April 1985, p. 150.
56 *Department of Employment Gazette* 96(6), June 1988, pp. 335–8.
57 See, for example, Hugh Clegg, *Trade Unionism Under Collective Bargaining*, Oxford, Blackwell, 1976, Chapter 6.
58 See, for example, Stephen Creigh, 'Strikes in OECD countries: a research note', *Industrial Relations Journal*, 13(3), Autumn 1982, pp. 67–71.
59 See, for example, Douglas A. Hibbs, 'Industrial conflict in advanced industrial societies', *American Political Science Review*, 70, December 1976, pp. 1033–58.
60 Geoffrey K. Ingham, *Strikes and Industrial Conflict*, London, Macmillan, 1974.
61 C. Kerr and A. Siegel, 'Inter-industry propensity to strike', in Allan Flanders (ed.), *Collective Bargaining*, Harmondsworth, Penguin, 1969, pp. 138–60.
62 W. Korpi and M. Shalev, 'Strikes, industrial relations and class conflict in capitalist societies', *British Journal of Sociology*, 30, 1979, pp. 164–87.
63 P. K. Edwards, 'The awful truth about strife in our factories: a case study in the production of news', *Industrial Relations Journal*, 10(1), 1979.
64 Tony Lane and Kenneth Roberts, *Strike at Pilkingtons*, London, Collins, 1971, p. 76.
65 Glasgow University Media Group, *Bad News*, London, Routledge & Kegan Paul, 1976, pp. 276–8. For a strong criticism of this particular study see Martin Harrison, 'Whose bias? Strikes, TV news, and media

studies', Research Paper no. 19, Department of Politics, University of Keele, 1984.

66 V. L. Allen, *Trade Unions and the Government*, London, Longman, 1960, pp. 213 and 216.

67 See, for example, Eric Hobsbawn, *The Forward March of Labour Halted?*, London, Verso, 1981, p. 14.

68 Paul Edwards, 'Britain's changing strike problem?', *Industrial Relations Journal*, 13(2), Summer 1982, p. 16.

69 Nicholas Jones, *Strikes and the Media*, Oxford, Blackwell, 1986, p. 207.

70 See, for example, Brian Towers, 'Posing larger questions: the British miners' strike of 1984–85', *Industrial Relations Journal*, 16(2), Summer 1985, pp. 21–2.

71 *New Statesman*, 18 January 1985.

72 Kenneth Newton, 'Mass media', in Henry Drucker, Patrick Dunleavy, Andrew Gamble, and Gillian Peele (eds), *Developments in British Politics*, London, Macmillan, 1986, p. 319. See also J. Tunstall, *The Media in Britain*, London, Constable, 1983.

73 W. E. J. McCarthy, 'The nature of Britain's strike problem', *British Journal of Industrial Relations*, 8(2), July 1970, pp. 224–36.

74 H. A. Turner, *Is Britain Really Strike Prone? A Review of the Incidence, Character and Costs of Industrial Conflict,* Occasional paper no. 20, Department of Applied Economics, Cambridge University, 1969.

75 See, for example, P. Galombos and E. W. Evans, 'Work stoppages in the United Kingdom 1951–1964: A quantitative study', in E. W. Evans and S. W. Creigh (eds), *Industrial Conflict in Britain*, London, Frank Cass, 1977, pp. 32–6.

76 N. W. Chamberlain and J. M. Schilling, *The Impact of Strikes: Their Social and Economic Costs*, New York, Harper & Row, 1954.

77 P. B. Beaumont, 'The right to strike in the public sector: the issues and evidence', *Public Administration Bulletin* no. 35, April 1981, pp. 21–38.

78 See, for example, Donald E. Cullen, *National Emergency Strikes*, ILR Paperback no. 7, New York School of Industrial and Labor Relations, Cornell University, 1968. See also John A. Ackerman, 'The impact of the coal strike of 1977–78', *Industrial and Labor Relations Review*, 32(2), January 1979.

79 Robert Hudson, 'The effects of dock strikes on UK international trade', *Applied Economics*, 13, 1981, pp. 67–77.

80 Jean Hartley, John Kelly, and Nigel Nicholson, *Steel Strike*, London, Batsford, 1983, p. 167.

81 *ibid.*, p. 167.

82 For a summary, see S. W. Creigh, 'The economic costs of strikes', *Industrial Relations Journal*, 9(1), Spring 1978, pp. 19–26.

83 K. G. J. C. Knowles, *Strikes*, Oxford, Blackwell, 1954, p. 262.

84 See, for example, J. Gennard, *Financing Strikers*, London, Macmillan, 1977.

85 J. W. Durcan, W. E. J. McCarthy, and G. P. Redman, *Strikes in Post War Britain*, London, Allen & Unwin, 1983; and Paul Edwards, 'Britain's changing strike problem?', *Industrial Relations Journal*, 13(2), Summer 1982, pp. 5–20.
86 Edwards, *op. cit.*, n. 68, pp. 18–19.
87 Durcan, McCarthy, and Redman, *op. cit.*, n. 85, pp. 178–80.
88 C. T. B. Smith, Richard Clifton, Peter Makeham, S. W. Creigh, and R. V. Burn, *Strikes in Britain*, London, HMSO, 1978.
89 Edwards, *op. cit.*, n. 68, pp. 17–18.
90 Neil Millward and Mark Stevens, *British Workplace Industrial Relations 1930–1934*, Aldershot, Gower, 1986, p. 263.
91 See, for example, H. A. Clegg, *The Changing System of Industrial Relations in Great Britain*, Oxford, Blackwell, 1979, pp. 273–7.
92 See, for example, H. A. Turner, Garfield Clark, and Geoffrey Roberts, *Labour Relations in the Motor Industry*, London, Allen & Unwin, 1967.
93 J. Shorey, 'The size of the work unit and strike incidence', *Journal of Industrial Economics*, 23(3), 1975; and J. Shorey, 'An inter-industry analysis of strike frequency', *Economica*, 43, 1976.
94 S. W. Creigh and P. Makenham, 'Foreign ownership and strike proneness: a research note', *British Journal of Industrial Relations*, 16(3), 1978.
95 David Blanchflower and John Cubbin, 'Strike propensities at the British workplace', *Oxford Bulletin of Economics and Statistics*, 48(1), February 1986, pp. 19–40.
96 P. K. Edwards, 'The strike-proneness of British manufacturing establishments', *British Journal of Industrial Relations*, 19, 1981, pp. 135–48.
97 See, for example: S. J. Prais, 'The strike-proneness of large plants in Britain', *Journal of the Royal Statistical Society (Series A)*, vol. 141, Part 3, 1978; and R. C. Geary, 'Prais on strikes', *Journal of the Royal Statistical Society (Series A)*, vol. 143, Part 1, 1980.
98 James E. Cronin, *Industrial Conflict in Modern Britain*, London, Croom Helm, 1979, pp. 23–6.
99 A. Ross and P. Hartmann, *Changing Patterns of Industrial Conflict*, New York, Wiley, 1960.
100 Cronin, *op. cit.*, n. 98, pp. 23–6.
101 Orley Ashenfelter and George E. Johnson, 'Bargaining theory, trade unions and industrial strike activity', *American Economic Review*, 59, March 1969, pp. 35–49.
102 See Michael Shalev, 'Trade unionism and economic analysis – the case of industrial conflict', *Journal of Labor Research*, 1(1), Spring 1980, pp. 133–73.
103 J. H. Pencavel, 'An investigation into industrial strike activity in Britain', *Economica*, 37, 1970, pp. 239–56.
104 For summaries see Durcan, McCarthy, and Redman, *op. cit.*, n. 85, pp. 216–29, and Cronin, *op. cit.*, n. 98, pp. 74–9.
105 See, for example, P. K. Edwards, 'Time-series regression models of

strike activity: a reconsideration with American data', *British Journal of Industrial Relations*, 16, November 1978, pp. 320–34; and K. Mayhew, 'Economists and strikes', *Oxford Bulletin of Economics and Statistics*, 41, February, 1979, pp. 1–19. Undoubtedly the strongest criticism is that of Hoyt N. Wheeler, 'Determinants of strikes: comment', *Industrial and Labor Relations Review*, 37(2), January 1984, pp. 263–9.

106 Edwards and Scullion, *op. cit.*, n. 45, pp. 276–7.

107 See, for example, Hoyt N. Wheeler, *Industrial Conflict: An Integrative Theory*, Columbia, South Carolina, University of South Carolina, 1985.

108 Edward Shorter and Charles Tilly, *Strikes in France 1830 to 1968*, Cambridge, Cambridge University Press, 1974.

109 Korpi and Shalev, *op. cit.*, n. 62, pp. 164–87.

110 These figures were provided by John MacInnes, University of Glasgow.

111 See P. K. Edwards, 'Size of plant and strike proneness', *Oxford Bulletin of Economics and Statistics*, 42(2), May 1980, pp. 145–56.

112 For a useful general discussion see K. D. George, R. McNabb, and John Shorey, 'The size of the work unit and labour market behaviour', *British Journal of Industrial Relations*, 15(2), July 1977, pp. 265–78.

113 Charles Perrow, 'The short and glorious history of organizational theory', *Organization Dynamics*, Summer 1973, pp. 9–10.

114 R. Blauner, *Alienation and Freedom*, Chicago, Illinois, University of Chicago Press, 1964.

115 Joan Woodward, *Industrial Organization: Theory and Practice*, London, Oxford University Press, 1965, pp. 50–67.

116 See, for example, Frederick Eisele, 'Organization size, technology and frequency of strikes', *Industrial and Labor Relations Review*, 27(4), July 1974, pp.560–71.

117 Harry Braverman, *Labor and Monopoly Capital: The Degradation of Work in the Twentieth Century*, New York, Monthly Review, 1974.

118 J. Purcell, 'The Management of Industrial Relations in the Modern Corporation: Agenda for Research', *British Journal of Industrial Relations*, 22(1), March 1983, pp. 2–3.

119 See, for example, J. Purcell, *Good Industrial Relations: Theory and Practice*, London, Macmillan, 1981.

120 Paul M. Marginson, 'The distinctive effects of plant and company size on workplace industrial relations', *British Journal of Industrial Relations*, 22(1), March 1984, pp. 1–14.

121 J. Hamill, 'Multinational corporations and industrial relations in the UK', *Employee Relations*, 6(5), 1984, p. 12.

122 For a useful summary see John Gennard, *Multinationals: Industrial Relations and the Trade Union Response*, Occasional Papers in Industrial Relations, Universities of Leeds and Nottingham, no. 1, 1976, pp. 7–17.

123 Thomas Kennedy, *European Labour Relations*, Lexington, Mass., D. C. Heath & Co., 1980, pp. 343–53.

124 Barbara Barnovin, *The European Labour Movement and European Integration*, London, Frances Pinter, 1986, p. 121–32.
125 Jacques Rojot, 'The 1984 revision of the OECD guidelines for multinational enterprises', *British Journal of Industrial Relations*, 23(3), November 1985, pp. 379–97.
126 R. Blanpain, *The OECD Guidlines for Multinational Enterprises and Labour Relations 1982–1984*, Deventer, Kluwar, 1985, p. 45.
127 See, for example, Richard L. Rowan and Duncan C. Campbell, 'The attempt to regulate industrial relations through international codes of conduct', *The Columbia Journal of World Business*, 18(2), Summer 1983, pp. 64–72.
128 See, for example, Kennedy, *op. cit.*, n. 123, pp. 331–42.
129 Herbert R. Northrup and Richard L. Rowan, *Multinational Collective Bargaining Attempts*, Industrial Research Unit, Wharton School, University of Pennsylvania, 1979, p. 533.
130 For a summary see Creigh (1984), *op. cit.*, n. 49, pp. 7–8.
131 See, for example, Peter J. Buckley and Peter Enderwick, *The Industrial Relations Practices of Foreign Owned Firms in Britain*, London, Macmillan, 1985.
132 John Purcell, Paul Marginson, Paul Edwards, and Keith Sisson, 'The industrial relations practices of multi-plant foreign owned firms', *Industrial Relations Journal*, 18(2), Summer 1987, pp. 130–37.
133 Peter Enderwick, 'Labour and the theory of the multinational corporation', *Industrial Relations Journal*, 13(2), Summer 1982, p. 32.
134 William Ouchi, *Theory Z*, Reading, Mass., Addison-Wesley, 1981, p. 58.
135 See, for example, Jeremiah J. Sullivan, 'A critique of theory Z', *Academy of Management Review*, 8(1), 1983, pp. 132–42.
136 Mark Thompson and Hervey A. Juris, 'The response of industrial relations to economic change', in Hervey Juris, Mark Thompson, and Wilbur Daniels (eds), *Industrial Relations in a Decade of Economic Change*, Madison, Wisconsin, IRRA, 1985, p. 384.
137 For a useful summary discussion see Everett M. Kassalow, 'Japan as an industrial relations model', *The Journal of Industrial Relations*, 25(2), June 1983.
138 *The Future of the Automobile*, The Report of MIT's International Automobile Program, London, Counterpoint, 1985, p. 215.
139 See, for example, Joseph M. Weiler, 'The Japanese labour relations system: lessons for Canada', in Craig Riddell (ed.), *Labour Management Co-operation in Canada*, Toronto, University of Toronto Press, 1986, pp. 111–49.
140 *The Future of the Automobile*, p. 216.
141 Mark Gregory, 'The no-strike deal in action', *Personnel Management*, December 1986, p. 31.
142 Michael White and Malcalm Trevor, *Under Japanese Management*, Heinemann, London, 1983.
143 See, for example, Peter Turnbull, 'The "Japanisation" of British

industrial relations at Lucas', *Industrial Relations Journal*, 17(3), Autumn 1986, pp. 193–206.
144 See, for example, S. Lukes, *Power: A Radical View*, London, Macmillan, 1974.
145 J. T. Dunlop, *Wage Determination Under Trade Unions*, New York, Macmillan, 1944, pp. 77–8.
146 C. E. Lindblom, 'Bargaining power in price and wage determination', *Quarterly Journal of Economics*, 62, May 1948.
147 See, for example, Hervey Juris and Peter Feuille, *Police Unionism*, Lexington, Mass., D. C. Heath, 1973.
148 Neil W. Chamberlain and James W. Kuhn, *Collective Bargaining*, New York, McGraw Hill, 2nd edn, 1965, Chapter 7.
149 *ibid.*, pp. 170–1.
150 See, for example, S. B. Bacharach and E. J. Lawler, *Bargaining Power, Tactics and Outcomes*, San Francisco, Jossey-Bass, 1981.
151 See, for example, R. M. Emerson, 'Power-dependence relations', *American Sociological Review*, 27, 1962, pp. 31–40.
152 L. R. Pondy, 'Organisational conflict: concepts and models', *Administrative Science Quarterly*, 17, 1967, pp. 296–320.
153 Mick Marchington, *Managing Industrial Relations*, London, McGraw Hill, 1982, Chapter 7.
154 Terry L. Leap and David W. Grigsby, 'A conceptualisation of collective bargaining power', *Industrial and Labor Relations Review*, 39(2), January 1986, pp. 204–6.

Chapter 7 Collective bargaining and the interaction with the environment

1 Alton W. J. Craig, 'A framework for the analysis of industrial relations systems', in Brian Barrett, Ed Rhodes, and John Bershon (eds), *Industrial Relations and the Wider Society*, London, Collier Macmillan, 1975, p. 17.
2 Sumner Slichter, James L. Healy, and E. Robert Livernash, *The Impact of Collective Bargaining on Management*, Washington, Brookings, 1960.
3 Richard B. Freeman and James L. Medoff, *What Do Unions Do?*, New York, Basic Books, 1984, Chapter 1.
4 Daniel J. B. Mitchell, *Unions, Wages and Inflation*, Washington, Brookings, 1980, p. 70.
5 The major work here is that of H. Gregg Lewis, *Unionism and Relative Wages in the United States*, Chicago, University of Chicago Press, 1963.
6 Freeman and Medoff, *op. cit.*, n. 3, Chapter 3.
7 *ibid.*, pp. 44–6.
8 *ibid.*, p. 54.
9 *ibid.*, p. 239.
10 For a useful summary statement see Mitchell, *op. cit.*, n. 4, Chapter 3.

11 See, for example, Thomas A. Kochan and David E. Helfman, 'The effects of collective bargaining on economic and behavioural job outcomes', in R. Ehrenberg (ed.), *Research in Labor Economics*, Greenwich, Conn., JAI Press, 4, 1981, p. 332; and Richard B. Freeman and James L. Medoff, 'The impact of collective bargaining: illusion or reality?', in Jack Stieber, Robert B. McKersie, and D. Quinn Mills (eds), *US Industrial Relations 1950–1980: A Critical Assessment*, University of Wisconsin, IRRA, 1981, p. 86.
12 H. Gregg Lewis, 'Union relative wage effects: a survey of macro estimates', *Journal of Labor Economics*, 1(1), 1983, pp. 1–27.
13 See, for example, Paul A. Geroski and Mark B. Stewart, 'Trade union wage differentials in the UK: a strange and sad story', Working Paper no. 157, Industrial Relations Section, Princeton University, October 1982.
14 M. Stewart, 'Relative earnings and individual union membership in the UK', *Economica*, 50(2), May 1983.
15 David Metcalf and Stephen Nickell, 'Will pay cuts bring more jobs?', *New Society*, 28 February 1985.
16 D. Metcalf, 'Trade unions and economic performance: the British evidence', Discussion Paper no. 320, Centre for Labour Economics, LSE, August 1988.
17 R. Layard and S. Nickell, 'The causes of British unemployment', *National Institute Economic Review*, February 1985, p. 72.
18 P. Minford, *Unemployment: Cause and Cure*, Oxford, Martin Robertson, 1983.
19 P. R. G. Layard and S. J. Nickell, 'Unemployment, real wages and aggregate demand in Europe, Japan and the US', Discussion Paper no. 214, Centre for Labour Economics, LSE, March 1985.
20 A. G. Hines, 'Trade Unions and wage inflation in the Unted Kingdom, 1893–1961', in B. J. McCormick and E. Owen Smith (eds), *The Labour Market*, Harmondsworth, Penguin, 1968, pp. 284–319.
21 *ibid.*, pp. 289–91.
22 A. G. Hines, 'Wage inflation in the United Kingdom, 1948–62: a disaggregated study', *Economic Journal*, 79, March 1969, pp. 66–89.
23 D. L. Purdy and G. Zis, 'On the concept and measurement of union militancy', in D. Laidler and D. Purdy (eds), *Inflation and Labour Markets*, Manchester, Manchester University Press, 1974, pp. 46–7.
24 Charles Mulvey and Mary Gregory, 'The Hines wage inflation model', *Manchester School*, 45, March 1977, pp. 29–49.
25 C. J. Parsley, 'Labor union effects on wage gains: a survey of recent literature', *Journal of Economic Literature*, 18, March 1980, pp. 22–6.
26 Alistair Dawson, 'The performance of three wage equations in post war Britain', *Applied Economics*, 15, 1983, pp. 92–5.
27 A. Ellis, J. M. Pearson, and P. D. Pershon, 'Trade unions and wage inflation in the United Kingdom: a re-estimation of Hines model', *Applied Economics*, 19(1), 1987, pp. 597–608.

28 See, for example, J. Taylor, 'Incomes policy, the structure of unemployment and the Phillips curve: the United Kingdom experience 1953–70', in M. Parkin and M. T. Sumner (eds), *Incomes Policy and Inflation*, Manchester, Manchester University Press, 1972.

29 Purdy and Zis, *op. cit.*, n. 23, pp. 58–9.

30 S. B. Bacharach and E. J. Lawler, *Power and Politics in Organisations*, San Francisco, Jossey Bass, 1980.

31 Terry L. Leap and David W. Grisby, 'A conceptualization of collective bargaining power', *Industrial and Labor Relations Review*, 39(2), January 1986, p. 205.

32 M. W. Reder, 'Job scarcity and the nature of union power', in B. J. McCormick and E. Owen Smith (eds), *The Labour Market*, Harmondsworth, Penguin, 1968, p. 133.

33 See, for example, Henry Phelps Brown, *The Origins of Trade Union Power*, Oxford, Oxford University Press, 1986, pp. 159–65; also C. J. Crouch and A. Pizzorno (eds), *The Resurgence of Class Conflict in Western Europe Since 1968*, London, Macmillan, 1978.

34 E. H. Phelps Brown, 'New wine in old bottles: reflections on the changed working of collective bargaining in Great Britain', *British Journal of Industrial Relations*, 11(3), November 1973, p. 334.

35 Freeman and Medoff, *op. cit.*, n. 3, Chapter 5.

36 David Metcalf, 'Unions and the distribution of earnings', *British Journal of Industrial Relations*, 20(2), July 1982, pp. 163–9.

37 Simon Kuznets, *Modern Economic Growth*, New Haven, Conn., Yale University Press, 1966, pp. 168–70.

38 Brian Burkitt and David Bowers, *Trade Unions and the Economy*, London, Macmillan, 1979, pp. 62–4.

39 See, for example, A. Glyn and B. Sutcliffe, *British Capitalism, Workers and the Profits Squeeze*, Harmondsworth, Penguin, 1972.

40 Burkitt and Bowers, *op. cit.*, n. 38, p. 71.

41 Keith Cowling and Ian Molho, 'Wage share, concentration and unionism', *Manchester School*, 50, June 1982, pp. 99–115.

42 M. Kalecki, *Essays in the Theory of Economic Fluctuations*, London, Allen & Unwin, 1939. For a general summary of this and other theories see N. Kaldor, 'Alternative theories of distribution', in B. J. McCormick and E. Owen Smith (eds), *The Labour Market*, Harmondsworth, Penguin, 1968, pp. 349–79.

43 M. Kalecki, 'Class struggle and the distribution of national income', *Kyklos*, 24, 1971, p. 1–9.

44 See, for example, Arne L. Kalleberg, Michael Wallace, and Lawrence E. Raffalouichi, 'Accounting for labor's share: class and income distribution in the printing industry', *Industrial and Labor Relations Review*, 37(3), April 1984, pp. 386–402.

45 Freeman and Medoff, *op. cit.*, n. 3, Chapter 12.

46 Metcalf, *op. cit.*, n. 36, pp. 10–12.

47 Lloyd Ulman, 'Collective bargaining and industrial efficiency', in R. E. Caves (ed.), *Britain's Economic Prospects*, Washington, Brookings, 1968, p. 340.

48 Harvey Leibenstein, 'Allocative efficiency and X-efficiency', *American Economic Review*, LVI, June 1966, pp. 392–415.
49 See, for example, Andrew Kilpatrick and Tony Lawson, 'On the nature of industrial decline in the UK', *Cambridge Journal of Economics*, 4, 1980, pp. 85–102.
50 *ibid.*, p. 87 and Ulman, *op. cit.*, n. 47, p. 342.
51 Phelps Brown (1986), *op. cit.*, n. 33, p. 4.
52 See, for example, B. Elbaum, and F. Wilkinson, 'Industrial relations and uneven development: a comparative study of the American and British steel industries', *Cambridge Journal of Economics*, 3, 1979, pp. 275–303.
53 C. F. Pratten, *Labour Productivity Differentials Within International Companies*, University of Cambridge Department of Applied Economics, Occasional Paper no. 50, 1976.
54 R. Wragg and J. Roberston, *Post War Trends in Employment, Productivity, Output, Labour Costs and Prices by Industry in the UK*, Research Paper no. 3, Department of Employment, London, 1978.
55 J. H. Pencavel, 'The distributional and efficiency effects of trade unions in Britain', *British Journal of Industrial Relations*, 15(2), July 1977, pp. 137–56.
56 R. E. Caves, 'Productivity differences among industries', in R. E. Caves and L. B. Krause (eds), *Britain's Economic Performance*, Washington, Brookings, 1980, pp. 135–98.
57 G. C. Wenban-Smith, 'Factors influencing recent productivity growth – report on a survey of companies', *National Institute Economic Review*, 1982, pp. 57–86.
58 See, for example, Theo Nichols, *The British Worker Question*, London, Routledge & Kegan Paul, 1986, especially pp. 55–64.
59 K. Williams, J. Williams, and D. Thomas, *Why are the British Bad at Manufacturing?*, London, Routledge & Kegan Paul, 1985.
60 P. K. Edwards, 'Managing labour relations through the recession', *Employee Relations*, 7, 1985, pp. 3–7.
61 U. G. Lintner, M. J. Pokorny, M. M. Woods, and M. R. Blinkhorn, 'Trade unions and technical change in the UK mechanical engineering industry', *British Journal of Industrial Relations*, 25(1), March 1981, pp. 19–30.
62 W. W. Daniel, *Workplace Industrial Relations and Technical Change*, London, Frances Pinter, 1987.
63 J. Northcott, P. Rogers, W. Knetsch, and de Klespapis, *Microelectronics in Industry: An International Comparison: Britain, France and Germany*, PSI, no. 800, London, 1985.
64 P. B. Beaumont, 'Selective perception, unions and organisational change', *Industrial Relations Journal*, 19(2), Summer 1988.
65 Freeman and Medoff, *op. cit.*, n. 11, Chapter 11.
66 See, for example, J. T. Addison and A. H. Barnett, 'The impact of unions on productivity', *British Journal of Industrial Relations*, 20(2), July 1982, pp. 145–62.
67 See, for example, Brian Bemmels, 'How unions affect productivity in

manufacturing plants', *Industrial and Labor Relations Review*, 50(2), January 1987, pp. 241–53.
68 Metcalf, *op. cit.*, n. 36, pp. 163–9.
69 Kevin Denny and Johnny Muellbauer, 'Economic and industrial relations explanations of productivity change: some evidence for the British manufacturing sector 1980–1984', mimeographed paper, Oxford University, 1988.
70 Michael Bruno and Jeffrey D. Sachs, *Economics of Worldwide Stagflation*, Oxford, Blackwell, 1985, p. 222.
71 D. Metcalf, 'Labour market flexibility and jobs: a survey of evidence from OECD countries with special reference to Great Britain and Europe', Discussion Paper no. 254, Centre for Labour Economics, LSE, October 1986.
72 Christopher Saunders and David Marsden, *Pay Inequalities in the European Communities*, London, Butterworth, 1981.
73 W. W. Daniel and Neil Millward, *Workplace Industrial Relations in Britain*, London, Heinemann, 1983, pp. 254–60.
74 Harry C. Katz, Thomas A. Kochan, and Kenneth R. Gobeille, 'Industrial relations performance, economic performance and QWL programs: an interplant analysis', *Industrial and Labor Relations Review*, 37(1), October 1983, pp. 3–17; and Harry C. Katz, Thomas A. Kochan, and Mark R. Weber, 'Assessing the effects of industrial relations systems and efforts to improve the quality of working life on organizational effectiveness', *Academy of Management Journal*, 28(3), September 1985, pp. 509–26.
75 *ibid.*, p. 4.
76 W. Richard Scott, 'Effectiveness of organizational effectiveness studies', in Paul S. Goodman and Johannes M. Pennings (eds), *New Perspectives on Organizational Effectiveness*, San Francisco, Jossey-Bass, 1977, pp. 63–4.
77 *ibid.*, pp. 73–4.
78 Thomas A. Kochan, *Collective Bargaining and Industrial Relations*, Homewood, Illinois, Irwin, 1980, p. 25.
79 *ibid.*, pp. 224–5.
80 Frederick H. Harbison and John R. Coleman, *Goals and Strategy in Collective Bargaining*, New York, Harper & Row, 1951.
81 Richard E. Walton and Robert B. McKersie, *A Behavioural Theory of Labor Negotiations*, New York, McGraw Hill, p. 185.
82 Milton Derber, W. E. Chalmers, and Milton Edelman, 'Assessing union management relations', *The Quarterly Review of Economics and Business*, 96, November 1961, pp. 27–40.
83 See, for example, J. T. Turner and J. W. Robinson, 'A pilot study of the validity of grievance settlement rates as a predictor of union–management relationships', *Journal of Industrial Relations*, 14, 1972, pp. 314–22.
84 See, for example, David Lewin, 'Theoretical perspectives on the modern grievance procedure', in Joseph D. Reid (ed.), *New Approaches to Labor Unions*, Greenwich, Conn., JAI Press, 1983, pp. 131–33.

85 David Lewin, 'Empirical measures of grievance procedure effectiveness', *Proceedings of the Industrial Relations Research Association*, Madison, Wisconsin, Spring 1984, pp. 491–9.
86 See, for example, Nigel Nicholson, 'Industrial relations climate: a case study approach', *Personnel Review*, 8(3), 1979, pp. 20–5; and Ali Dastmalchian, Raymond Adamason, and Paul Blyton, 'Developing a measure of industrial relations climate', *Relations Industrielles*, 41(4), 1986, pp. 851–9.
87 Dastmalchian, Adamson and Blyton, *op. cit.*, n. 86, p. 852.

Chapter 8 The changing role of the State in the industrial-relations system

1 P. B. Beaumont, 'The role of the state in industrial relations: a European perspective', Discussant's Paper at the First Industrial Relations Congress of the Americas, Quebec, 1988 (mimeographed).
2 Wolfgang Streeck, *Industrial Relations in West Germany*, London, Heinemann, 1984, pp. 146–55.
3 Colin Crouch, 'Conservative industrial relations policy: towards labour exclusion?', in Otto Jacobi, Bob Jessop, Hans Kastandick, and Marino Regini (eds), *Economic Crisis, Trade Unions and the State*, London, Croom Helm, 1986, pp. 146–7.
4 Marino Regini, 'Political bargaining in western Europe during the economic crises of the 1980s', in Otto Jacobi, Bob Jessop, Hans Kastandick, and Marino Regini (eds), *Economic Crisis, Trade Unions and the State*, London, Croom Helm, 1986.
5 Jill Rubery, 'Trade unions in the 1980s: the case of the United Kingdom', in Richard Edwards, Paolo Geronna, and Franz Todtling (eds), *Unions in Crisis and Beyond*, Dover, Mass., Auburn, 1986, p. 66.
6 P. B. Beaumont, 'The Thatcher/Reagan administration approaches in labor relations', *Proceedings of the Industrial Relations Research Association*, New York, 1988.
7 Richard Scase, 'Introduction', in Richard Scase (ed.), *The State in Western Europe*, New York, St Martin's Press, 1980, p. 11.
8 Jonathan Zeitlin, 'Shop floor bargaining and the State: a contradictory relationship', in Steven Tolliday and Jonathan Zeitlin (eds), *Shop Floor Bargaining and the State*, Cambridge, Cambridge University Press, 1985, pp. 1–45.
9 Norman McCord, *Strikes*, Oxford, Blackwell, 1980, Chapter 2.
10 Ian G. Sharp, Industrial Conciliation and Arbitration in Great Britain, London, Allen & Unwin, 1950, p. 5.
11 E. H. Phelps Brown, *The Growth of British Industrial Relations*, London, Macmillan, 1959, p. 28.
12 ILO, *Conciliation in Industrial Disputes: A Practical Guide*, Geneva, ILO, 1973.
13 Thomas A. Kochan, 'Collective bargaining and organizational behaviour research', in Barry M. Staw and Larry L. Cummings,

Research in Organizational Behaviour, Greenwich, Conn., JAI Press, vol. 2, 1980, pp. 145–6. See also ILO, *op. cit.*, n. 12.

14 Thomas A. Kochan and Todd Jick, 'A theory of the public sector mediation process', *Journal of Conflict Resolution*, 22, June 1978.

15 Jean M. Hiltrop, 'Dispute settlement and mediation: data from Britain', *Industrial Relations*, 24(1), Winter 1985, pp. 139–46.

16 See, for example, J. F. B. Goodman and J. Krislov, 'Conciliation in industrial disputes in Great Britain: a survey of the attitudes of the parties', *British Journal of Industrial Relations*, 12(3), November 1974.

17 See L. C. Hunter, 'Economic issues in conciliation and arbitration', *British Journal of Industrial Relations*, 15(2), July 1977, pp. 240–1.

18 *ibid.*, pp. 233–8.

19 Michael Jones, Linda Dickens, Brian Weekes, and Moira Hart, 'Resolving industrial relations disputes: the role of ACAS conciliation', *Industrial Relations Journal*, 14(2), Summer 1983, pp. 6–17.

20 Neil Millward and Mark Stevens, *British Workplace Industrial Relations, 1980–1984*, Aldershot, Gower, 1986, pp. 180–92.

21 Thomas A. Kochan, *Collective Bargaining and Industrial Relations*, Homewood, Illinois, Irwin, 1980, p. 288.

22 Joseph Krislov, 'Supplying mediation services in five countries: some current problems', *Columbia Journal of World Business*, 18(2), Summer 1983, p. 56.

23 See, for example, Clark Kerr, 'Industrial conflict and its mediation', *American Journal of Sociology*, 60(3), 1954. See also W. E. J. McCarthy and N. D. Ellis, *Management by Agreement*, London, Hutchinson, 1973, Chapter 7.

24 Kochan, *op. cit.*, n. 21, pp. 434–5.

25 John Purcell, 'The lessons of the Commission on Industrial Relations' attempts to reform workplace industrial relations', *Industrial Relations Journal*, 10(2), Summer 1979, pp. 4–22.

26 *ACAS Annual Report 1981*, London, HMSO, 1982, p. 56.

27 Calculated from figures reported in Allan Flanders, *Trade Unions*, London, Hutchinson, 1968, p. 101.

28 See, for example, Peter Feuille, 'Selected benefits and costs of compulsory arbitration', *Industrial and Labor Relations Review*, 33(1), October 1979.

29 Sharp, *op. cit.*, n. 10, p. 359.

30 S. J. Frankel, 'Arbitration in the British Civil Service', *Public Administration*, 38, Autumn 1960, pp. 204–7.

31 See, for example, P. B. Beaumont, 'Union–management collusion and Schedule 11 awards', *Industrial Relations Journal*, 10, Spring 1979.

32 *Annual Report of CAC 1979*, London, HMSO, 1980, p. 25.

33 *ACAS Annual Report 1980*, London, HMSO, 1981, p. 26.

34 P. B. Beaumont and J. Leopold, 'Public sector industrial relations: recent developments', *Employee Relations*, 7(4), 1985, p. 36.

35 *ibid.*, pp. 33–4.

36 Institute of Directors, *Settling Disputes Peacefully*, London, 1984.
37 See, for example, Kochan, *op. cit.*, n. 21, pp. 295–7.
38 See, for example: Sir John Wood, 'Last offer arbitration', *British Journal of Industrial Relations*, 23(3), November 1985, pp. 415–24; and Ramsumair Singh, 'Final offer arbitration in theory and practice', *Industrial Relations Journal*, 17(4), 1986, pp. 329–38.
39 See, for example, the three papers in the section on arbitration and negotiation process in *American Economic Review, Papers and Proceedings*, 77(2), May 1977.
40 J. Meade, *Wage Fixing*, London, Allen & Unwin, 1982.
41 See, for example, P. Minford and D. Peel, 'Compulsory arbitration procedures and incomes policy', *Three Branks Review*, no. 137, 1983, pp. 3–16 and P. J. Dolton and J. G. Treble, 'On final offer and not quite compulsory arbitration', *Scottish Journal of Political Economy*, 23(2), June 1985, pp. 181–90.
42 See, for example, Morley Gunderson, *Economic Aspects of Interest Arbitration*, Ontario Economic Council Discussion Paper, 1983, pp. 43–7.
43 For a useful summary see M. J. Artis, 'Incomes policies: some rationales', in J. L. Fallick and R. F. Elliott (eds), *Incomes Policies, Inflation and Relative Pay*, London, Allen & Unwin, 1981, pp. 6–22.
44 Robert J. Davies, 'Incomes and anti-inflation policy', in G. S. Bain (ed.), *Industrial Relations in Britain*, Oxford, Blackwell, 1983, p. 432.
45 See, for example, Leo Panitch, *Social Democracy and Industrial Militancy*, Cambridge, Cambridge University Press, 1976, pp. 260–1.
46 John H. Pencavel, 'The American experience with incomes policies', in J. L. Fallick and R. F. Elliott (eds), *Incomes Policies, Inflation and Relative Pay*, London, Allen & Unwin, 1981.
47 Davies in Bain (ed.), *op. cit.*, n. 44, p. 433.
48 John Burton, *Wage Inflation*, London, Macmillan, 1972, p. 78.
49 *ibid.*, pp. 73–7.
50 Davies in Bain (ed.), *op. cit.*, n. 44, pp. 433–5.
51 Although for a rather different set of findings see D. Metcalf, 'Unions, incomes policy and relative wages in Britain', *British Journal of Industrial Relations*, 15(2), July 1977, pp. 164–9.
52 For some summary statements, see: R. J. Davies in Bain (ed.), *op. cit.*, n. 44, pp. 441–7;Brian Towers, *British Incomes Policy*, Universities of Leeds and Nottingham, Occasional Papers in Industrial Relations, no. 3, 1978; and R. F. Elliott and J. L. Fallick, 'Incomes policies, inflation and relative pay: an overview', in J. L. Fallick and R. F. Elliott (eds), *Incomes Policies, Inflation and Relative Pay*, London, Allen & Unwin, 1981, pp. 246–63.
53 Derek Robinson and Ken Mayhew, 'Introduction' in Derek Robinson and Ken Mayhew (eds), *Pay Policies for the Future*, Oxford, Oxford University Press, 1983, p. 6.
54 K. Holden, D. A. Peel, and J. L. Thompson, *The Economics of Wage Controls*, London, Macmillan, 1987, Chapter 2.
55 See, for example, S. G. B. Henry, 'Incomes policy and aggregate

pay', in J. L. Fallick and R. F. Elliott (eds), *Incomes Policies, Inflation and Relative Pay*, London, Allen & Unwin, 1981, pp. 32–42.

56 Robert J. Flanagan and Daniel J. B. Mitchell, 'Wage determination and public policy', in Thomas A. Kochan, Daniel J. B. Mitchell, and Lee Dryer (eds), *Industrial Relations Research in the 1970s: Review and Appraisal*, Madison, Wisconsin, IRRA, 1982, pp. 77–8.

57 J. D. Whitley, 'A model of incomes policy in the UK, 1963–79', *Manchester School*, March 1986, pp. 31–64.

58 S. B. Wadhwani, 'Wage inflation in the United Kingdom', *Economica*, 52, 1985, p. 201.

59 F. T. Blackaby, 'An array of proposals', in Frank Blackaby (ed.), *The Future of Pay Bargaining*, London, Heinemann, 1980, pp. 64–91.

60 See Flanagan and Mitchell in Thomas A. Kochan, Daniel J. B. Mitchell, and Lee Dyer (eds), *Industrial Relations Research in the 1970s: Review and Appraisal*, Madison, Wisconsin, IRRA, 1982, pp. 80–1.

61 Richard Layard, *How To Beat Unemployment*, Oxford, Oxford University Press, 1986, Chapter 10.

62 See, for example, Nick Bosanquet, 'Tax-based incomes policies', in Derek Robinson and Ken Mayhew (eds), *Pay Policies for the Future*, Oxford, Oxford University Press, 1983, pp. 33–50.

63 This discussion is heavily based on P. B. Beaumont, 'Industrial relations in the public sector', in Brian Towers (ed.), *Handbook of Industrial Relations Practice*, London, Kogan Page, 2nd edn, 1988.

64 'Public sector trade unions', *IDS Public Sector Digest*, 1988.

65 *ibid.*

66 Beaumont and Leopold, *op. cit.*, n. 34, p. 17.

67 IDS Public Sector Unit, *Public Sector Pay: Review of 1987, Prospects for 1988*, London, IDS, February 1988.

68 *ibid.*

69 National Board for Prices and Incomes Report No. 122, *Fourth General Report*, July 1969, Cmnd 4130, London, HMSO, p. 31.

70 N. Foster, S. Henry, and C. Trinder, 'Public and private sector pay: a partly disaggregated study', *National Institute Economic Review*, no. 197, February 1984; and R. Layard, 'Public sector pay: the British perspective', Discussion Paper no. 229, Centre for Labour Economics, LSE, January 1986.

71 R. F. Elliott and P. D. Murphy, 'The relative pay of public and private sector employees, 1970–1984', *Cambridge Journal of Economics*, 11, 1987, pp. 1907–32.

72 David G. Blanchflower, Andrew J. Oswald, and Mario D. Garrett, 'Insider power in wage determination', mimeographed paper, 1988.

73 See, for example, Robert Bacon and Walter Eltis, *Britain's Economic Problem: Too Few Producers*, London, Macmillan, 2nd edn, 1978.

74 Institute of Personnel Management and IDS Public Sector Unit, *Competitive Tendering in the Public Sector*, October 1986, pp. 17 and 26.

75 David Thomas, 'Privatisation and the unions', *New Society*, 21 June 1984, p. 479.
76 *National Institute Economic Review*, no. 111, February 1985, pp. 17–18.
77 See, for example, J. Lloyd, 'The two faces of the miners' strike', *Personnel Management*, June 1985, pp. 32–6.
78 CPS, *Essential Services – Whose Rights?*, May 1984. More generally, see J. Lover, 'The anti-strike hit list', *Management Today*, January 1985.
79 Michael Fogarty with Douglas Brooks, *Trade Unions and British Industrial Development*, PSI Research Report, 1986, p. 151.
80 See P. B. Beaumont, 'The Government as a model employer: a change of direction in Britain', *Journal of Collective Negotiations in the Public Sector*, 16(3), 1987, pp. 185–6.
81 See, for example, G. K. Fry, *The Changing Civil Service*, London, Allen & Unwin, 1985, Chapter 8.
82 See, for example, Tiziano Treu (ed.), *Public Service Labour Relations: Recent Trends and Future Prospects*, Geneva, ILO, 1987.

Chapter 9 Beyond collective bargaining

1 See, for example, Thomas A. Kochan, David B. Lipsky, and Lee Dyer, 'Collective bargaining and the quality of work: the views of local union activists', *Proceedings of the Industrial Relations Research Association*, Winter 1974, p. 150.
2 Thomas A. Kochan, *Collective Bargaining and Industrial Relations*, Homewood, Illinois, Irwin, 1980, pp. 359–60.
3 Cited in P. B. Beaumont, *Safety at Work and the Unions*, London, Croom Helm, 1983, p. 57.
4 *ibid.*, pp. 56–7.
5 See, for example, Allan Flanders, *The Fawley Productivity Agreements*, London, Faber, 1964, pp. 241–2.
6 Beaumont, *op. cit.*, n. 3, Chapter 5.
7 See, for example, Neil Millward and Mark Stevens, *British Workplace Industrial Relations 1980–1984*, Aldershot, Gower, 1986, pp. 147–50.
8 See, for example, Thomas A. Kochan, Lee Dyer, and David B. Lipsky, *The Effectiveness of Union–Management Safety and Health Committees*, Kalamazoo, Michigan, Upjohn Institute for Employment Research, 1977; and J. W. Leopold and P. B. Beaumont, 'Health, safety and industrial relations: a UK study', *New Zealand Journal of Industrial Relations*, 8(2), August 1983, pp. 135–46.
9 Milton Derber, *Labor–Management Relations at the Plant Level Under Industry Wide Bargaining*, Urbana, Illinois, University of Illinois Press, 1955, p. 80.
10 H. Ramsay, 'Cycles of control: worker participation in sociological and historical perspective', *Sociology*, 11, 1977, pp. 418–506.
11 T. A. Kochan and L. Dyer, 'A model of organizational change in the

context of union–management relations', *Journal of Applied Behavioural Science*, 12, 1976, pp. 57–78.

12 See, for example, John MacInnes, 'Conjuring up consultation: the role and extent of joint consultation in post war private manufacturing industry', *British Journal of Industrial Relations*, 23(1), March 1985, pp. 93–113.

13 Millward and Stevens, *op. cit.*, n. 7, pp. 138–41

14 For a useful summary of this draft proposal see Michael Gold, 'EEC employment and company law: recent developments and prospects', in Michael Armstrong (ed.), *The Personnel and Training Databook 1984*, London, Kogan Page, 1984, p. 53.

15 See, for example, Michael Fogarty with Douglas Brooks, *Trade Unions and British Industrial Development*, London, PSI, 1986, pp. 78–80.

16 See, for example, *ACAS Annual Report 1985*, London, HMSO, 1986, p. 48. See also *Industrial Relations Review and Report* no. 396, 14 July 1987, pp. 2–7.

17 P. B. Beaumont and D. R. Deaton, 'The extent and determinants of joint consultative arrangements in Britain', *Journal of Management Studies*, 18(1), January 1981, pp. 49–74.

18 P. B. Beaumont and R. I. D. Harris, 'High technology industries, non-union status and human resource management policies: the British picture', *Department of Economics, Queen's University of Belfast*, mimeographed paper, 1987.

19 Millward and Stevens, *ibid.*, pp. 142–7.

20 Mick Marchington, 'A review and critique of research on developments in joint consultation', *British Journal of Industrial Relations*, 25(3), November 1987, pp. 339–52.

21 Richard E. Walton, 'From control to commitment in the workplace', *Harvard Business Review*, March–April 1985, pp. 77–84.

22 Tony Lane, 'Economic democracy: are the trade unions equipped?', *Industrial Relations Journal*, 17(4), Winter 1986, p. 326.

23 *ibid.*, pp. 321–8.

24 G. S. Bain, 'The United Kingdom experience on employee participation and involvement', Paper presented to a seminar organised by the Northern Ireland Labour Relations Agency, 1985.

25 Peter Brannen, *Authority and Participation in Industry*, London, Batsford Books, 1983, pp. 113–4.

26 John Child, *Organization*, London, Harper & Row, 2nd edn, 1984, p. 248.

27 John Storey, 'The management of new office technology: choice, control and social structure in the insurance industry', *Journal of Management Studies*, 24(1), January 1987, pp. 44–5.

28 See, for example: Child, *op. cit.*, n. 26, Chapter 9; and Arndt Sorge and Malcolm Warner, *Comparative Factory Organisation*, Aldershot, Gower, 1986, Chapter 10. And for the US see Richard E. Walton, 'New perspectives on the world at work', *Human Relations*, 35(12), 1982, pp. 1073–84.

29 H. Braverman, *Labor and Monopoly Capital*, Monthly Review Press, New York, 1974.
30 R. C. Edwards, *Contested Terrain: The Transformation of the Workplace in the Twentieth Century*, New York, Basic Books, 1979.
31 Arthur Francis, *New Technology at Work*, Oxford, Oxford University Press, 1986, p. 106. See also Graeme Salaman, *Working*, Chichester, Ellis Horwood, 1986, p. 18.
32 *ibid.*, pp. 110–11.
33 Braverman, *op. cit.*, n. 29.
34 See, for example, Craig R. Littler, *The Development of the Labour Process in Capitalist Societies*, London, Heinemann, 1982, Chapter 3. See also S. J. Wood (ed.), *The Degradation of Work? Skill, Deskilling and the Labour Process*, London, Hutchinson, 1982.
35 Francis, *op. cit.*, n. 31, Chapter 5.
36 These terms come from S. H. Slichter, J. J. Healey, and E. R. Livernash, *The Impact of Collective Bargaining on Management*, Washington, Brookings, 1960, Chapter 12.
37 See, for example, Gerald G. Somers, Edward L. Cushman, and Nat Weinberg (eds), *Adjusting to Technological Change*, New York, Harper & Row, 1963.
38 This summary statement comes from Paul Willman, 'Bargaining for change: a comparison of the UK and USA', Occasional Paper no. 2, Industrial Relations Group, University of Durham, 1982, p. 4.
39 See, for example, Tony Mainwaring, 'The trade unions response to new technology', *Industrial Relations Journal*, 12(4), July/August 1981, pp. 7–26.
40 R. Williams and F. Steward, 'Technology agreements in Britain: a survey 1977–83', *Industrial Relations Journal*, vol. 16, no. 3, 1985, p. 58–73.
41 Ian Benson and John Lloyd, *New Technology and Industrial Change*, London, Kogan Page, 1983, p. 176.
42 See, for example, A. Davies, 'Management–union participation during micro-technological change', in M. Warner (ed.), *Microprocessors, Manpower and Society*, Aldershot, Gower, 1984, pp. 149–71.
43 Paul Willman, *New Technology and Industrial Relations: A Review of the Literature*, Department of Employment Research Paper no. 56, 1986, pp. 12–16.
44 Millward and Stevens, *op. cit.*, n. 7, pp. 46–7.
45 Colin Gill, *Work, Unemployment and the New Technology*, Cambridge, Polity Press, 1985, p. 129.
46 Eric Batstone and Stephen Gourlay, *Unions, Employment and Innovation*, Oxford, Blackwell, 1986, pp. 276–7.
47 Colin Gill, 'New technology and industrial relations', in Brian Towers (ed.), *A Handbook of Industrial Relations Practice*, London, Kogan Page, 1987, p. 78.
48 See, for example: Paul Osterman, ' "Technology and white collar employment", a research strategy', *Proceedings of the Industrial*

Relations Research Association, Winter 1985, pp. 52–9; and Thomas A. Kochan and Boaz Tamir, 'Collective bargaining and new technology', Paper presented to the 7th World Congress, International Industrial Relations Association, Hamburg, September 1986.

49 See, for example, H. Ramsay, 'Participation: the shopfloor view', *British Journal of Industrial Relations*, 14(2), July 1976, pp. 128–41.

50 Alan Fox, *Man Mismanagement*, London, Hutchinson, 1974.

51 Paul K. Edwards, 'Factory managers: their role in personnel management and their place in the company', *Journal of Management Studies*, 24(3), September 1987, pp. 479–501.

52 Howard F. Gospel, 'Managerial structures and strategies: an introduction', in Howard F. Gospel and Craig R. Littler (eds), *Managerial Strategies and Industrial Relations*, London, Heinemann, 1983, pp. 11–20.

53 Millward and Stevens, *op. cit.*, n. 7, pp. 163–7.

54 See 'The Vista survey of employee communications in British industry' (Winter 1986), summarized in *Industrial Relations Review and Report* no. 395, July 1987.

55 Compare 'Involving the staff', *Department of Employment Gazette*, March 1987, pp, 147–9 and *Industrial Relations Review and Report* no. 396, 14 July 1987. See also F. Mitchell, K. I. Sams and P. J. White, 'Research note: employee involvement and the law: Section 1 of the 1982 Employment Act', *Industrial Relations Journal*, 17(4), Winter 1986, pp. 362–7.

56 Ramsay (1977), *op. cit.*, n. 10.

57 'Profit sharing and labour co-partnership in 1928', *Ministry of Labour Gazette*, XXXVII(7), July 1929, p. 234.

58 Jean Remus, 'Financial participation of employees: an attempted classification and major trends', *International Labour Review*, 122(1), January/February 1983, pp. 1–22.

59 *Industrial Relations Review and Report*, no. 428, 15 November 1988, p. 13.

60 See, for example, Martin L. Weitzman, *The Share Economy: Conquering Stagflation*, Cambridge, Mass., Harvard University Press, 1984.

61 Martin L. Weitzman, 'Share arrangements and macroeconomics', *Proceedings of the Industrial Relations Research Association*, Winter 1986, p. 146.

62 Useful summary discussions include Saul Estrin, Paul Grout, and Sushil Wadhwani, 'Profit sharing and employee share ownership', *Economic Policy*, no. 4, April 1987, pp. 13–52; Daniel J. B. Mitchell, 'The share economy and industrial relations', *Industrial Relations*, 26(1), Winter 1987, pp. 1–17; and D. G. Blanchflower and A. J. Oswald, 'Profit sharing – can it work?', Discussion Paper no. 255, Centre for Labour Economics, LSE, October 1986.

63 M. J. F. Poole, 'Factors affecting the development of employee financial participation in contemporary Britain: evidence from a

national survey', *British Journal of Industrial Relations*, 26(1), March 1988, pp. 21–36.
64 Beaumont and Harris, *op. cit.*, n. 18.
65 D. Blanchflower and A. Oswald, 'Profit related pay: prose discovered?', Discussion Paper no. 287, Centre for Labour Economics, LSE, July 1987.
66 *Employment Gazette*, 96(10), October 1988, pp. 573–5.
67 *Industrial Relations Review and Report*, no. 423, 30 August 1988, p. 10.
68 For an interesting discussion of this interpretation of the quality of working life movement see Michael Rose, *Re-working the Work Ethic*, London, Batsford, 1985, Chapter 8.
69 See, for example, Sheila Rothwell, 'Human resources management', *Journal of General Management*, 12(3), Spring 1987, pp. 90–8.
70 David E. Guest, 'Human resource management and industrial relations', *Journal of Management Studies*, 24(5), September 1987, p. 505.
71 Charles Leadbeater and John Lloyd, *In Search of Work*, Harmondsworth, Penguin, 1987.
72 See, for example, Jack Fiorito, Christopher Lowman, and Forrest D. Nelson, 'The impact of human resource policies on union organizing', *Industrial Relations*, 26(2), Spring 1987, pp. 113–26.
73 Tom Burns and G. M. Stalker, *The Management of Innovation*, London, Tavistock Publications, 1959.
74 Randall S. Schuler and Susan E. Jackson, 'Linking competitive strategies with human resource management practices', *Academy of Management Executive*, 1(3), August 1987, pp. 207–19.
75 Guest, *op. cit.*, n. 70, p. 518.
76 Edward E. Lawler, 'Increasing worker involvement to enhance organizational effectiveness', in Paul S. Goodman (ed.), *Change in Organizations*, San Francisco, Jossey-Bass, 1982, p. 307.
77 Edward E. Lawler, *High-Involvement Management*, San Francisco, Jossey-Bass, 1986, Chapter 10.
78 D. R. Deaton, 'Management and industrial relations', unpublished report on the 1980 Workplace Industrial Relations Survey, University of Warwick, mimeographed, December 1981. See also Beaumont and Harris, *op. cit.*, n. 18.
79 See, for example, D. W. Owen, M. G. Coombes, and A. E. Gillespie, 'The urban–rural shift and employment change in Britain, 1971–81', in Mike Danson (ed.), *Redundancy and Recession*, Norwich, Geo Books, 1986, pp. 23–48.
80 P. B. Beaumont and B. Townley, 'Greenfield sites, new plants and work practices', in V. Hammond (ed.), *Current Research in Management*, London, Frances Pinter, 1985, pp. 163–79.
81 *Group Working and Greenfield Sites*, London, Incomes Data Services, 1984.
82 Chris Hendry, Andrew Pettigrew, and Paul Sparrow, 'Changing

patterns of human resource management', *Personnel Management*, November 1988, p. 38.

83 *Industrial Relations Review and Report*, no. 428, 15 November 1988, p. 16.

84 Kurt Lewin, *Field Theory in Social Science*, New York, Harper & Row, 1951.

85 For a recent example see Michael Burawoy, 'Between the labor process and the state: the changing face of factory regimes under advanced capitalism', *American Sociological Review*, 48, 1983, pp. 487–605.

86 Robert E. Cole, 'The Macropolitics of organizational change: a comparative analysis of the spread of small group activities', *Administrative Science Quarterly*, 30(4), December 1985, pp. 460–85.

87 Katherine I. Miller and Peter R. Monge, 'Participation, satisfaction and productivity: a meta-analytic review', *Academy of Management Journal*, 29(4), December 1986, pp. 732–33.

88 E. A. Locke and D. M. Schweiger, 'Participation in decision making: one more look', in Barry M. Staw and Larry L. Cummings (eds), *Research in Organizational Behaviour*, Greenwich, Conn., JAI Press, 1, 1979, pp. 265–339.

89 John R. Cable and Felix R. Fitzroy, 'Productivity efficiency, incentives and employee participation: some preliminary results for West Germany', *Kyklos*, 33, 1980, pp. 110–21.

90 Toby D. Wall, Nigel J. Kemp, Paul R. Jackson, and Chris W. Clegg, 'Outcomes of autonomous work groups: a long-term field experiment', *Academy of Management Journal*, 29(2), June 1986, p. 298.

Chapter 10 Back to the future?

1 Derek L. Bosworth and Peter J. Dawkins, *Work Patterns*, Aldershot, Gower, 1981, p. 73.

2 Guy Routh, *Occupations and Pay in Great Britain, 1906–79*, London, Macmillan, 2nd edn, 1980, p. 200.

3 *Redundancy Arrangements: The 1986 ACAS Survey*, Occasional Paper no. 37.

4 *IDS Focus*, no. 43, May 1987, p. 6.

5 For a recent example in Britain see Michael Poole, W. Brown, J. Rubery, K. Sisson, R. Tarling, and F. Wilkinson, *Industrial Relations in the Future*, London, Routledge & Kegan Paul, 1984.

6 *The Times*, 7 September 1987.

7 *Industrial Relations Review and Report*, no. 423, 15 November 1988, p. 12.

8 James Robertson, *Future Work*, Aldershot, Gower, 1985, pp. 17–20.

9 Charles Handy, *The Future of Work*, Oxford, Blackwell, 1984.

10 D. Metcalf, 'On the measurement of employment and unemployment', *National Institute Economic Review*, August 1984.

11 See, for example, K. G. Knight, *Unemployment: An Economic*

Analysis, London, Croom Helm, 1987, Chapter 9. See also Layard and Stephen Nickell, 'An incomes policy to help the unemployed', *The Economic Review*, 5(2), November 1987, pp. 12–20.

12 David Rose, Carolyn Vogler, Gordon Marshall, and Howard Newby, 'Economic restructuring: the British experience', *Annals of the American Academy of Political and Social Science*, no. 475, September 1984, p. 153.

13 See, for example, Martin Harrop, 'Voting and the Electorate', in Henry Drucker, Patrick Dunleavy, Andrew Gamble, and Gillian Peele (eds), *Developments in British Politics*, London, Macmillan, 1986, pp. 58–9.

14 *The Times*, 5 September 1988.

15 John Atkinson, 'Manpower strategies for flexible organizations', *Personnel Management*, August 1984.

16 *Industrial Relations Review and Report*, no. 410, 16 February 1988.

17 T. Burns and G. S. Stalker, *The Management of Innovation*, London, Tavistock, 1959.

18 Peter Ingram, 'Changes in working practices in British manufacturing industry in the 1980s: a study of employee concessions made during wage negotiations', mimeographed paper, CBI, 1988.

19 *Industrial Relations Review and Report*, no. 415, 5 May 1988.

20 *Industrial Relations Review and Report* no. 423, 30 August 1988.

21 See Alan Arthur's 'Egalitarianism in the workplace?', in V. Hammond (ed.), *Current Research in Management*, London, Frances Pinter, 1985, pp. 130–43.

22 W. W. Daniel, *Workplace Industrial Relations and Technical Change*, London, Pinter, 1987.

23 *The Thatcher Years: The Policies and the Prospects*, FT Business Information Ltd, 1987, cited in *IDS Focus*, no. 44, August 1987, p. 4.

24 Dennis Kavanagh, *Thatcherism and British Politics: The End of Consensus?*, Oxford, Oxford University Press, 1987, p. 244.

25 Kent Matthews and Patrick Minford, 'Mrs Thatcher's economic policies 1979–1987', *Economic Policy*, no. 5, October 1987, pp. 59–92.

26 Michael Moran, 'Industrial relations', in Henry Drucker, Patrick Dunleavy, Andrew Gamble, and Gillian Peele (eds), *Developments in British Politics*, London, Macmillan, 1986, p. 294.

27 John Kelly, *Trade Unions and Socialist Politics*, London, Verso, 1988, p. 282.

28 *IDS Focus*, no. 44, August 1987, pp. 4–13.

29 *The Times*, 2 December 1988.

30 Matthews and Minford, *op. cit.*, n. 25.

31 *The Thatcher Years*, cited in IDS Focus, no. 44, August 1987, p. 3.

32 *ibid.*, p. 85.

33 Richard Freeman, 'On the divergence in unionism among developed countries', mimeographed paper, Harvard University, October 1988.

34 Stephen Evans, 'The use of injunctions in industrial disputes, May

1984 – April 1987', *British Journal of Industrial Relations*, 25(3), November 1987, pp. 419–35.
35 Thomas A. Kochan, Harry C. Katz, and Robert B. McKersie, *The Transformation of American Industrial Relations*, New York, Basic Books, 1986.
36 P. B. Beaumont, 'Management opposition to union organisation: researching the indicators', *Employee Relations*, 8(5), 1986, pp. 33–4.
37 These figures come from the *Annual Reports of ACAS* for 1980 (p. 65) and 1986 (p. 26).
38 *ACAS Annual Report* for 1986 (p. 27).
39 See, for example, W. T. Dickens and J. S. Leonard, 'Accounting for the decline in union membership', Working Paper no. 175, Department of Economics, University of California, Berkeley, 1983.
40 Kelly, *op. cit.*, n. 27, p. 282.
41 See Michael Piore and Charles Sabel, *The Second Industrial Divide*, New York, Basic Books, 1984.
42 See, for example, John Lloyd, 'Can the unions survive?', *Personnel Management*, September 1987, pp. 38–41.
43 Handy, *op. cit.*, n. 9, p. 128.
44 Michael Fogarty with Douglas Brooks, *Trade Unions and British Industrial Development*, London, PSI, 1986, Chapter 5.
45 Peter Hain, *Political Strikes*, Harmondsworth, Penguin, 1986, p. 322.
46 Brian Towers, 'British Trade Unions: Crisis and Response', in Brian Towers (ed.), *A Handbook of Industrial Relations Practice*, London, Kogan Page, 2nd edn, 1987, p. 30.
47 See, for example, Tony Lane, 'Economic democracy: are the unions equipped?', *Industrial Relations Journal*, Winter 1986.
48 Lloyd, *op. cit.*, n. 42, p. 41.
49 Robert Taylor, 'Trade unions and the Labour Party: time for an open marriage', *Political Quarterly*, 58(4), Octover–December 1987, pp. 429–30.
50 Neil Millward and Mark Stevens, *British Workplace Industrial Relations 1980–1984*, Aldershot, Gower, 1986, p. 70.
51 *Industrial Relations Review and Report*, no. 401, 29 September 1987, p. 13.
52 Alice H. Cook, 'International comparisons: problems and research in the industrialised world', in Karen Shallcross Koziara, Michael H. Moskow, and Lucretia Dewey Tanner (eds), *Working Women*, Madison, IRRA, University of Wisconsin, 1987, p. 366.
53 Sheila Rowbotham, Lynne Segal, and Hilary Wainwright, *Beyond the Fragments*, London, Martin Press, 1979, pp. 95–6.
54 Taylor, *op. cit.*, n. 49, p. 426.
55 Hain, *op. cit.*, n. 45, pp. 237 and 293–6.
56 For a useful summary of recent union initiatives in the US see Charles J. McDonald, 'The AFL-CIO blueprint for the future – a progress report', *Proceedings of the Industrial Relations Research Association*, Winter 1986, pp. 276–82.
57 *Review of the TUC's Education Service*, TUC, Congress House, 1987.

58 *Industrial Relations Review and Report*, no. 417, 1 June 1988, p. 11.
59 Kelly, *op. cit.*, n. 27. Chapter 10.

Appendix

1 Kevin Hawkins, *Case Studies in Industrial Relations*, London, Kogan Page, 1982.
2 Chris Clegg, Nigel Kemp, and Karen Legge (eds), *Case Studies in Organizational Behaviour*, London, Harper & Row, 1985.
3 Shaun Tyson and Andrew P. Kakabadse (eds), *Cases in Human Resource Management*, London, Heinemann, 1987.
4 G. D. Green, *Case Studies in Industrial Relations*, London, Pitman, 1988.

Index